ON HIGHER EDUCATION

The Academic Enterprise in an Era
of Rising Student Consumerism

PREPARED FOR THE CARNEGIE COUNCIL
ON POLICY STUDIES IN HIGHER EDUCATION

David Riesman

ON HIGHER EDUCATION

*The Academic Enterprise in an Era
of Rising Student Consumerism*

Jossey-Bass Publishers

San Francisco • Washington • London • 1980

ON HIGHER EDUCATION
The Academic Enterprise in an Era
of Rising Student Consumerism
by David Riesman

Copyright © 1980 by: The Carnegie Foundation
for the Advancement of Teaching

Jossey-Bass Inc., Publishers
433 California Street
San Francisco, California 94104

Jossey-Bass Limited
28 Banner Street
London EC1Y 8QE

Copies are available from Jossey-Bass, San Francisco,
for the United States and Possessions, and for Canada,
Australia, New Zealand, and Japan.
Copies for the rest of the world are available
from Jossey-Bass, London.

Library of Congress Cataloging in Publication Data

Riesman, David, 1909–
    On higher education.

    Bibliography: p. 381
    Includes index.
    1. Universities and colleges—United States.
2. College, choice of—United States. I. Title.
LA227.3.R53   378.73   80-8007
ISBN 0-87589-484-4

Manufactured in the United States of America

JACKET DESIGN BY WILLI BAUM

FIRST EDITION

Code 8046

The Carnegie Council Series

The following publications are available from Jossey-Bass Publishers.

Contents

Foreword

This book is proof again, if proof is needed—and it is not, that David Riesman is the best informed, most insightful, most interesting commentator on higher education in the United States. And he has no peer in any other nation.

In 1968, he and Christopher Jencks published *The Academic Revolution* (New York: Doubleday, 1968). Coming out when it did, the title was taken by some (and that was often the only thing they knew about the volume) to mean that it dealt with the student revolt then going on. It did not. It was, rather, about the prior "rise of faculty domination" in the college and university world. This present book, however, is about the student revolt, and much else, but particularly about the "decline" of faculty influence. It is about the new supremacy of the student market as the earlier book was about the rising dominance of the faculties. This shift from academic merit to student consumerism is one of the two greatest reversals of direction in all the history of American higher education; the other being the replacement of the classical college by the modern university a century ago.

This study does for the late 1960s and the 1970s what the earlier book did for the late 1950s and most of the 1960s—and that is to serve as the best single commentary by far on higher education in America at this important transition in its history. The two volumes taken together will stand among the very few classics of the post-World War II period.

The Carnegie Council on Higher Education and the Commission before it have benefitted so greatly from the assistance of

David Riesman. He was a member of the Commission and was a constant and essential guest participant at meetings of the Council. He commented at length and with deep perception on almost every draft report of both the Commission and Council. Those collected comments by themselves are an historical record of great value.

This is the third volume that David Riesman has contributed to the Carnegie series. The first, *Academic Transformation*, he edited with Verne Stadtman (New York: McGraw-Hill, 1973). It included descriptions of "seventeen institutions under pressure" in the late 1960s and early 1970s. To the second, *Education and Politics at Harvard*, written with Seymour Martin Lipset (New York: McGraw-Hill, 1975), he contributed the section on "Educational Reforms at Harvard: Meritocracy and Its Adversaries."

It is fitting that David Riesman should help to conclude the Carnegie review of higher education, as he helped to introduce it and as he contributed at all times along the way, with the greatest of knowledge, the deepest of understanding, and the most profound interest in and goodwill toward American higher education.

CLARK KERR
Chairperson, Carnegie Council
on Policy Studies in Higher Education
1974–1980

Preface

This book grew out of Clark Kerr's invitation to me on behalf of the Carnegie Council to spell out what I had often voiced at our meetings about the growth of student "consumerism" in higher education, including students' increased litigation against colleges and increased federal efforts to protect student interests by regulating institutions. Now, several drafts later, *On Higher Education* elaborates on several other concerns as well. Those of us who have been teaching for a number of decades have wanted to encourage a wide-angled curiosity in our students by building on their already developed literacy, quantitative ability, and capacity to handle historical texts, and by helping them find intellectual excitement in the scientific and scholarly horizons of astronomy and biology, demography and economics. We have hoped that our students would become good citizens, aware of our culture's history yet with their native ethnocentrism challenged by substantial knowledge of another culture. And Americans in general have retained a residual faith that in education lies the cure for our national ills, whether social inequality, lack of productivity, widespread boredom, or nihilism. Unfortunately, our hopes have often outrun our realizations. In this book, I seek to examine why reality has not lived up to desire, in the expectation that if we understand our situation more fully, we may be able to react more rationally to it. I trust readers will find in it some suggestions of incremental steps that can be taken to improve postsecondary education, as well as some warnings about roads that have gone nowhere or are likely to go nowhere in this direction.

This book was originally intended to be a guide for those students who are prepared to make an active choice of college rather than to attend the nearest available or the most prestigious institution. It also aimed to persuade them of the value of wise decisions, both in choosing a college and in choosing the level of effort to exert while in college. But as the book developed and took on, as books will do, a life of its own, I realized that I was writing it for more than students. I found myself addressing all those now working in higher education, those who are considering careers in higher education, those with a natural or potential stake in higher education (such as parents who seek to guide their children's choice of college or guidance counselors charged to aid this choice), those who shape educational policy (including trustees, state coordinating boards, and federal officials), and, beyond these audiences, as with all my writing, those who are curious about our society and its institutions and who have a civic concern for our society's future.

I seek to alert readers to what is happening to American higher education as the number of colleges and universities oversupplied with applicants wanes and as students turn from being supplicants for admission to courted customers, even if they are neither athletes nor Merit Scholars, neither student body presidents nor those particularly rara avises, oboists. I seek to analyze the consequences for teaching and learning of the likelihood, as institutions compete frantically with each other for body counts, that faculty members and administrators will hesitate to make demands on students in the form of rigorous academic requirements for fear of losing "FTE"s—full-time equivalent students.

I aim to show that the "wants" of students to which competing institutions, departments, and individual faculty members cater are quite different from the "needs" of students, and to point out to students the danger of viewing themselves primarily as passive consumers of education rather than as active producers of their own education and as resources for educating each other and even faculty.

I examine the prospects for faculty morale when market forces dictate changes not only in whole curricula but also in modes of instruction. At its worst, I envisage Hobbes' war of all against all, as faculty members compete to capture the student market on which their own reputation or their department's opportunities depend. At best, I foresee hazards to the future of scholarship as many of today's able students seek the apparent safety of the professions of law, medicine, or management rather than the risks of a chancy academic career. And I fear the gains from collective bargaining are apt to be minimal in securing for faculty members the power attributed to unionization in other sectors of society, while the losses may be not inconsiderable.

I discuss the haphazard and ill-informed ways in which students choose colleges—in the minority of instances where they make any active choice at all—as well as possible means for improving student choice. Since students are so often misled in their choices, I have long encouraged federal as well as regional and state efforts to protect their rights; but in this book I advocate other federal initiatives than trying to regulate institutional procedures from Washington or from the federal judiciary—among them, the possibility of strengthening the regional accrediting associations, supporting the efforts of high school guidance counselors in helping students make optimal choices, and assuring better information not only from individual colleges but, even more important, from groups of colleges, such as those that make up the College Entrance Examination Board, on the basis of which students can better choose among institutions.

I should emphasize that, despite my concern about the current expansion of student power, I do not view total student subordination to faculty as idyllic either. When student applicants were plentiful, as they were in recent decades, they were often mistreated and shortchanged, both by institutions and by individual faculty members. Today, in an era of increasing student hegemony, students are not always wise in the use of their greatly enhanced market power and shortchange themselves, while advantage can still be taken of them by unscrupulous instructors and institutions. Like any other interest group, the student estate often does not grasp its own interests, and those who speak in its name are not always its friends.

For this reason, at various points I suggest remedies for those instances where students' market power does not protect them against deceit and works against their own long-run interests, while at the same time making use of already available models for sustaining faculty morale and student scholarly achievement. I note instances where colleges and universities, both public and private, have fought against the notion that all that students seek is a credential rather than a demanding education. Their boats have not been beached but instead have risen as they have successfully gone against the ebbing tide by raising requirements. Our task, as I see it, is to strike a balance between the need for consumer protection where students are defrauded and the need to limit student power so as to minimize the impact of Gresham's law on higher education as a whole—and thus preserve enclaves where students and faculty can work together, despite some inevitable tension, in ways that permit the more experienced to assist creatively in students' education.

To put this task in perspective, the first chapter illustrates faculty hegemony in past decades by describing institutions in which students have subordinated themselves willingly or grudgingly to faculty norms and verdicts, including Harvard Law School (to some extent still an almost undiluted meritocracy), Reed, Swarthmore, the College of the University of Chicago, and, at least in the past, the City College of New York.

Chapter Two sketches the sources of faculty hegemony and of the recruitment of students from wider and wider catchbasins, including the G.I. Bill, in permitting veterans to move toward prestigeful and selective institutions; the College Entrance Examination Board, in helping institutions judge applicants and students determine where they could avoid being either overmatched or insufficiently challenged; and those Jewish students who, unattached by family or religious tradition or state loyalty to local institutions, helped set the intellectual pace of the most cosmopolitan institutions and encouraged the cosmopolitan attachment of faculty members to their disciplines rather than to older institutional loyalties.

Chapter Three dissects the rise and consequences of student disaffection during the 1960s, stemming in part from intense student competition for preferment and in part from anti–Vietnam war resistance. It compares the two main branches of the student movements—the activist wing and the countercultural wing—that often made common cause in antiuniversity attacks; it also describes the emergence of faculty resistance, including resort to unionization—a tactic that appeared sufficiently "proletarian" to appeal to liberal faculty while sealing faculty ranks against outside influence, including that of students.

Chapter Four discusses the situation institutions now face in competing for student customers, including the new-found market of older students. It notes the benefits of student power in expanding the curriculum but criticizes the consumerist onslaught on standardized testing, as epitomized by attacks on the Educational Testing Service, and it points out the advantages for students themselves of standardized testing.

Turning to examples of remaining faculty power, Chapter Five focuses on the evangelical colleges, many of which are still able to hold a tight rein on student extracurricular conduct and maintain a sense of coherence because they have a loyal group of alumni and a student body that is willing in some measure to abide by their restraints.

Chapter Six examines the community colleges—the institutions with perhaps the strongest power of survival and growth, in part because of the minimal commitment they ask of students and the correspondingly minimal risk to students of possible failure and wasted effort. Unlike some critics of community colleges who see them as designed by the elite to keep the disadvantaged from aspiring to and achieving more rewarding careers, I see them serving not only as a ceiling on students' aspirations but as enclaves where unsure students can gain the self-confidence they need for further work.

Chapter Seven takes up the question, adumbrated in all that has gone before, of the freedom students have in the academic marketplace when the use of a free market requires accurate knowledge on which to base decisions. Even when students have access to ample information, great numbers of them—even graduate students—do not make use of it, and parents often discourage their children from being exploratory and venturesome in college choices by urging them to remain at home, attend a local college that is "good enough," and minimize the family's financial sacrifices.

Chapter Eight discusses ways of providing more adequate information to guide student choice. It notes the potential role

of high school guidance counselors as well as what students themselves can do in the way of consumer research on colleges, and it
reviews the neglect of academic advising within colleges. Like remedial teaching of reading, writing, and mathematics, advising is
handicraft labor, and, for academics who like to perform before an
audience, it is of limited gratification because invisible. But I
believe that faculty energies would often be well spent directed
toward good advising, almost as much as toward the improvement
of teaching, recognizing how important teaching obviously is.

Chapter Nine examines the largely untapped power of students in affecting educational reform and suggests that students
can do far more to improve their own education than any amount
of imposed curricular reform with a capital "R." It offers illustrations of student self-help, and of faculty assistance, in stimulating
students to be active self-starters in regard to their education rather
than drifting into passive, if not alienated, consumerism.

Chapter Ten turns to the role that accrediting agencies—
and, in particular, the regional associations that accredit entire
institutions—can play in improving both education and student
information. The chief area in which I look for such potential is in
an effort to control the increasingly rapacious recruitment of students from abroad, especially, of course, those believed to be able
to pay their own way. I use the instance of non-American students
who are mismatched culturally if not academically at many of the
institutions they attend as a kind of extreme example of the mismatching of students and institutions that also occurs with students
from within the boundaries of the United States.

Finally, Chapter Eleven probes the potential for effective
federal consumer protection of students and for assistance in improving student choice—through improved high school counseling
and centers for information and advice—without deleterious regulation of institutions.

Throughout the book I seek to puncture overgeneralizations
(including some of my own earlier ones) by calling attention to
what is always a fruitful source for sociological analysis—namely,
the deviant case. For example, I comment on the need to disaggregate among black students, who differ enormously in the subcultures from which they are drawn to college, just as do other

racial and ethnic groups, rather than considering them an undifferentiated "community," and recruiting them, as predominantly white institutions have too often done, in a way I regard as condescending, to satisfy abstract ideas about institutional responsibility or affirmative action requirements. Similarly I look at that minority of community college students who, stimulated by their experience of success in college, gain the self-confidence necessary to transfer to private as well as public institutions, earn the baccalaureate, and even go on for advanced degrees.

Such disaggregation leads to few prescriptions, and I have no panaceas to offer. I believe in incremental improvements particular to a time and a locale rather than in packaged reforms applicable anytime everywhere. Moreover, my previous books lead me to exercise restraint regarding predictions and remedies in this one. We sociologists are capable of giving an explanation for an event that has occurred (whether the explanation is correct or not is another story—and it is likely to be simplistic). But we are not much better than anyone else at foretelling events—and perhaps even worse when we are afflicted by hubris. *The Lonely Crowd* (1950) offers a good example. In it, my coauthors and I assumed that the decline of population in the advanced industrial countries prior to the Second World War would continue despite the postwar baby boom, and we suggested that the ghost of Malthus may have been put to rest by advances in technology that promised continued increases of postindustrial abundance. But we were off by two decades in our population projections, and shortly after *The Lonely Crowd* appeared, I came to the conclusion that we were postindustrial in our attitudes long before we could afford its luxuries in our economy.

In the field of postsecondary education, which has been the main arena for my research since 1954, I was equally prone to trend thinking that turned out to be overstated if not entirely mistaken. Thus in my first book on education, *Constraint and Variety in American Education* (1956), I employed the imagery of "the academic procession" in which all institutions are striving to imitate what they see as the academic leaders, although often mistaking them or seeing them as they were in an earlier era. But the idea of a single procession later seemed to me a profound overgeneralization: there were not only discontinuities but different models at different locations in the academic division of labor. Not all evangelical colleges wanted to become secular and follow the model of Amherst or Wesleyan, and few community colleges wanted to become four-year colleges. As Richard Johnson has pointed out (1979), if community colleges have a model, it may be Miami-Dade, with its 55,000 students on three campuses in Florida, or it may be Foothill, with its handsome buildings crowning a hilltop south of Palo Alto in California—but not a university.

Similarly, when Christopher Jencks and I completed *The Academic Revolution* in 1968, I should have recalled from the work of Seymour Martin Lipset that when social movements are at their peak, they are also at their most over-extended and most likely to falter. Taking for a permanent development what has turned out to be a temporary spurt in the demand for faculty and hence in their bargaining power, we viewed the academic revolution as the victory of the academic disciplines, organized in departments, over all the other contending powers in major universities. Even by the time *The Academic Revolution* was published, however, we realized its title was inappropriate: students were already asserting their powers at the expense of institutions and of those faculty members who were not of their party. As we noted in the preface to the paperback edition in 1969, had the first edition come out a year later, we would have entitled it The Academic Enterprise. In retrospect, I would agree with Laurence Veysey (1973b) that the major academic revolution occurred in American higher education between 1890 and 1910, when the department—still the major bulwark and building block (or stumbling block) of academic life— became the base for faculty allegiance and power.

In 1969, I wrote an essay on "The Collision Course of Higher Education" in which I argued that, with the coming demographic decline, decreased philanthropic support, and steadily rising costs, we would shortly see many private colleges close, while campus dissidence and disturbance would lead legislators and taxpayers to infuriated tax revolts. But if *The Academic Revolution* has been too sanguine about the triumph of professors and the disciplines, "The Collision Course of Higher Education" was prematurely pessimistic about decline: by its logic, half the private colleges in America should now have closed their doors, in California Proposition 13 would have been abetted by Proposition 9, and similar backlash legislation or referenda would be in effect in all other states.

Although I have been chastened by these errors of prophecy, I retain some self-confidence on the basis of other more accurate predictions, and I find it difficult not to seek to influence the future by disaggregating overgeneralizations, offering tentative suggestions, and warning of avoidable dangers. One can maintain a view of the human condition as filled with individual and social tragedy and yet not succumb either to dogmatic determinism or to resigned cynicism. I do not share the generally defeatist mood that prevails so widely among educated people who have learned to be as cynical as less-educated people are about the future. The swing in the mood of many faculty over the past fifteen years from euphoria to paranoia has been sharper than the actual changes in institutional boom and bust warrant. Academic institutions have been harmed less by demographic decline, inflation, and taxpayer revolts than I had thought likely a dozen years ago, and while inflation has hurt many faculty members more than it has hurt members of unions whose salaries and wages are pegged to cost-of-living indices, most academics still live at a level well above the average American, if not on a par with most lawyers or physicians. If we fail to communicate our excitement and privilege in being paid for a life of scholarship and the pleasure of sometimes being able to widen both intellectual and occupational horizons for our students and, instead, like many novelists and playwrights, proclaim and satirize the inevitable frustrations, the avoidable pettiness, and unnecessary internecine jungle fighting of academic life—all readily available targets—we shall scarcely make an academic career look inviting to our students, and we will thus hobble our own calling for the future.

Some professors of my generation, approaching retirement after the opportunity of teaching in highly selective and demanding research universities during the recent decades of near total faculty hegemony, regard the past with nostalgia and the present era of expanding student power with profound disaffection. For me, however, the future is always in some measure open. Although we must avoid quixotic experiments clearly doomed to failure and thus contributing to heightened despair, we will not know the possibilities of openness until we do experiment. Of despair, we already have full measure. Indeed, despair is so commonly over-generalized that one way of defining my aim in this book is to describe it as an effort not to reduce our expectations but to dis-aggregate among them and to nourish and sustain such of them as are within reason. I believe passionately in reason, and I believe we cannot achieve our expectations except by implementing them rationally—by which I do not mean employing any less passion or conviction.

Cambridge, Massachusetts   DAVID RIESMAN
October 1980

Acknowledgments

Without the unwavering support of Clark Kerr, this book would not have come into existence. I was in his audience when he came to Harvard in 1963 to deliver his Godkin Lectures, which became his classic *The Uses of the University,* and since that time I have had repeated opportunities to learn more about higher education through his initiative. In 1963, he invited me to visit the three new campuses the University of California was establishing at Irvine, San Diego, and Santa Cruz, and I was able to follow up this opportunity by more extended visits to San Diego and by making Santa Cruz a main locale for further research (Grant and Riesman, 1978, pp. 77–134, 253–290).

My membership on the Carnegie Commission on Higher Education gave me the opportunity from 1967 to 1973 to work with Clark Kerr and a group of other dedicated academic leaders and scholars and, by virtue of the commission's policy of meeting in different parts of the country and inviting local college and university presidents to meet with us and address us, the chance to broaden my knowledge of the academic landscape. I learned a great deal from my fellow commissioners; this benefit was intensified by the presence at our meetings of some exceptionally perceptive members of the Carnegie Corporation, notably David Z. Robinson, Alan Pifer, Alden Dunham, and Richard Sullivan. During 1973–74, while I was on leave of absence from Harvard, Dr. Kerr invited me to spend some intermittent weeks at the headquarters of the Carnegie Commission's successor, the Carnegie Council for Policy Studies in Higher Education, and during my visits he arranged for me to meet members of the Berkeley faculty, the University of California administration, and educators in the San Francisco Bay area who could contribute to my understanding. For example, a luncheon that he arranged with David Saxon, president of the university, alerted me to the problems of competition for transfer students between the campuses of the university and those of the California State University and Colleges—an issue I then followed up in correspondence with Allan Herschfield at Berkeley and Karl Lamb and Herman Blake at Santa Cruz.

I profited from subsequent meetings of the Carnegie Council to which I was invited even though I was not formally a member and which I attended if they fitted into my teaching schedule at Harvard. As a discussant and critic of draft papers prepared for the Council, I often found myself playing the role of Cassandra, puncturing what I regarded as overly buoyant declarations and drawing attention to concrete examples of academic demoralization and violations of what Edward Shils has termed "the academic ethos" (1977). Thus while the Council titled its final report *Three Thousand Futures*, foreseeing the prospect that the nation's 3,000 accredited colleges and universities can not only stay in business but maintain their individual distinctiveness and collective diversity in the years ahead, I am inclined to anticipate their having fewer separate prospects—not 3,000 distinctive futures, but perhaps a third that many.

Clark Kerr is a man of greater sensitivity than often appears; criticism stings; and yet he has always responded to mine with generosity and openness. Indeed, his sanguinity has provided a useful corrective to my pessimistic outlook. He shares the general American belief that, if one can define a problem, will and goodwill can discover a solution. Apart from our Carnegie-related duties, he and I have worked together on what Friends would term "concerns" with nuclear disarmament and other international issues, such as the treatment of the Vietnamese during and since the Vietnam war, both in Vietnam and the United States, and of Iranian students in this country during 1980. His interest in the non-American world has helped deprovincialize the concerns of all of us. My own regret is that I was unable to complete this book, despite his sustained confidence in me as I struggled with it, prior to the completion of his direction of the Carnegie Council's work.

The manuscript for this book went through many drafts. Verne Stadtman read the manuscript straight through at an early stage and provided immensely helpful suggestions. Barry Munitz, John Bunzel, and Larry Litten read all or substantial parts of the manuscript and offered painstaking criticisms. I am indebted to them, as I am to Martin Trow, Laurence Veysey, and Gerald Grant, for their repeatedly helping me in recent years to deepen my understanding of American higher education.

I checked various segments of the manuscript that concerned particular institutions or types of institutions with individuals possessing special knowledge of them. Thus I am indebted to Alexander Astin for specific comments on community colleges, on student transiency, and on the importance of residential institutions, and to both him and Helen Astin for their friendly and supportive criticism of my work over the years. Neal Berte made helpful comments in areas relevant to his experience at New College of the University of Alabama and Birmingham Southern College. Paul Bragdon was indefatigable in digging out material on Reed College. David Cavers helped me interpret and make more accurate my account of Harvard Law School of an earlier day. Lloyd Watkins confirmed the growing attractiveness of Northern Illinois University as it became more selective and more academically demanding. Robert M. O'Neil corrected my assessments of the universities in the University of Wisconsin system and, as a member of the Carnegie Council, discussed the role of the voluntary accrediting associations on several occasions as a result of his own observations and experience. Others who contributed to my knowledge of accreditation were E. K. Fretwell, Frank Newman, Daniel Evans, Kenneth O. Young, Craig Eisendrath, and Albert Ullman. James Whalen clarified my interpretation of the struggles over unionization at Ithaca College. Paul Gagnon has also enlarged my comparative reach by his writing and many discussions of contemporary postsecondary education, including "recurrent education," in France. Both he and Donald O'Dowd have contributed to my understanding of some of the kinds of faculty grievances which result in unionization in the public sector, while Harry Marmion, Jr., has been equally helpful concerning the sources and aims of union activities in the private sector. Alberta Arthurs and Louis

Barnes were helpful in my understanding of the prospects for private women's colleges. And my understanding of Davidson College profited from discussions with John Bevan, T. C. Price Zimmerman, and J. Nichols Burnett.

Michael Usdan, Nan Robinson, Donald Winandy, and their colleagues of the Connecticut Commission on Higher Education have aided my understanding of the forms taken by competition between public and private institutions in a state where the latter are strong, and where there are many conflicts also within and among the segments of the public sector. Similarly, I have benefited from the work of T. Edward Hollander, chancellor of higher education for New Jersey, and also from comments concerning the county or community colleges of that state by my long-time friend and generous critic, Alden Dunham. Laura Clausen, Edward Wright, Jr., and Sybil Smith facilitated my understanding of problems of competition and coordination in Massachusetts.

Among members of the Carnegie Council staff, Martin Kramer and Margaret Gordon were helpful to me on issues of federal aid to students and the difference this aid makes to particular categories of students and types of institutions, and Arthur Levine and I shared a preoccupation with the growing spirit of consumerism among students. Among Martin Trow's associates on the surveys of faculty, graduate students, and undergraduates undertaken for the Carnegie Commission and the Carnegie Council, I had the benefit of discussions particularly with Oliver Fulton.

My long-time preoccupation with the situation of foreign students in the United States, in terms of both their recruitment and their matching with institutions that will be culturally as well as academically suitable for them, has benefited from the comments of Thomas Ragle, David Hopkins, and Barbara Burn; an interest in the fates of foreign students both in this country and on their return and in what they can contribute to deprovincializing a still ethnocentric America has long been shared with my friend and fellow Carnegie Commission member, James A. Perkins. Margaret MacVicar and Sheila Tobias are among a number of friends who have shared my interest in securing a greater competence in mathematics, science, and high technology among women, starting with overcoming "math anxiety" in elementary and secondary school.

Concerning affirmative action, particularly for blacks, and the often ambivalent role of black studies departments both in insulating black students and in offering them sanctuary within predominantly white institutions, I have benefited from the extensive study of such programs by Wilson Record and from exchanges with, as well as writings by, Thomas Sowell, while Ernst Borinski has contributed to my knowledge of black studies programs in the predominantly black colleges.

On questions of admissions policies, I have been for years indebted to the work of Humphrey Doermann and of my Harvard colleague, Dean Whitla. I have also drawn on a series of exchanges with William Turnbull, Warren Willingham, and Rex Jackson; I have benefited from similar exchanges with Robert E. Klitgaard regarding his assessment of both the present state and the future prospects of attracting into academic life students of the highest ability—in terms of both personal qualities and academic accomplishment. Edwin Taylor generously shared with me his unpublished monograph, "What to Ask of a College," aimed with wit and wisdom at giving students a better idea of how top-flight research universities are structured and how to make use of their opportunities while escaping their pitfalls. And Carl Kaysen, another member of the Carnegie Commission, clarified my understanding of the kind of assessments eminent mathematicians can make of each other; more significantly, both directly and in his role as Vice Chairman and Director of Research of the Sloan Commission on Government and Higher Education, he and members of his Commission's staff enlightened me on government relations with higher education and vice versa.

The reliability and resourcefulness of Phyllis Keller were unfailing in responding to my questions about Harvard in general as well as about affirmative action policies and the role of women in higher education. And in shifting much of my teaching from sociology to the Graduate School of Education at Harvard when in 1976 I reached what is there called semiretirement, I had the benefit of working with a remarkable group of scholars of higher education: Richard Chait, Frederic Jacobs, Charlotte Kuh, George Weathersby, my old friend and departmental colleague Nathan Glazer, and, in the last several years, another old friend, Stephen Bailey.

For two decades, Japan has been my "other country," in terms of useful comparisons and contrasts with the United States, and here my guide has often been my friend Hidetoshi Kato. Glen and Sakie Fukushima have assisted my understanding of the role of the examination system in Japan and the forms of selectivity and meritocracy in that country. And my friend and colleague Ezra Vogel has read the references to Japan in this volume and has in general helped diminish my ignorance of its culture.

My indebtedness to the capable historians who have written about American higher education is particularly great. I have already mentioned Laurence Veysey, who through his writings and frequent discussions has taught me not only about the history of higher education in the United States but also about how to put that knowledge in the context of the intellectual life of this country and of Europe. Frederick Rudolph, whose historical analysis *Curriculum* (1977) was commissioned by the Carnegie Council, has also greatly influenced the present volume. I have profited as well from the work of Hugh Hawkins on Harvard and Johns Hopkins, from Robert McCaughey about Harvard and education in general, from Walter Metzger and his former colleague, the late Richard Hofstadter, from my colleagues Bernard Bailyn and Patricia Graham, from Burton Clark in his role as historian (1970), from Geoffrey Blodgett, especially concerning Oberlin's history, and from Lawrence Cremin and Diane Ravitch, who, although dealing primarily with precollegiate education, have helped shape my thinking about the relation of education to society and vice versa. I am indebted as well to the historian-sociologists of science, notably Joseph Ben-David and the group stimulated by the work of Robert K. Merton and Harriet Zuckerman.

Burton Clark has also helped focus my attention on community colleges both through his own work and that of his colleagues and students. Howard London (1978) has been especially helpful in his published writing and in many private exchanges. I am also indebted to one former community college president, Joseph Cosand, a member of the Carnegie Commission, who helped introduce me to the study of community colleges, a task later taken up by Nolen Ellison, a member of the Carnegie Council, and by Leslie Koltai, head of the Los Angeles community college system. Three community college presidents, Jonathan Daube, Harold Shively, and George Vaughan, have helped my understanding, and so have Edmund Gleazer, Jr., and Roger Yarrington.

I have also relied, especially as travel has become more difficult and I have had to become in part an "armchair ethnographer," on field reports from others, both on many friends who are college and university presidents or faculty members and who have continued to inform me about developments at their institutions and on an increasingly capable corps of journalists covering (or formerly covering) education, such as Edward Fiske and Gene Maeroff of the *New York Times*; William Trombley of the *Los Angeles Times*; Luther J. Carter, Constance Holden, Deborah Shapley, Nicholas Wade, and John Walsh of *Science*; Malcolm G. Scully and Beverly T. Watkins and their colleagues of *The Chronicle of Higher Education*; and the continuously helpful reportage of *Change* magazine, whose founder and former editor, George Bonham, has been an endlessly generous informant and critic of my work.

I fear I have left out of these acknowledgments a number of individuals who have helped at some point regarding specific topics, some of which have been eliminated from the final manuscript of this book for purposes of condensation, or whose own writing on higher education has influenced me, even if I have been unable to cite their books and articles in connection with the topics I treat in these pages. My indebtedness to them is nonetheless great.

I owe a special debt to two research assistants: Martha MacLeish Fuller, who has served in that capacity for a number of years and who did some of the interviewing concerning college choice and community colleges in the Boston area from which I draw in later pages, and William Neumann, an advanced graduate student in cultural foundations of education at Syracuse University, who moved to Boston to see his wife through a doctoral program in sociology at Boston University and who was for two years my versatile assistant in traveling to colleges and universities throughout the country. My secretary, Lynn McKay, typed the endless drafts of the manuscript, kept its evolving sections in manageable order, and worked tirelessly to check entries in the bibliography. And at Jossey-Bass, Gracia Alkema, Rephah Berg, and JB Lon Hefferlin have contributed exceptional talent and scrupulous care as editors.

It should be obvious that neither the many people who generously read and criticized the draft, or portions of it, nor those on whose written work I have drawn bear any responsibility for what I have written; sins of commission and omission are mine alone.

Finally, I am indebted for financial support that made this book possible to a number of generous and patient foundations. For two years of my semiretirement from Harvard, when, on reaching the age of 66, I chose the option of taking half-time duties and half salary for four years, the balance of my salary was reimbursed to Harvard by the Carnegie Foundation for the Advancement of Teaching. This money not sufficing to finish the work, the Exxon Education Foundation stepped in generously with a grant, later supplemented, that made possible the extension of the work to community colleges and underwrote some of the costs of transcribing the numerous drafts, corresponding with institutional and government officials, and undertaking a minimum of travel to complete the work. Robert Payton, president of the foundation, was unfailingly helpful, as later on was my friend and former Harvard colleague, Leon Bramson, who served for two years as program officer for the foundation. The Permanent Charity Fund of Boston, under the leadership of Fred Glimp and later of Geno Ballotti, made several contributions for support of this work, and a grant from the Lilly Endowment and the strong encouragement of Laura Bornholdt at the endowment were also essential in permitting me to complete it.

DAVID RIESMAN

The Author

David Riesman's interest in education stems from a number of sources: his father's concern with medical education as a professor of clinical medicine and later of the history of medicine at the University of Pennsylvania Medical School; his mother's continuous efforts on behalf of her alma mater, Bryn Mawr; his parents' acquaintance with John Dewey and Arthur Morgan; and his own experience at William Penn Charter School, which he attended from 1919 to 1926 and which offered little music and less art, and where, as he says, he studied Latin for seven years and Greek for three by rote, without being introduced in any real sense to classical civilization.

His view of Harvard College as an undergraduate from 1927 to 1931 was hardly less critical but was redeemed by his work on the Harvard *Crimson*, where he made education his beat; by his serving as speaker-chairman of the Harvard Liberal Club during his sophomore year and inviting a series of academic innovators to come to Harvard to lecture, including Alexander Meiklejohn who was then beginning his experimental college at the University of Wisconsin; and by his writing an essay in his senior year for Irving Babbitt, comparing the educational theories of Goethe and Rousseau.

He was not less critical of Harvard Law School, into which he drifted after college and where he edited the *Harvard Law Review* and to which he invited Karl Llewellyn, the professor-reformer at Columbia to address an overflow audience on how legal education could be made more realistic and more clinical. On a post–law school fellowship during 1934–35, he studied with Carl Friedrich, who had done his dissertation at Heidelberg under Alfred Weber and who introduced Riesman to European social science as well as to such American thinkers as Thorstein Veblen, and whose encouragement was decisive in persuading him that he might become a professor.

After clerking for Supreme Court Justice Brandeis and practicing with Lyne, Woodworth & Evarts in Boston, he taught law at the University of Buffalo Law School. Sensing that its "first generation" students would mostly become local practitioners, he taught them local rather than "national" law, including a seminar on the ordinances of the City of Buffalo. He wrote about legal education and discussed it at meetings of the Association of American Law Schools but found that his scholarly interests in cross-cultural studies of defamation and of the meaning of words was of greater interest to social psychologists and sociologists than to other law professors. A visiting research fellowship at Columbia Law School gave him a chance to meet Robert and Helen Merrill Lynd, Paul Lazarsfeld, Margaret Mead, and others with whom he felt more colleagueship than with most professors of law or political scientists. After serving as deputy assistant district attorney for New York City and with the Sperry Gyroscope Company during World War II, he had the opportunity to teach on the social science staff of the College of the University of Chicago without securing what would have been requisite a few years later: a Ph.D.

At Chicago he apprenticed himself to Everett Hughes, auditing his sociology courses in field work methods and in the study of occupations and professions. During partial leaves of absence spent at Yale in 1948 and 1949, with Nathan Glazer he visited schools and interviewed students, some of whose portraits, along with those of their schools, appeared in *Faces in the Crowd* (1952). Then as the on-site member of a University of Chicago research group conducting a community study in Kansas City, Missouri, he had an opportunity to visit nearby academic institutions, including the University of Missouri, the University of Kansas, and Kansas State University. In succeeding years he travelled to increasing numbers of institutions, subscribing in advance to the student newspaper, studying the catalogue and other printed materials, and then conducting what has been termed "blitzkrieg ethnology"—inevitably partial interviews and discussions—but often followed up by return visits and continued correspondence.

The full diversity of American higher education became evident to him only through his assistance between 1955 and 1957 to the Academic Freedom Study, commissioned by the Fund for the Republic at the height of anticommunist attacks on scholars, and conducted by Paul Lazarsfeld through a questionnaire survey of social scientists in a random sample of all accredited four-year colleges and universities. By reading the several thousand survey responses, interviewing respondents at some forty institutions, and sending out another questionnaire to other respondents, he realized that the cosmopolitan academic concern about McCarthyism was stratospheric on many campuses, where not even a fellow traveler had ever penetrated and where apprehension was more often local than national and frequently more religious, racial, or social than political. His first book on education, *Constraint and Variety in American Education* (1956), gained much of its substance as a result of that study.

After moving to Harvard in 1958 to inaugurate the Henry Ford II Professorship of Social Science, he recruited Christopher Jencks, then a graduate student in education, to help him study the way in which the University of Massachusetts at Amherst and Boston College were affected by the immense resources and national prestige of Harvard and the Massachusetts Institute of Technology. Their collaboration extended to ethnographic studies of colleges and universities from coast to coast and resulted in *The Academic Revolution* (1968). His subsequent collaboration with Gerald Grant led to *The Perpetual Dream* in 1978, and his participation with Grant and others in a study of competence-based education under the auspices of the Fund for the Improvement of Postsecondary Education resulted in *On Competence* (Grant and others, 1979).

As a member of the Carnegie Commission on Higher Education and more recently as an associate of the Carnegie Council on Policy Studies in Higher Education, his concern about the growth of consumerism in higher education led him to agree to undertake the present volume. It began in 1976 as a limited analysis of the rise of student power under the title, "The Academic Counterrevolution," and it now appears, following his retirement in 1980 at age 71 and the assumption of the Carnegie Council's work by its parent Carnegie Foundation for the Advancement of Teaching, as the final volume in the Carnegie Council series of policy studies on higher education.

For Clark Kerr

ON HIGHER EDUCATION

The Academic Enterprise in an Era of Rising Student Consumerism

PREPARED FOR THE CARNEGIE COUNCIL
ON POLICY STUDIES IN HIGHER EDUCATION

1

The Era of Faculty Dominance and Its Decline

When Christopher Jencks and I sent *The Academic Revolution* to press in 1967, American higher education (since democratically renamed "postsecondary" education) was, in its more selective segments, at the very peak of undiluted meritocratic competitive pressures. The faculties of the major public and private universities and of the top-flight private liberal arts colleges had triumphed over most sources of outside interference: trustee control; religious control, as by the Catholic religious orders or a few dioceses or by the boards of the "mainstream" Protestant churches; and control by the predilections of the major foundations and federal agencies. Thus, while trustees retained more than nominal control over the selection of the chief executive, they increasingly consulted with faculty and even with students; moreover, the candidates were generally chosen from the ranks of faculty. Indeed, except for a few lawyers (mainly prior law professors), college and university presidents so invariably had the Ph.D. degree that it was something of a novelty when John Corbally became president of a world-class state university (Illinois) with the handicap of a Doctor of Education degree.[1] Faculties were generally willing to leave investment policy to trustees, except when such policy became politicized, as with

[1] For a survey of literature on changing recruitment of chief executive officers in academia and a report of new research on the topic, showing the overwhelming origins of presidents from among the faculty, see Cohen and March (1974, chap. 2) and Kauffman (1980).

investments in companies dealing with South Africa; similarly, trustee decisions concerning matters of budget or plant investment and maintenance could at times become subject to faculty scrutiny. And at the national level, faculties had disciplined both the large private foundations and such federal agencies as the National Science Foundation and, to a lesser degree, the National Institutes of Health into granting stipends on a merit basis and research grants on a competitive basis, subject to peer review.

Although a faculty member's capacity as a teacher, at least at a minimum level, was rarely as neglected as legend would have it, departments and whole institutions sought to become more distinguished by using the expansion of their student enrollments to recruit more faculty members than would have been necessary on the basis of earlier teaching loads and student/faculty ratios, thus allowing the build-up of graduate and research programs, which grew even more rapidly than undergraduate enrollments. (In the private sector, the leading institutions expanded their undergraduate colleges only slightly. However, somewhat comparable processes operated in the public sector in order to allow recruitment of distinguished faculty members who could make use of teaching assistants to spare themselves the handicraft labor of working with any but the most committed and adept undergraduates.)

Everywhere, tenure was granted at ever younger ages to those who had given visible evidence of what came to be called "productivity." (It made a difference, to use a dairyman's metaphor, whether productivity was defined in Devonshire, Jersey, or Holstein terms—that is, in terms of high density and quality, as against more diluted and bulkier output. The more selective and self-confident the institution, the more it felt it could judge quality without reference to quantity. However, even the most distinguished American universities have lacked the calm of the ancient British universities of Oxford and Cambridge, so secure in their status that they could afford even a touch of scorn for excessive zeal in terms of quantity, if quality was high.)[2] Deans and presi-

---

[2] Rathbone (1980) has delineated in a vivid and penetrating way the difference between the assured hierarchical tradition of Oxford and the gnawing fears even of so eminent an American university as Harvard that its rivals will overtake and surpass it—as indeed, in particular schools and departments, Stanford and Berkeley

dents were useful in mobilizing resources to keep people whom other institutions sought to capture and to recruit people whom other institutions might want to keep—but as Clark Kerr complained in *The Uses of the University* (1963), administrators had very little power to shape the institution's priorities: these lay in the hands of the departmentally organized tenured faculty.

Trustees in private institutions could be shaped by cooptation; in public ones, they could sometimes be shamed into noninterference, although there were notable exceptions, as in Illinois and Colorado, where regents are publicly elected; or in Texas, where the regents of the University of Texas were generous but periodically bossy. Legislatures in the several states could be cajoled into competing with other states to raise salaries and match federal dollars to build handsome state institutions; federal legislators could be defended against counterattack from philistines by arguing the advantages for defense or for practical health, agricultural, and technological advance of subsidizing research and prospective researchers.[3]

The students remained the one relatively unsubdued constituency, except in that handful of institutions where an influential plurality were themselves planning to become professors. (Reed College is a good example: the minority who reached the senior year did so by already having become protograduate students.) Everett Hughes and his coworkers Howard Becker and Blanche Geer showed in gamy detail how at the University of Kansas medical school (Becker and others, 1961) and the undergraduate college of the same university, students "made the grade" (Becker, Geer, and Hughes, 1968) and met professorial imperatives—although only up to a point, remaining primarily oriented to the

---

and other institutions have. All American institutions, Rathbone notes, are at every moment engaged in anxious efforts to retain or improve their status in America's more egalitarian and competitive society, and few professors or departments are exempt.

[3] For the very much altered situation today, when there is danger that faculties will be declining or at best static and that tenure appointments will be rare, see the following reports by the Carnegie Council on Policy Studies in Higher Education: von Rothkirch (1978); Radner and Kuh (1978). For a study raising questions of whether academic careers are continuing to attract, as they did during the period of faculty triumph, the ablest undergraduates—even to fields that are still expanding—see Klitgaard (1979).

collegiate and vocational subcultures. (For a different perspective on student attitudes in medical school, see Merton, Reader, and Kendall, 1957.)

In considering student attitudes in general, the well-known typology of Burton Clark and Martin Trow is helpful. Clark and Trow classify students along two dimensions: whether they are much or little involved with ideas and whether they are much or little identified with their institution. It labels students much identified with both as "academic," those much identified with ideas but little with their college as "nonconformist," those much identified with their college but little with ideas as "collegiate," and those little identified with either as "vocational." (See Clark and Trow, 1966, pp. 19–26.)

Neither the medical students described in *Boys in White* nor the undergraduates in *Making the Grade* were, in the late fifties, openly defiant toward their teachers. The medical students wanted to get through medical school and out into practice and only in the rarest cases to become research medical scientists; they saw faculty members as individually demanding virtual full time from every student; they concluded that they could manage and get through only if they cut corners vis-à-vis every expectation put on them, even if this meant skipping material that they might sometime require in the actual practice of medicine. The undergraduates at the University of Kansas also wanted to get out, not merely with what in England would be termed a "pass" degree, but with a good grade-point average for themselves and, if Greeks, collectively for their fraternities and sororities.

It is important to have a sense of scale in considering the Clark-Trow typology. The University of Kansas is typical of the bulk of state universities at the undergraduate level, attracting reasonably affluent students who can pay the costs of residential living. (The only flagship state universities in metropolitan areas are the University of Minnesota, the University of Washington, UCLA, with a few residential dormitories in Los Angeles, and Ohio State University in Columbus; all others are in small towns or at least are nonmetropolitan.) In these institutions and in many similar, private research universities, excluding those of the very most selective sort, students were willing to comply with faculty expectations, and faculties were willing to offer a modicum of undergraduate instruction, often with the help of a corps of teaching assistants. In other words, a tacit bargain was struck in which students did not resist faculty expectations of a certain level of effort, but neither did they internalize faculty norms, nor were most faculty members especially interested in the effort it would have taken to integrate students into the faculty's subcultures and to socialize the undergraduates—or, as some would later learn to say, coopt them. This kind of faculty effort and student response was always a marginal exception, quantitatively illustrated by the fact that the University of Kansas has 17,000 undergraduates and Reed College 1,100. Another way of putting it would be to say that Reed, about which more will be said later, is at one end of a continuum, at the other end of which might be put one type of liberal arts or transfer program at a public community college, all of whose students are commuters working part-time, many of them married, with limited institutional commitment, some of them openly defiant of faculty expectations (London, 1978). The percentage of students enrolled in institutions where faculty hegemony prevails and is actively supported by a high proportion of the undergraduates might, by a generous estimate, be 5 percent of all enrolled students—but that amounts to something like half a million full-time students, among whom are some of the most academically talented and ambitious. A disproportionate percentage of the academics of recent generations have come from that small fraction who had been taught by faculty members with a desire not merely to offer instruction, whether routinized or entertaining, but to introduce students into what in an earlier era would have been termed the "mysteries" of their craft.

It should also be recognized that any typology is an abstraction, so that actual students and faculty members are apt in some measure to blend the attitudes of other "types." Just as there were students at the University of Kansas who were academically oriented and might also be nonconformist and resistant to what they saw as faculty routine, so at Reed College there developed in the late 1960s a minority of faculty members who split off from Reed College to found the Alternative Learning Community in Portland, Oregon, and to make common cause with students actively hostile to the Reed College ideal as it had existed since the college opened.

The schism at Reed illustrates the first of two major phenomena that in sequence, and to some extent concurrently, have altered the power of what Lord Ashby has termed the "student estate" relative to that of what we might term the faculty estate or the institutional estate, vastly increasing the power of students vis-à-vis their teachers. One of these is loosely described by the term *the counterculture;* the other is defined by the realities of demography.

In higher education, the ideological movement of the counterculture toward freedom from all restraints on individual behavior found expression not only in student-designed majors and student-run courses but also in the creation of institutional forms (despite the general preference for formlessness) to defend student "rights," such as student-financed public-interest law firms in the universities, student lobbies in state capitals and in Washington, legal protection against actual and presumed educational abuses by institutions or individuals (for example, the Buckley Amendment), student representation on boards of trustees and curriculum committees, and, in many institutions, significant student influence on faculty retention and promotion, either by evaluations or by direct participation. (For a succinct survey of student activity of these sorts, both in Washington and in various state settings, see National Student Educational Fund, 1979.)

Students could not have achieved these victories without substantial support from at least a minority of faculty members, often themselves recently students, and administrators who either believed that students were right, found it expedient to act as if they did, or had lost confidence that they themselves could distinguish right from wrong. Students could not have won such hegemony if parents had not frequently abdicated their authority—often siding with their children against secondary school teachers over matters of student discipline, and at the postsecondary level unwilling to support institutional demands where these conflicted with student preferences—including preferences for temporarily stopping out or dropping out of college entirely.

The counterculture—unlike, for instance, student protests against the Vietnam war or other particular social evils—has not been an ephemeral movement, but rather one that has profoundly changed our whole society. In an earlier day it was an affair of the affluent, bitterly resented by stable working-class and middle-class students and by their parents. More recently, however, in most parts of the country, the counterculture, like other movements in an egalitarian society, has been downwardly mobile, influencing the sexual and pharmacological behavior of once-resistant social-class groups and, with the declining physical and psychological or cultural age of puberty, reaching ever-younger cohorts. (For a fuller discussion of the historical roots and current reactions to elements of the counterculture, see Riesman, 1980a, including references there cited, and responses by Berger, 1980, and Maccoby, 1980.)

The resistance to requirements reached its height, especially in the most selective and therefore competitive institutions, at the very same time that the demographic bulge due to the baby boom brought a vast expansion in the number of those attending college and an even greater expansion in the number of those going on to graduate school because jobs teaching the new entrants were available.[4]

By the middle 1960s, it was clear to discerning demographers that birthrates, especially among the educated, were beginning to fall rapidly and hence that the end would soon come to the surge of post–high school youths who might be candidates for postsecondary education. Public institutions continued on what seemed to the economist Allan Cartter and to me a binge of reckless expansion that lasted into the early 1970s. Even the private colleges and universities, though they could not afford to behave so lavishly, built dormitories and science buildings and assumed constant or even increasing applicant pools—at a time when not only was the private share of the whole educational market continuing to contract, as it had been doing since the Second World War, but it was clearly wishful thinking to believe that any but a small number of private

---

[4] For a discussion of the resentments built up, often unconsciously, during the period of rapid expansion—a time also when many students were in college involuntarily as a shelter from the Vietnam war draft—see Grant and Riesman (1978, chap. 6). In several essays, Moynihan (1973, pp. 420–430) has also emphasized the demographic elements in movements of protest, seeing the very size of youthful cohorts as making the tasks of adult socializers more difficult. For statistical data on the seldom-recognized differences in fertility by ethnic and racial groups, with reference to the consequences of family size on IQ and academic performance, and the enormous variations among different ethnic groups by median age, see Sowell (1978, pt. 2).

liberal arts colleges would be able to increase or even maintain their "market share" of highly qualified applicants.

Indeed, my efforts to call the attention of executives and faculty members of both private and public institutions to obvious demographic facts in the period after 1967 were met almost uniformly with a roseate set of expectations for the future. Although in states like California 80 percent of high school graduates were already attending postsecondary institutions, there was hope that even this draft-inflated figure would continue to increase, despite the grudging recognition that many were graduating from high school thanks to social promotion, disliked school, and had neither taste nor preparation for further education. (In the peak year of 1970, in the country as a whole, the proportion of the age cohort enrolled in postsecondary education did not exceed 43 percent; see Veysey, 1980.) Then there was the hope that adults could be attracted back to college, sometimes in evening and weekend programs, sometimes through external degree or distance-learning strategies (see Bonham, 1978)—often with the self-serving assumption that everyone who did not have a college degree desired one. Presidents who placed their hopes in the so-called adult market assumed that *their* institutions would capture that market—and indeed, there was such a market, especially among older women who had dropped out of college to marry or who had otherwise missed out on education but had the wish and aptitude to enter or reenter the labor force with better credentials. (In the United States—in marked contrast, for example, to Japan—girls have taken to school much more readily than boys have, and in a number of contexts girls have been favored with more education than that granted their brothers. This was true on the farm, where the boys' and young men's labor was needed, while young women prepared for the possibility of teaching school until they married or indefinitely, if they did not marry. In a growing Catholic population also, young women had the alternative of the religious life, which made available careers as teachers in the growing parochial school systems, where for a long time, as a Boston study shows [Oates, 1978], girl pupils markedly outnumbered boys; until quite recently, the young Catholic woman's entry into a teaching order was a kind of "women's liberation" from traditional Catholic demands for stay-at-home motherhood. On the proportion of women teaching in postsecondary education before the post–World War II era of domesticity and the baby boom, see Bernard, 1964.) What was irrational was the one-person chess of the institutions that did not consider that equally vigilant and aggressive recruiters from other institutions would be pursuing the same absolutely large but still insufficient cadre of prospects, thus in effect canceling out, while rendering ever more expensive, one another's marketing tactics.

As enrollments by the middle 1970s began to taper off and, among white males, actually to fall, all but a few highly attractive institutions discovered that they could not restore requirements abandoned in the earlier era of protest, since any requirement had in general (we shall note a few small exceptions later) the effect of keeping some prospective student customers away who believed in their "rights" and who enjoyed the privilege of shopping at the academic bazaar beyond vocational imperatives. Even in overapplied institutions, which had sufficiently eager si pplicants so that requirements could have been imposed or reimposed, faculty members could rarely agree on what constituted an appropriate education, and the requirements have often remained forms of distributing student traffic among various departments in accordance with the departments' political strength, although even in such institutions they are not entirely independent of students' pressure for their freedom to choose their own course of study.

In most institutions, whose applicant pools were not large enough to permit a high degree of selectivity, that student insistence on freedom—the student as customer—gained overwhelming political strength. In private as well as public institutions, faculty members depended for personal and departmental survival on their attractiveness to students, whose relative market power increased as their numbers declined in classrooms and dormitories.

A more appropriate analogy for the relation between student and teacher than that of customer and marketer is that of athlete and coach, when the coach's interests lie in developing the student's powers rather than in exploiting them for the coach's own glory. Even today, one can find American students who, weary of the overoptioned life, seek a master who will teach them self-mastery. Just as some Americans subordinate themselves to Zen disciplines both in the United States and in the Far East, one can find a similar style of student self-subordination among those who want to achieve the highest peaks of artistic virtuosity. The generations of American composers who studied in Paris with Nadia Boulanger were witness to the extraordinary attraction she exercised over students of composition by the notoriously difficult demands she placed on them to work with an intensity as if not only their careers but their very lives hung in the balance. They knew that she had no patience with teaching them to be "creative" or even with reading their compositions; rather, she would subject them to drill and exercises in harmony and counterpoint that would make them masters of the techniques they needed—in other words, the basic skills of musicianship so thoroughly learned as to form the basis for later independence and, where musically desirable, the conscious breaking of rules in contrast to sloppy nonadherence to rules unknown. Such skills seem still today to be best taught by the apprentice method, which goes back to the earliest days of the Greek academies.

In contrast to such voluntary discipleship, as Willard Waller noted long ago in his classic book *The Sociology of Teaching* (1932), when schooling becomes compulsory, some conflict between involuntary captives and their teachers becomes unavoidable. There is probably no society where more than 15 percent of students, especially among boys, really enjoy school and subordinate themselves to its demands willingly and even joyfully.[5] The classic conflict described by Waller of the competing agendas, only slightly overlapping, dividing teachers and students, is ancient—preceding by centuries the practice at the University of Bologna of students' hiring their own professors, paying them fees according to

---

[5] Japan may be something of an exception. In spite of complaints about what is termed "the infernal examination system" and the tremendous competitive pressures from kindergarten through the precollegiate years, students and parents work together to prepare for the examinations that will determine entry to the major government (and a few leading private) universities, which will in turn lead to high position in the civil service or corporate life. A kind of retroactive resentment shows up in the behavior of the students once they have entered university and life becomes easier, at times even rebellious. Still, there is pride in a system that brings the whole population to high standards of literacy and numeracy, and its undiluted meritocratic quality gives it the aura of fairness even though objections are raised on

their performance, and dismissing them when they proved un-satisfactory. In reviewing *The Oxford Book of Oxford* (Morris, 1978), the Cambridge historian J. H. Plumb illustrates these different agendas between young and old: "For centuries, youth paid an astonishing deference to age," he notes, while the dons "tolerated a fantastic amount of horseplay in the young. . . . So long as [the dons] kept their privileges to rule, to teach what they liked, to examine how they liked, and to impose their own quaint social discipline with regard to women and sex, they were willing to dis-miss drunkenness and riot as mere aristocratic horseplay." Earlier, young and old "kept their worlds apart, one subject to the other, but ever tolerant of the other's excesses. . . . Now these worlds are in collision" (1978, p. 12).

Faculty Dominance in Professional and Graduate School

Student Subordination at Harvard Law School. At some American in-stitutions, many students have long acquiesced willingly to faculty power; but to observe them before the height of the era of faculty hegemony, researchers would have had to look elsewhere at a col-lege of arts and sciences or even a medical school of a moderately selective and demanding state university such as Kansas, as Hughes and his associates did. If they had instead examined the climates of the half-dozen major national law schools, they would have emerged with a very different picture. Students in these settings, rather than using coping behavior to counteract faculty expecta-tions that they thought unreasonably high and performing at a level of effort consensually deemed appropriate, eagerly internal-ized the values of the faculty and judged themselves accordingly.

---

the score of the élan and creativity that may be lost in student subordination to often pedantic drillmasters. And of course, the Japanese schools are part of a whole social structure in which there are today only vague stirrings concerning the concept of *itigai*, or self-realization; the society rests on at least overtly harmonious relations within the family and within the peer group of age mates in school and in later life. Obedience to group norms, rather than to anarchic individual desires, seems essen-tial if a hundred million people are to maintain productivity and social order in a country smaller than Montana and with no natural resources. A Japanese Zen master, with his penalties ranging from sarcasm to physical beatings, to whom disciples willingly subordinate themselves, is but an extreme example of a more general national pattern.

For one thing, there is an inherent difference between medical schools and law schools. The former have been increasingly selective at the point of entry ever since the Flexner reforms. But once admitted, students who make a reasonable effort are rarely failed out. And the faculty members are specialized: the obstetricians and the psychiatrists, the orthopedic surgeons and the gastroenterologists all want a cohort of students, as of interns and residents, who will work on the wards with them in the clinical years or assist in the operating room. Grades are not of such monolithic importance as to overshadow performance on the job; it is this that will help obtain the letters of recommendation for coveted internships in famous teaching hospitals. In fact, in many situations, students are forced by the nature of medical training to cooperate with one another: in dissecting a cadaver, in patient care on the wards. Their competition is past once each has won a place in a medical school.

In contrast to medical schools, law schools are like accordions: almost infinitely expansible, relatively inexpensive to start and to run. And for many years, Harvard Law School (to take the largest and most internally competitive) admitted students rather freely to the first-year class and then warned the neophytes that a third of them would be washed out by examinations that came only at the end of the year and were impersonally graded in numbered bluebooks out of which the student received an average measured in decimal points. (The bluebooks were not returned nor any comments given to the students, so that the single number that averaged all the examinations was the only feedback students received, other than the happenstance and often tormenting encounters with professors in class, who asked them to state cases and then pulled apart their ability to be succinct and sufficiently critical —activities that could be deeply humiliating but had no bearing on the final grade.)

Moreover, within the law schools lies a prize as coveted as an internship at a prestigious teaching hospital—namely, the Law Review. Staffs of the Law Reviews were originally chosen solely on the basis of grades within a rather narrow range,[6] though in some

---

[6] When I attended Harvard Law School, the range of grades that determined whether one "made" Law Review was narrow: most of the members of the Law Review had first-year grades between 75.5 and 77.5, with grades over that so rare as

schools (including Harvard) they are now chosen in part by grades and in part by competition through samples of one's writing. The Law Reviews not only provided in some ways a superior education to the last two years of law school, cultivating the abilities to write, to edit, and to be edited, but were the gateway to becoming clerks to appellate justices, members of the leading law firms anywhere, and occupants of many desired positions in government service— in the Department of Justice, the Securities and Exchange Commission, and other lawyer-staffed agencies. (For an argument that the Law Review graduates who become law clerks, even to the Supreme Court justices, have gained that omnicompetent arrogance which is one of the marks of the successful lawyer and that many who "leaked" information about their Supreme Court employers to the authors of *The Brethren* [Woodward and Armstrong, 1980] had been given this overweening and, in this instance, unethical outlook by their law school success, see Lynch, 1980.)

At a time when in Harvard College a gentleman's C was only beginning to lose its reputable quality, for there still were gentlemen, and the C still contained elements of *virtù* in the Roman sense (see Thelin, 1976), Harvard Law School had become completely meritocratic. The penalties for doing inadequate work were unequivocal: namely, dismissal of as many as a third of the entering class—a more severe mortality than practiced by those state universities that by law had to admit everybody who was a high school graduate and then used students' first term as a de facto College Board examination. Out of an entering class of 700, only several dozen could achieve Law Review status, with another, smaller cadre added at the end of the second year. In this earlier era there were consolation prizes in the form of opportunity to take part in mock appellate trials (moot court) or in legal aid work, which has since become a major focus of many major law schools.[7]

---

to be a statement that no one in this cohort would be likely to equal the legendary grade of 89 achieved by Louis D. Brandeis and, many years later, by James M. Landis (later a Harvard Law School professor, dean, and high government servant).

[7] Northeastern University Law School in Boston, founded in 1968, operates on that University's co-op pattern of a term at school and an internship term, with internships arranged in law offices of various sorts. Antioch School of Law in Washington, D.C., was founded in 1971 by two Yale Law School graduates, Jean Camper Cahn and Edgar Cahn, Jr., who conceived the idea of a school that, from the very first

The form of teaching that characterized Harvard Law School in an earlier era was termed socratic (on the mistaken assumption that Socrates allowed his adversaries, such as Thrasymachus, ever to gain the upper hand in debate), but perhaps it could be better termed sarcastic: many professors would quiz a student on the "finding" of the case while other students looked on in a mixture of gloating and fear lest they too be called on. The faculty was almost universally made up of professors who had themselves made the Law Review, if not at the home institution, then at the one or two others grudgingly deemed marginally comparable. Indeed, students were aware of the one or two members of the faculty who suffered, whatever their national or even world-class distinction, from the knowledge that they had not been members of the Law Review when they themselves were law students. It was also possible to observe law students who, for example, had been Rhodes Scholars of luminous talents and who then faded into feelings of gray mediocrity when they did good but not outstanding work as defined in the single currency of scrupulously bestowed law school grades. Similarly, although in my opinion it was more difficult at that time to earn a summa at Harvard College than to make the Law Review at one of the national law schools, it was possible to observe failure under the later verdict nullifying success under the former one (or the kudos of a Rhodes Scholarship)—its very severity proof that one was, what the most sensitive students frequently feel they are, at bottom a fake, indicating that the success one has had previously was a fluke.

Students did form little groups to review for the year-end examinations on which everything depended, but unlike the medical students in *Boys in White* or work groups in general, they formed no solidary cohort to protect themselves from faculty pressures or from their own internal pressures to avoid failure and to achieve success.

---

year, would be at the same time a law firm—thus, a clinical law school going beyond most medical models. Unfortunately, the pedagogically radical ideal never had a genuine trial, since the school also actively recruited minorities and, given the times and the milieu, had a loose and participative regimen. When the Cahns attempted to tighten control, the faculty unionized, and the most recent chapter in an unhappy sequence is the dismissal of the founders by President William Birenbaum of the parent institution in Yellow Springs (see Myers, 1980).

Even in the most demanding undergraduate colleges, of which California Institute of Technology would be a dramatic example, although the main avenue to success is plainly academic, there are alternative routes to modest acclaim—for example, musical performance, student journalism, or exercise of leadership. But in professional schools in general, where consensus on top performance is high and (in contrast to many medical schools) unidimensional,[8] the situation changes dramatically; this is true of graduate schools of business and management, many Ph.D. programs in arts and sciences, doctoral programs in engineering, and other major professional postbaccalaureate schools, as well as law schools. Students entering law school from elite liberal arts colleges where their wide curiosities and interests had been valued or even taken for granted by faculty members experienced culture shock in the cutthroat atmospheres of law schools where those very curiosities and interests were felt as a threat—as childish things to be put aside. On their side, the major law schools saw their task as taking students who had coasted by on a gentleman's C—or had done better with full time to explore areas of amateur interest in or out of the curriculum—and saying to them: "Now is the time to put undergraduate concerns away; this is boot camp, and a model for life. If you think our demands unduly stressful and competitive, so is life itself." (One difficulty with this rationale is that in fact law school is much more competitive than most aspects of American life, as well as more meritocratic and far more rationalistic.) I believe that it is not the business of schools to be lifelike, to simulate the "real world," but rather to create a situation of tension vis-à-vis the diversities of that world. Law schools in the era of undiluted meritocracy conveniently took for granted that there was but a single real world (a view that embraced a set of assumptions about their student bodies—and the world—which were untested by research).

[8] Barbara Lerner, a lawyer and psychologist, discusses the special case of the law school aptitude test in an essay (1980) largely devoted to defending the use of tests in both undergraduate and graduate admissions. She comments that the leading law schools, such as Harvard, no longer have any substantial attrition because performance on the LSAT is closely linked to ability to do the work required in law school and, with an obvious allowance for the influence of motivation and other personal characteristics, much of the diurnal work of many lawyers.

Indeed, law professors even today are not for the most part researchers (though this is rapidly changing in some of the leading law schools, including Harvard); they publish periodic "book reviews" of what the appellate courts decide, and they occasionally collect these decisions in annotated (and increasingly erudite) textbooks to be used in teaching. Many have seen one purpose of the first-year law courses as teaching students to distinguish their sentiments and their sentimentality from legal reasoning and hence to become debaters able to argue either side of a case. For those entering members of the class who believe that law and justice are identical and that what is right must also be what is legal, such teaching, though it may seem that of a sophist, can be justified as a protection against moralistic oversimplification and naive idealism. Many faculty members have believed that in class discussion and, above all, in the examinations it has been possible to make a unilinear judgment of a student's ability to "think like a lawyer."

Students with the proper verbal acuteness and power of abstract reasoning could fairly quickly learn the appropriate cognitive habits that allowed the ablest professors, with practiced effortlessness, to show their superiority to particular judges (ordinarily, in the American grain, the product of lower social origins and the lesser law schools) whose opinion (much of it *obiter dicta*) frequently bore little relation to the actual ruling—which often was itself contradictory or anomalous.

Even in the heyday of this system, now much attenuated, there were students who refused to be subordinated by it. Some, unwilling to put their adequacy to what they regarded as a limited test, rejected the "game" of law school entirely; some engaged in the psychological equivalent of oversleeping the examination, pretending that they were uninterested in the verdict, and of course occasionally avoiding it by voluntary departure. Having played the game successfully, I could also afford to reject it, and at one point I sought to organize an independent Law Review chosen from among those known to be excellent writers whose grades were not quite of Law Review caliber but who would certainly have made Law Review at a smaller school. I arranged to bring gifted, poetic, puckish Karl Llewellyn, then of Columbia Law School, to talk to a mass meeting of students on "What's Wrong with Harvard Law

School," a meeting the dean, the formidable Roscoe Pound, sought to obstruct. The size of the group attending the meeting indicated unhappiness with the gray monotone of unrelieved and anxious study, but it was many years before critics such as the psychoanalyst Alan Stone (1971) or Duncan Kennedy, a Yale Law School graduate who has written scathingly about the socratic style (1970), were given tenure on the Harvard Law School faculty.

But by that time, though some legacies of the older law school pattern remained, there had been a great loosening of the curriculum and a broadening of the faculty, so that it included a number of distinguished scholars, for example, in Chinese, Korean, and Japanese law (Jerome Cohen) and Soviet law (Harold Berman) and philosophically oriented non-Americans (Charles Fried, Roberto Ungar); the very presence of faculty members such as Duncan Kennedy and Alan Stone was testimony to the altered climates, now pluralistic, of the school. The law school was on its way to becoming, like other major professional schools, a mini-university.

Undiluted Academic Meritocracy: The Case of Mathematics. After Harvard Law School and those that follow its lead more or less strictly, the next place to look for the subordination of students to a univocal decision about their adequacy is in certain departments of graduate schools of arts and sciences in eminent research universities. There are certain fields—mathematics, for example—in which many articulate persons on the "arts" side of C. P. Snow's famous "two cultures" divide (in Western Europe more than in China or Japan) never even reach the treeline, let alone see the towering peaks above the treeline. In a department of mathematics or such a school of mathematicians as is to be found at the Institute for Advanced Study at Princeton, the consensus on who does good work and what constitutes good work is reached early—in a university, quite often when a student is an undergraduate or even earlier. Mathematics has much of the quality of a game, analogous to chess, though played against an "invisible college" that is working on its own autonomous developments on the branching tree of ever more recondite subspecialties. There is something boyish about the game; for reasons marginally genetic and in large part cultural, few women in Western culture have been good at it; when they reach the treeline, like many men, they give up the "pure" game either for applied work in a less prideful field or for another kind of applied work that is only nominally within the field—namely, mathematics education or science education. For the able practitioner, the work can sometimes be performed in intense, brief spurts, allowing much time for the cultivation of other interests—musical, literary, athletic, or whatever.

It is a common view that mathematicians do their best work when young and that practitioners of enormous distinction who remain alert as senior persons in the field, such as André Weil or the late John von Neumann or the late Marston Morse, are exceptions. This judgment rests on a failure to take account of the fact that most mathematicians—like most scientists in general—are young, so that naturally they produce most of the work. There is no satisfactory evidence that "productivity"—usually based on citation indexes, with all their limitations—declines after the age of about thirty-five, but rather evidence that in a high-consensus field distinction can come and be clear to all when one is quite young.

Perhaps a quarter of mathematicians seek to make careers as researchers—a proportion not greatly different from that in other academic fields (Trow, 1975b, chap. 2). Those who have decided that they lack the gift, energy, or support to continue primarily as researchers, who do a limited amount of teaching in major universities, have sometimes already redefined themselves as nonpublishing teachers or moved toward applied mathematics or statistics or to theoretical physics, perhaps even to sink as "low" as economics or (in snobbish faculty ungenerosity) academic administration. Older researchers may continue to publish articles at a declining rate or in collaboration with younger scholars; they may take on responsibilities in the American Mathematical Society or, if outstanding scholars, the National Science Board.

One result of the difficulty of securing a Ph.D. degree in mathematics (as an article in *Science* noted a number of years ago) is that there have been until recently too few Ph.D.s in mathematics to meet the requirements for accreditation (including having a set proportion of Ph.D.s on the faculty) of all the liberal arts colleges in America, most of which needed teachers of mathematics who held the doctorate as an essential curricular component. But those with the qualifications for becoming "mere" teachers of mathematics are in some graduate departments not encouraged to pursue "merely" plodding work that might allow students the "finger exercise" credential of the Ph.D. degree. For in the really distinguished departments of mathematics, only work deemed original is regarded as deserving of the Ph.D. degree—as "originality" is supposed to be the hallmark of the doctorate in all fields (a little like the Doctorat d'Etat in France) but is reached in very few. In the immediate post-Sputnik era a few mathematicians found a new vocation in upgrading the level of mathematics teaching in leading elementary and secondary schools—developing the so-called "new math." Professor Biberman of Illinois was one of the leaders; then Professor John Kemeny, now president of Dartmouth, took the lead in creating a doctorate specifically geared to turning out teachers of mathematics who had inventiveness in this respect.[9]

Nevertheless, when students began to come to college with virtually no quantitative preparation, few mathematicians turned out to have much interest in teaching or in letting others teach what used to be called "bonehead math"—that is, mathematics for the mathematically inadequate. Although mathematicians enjoy one another's company and engage in a great deal of "office gossip" and "shop talk," they tend to be anarchic people who have grown up as precocious boys. Gifted and imaginative, often musical and widely cultivated, they have been in my experience at my own

---

[9] In the leading research universities, one can find a somewhat comparable constellation in the relation between those graduate students who are interested in, and gifted at, teaching foreign languages and those who are interested in literature and criticism; prestige goes only to the latter. The former, who really enjoy the teaching of language and may have a gift for nuance evident in their translations, may have to pretend to an interest in literature in order to be taken seriously, to qualify for the doctorate, and certainly to receive tenure at a major university. Yet, as in mathematics, the need of the majority of students is for the teaching of languages and basic skills, skills that do not advance the discipline defined as concentrated on the literary and artistic high culture.

Carl Kaysen has pointed out (personal communication, 1980) that a number of mathematicians at the Institute for Advanced Study (of which he is a former director), notably Deane Montgomery, have taken a genuine interest in advancing the teaching of mathematics and have sought to bring there as annual members visitors who are not in the most elite institutions (or, in the metaphor I have used, above the treeline) but whose impact on the teaching of their colleagues and students can be considerable if given the time and opportunity to work with the more generous mathematicians at the Institute for Advanced Study.

institution among those most vehemently opposed to all requirements imposed on undergraduates. One reason may be that they
see mainly people who are talented, if not highly gifted. I have
been on committees with mathematicians who have recommended
virtual open admissions at Harvard. They are eager to welcome
"authentic ghetto blacks," assuming that they will not have to teach
such individuals, so that, unconsciously rather than maliciously,
they are antielitist at the expense of "slum" fields such as sociology.
If I speak with some feeling, it is not because these mathematicians
derogate sociology—a derogation which I am used to and which is
often all too justified. It is because some of them found it difficult
to allow Deborah Hughes-Hallett, a gifted teacher for those suffering from what Sheila Tobias later dubbed "math anxiety" (Tobias,
1978, pp. 17–18), to teach Math A, a remedial course. The course
was accepted on the ground that it would be helpful for nonwhites,
but actually it has been more sought after by young women wanting to go to medical school or to understand something about
economics than by many of those less well-prepared blacks
who understandably find it humiliating to take what is labeled a
remedial course if they are not required to. It is on such grounds
that many vocal mathematicians opposed Harvard's core curriculum, adopted by faculty vote in the spring of 1978: they argued
that Math A could operate only on a voluntary basis and that it was
impossible to bring to mathematics students for whom the course
would be required. Some may have been projecting their own
anarchistic tendencies on the incoming students, who of course
were free to choose among many good colleges that had no such
requirement in mathematics.

Each specialty in academic life, as in society in general,
depends heavily on self-selection for its recruits. (For a study of
changes in career plans among entering students as they match
their interests and qualities against those already in an academic
field, see Goldsen and others, 1960.) Certain occupational groups,
for example, may be more alike across otherwise dissimilar societies
than like the counterparts in other fields in their own societies.
Nevertheless, it would of course be unfair to regard mathematicians as a unified cadre, at Harvard or elsewhere. At Dartmouth,
as already implied, some mathematicians have been willing to do

battle against the ideological defenses many students offer against becoming adequate—not geniuses but simply adequate—in quantitative work. Thus inadequacy may even be offered as proof of one's being humane and creative![10] Also the verdict of inadequacy on a mathematics student lacks the personal trauma of most such verdicts in a law school; here, as in many other aspects of the national life, those who suffer most may be those who are near enough the top to have a chance for it and who yet know, because the top is so clearly delineated, that they will never get there. The top, like Mount Everest, is a world top; mathematics is an international game, and members of any country can play, although some countries have Sherpas to guide people at least up to the treeline and others do not. And the difference between the Olympics and academic work is clear: in the Olympics, one's action is for the glory of the group, even though one may become a celebrated individual hero; in mathematics, as in so much else in scholarship, one works alone. Even the institution that nurtured the mathematician may not get the credit, for the Fields Medal may come when he has already gone elsewhere, although there is some counting of coups by institutions and of course by countries. Still, it is a sport in which at the top there are few if any coaches, only rivals.

The British mathematician Hardy quipped that the great thing about mathematics was that it was no damn use. Like Mount Everest, it was simply there. Of course, he was completely wrong, but that spirit still prevails, and in America this very fact helps give mathematicians a beleaguered quality, working against what they see as the pragmatic and utilitarian American grain.

During the 1950s and much of the 1960s, many fields came as close to mathematics as they could in their effort to impose at the graduate level equally severe standards of what was good work. In sociology, for example, it is obvious that a variety of talents can be useful, including the gift of tact as an interviewer, skill as a

[10] Some natural scientists have begun eloquent counterattacks against the effort to stereotype them as unfeeling, extravagantly rationalistic technocrats. See, for example, Thomas (1974, 1979). There is, however, a substantial cohort of talented scholars, a number of them concentrated at MIT and Harvard, who have turned against science, as in the attacks on any research on DNA. Some see work in genetics as having inevitably racist connotations—their enemies sometimes call them "Lysenkoists."

survey researcher, erudition in history and comparative culture, and theoretical clarity. Some graduate schools of sociology nevertheless became minor monoliths, setting up a unidimensional standard of excellence few could attain and sending the majority off without the doctorate, some to teach in community or unselective four-year colleges, others to fall by the wayside—from their mentors' perspective—into market research, work for a government agency, or similar fields. Although these jobs were often well paid and intrinsically satisfying, their occupants, indoctrinated by their training, regarded them as second-best.

At the undergraduate level also, in the high-consensus fields of mathematics and the natural sciences, students at selective university colleges even today accept the verdicts on their capacities as measured by a grade, much as students at Harvard Law School did. (Some branches of economics, the most conceptually and mathematically "advanced" of the social sciences, can in a major university be included here.) I have had the frequent experience of conversing with students in Harvard College who had entered the college with the intention of specializing in one of the scientific subfields until they received an A-minus or, even more fatal, a B-plus on an examination in their subject. To them, such a verdict, like the verdict of Harvard Law School, is irrefutable evidence of inadequacy. It has done no good to point out that on a world scale such students are still among the brightest natural scientists to be found on the planet and that natural science is a large enough mansion—the partitions between rooms being under continual movement—to provide room for students of a variety of gifts. Occasionally I have said to such a student: "Suppose that in fact the judgment passed on you by your professor is a mistake, and the professor is wrong?" Now I rarely raise such a question, because I have found that students either reject it or are shaken by it: if a professor's judgment in a consensual field like mathematics or physics cannot be relied on, entropy has already set in, and the order of the universe cannot be restored. The students' self-doubts, which most of us harbor in greater or lesser degree all our lives, may often lead them to prefer the judgment that it is they who are mistaken.

Nonconsensual Fields and Diminution of Student Subordination. In consensual fields, students would prefer to believe they are inadequate rather than even consider the possibility that a professor might make a mistake. In "wisdom," or nonparadigmatic, fields, such as the social sciences, professors' judgments can be and often are questioned.[11] This is especially likely if the student has put in a great deal of work, for students bring with them a legacy of the high school ethos that hard work should win a good grade. Given a certain amount of talent, hard work does win a good grade—indeed, a top grade—in mathematics and the natural sciences. But in the humanities and the nonconsensual social sciences, students find it hard to accept the relativistic and noncongruent values of professors in selective colleges, in which hard work even by able students does not suffice—the frames of reference are too relativistic, the judgments of creativity too hard to predict (Perry, 1970). Thus, there is a sharp break between the attitudes held by most high school seniors and the kinds of assessment mutually made by students and faculty at selective institutions, examples of which I discuss below. For in these institutions, not only can students not win distinction by high ability and hard work, as they did in high school; something more is needed, some indefinable grace, that sign of election for which the Calvinists strove. Similarly, faculty members cannot win the approbation of students (who become increasingly critical as they proceed through the curriculum) simply by being considerate and decent, if they are not also clearly scholarly and are regarded as such by peers.

I shall discuss as an example the field of sociology. Though

[11] It should be apparent that I am speaking here in general and hence overaggregated terms. A consensus in a paradigmatic field breaks down as new data and interpretations are brought forward (Kuhn, 1962). And I have already indicated that some segments of economics—and, I would add, of experimental psychology—are closer in these respects to the natural sciences than to such fields as anthropology, clinical psychology, or history, just as in sociology there are fierce arguments about demography but reasonable consensus on actual data concerning fertility rates, if not concerning the social-psychological, cultural, and ecological conditions that influence these. However, I have sometimes come across students with more than a little touch of paranoia combined with narcissism, who believe themselves to be unrecognized geniuses whose lack of recognition in high-consensus

there might be departments of sociology that, dominated by a gifted perfectionist, could create a single-minded ethos, the United States is much too large and decentralized for any single pattern in a nonconsensual field to assume national hegemony. (There has for many years been a widespread belief that sociology is dominated by some sort of "Eastern establishment," seen as positivistic in one era, as conservative—if not reactionary and complicitous—in another. However, since sociology demands relatively little ability of its entrants, contrasted with economics or the hard sciences, and has highly divergent ideological and pedagogic styles, a single "establishment" could hardly set and maintain standards for the field.) Even so, many departments of sociology have been able to create, on the one hand, "schools" of disciples, evangelists of the doctrine or method as practiced in the department, and often, on the other hand, much larger numbers of those who dropped out in fact or feeling because they either could not discover the pluralistic niches in a seemingly monolithic department or could not regard such niches as academically respectable.

The time taken to complete the degree is often an important factor in the balance of self-esteem and self-deprecation with which a student works his or her way through graduate school. One of the large attractions of law school is the fact that it requires three years only. Since the first degree in law does not require a work of scholarship, one might regard it as simply a postbaccalaureate bac-

---

areas is due to their professors' envy or vindictiveness. In such cases, inner self-doubts are turned outward, against the alleged victimizers.

There is a danger, as the social psychologist Donald Campbell warns in a recent article (1979–80), that in a period of declining enrollments departments in reviewing junior faculty members will tend to favor those whose interests are closest to the departments' central or core concerns, rather than those who have developed alliances with neighboring fields and have the potential of cultivating what Campbell calls "a novel narrowness." Campbell notes that the temptation to appoint to scarcer tenure positions those whose allies are the departments' central members is likely to be heightened by the availability of able faculty members who can now be recruited by universities wishing to increase their reputations as research institutions because such faculty members have more difficulty in finding posts in a relatively static market at the already high-prestige institutions. Scholarship is likely to suffer when decisions are made only on a departmentwide rather than an institutionwide basis—of course, one would not want to ignore the departmental judgments as one element in quality control at the threshold, but to rely on such judgments exclusively may lower the ceiling.

calaureate—three more years of collegelike courses and examinations. Law schools are even more like college today than in the earlier day described above: their near-total reliance on "socratic" teaching by the case method and their narrow definitions of what is good work and what is good teaching have been diluted by bringing in the social sciences or other styles of work, including the practitioner forms mentioned. In mathematics, as in law, little time is needed to secure a degree—some can do it in a single year, and few take more than four. In many of the natural sciences also, even the first-year graduate student may get on the track of a senior professor and obtain a thesis out of a series of articles published with a team, judgment on the student's own contribution being made collectively by his or her mentors. But in more individualistic fields, such as history or literature or sociology, the longer one waits to finish one's degree, the more brilliant one may feel one must be in order to justify the delay.

Furthermore, in many departments, the courses one takes resemble law courses in showing up the deficiencies of the material one reads, even the work of the great writers of the field. Consequently, the graduate student is apt to feel that nothing he or she can produce will live up to the already internalized standards by which even Durkheim's *Suicide* or Weber's *Protestant Ethic and the Spirit of Capitalism* can be attacked. This constant exercise of criticism leaves the implication that there is really no work that is good enough to stand up against either the ideological or methodological critiques that have become prevalent today.

As already indicated, the undiluted subordination of students, illustrated in the extreme by Harvard Law School of an earlier day and to a lesser degree by departments of mathematics, is, by the very nature of those attracted into the field, rarely found even in the most monolithic departments of sociology. Many students have come with a variety of backgrounds, including interim periods of teaching or other work, from a variety of undergraduate institutions, where they may have majored in subjects more intrinsically difficult than sociology at its average level—mathematics or a natural science, for example. Many have mastered such a difficult foreign language as Japanese or have served in the Peace Corps and learned Wolof or Fula. Under these conditions, there is likely to develop, if not a full-blown student subculture of an oppositional sort, at least cadres of students who "think otherwise" than what passes for sociology among the more impressive and oppressive mentors.[12]

Most graduate schools of arts and sciences have had a saving grace that has protected the self-esteem of many, even while shaking the self-esteem of others: the ability quite early in one's career to become a teaching assistant and to validate one's knowledge, if not one's originality, through teaching. (In the natural sciences, the best students have found a similar outlet by becoming research assistants.) The race for distinction has thus not been quite unidimensional, despite the near-universal judgment that only research and scholarship counted and not teaching. Even at the height of the post-Sputnik meritocratic era, teaching was not completely ignored, and it gave those who did it a legitimate alternative to the ever-renewed obligation to be original in print. Of course, teaching could become a substitute for research and that way lead to a downward mobility far steeper than that of the mathematicians who ended up as economists or sociologists; it could take one to a community college via a consolation M.A. degree while one remained the perpetual floating ABD (All But Dissertation) person. Today in many departments of sociology and other "soft" fields, the Ph.D. degree itself is sometimes given as a consolation prize

[12] In fields unlike mathematics in that experience of life counts for something and child prodigies may not possess superior insight, there is every reason for graduate departments to accept people who have not studied the subject as undergraduates. One way of putting it is to say that, as a field of full-time study, sociology is rarely eight years deep; in certain subfields, a gifted and highly motivated graduate student can reach relatively quickly the point of being able to make an independent contribution. In other words, to get to the timberline in sociology does not take intensive study, provided one sees it as a series of subdisciplines loosely linked by a common departmental name. The ceiling for outstanding achievements is unlimited, as in all fields of scholarship, but the threshold from which one can make a contribution to knowledge is relatively low in comparison with more consensual fields. Contrary to what is often thought, this has nothing to do with the period of time during which the subject has been studied; sociologists can still learn about friendship from Aristotle, as political scientists can learn about their subjects from Plato, Aristotle, Vico, Machiavelli, and Hobbes, whereas only the rare scientist in a paper published in a refereed journal will cite work going back as early as, let us say, 1960, and only the most unusual and cultivated will have any extensive knowledge of the history of the subject or the epistemological issues raised in other cultures and in other times. (See Kevles, 1978, chap. 22.)

even to students of minimal ability who produce acceptable prose. Such individuals may find their way to community colleges, perhaps concealing their possession of the doctorate as a symbol of being "overqualified." (For a study casting doubt on the judgment that community college faculty members are necessarily more effective who share a general community college ethos that is hostile to research and scholarship—an ethos by no means universal among community colleges, which differ as much from one another as four-year colleges do—see Morrison and Freedman, 1978.)

However, if teaching also went badly, the rout of one's hopes and sense of adequacy could be virtually complete—and one might end up saying, with Allen Wheelis' semifictional psychoanalyst in *The Quest for Identity,* "Any honest work is better than this" (1958, chap. 7). But for others, teaching served to rescue one's failing self-esteem and to provide a break from the struggle to find a thesis topic and sustain one's work on it, thus easing the path toward becoming a teacher-scholar-researcher (see Riesman, 1979d). By teaching, furthermore, one avoided isolation; one was not holed up in a study or a cubicle in the library, staring at the walls.

Academic Apprenticeship in Selective University Colleges

There are a few postsecondary institutions that are highly selective in the sense of having large applicant pools. These include the so-called Ivy League universities plus Stanford; the "Little Ivies" (Wesleyan, Williams, Amherst, to which Bowdoin and Middlebury must be added); Swarthmore, Bryn Mawr, and Haverford, Wellesley and Barnard, Duke and Vanderbilt, Notre Dame and the College of the Holy Cross, Pomona, Harvey Mudd, Rice and MIT and Cal Tech—all of these, along with Spelman (for its predominantly black applicants), are private. In the public sector, selectivities of varying types exist—for example, by demanding a certain high school level, as at the University of California, or a certain grade-point average and test scores, as at the Universities of Washington, Virginia, and Vermont, which, along with the University of Michigan and other major state universities, such as Wisconsin at Madison, have considerably higher requirements for out-of-state students.

It often surprises people to learn that Cal Tech has students whose verbal SAT scores are at or above the 700 level, while their quantitative scores are close to the ceiling; it is the most selective institution in the country (aside from tiny two-year Deep Springs College). In general, both private and public institutions oriented toward technology, architecture, and the natural sciences have a high threshold because of self-selection, even if an entire land-grant university may receive students of much lower aptitude (as measured by tests) for its nonquantitative colleges or programs. The University of California has relatively high selectivity, accepting the top eighth among high school graduates plus those qualified through College Boards; even so, there are differences among the nine campuses, with some—Berkeley, UCLA, Davis, Santa Barbara—unevenly overapplied and others desperately short of students.[13]

But selectivity in the sense of proportion of applicants turned away is correlated with academic intensity only in the small band of heavily overapplied, primarily private institutions of the sort just mentioned. It is in colleges of this sort, numbering by generous

[13] Laurence Veysey, himself a professor of history at the University of California at Santa Cruz, has described how in 1965, this then-new campus was by far the most heavily overapplied of the nine campuses, appealing as it did both to some academically highly alert students who disliked competition and were not anxious about their postbaccalaureate futures and also to the devotees of the counterculture; by 1977, Santa Cruz was so short of applicants, as well as having high attrition among those it did recruit, that there was talk that it might have to close. Its substitution of written evaluations for grades was, as surveys showed, clearly a factor in reducing applicants at a time of vocational uncertainty, but the students who were enrolled and many faculty members fought to retain the no-grade policy, not willing to make the concessions necessary for survival and not sure these would work in any case. However, by 1979, under the new admissions director, Richard Moll (who had first put Bowdoin College on the map in part by having the college declare that it was not necessary to take the SAT and then helped Vassar College recruit an excellent cohort of male students), the short-run dangers to Santa Cruz's survival were avoided by a drastically rewritten catalogue, eschewing photographs of longhaired, barefoot students and scantily clad bodies lying in the sun, and emphasizing the solid academic core that has always existed at Santa Cruz rather than the interdisciplinary courses of the various colleges geared to supposed contemporary relevance (Veysey, 1980). The ups and downs of enrollment and attrition at Santa Cruz, being new and without a traditional clientele, illustrate dramatically the volatility of enrollments in residential institutions, as well as the difficulty of altering established imagery even if faculty members do not feel that their new-found tradition is compromised.

count under 100 altogether, that the faculty and the academic program carry weight (Astin, 1977b).

Reed College is among the institutions, virtually all of them small and private, where most entering students have been prepared to apprentice themselves to faculty members who made high demands on their sense of discipline and sought to convey what Trow, in a penetrating essay (1976b), has described as the moral temper of the academic disciplines themselves.[14] Reed College, begun in 1911 in that Western outpost of New England Puritanism and Protestantism known as the state of Oregon, began in what could be seen in one perspective as a colony or farm team for the major graduate schools and in another perspective as what might be called a university college that would be unequivocally at odds with the prevailing collegiate traditions of undergraduate education—traditions by no means moribund even today (Foster, 1911). Reed was to be a place for scholar-teachers, without fraternities and sororities, without football, without the frills and frivolities we lump under the term *collegiate*. This is not to say that it was "purely academic." As Burton Clark (1970) describes matters in his delineation of Reed's history, faculty members such as William Ogburn, later professor of sociology at Columbia and then at Chicago, sought to tie the college into the ongoing municipal problems of Portland—much as the founders of "The Wisconsin Idea" sought

---

[14] It would be a valuable undertaking to determine the extent to which the implicit academic code of ethical responsibility that Trow espouses is actually carried out in practice. Even in the "hard" sciences, we all know of breaches—for example, in hasty races for priority. Common in less consensual fields are tendentiousness, avoidance of obvious facts, and pretentious dogmatism. Presumably much less common—one learns of such instances only by chance, perhaps inaccurately, through gossip—are instances of suppression or obfuscation of research results that the researcher or others fear might be used, if published, to support reactionary views or policies or would displease one's sponsors, colleagues, liberal funding agencies, or powerful intra- and extra-academic pressure groups. Moreover, the code itself can be used, as Trow would be the first to recognize, as a way of quickly dismissing research that departs from conventional methodological patterns though it scrupulously adheres to what I myself would define as the true nature of science— namely, doing work appropriate to the subject, rather than following the methodological monopoly that in many fields is termed "science." In Trow's terms and in mine, "science" requires looking for negative evidence, or what Trow terms "inconvenient facts," submitting one's conclusions to one's colleagues, and being ready to revise conclusions in the light of new evidence.

to relate the university to the necessities of the state, as interpreted at its major university center. (See McCarthy, 1912; for discussion, see Hofstadter, 1963, pp. 199–204.)

In the early days, Reed faculty members played intramural sports with students; later, such informal faculty/student relations were more apt to occur in bull sessions that could last all night, though with the assumption that both students and faculty would be in class the next morning prepared to discuss the assignment (John Pock, professor of sociology at Reed College, personal communication, 1980). Although in the early days professors were given the title *Mister,* as against the current habit of first-naming, the faculty did not behave like remote professors in major postbaccalaureate institutions. And over a long period Reed has maintained one of the best undergraduate general-education programs in the country, although it has not marched under that label. But Reed has in the past resembled Harvard Law School in the degree to which students who could not surmount its steeply inclined gradient have felt themselves to be unlikely prospects for passing the qualifying examination ("The Quals") required before one could enter the senior year. And in that year everyone has been expected to write a thesis and to defend it orally before faculty members. Characteristic in part of the West Coast styles of transiency, but also reflecting its arduousness, Reed has had a relatively high rate of attrition, though no higher than far less demanding institutions (Mitzman, 1979). Thus, Reed has in no sense been a "total institution," to use a frequent but invalid analogy implied by antagonists of the academic revolution. Its faculty members were prepared to help students enter other fields than Ph.D. programs even before the drop in the market for Ph.D.s, although of course it should be added that many professional schools, as in business administration and public policy, have become more discipline-oriented and intellectual. Thus, whatever their postbaccalaureate destination, Reed students have been unusually willing and eager to subordinate themselves to their dedicated mentors. A very high proportion of Reed's small number of graduates have been leading scholars and scientists who received their postbaccalaureate training in the major graduate schools.

Reed College could not offer the "prize at the end of the road" of a medical or law degree; it could offer only the distinction of having graduated from a demanding university college, monolithic in its academic rigor, but not in the modes of life ("life-styles" in current parlance) pursued on campus or in activism in the city of Portland—a distinction recognized in academia but not in the country as a whole.

On seeing the first issue of the short-lived *Reed Journal of History and the Social Sciences,* I was somewhat critical of what seemed to me its hyperprofessionalism. It showed what I did not think needed to be shown: that Reed undergraduates could produce articles comparable in style and substance to those in the major journals. I expressed my wish that some students, since they were going on to graduate school anyway, might use their undergraduate opportunities for a somewhat more exploratory, if less heavily annotated, mode of work. Further reflection led me to regret that judgment. It is important for undergraduates, whatever they may do later, to be able to read reports of research with an understanding of the logic of inquiry, and one can learn this best by engaging in a small-scale piece of social research oneself. Furthermore, shortly after the journal began, the counterculture arrived along with radical activism at Reed as elsewhere, and in retrospect the journal illustrates that it is possible, even in the less consensual fields, for undergraduates to do scholarly work that may maintain a thesis but submit to the moral imperatives of science in the terms suggested by Martin Trow (as mentioned earlier in these pages). Today, as one attends to the combination of rhetoric and sentimentality in the oral discourse of semiliterate undergraduates in the "softer" social sciences, one could long for a journal with as much starch as that one. (For a description of the damage temporarily done to Reed College in the late 1960s by a combined cohort of faculty-administration-student revolutionary activists and hedonistic counterculturists, see Goldsmith, 1971.)

The very fact that Reed College does not have graduate teaching fellows, but a dedicated and scholarly faculty, turns out for some students going on to graduate school, especially in several of the natural sciences, to be a mixed blessing, at least in the initial year. Consider a physics major at Reed who has had the benefit of a fine physics department and who has been best in league, coming to the graduate department of physics at Berkeley or MIT or Harvard. Precisely because such a student has not been in a large cohort of fellow students and has not been taught by teaching fellows who know the latest preprint research findings or theories being circulated among the members of invisible colleges of scholars in each specialty, the student is in the same position during the first postbaccalaureate year as the high school valedictorian who arrives at Reed as a self-confident freshman, only to find that the entering class is full of valedictorians who appear even more talented. But the Reed student who can survive the first postbaccalaureate year can then come into his or her own, with the added benefit of the wide range and cultivation that a Reed education provides.

One finds few analogues of Reed College among baccalaureate institutions in the pre–World War II era. Swarthmore, also described by Burton Clark, divided its student body, in the British or Australian style, into those pursuing pass and those pursuing honors degrees. The latter spend their final two years in seminars and are examined by external examiners; they attain a protograduate finish and style of exceptional quality. However, they eat in the same dining hall, read the same student paper, and often live in the same dormitory as able but merely "ordinary" Swarthmore undergraduates, people who are entering such callings as business or engineering, devalued at Swarthmore.

In the late 1960s such a division came increasingly into disrepute among honors and pass students alike. Despite the extra work demanded of the honors cohort, this cohort became defined as "elitist" by the increasingly powerful egalitarian ethos, which does not recognize any distinction of status or privilege. Honors programs elsewhere, such as the Echols Scholars at the University of Virginia, came temporarily into similar disrepute. In the last few years, however, there has been a revival of support for such programs, especially in large state universities and also at Swarthmore College. (See, for example, the mimeographed journal *Forum for Honors,* published at Ohio State University. Advocates of these programs meet periodically for discussion of problems and for mutual support.)

More like Reed in its monolithic quality, but successful in recent years in drastically decreasing attrition, is St. John's College in Annapolis, Maryland. Its undiluted Great Books program and seminars and totally required curriculum provide an education

that eschews disciplinary professionalism and finds its high seriousness instead in the subordination of students and faculty members
to the identical required program. Thanks to this mutuality, students and faculty have the opportunity for noncurricular discussion of the ideas generated in the seminars and readings. One
cannot say that students at St. John's are subordinate to faculty in
the same way as at Harvard Law School, for both students and
faculty see themselves as the acolytes to the "Great Books" of learning (including science, ancient and modern) from the time of the
Greeks down to the present. They are subordinate in the way that
an orchestra and its conductor (with the exception of Leopold
Stokowski!) regard themselves as subordinate to the music of the
composer, the mentor being only a little more advanced as a coach
in the intricacies of performance. In the same way, the St. John's
tutors are coaches. As they come from different specialties and are
themselves at the outset learning the whole St. John's curriculum,
in each portion of which they must eventually teach, they are in no
way superior to the ablest undergraduates.

The St. John's example makes clear what was left unclarified
in *The Academic Revolution.* The victory of the academic does not
necessarily mean the victory of particular academicians, but rather
of a particular curriculum, which is accepted by those who stay the
course and to which faculty as well as students may feel obligated
(see Veysey, 1979). At Harvard Law School, students in an earlier
day emerged with a feeling that they would never have the breadth
of knowledge of the late Samuel Williston or the barbed and brilliant tongue of James Casner. Similarly, students at St. John's
suffer from a combination of humility vis-à-vis Plato and arrogance
vis-à-vis those for whom Plato is not a series of questions but only a
name that has passed into general currency, whose views, we are
told, influence our daily lives but of which most of us are innocent.

When the Annapolis campus had more applicants than it
could accept, the critical scale being 400 students, rather than expand in a crowded city with the Naval Academy next door, it established a new campus in Santa Fe, New Mexico, with the absolutely identical curriculum—an identity assured by emigrés from
Annapolis and constant transfer—and with the supervision of one
president for both institutions.

When some years ago I visited the Santa Fe campus, adher-

ence to the Annapolis model seemed relatively strict. My suggestion was rejected that the new campus might take advantage of its
location to introduce some of its students, without abandoning its
basic core, to the complex interrelations of the subcultures of the
area (Spanish Americans and Chicanos; indigenous Anglos and
tourist Anglos; various Indian groups—not always hospitable to
temporary visitors; hippies and ascetics). Some members of the
faculty were willing to consider the idea, and Santa Fe has since
then become somewhat freer in departures from the Annapolis
model, but at the time I was there the majority feared any concession to what seemed like the conventional plea for localism and
"relevance." It is understandable that the fundamental reform
pioneered by St. John's College would be held onto all the more
firmly because its faculty makes such sacrifices to the demands of
the curriculum (demands that are in any case high in a small,
liberal arts, teaching-oriented college) that only rarely can a tutor at
St. John's maintain academic visibility in the discipline in which he
or she was originally trained.[15] (For fuller discussion, see Grant and
Riesman, 1978, pp. 40–76.)

Robert M. Hutchins achieved more through his friends Scott
Buchanan and Stringfellow Barr at St. John's College than in the
undergraduate college of the University of Chicago; but the latter
(along with its struggling adjunct, Shimer College, which has
moved from its pastoral location in Mount Carroll, Illinois, to
Chicago) came fairly close to a totally coherent curriculum during
the "Hutchins era." Following the lead of the general-education
program at Columbia, the program developed under Hutchins
was even more effective than Columbia's in subordinating its student body to its relatively monolithic style of verbal acuteness and
pure, nondepartmental academicism. As at Reed, Hutchins saw
football as an enemy and got rid of it, but without substituting what
Reed had had—namely, an active faculty-student intramural program. (Hutchins' scorn for "jocks" fed academic snobberies then

---

[15] Eva Brann, Addison E. Millikin Tutor on the Annapolis campus, is one of the
college's most distinguished scholars, trained in Greek archeology, who recently
published a book on education. See Brann (1979) and discussion in Itzkoff (1980).
Curtis Wilson has retained distinction in his original specialty of the history of
science.

and now.) As at Reed College, the Hutchins college had its glories for those who stayed the course, with an attrition approaching 50 percent. The sources of attrition (which at Reed has been especially common among young women not good at verbal games or not eager to play them) reflect the very subordination of the students to undiluted academic meritocracy that has been characteristic at Chicago. There has been little if any grade inflation, and a number of students have decided, after two years of getting B's and C's for work that would win them A's in most institutions, to transfer and get their degrees elsewhere, with high rewards in the form of grades and less anxious efforts.[16]

The undergraduate college of the University of Chicago, as it was reshaped under the egis of Hutchins but under the actual leadership of a group of unusually erudite and brilliant faculty members after the Second World War, did not offer only small seminars concentrating on a predetermined canon; nonetheless, there were many similarities to St. John's College. The era of academic specialization and the consequent departmentalism had long since arrived, yet the leading intellectual mentors of the college at Chicago were often polymaths. They included such scholars as Edward Shils, who was the virtual, though not the nominal, leader of the staff of the final course in the three-year social sciences sequence;[17] Joseph Schwab, at home in philosophy and in the natural and biological sciences, a powerful influence on many junior colleagues and undergraduates; and Benjamin Bloom, drawn in by that remarkable Midwestern impresario of intellect, Ralph Tyler, to become college examiner—working with the staffs of the various course sequences to provide external examinations

[16] See Spady (1967). For a picture of what was invigorating about Chicago, see the sympathetic account by Nisbet (1964). And for an illustration (originally delivered as an address at the invitation of *Salmagundi* magazine, published at Skidmore College) in which the Chicago style in its combination of brilliant virtuosity and severity is exhibited, see the remarkable book by Philip Rieff, *Fellow Teachers* (1973). Rieff, founder of the short-lived admirable *University of Chicago Magazine* while still a student, took both his undergraduate and graduate degrees at Chicago.

[17] Shils, a man of cosmopolitan erudition, had been a graduate student in the Graduate Department of Sociology and Anthropology, where memories of such notable cosmopolitan and versatile men as Robert Park and W. I. Thomas were fresh in the minds of their students, such as Everett Hughes and Robert Redfield. See, for example, Shils (1975).

(as in the Swarthmore honors program). These examinations allowed teachers to separate their roles as teachers from their roles as assessors (although never completely), much as Oxford and Cambridge dons are able to do.

Columbia College had an earlier, even more inventive general-education program that also had notable scholar-teachers who crossed divisional boundaries between the humanities and the social sciences, much as happened occasionally at Chicago. Columbia attracted many brilliant students, especially from the metropolitan New York area, even while, like Chicago, it lost much of the social elite, so that Columbia remained "Ivy League" only in rather nominal and athletic terms. Some faculty members, such as Lionel Trilling, who was devoted especially to Columbia College, lived in the immediate area, but many scattered to the suburbs, whereas at Chicago virtually all the teaching staff lived in the immediate neighborhood of the university, adding to the intensity of the institution's intellectual life. (Daniel Bell, whose book on general education [Bell, 1966] remains, in my opinion, the best book available on that topic, taught in the college at Chicago, eventually going on to get his doctorate in sociology and teach courses, among others, jointly with Lionel Trilling at Columbia.)

Chicago was for the Middle West, and to a lesser degree for the rest of the country, the institution that attracted those students whom high school principals and counselors regarded as troublesome, precocious brats. But once at the college, where they could move at their own pace through examinations, sometimes without a high school diploma, and sometimes could be admitted to graduate school without a baccalaureate degree, they became some of the most eager disciples of the most celebrated of the college faculty. To be sure, many of these students became activist radicals in the late 1960s, but much of their energy was devoted to extramural events, such as the Democratic party convention of 1968 or black struggles in the neighboring Woodlawn area. When some turned against the university itself and invaded the administration building in 1969, President Edward Levi was able to maintain faculty support in making no concessions whatever to the students, insisting that he would not negotiate with them, and later dismissing a number of them in the face of angry protests from parents and from many fellow students.[18]

Students were attracted by the faculty, sometimes awed and intimidated, and sometimes more simply exhilarated. They took it for granted that if a book was mentioned in a lecture it was up to them to know at least something about it—and because the same curriculum was required for all, as at St. John's, private discourse was often a spillover from the classroom. It was a culture of verbal virtuosity, which could be dramatized as in the Mike Nichols and Elaine May wit and wisdom of the Second City theater company;

---

[18] It anticipates our story, but it may be appropriate here, to note that in the judgment of many, including myself, the University of Chicago is the major American research university to have emerged relatively unscathed and intellectually and morally intact from the student-faculty turbulence of the late 1960s and early 1970s. There are many reasons, including not only the firm leadership of President Levi and the scholarly orientation of the larger part of the student body, but also a general climate of mutual intellectual exchange among the faculty both of the college and of the graduate divisions—all in a rather small university by national norms, and including the medical school on the same campus. This faculty had already tested its senior members in the era of McCarthyism and developed an atmosphere in which, despite sharp differences both of disciplinary "school" and of political persuasion, the whole culture of the institution expected a readiness to listen to opposing viewpoints. (This judgment might be denied by some graduate faculty members, who regarded the students who came to them from the undergraduate college as arrogant, in part because of the very skepticism concerning the boundaries between academic disciplines nourished in the college.)

In 1978–79, the civil and civic culture of Chicago nearly collapsed when students and faculty members learned that, under President Hanna Gray's interim predecessor, a faculty committee had chosen Robert McNamara, president of the World Bank, to address members of the institution and receive a prize for his contribution to international development. Students who had missed out on the anti–Vietnam war protests and who, as at other leading institutions, harbored a powerful nostalgia for the "war" they were too young to fight, were abetted by faculty members with various reasons for disliking McNamara; they had an image of him as the leader in the war in Vietnam as well as someone who now espouses "modernization" and who has a mind like a computer, an inhuman technocrat—a picture of the man which I regard as false—fought to have the invitation withdrawn. Failing in that, they sought to block the speech and, later, the exit of trustees and many faculty members in evening dress from the prize occasion. However, President Gray managed to see that the invitation was not withdrawn, thanks to a modicum of intelligent and forceful faculty support, while having money and lawyers on hand immediately to bail out the students arrested in the demonstration that blocked University Avenue after the address, thus maintaining the Chicago tradition of freedom of speech while sheltering students as yet unsocialized to that tradition.

but it made no more effort to be strong in the arts than in intercollegiate athletics.

Like Reed and Swarthmore, the college of the University of Chicago stands high among those primarily small private, undergraduate liberal arts colleges that, in the famous studies done at Wesleyan, showed high "productivity" among various baccalaureate institutions, as measured by the proportion of their graduates going on to become scientists and scholars (Knapp and Goodrich, 1952; Knapp and Greenbaum, 1953).[19]

All the colleges described so far have been private and selective or self-selective, not only in appearing formidably arduous to prospective students but also in discouraging many who found the atmosphere too rarefied, even dehydrated. The only public non-residential institution that figures in this galaxy was at the time a wholly undergraduate commuter college—namely, CCNY—and, indeed, it was not an institution that for the entire student body brought about the kinds of internalization of faculty values which have been our main concern here. Rather, it was a minority cohort of City College students, mainly Jewish but including also such ambitious intellectuals as James Baldwin and Daniel Patrick Moynihan, who were attracted to the intellectual life—but of this they found only smidgens among the faculty, of whom some of the most famous, such as the philosopher Morris Cohen, behaved like Grand Inquisitors who could demolish students. It was one generation of mainly Eastern European Jews, the first generation of college-goers in their families, who created the ethos of City College for their own cohort, while many others of the same generation simply sought the college as a passport to upward vocational mobility and not to join an intellectual subculture. CCNY thus combined, in the Clark-Trow typology, the vocational and the

---

[19] As is often pointed out, these studies do not control for "input," yet if one controls this factor as very roughly measured by College Board scores, the small, often Midwestern, private liberal arts colleges have turned out in relation to the size of their graduating classes a remarkable number of distinguished academicians, in comparison with equally high-scoring students at more socially prestigious institutions in the Ivy or Little Ivy Leagues, although CCNY, of course a public college, was as "productive" as the small private colleges. See Jencks and Riesman (1968, pp. 493–500).

academic yet often simultaneously nonconformist (see Freedman, 1980, and Glazer, 1973).

Scholarly Atmosphere of the Top-Flight Liberal Arts Colleges

There are a number of rather speculative hypotheses about why these liberal arts colleges, many of them small, turned out (in the Wesleyan studies just cited) to produce so high a proportion of leading scholars and scientists. A high degree of self-selection is at work when students choose to attend colleges that in their own localities have the reputation of refuges for academic "oddballs," as Reed, Antioch, and others have had. And certainly the absence of teaching fellows has meant not only that ties between students and faculty mentors can be close but also that the latter quite commonly nourish academic ambition in their students and bring them early into undergraduate research enterprises.

Disciplines vary considerably in the ease with which undergraduates can be brought into active research. A recent study indicates that, among the disciplines in first-rate liberal arts colleges, biologists are notable in their involvement of students in published research (Fulton and Trow, 1975), and in visiting such colleges I myself have observed the extent to which biologists and those in related fields, including some chemists, do draw undergraduates into their research, take them to professional meetings, and publish papers jointly with them. I suspect that biology in the period covered by this study has been so fluid and fissionable that students have been able to approach the research frontier while still undergraduates. Moreover, some branches of contemporary physics require equipment too elaborate even for most research universities, such as Stanford's linear particle accelerator.

In the traditional humanities, it is more difficult for students to make original critical contributions, although in the arts and in creative writing, the "little magazines" that publish student poetry, photography, and writing; the art studios that exhibit painting, sculpture, pottery; the musical composition—even in schools that do not include a conservatory—are often notable. I myself believe that much more could be accomplished by undergraduates in sociology because—as would also be true with oral history—there is so much that is unknown about American life that a student of any observational power could make a contribution. When I began teaching at Harvard College in 1958, so shy and subordinate were the majority of nonspecialist students that they could not believe this (see Riesman, 1979d); it was necessary for me to publish three successive volumes of undergraduate papers to make evident the variety of areas in which students could add to knowledge and interpretation. (For a recent discussion of an analogous theme, see Stebbins, 1978, and appended comments.)

The top-quality liberal arts colleges have attracted not only faculty members interested in scholarly teaching but also a number who continue to do research visible in their disciplines; the latter, in the absence of graduate students, are often happy to draw gifted undergraduates into their small research enterprises and hence to serve as role models for them. (For a sensitive discussion of the various kinds of role models, some of them harmful to students who are not always sufficiently aware of the risks of such a model, see the discussion by a former Bennington College psychologist: Adelson, 1962. See also Heath, 1964.) A comment by Verne Stadtman, associate director of the Carnegie Council, is in line with my own observations: "Gifted students may not feel as intimidated on such campuses. They will more readily come to terms with their own abilities as being somewhat superior. At larger research institutions, compared to internationally famous scholars and frequently published aspirants, they may be less sure of themselves" (Stadtman, personal communication).

The converse of this seduction of the academic was observed at Vassar College in the studies undertaken there in the 1950s by a team of researchers led by Nevitt Sanford and Mervin Freedman. Those studies suggested that some women avoided close commitment to faculty members because of fear of letting them down, either by inability to perform in graduate school according to what their Vassar teachers expected of them or out of ambivalence about becoming bluestockings, subject to the harsh verdict of the late M. Carey Thomas at Bryn Mawr that "only our failures marry."[20]

---

[20] None of the women's colleges, not even Bryn Mawr with its graduate school, ever achieved the monolithic subordination of students to faculty I have been describing for such exceptional undergraduate colleges as Reed, St. John's, or Chicago. Even Bryn Mawr attracted some debutantes and socialites, who were not out to prove on

But there is another reason that such liberal arts colleges as the College of Wooster in small-town Ohio or Carleton in Northfield, Minnesota, or Grinnell in Grinnell, Iowa, or Oberlin in the small town of the same name should have produced such a disproportionate number of academics in an earlier era: professors were the only adult models around, as the distractions of metropolitan life were absent—distractions that also might provide other models, such as big-city journalism or the arts, for gifted nonconformist but also academic intellectuals. In a later era, moreover, Princeton, Georgetown, Harvard, and other universities made visible the alternative career of government service, including the Foreign Service. Cornell, Illinois, and Wayne State University offered opportunities made especially attractive in the great era of labor organizing during the New Deal to become a labor intellectual, through their schools and programs in industrial and labor relations—and if one could not work for a union, one might work for the National Labor Relations Board or one of its state analogues. Antioch College in an earlier period provides the possibility of deviant-case analysis, for its off-campus internships gave students opportunities to try out a variety of careers; and yet Antioch is one of the institutions that figure in the Wesleyan studies as sending many people on to Ph.D. programs, thus indicating that its encapsulated on-campus program in isolated Yellow Springs in conservative southeastern Ohio and its dedicated, scholarly faculty overcame for many students the temptations to other careers opened up by off-campus co-op jobs. (During the 1960s and early 1970s, under the presidency of James Dixon, Antioch College turned toward activism and away from scholarship [Grant, 1972a]. For a succinct account of Reed, past and present, see Mitzman, 1979; for both these institutions plus Swarthmore, see Clark, 1970.)

---

every occasion that able women could beat men at their own games. For an account of changing styles among Bryn Mawr alumnae, see Riesman (1976). (For evidence, for example, that girls and women are generally more involved in their personal relations than boys and men and are therefore more vulnerable, see Scarf, 1980; see also Weiss, 1973.)

2

Sources of
Faculty Hegemony

As many Americans are aware, other countries have made a sharp demarcation between the pursuit and the transmission of knowledge. In the Soviet Union, the leading academicians are in research institutes and not in the universities, even in major centers such as Moscow or Leningrad. Members of the sacrosanct elect of the Collège de France may give an occasional lecture, but little teaching is required of them. At least until recently, most of Japan's research has gone on in industrial laboratories and some in government laboratories, rather than in the major universities, whose postbaccalaureate doctoral programs are relatively small-scale.

In his discerning and wide-ranging essay focusing on post–World War II changes in the organization of the curriculum, Veysey (1973b, p. 17) notes that in the 1950s for the first time "research chairs became fairly common, at least toward the top of the academic system." However, in my own limited observation, holders of such research chairs have seldom devoted themselves exclusively to research; they were freed from the ordinary round of classroom and committee duties, but they generally have given lecture series at their own and other institutions. And, being in a university setting, they were available to the more hardy and persistent students.

In the United States, of course, much research as well as development goes on in industry—in the laboratories of pharmaceutical companies, of RCA, of General Electric. Indeed, few if any American universities can match either the distinction or the facilities of Bell Labs or of "think tanks" as eminent as the Rand Corporation, SRI International (formerly the Stanford Research Institute), or Brookings. Nevertheless, in the United States most of the major research not geared to direct application is university-based, including that by research scientists in university-connected medical schools. Virtually all the hundred American Nobel Prize winners in science and medicine have been located in research universities, and the idea of American academics as prize-winning scholars has not only permeated faculty life in all but the most unpretentious of undergraduate colleges but also provided faculty members in a large number of even the noneminent research universities and liberal arts colleges with an authority that inspires some students and awes others.

In 1876 Johns Hopkins opened on what Americans interpreted as the German model of a "real" university, focusing its attention on graduate work and research. (For its beginnings, see, for example, Hawkins, 1960.) But Daniel Coit Gilman soon discovered, as G. Stanley Hall at Clark and William Rainey Harper at Chicago were later to realize, that in the American setting one needed an undergraduate student body to support an edifice of graduate study and scholarship. The structure of this edifice, begun by these pioneers in the late nineteenth century, was in place before the Second World War,[1] but the enormous expansion of research as a major source of support and of eminence for faculty members at both public and private universities came about during and after the war, especially with the postwar soaring of undergraduate enrollment. This growth in enrollment, along with direct federal and corporate funding, helped to build the pyramid of graduate study and research that characterizes today's American university, as exemplified by virtually all the members of the Association of American Universities. These fifty institutions cooperate in pushing for federal and state support for the research enterprise while competing for the most eminent or promising faculty members, able and ambitious graduate students, and federal

---

[1] Veysey (1973b) has argued forcefully that the truly significant "academic revolution" occurred during the decades from 1870 to 1910, between the opening of Johns Hopkins University and the First World War, and that the later growth was built upon this preexisting structure.

and state funds for research. But none of them overlooks the importance of its undergraduates, even when, as Berkeley's reputation shows, it appears to offer many of them only benign neglect. Indeed, many of the large public universities receive state funds for operating expenses on the basis of their number of full-time equivalent students, often with extra per-capita funding for graduate students, many of whom can then be employed as teaching assistants. In addition, the exceptionally generous philanthropic support—and this is true of the major private as well as public institutions—comes primarily from alumni of the undergraduate program, either directly from their personal gifts or from corporate donations over which they have leverage. (Some corporations will match the gifts of an employee who is an alumnus.)

Thorstein Veblen, who had found Carleton College stiflingly pious as an undergraduate and who had eagerly gone to Johns Hopkins when it opened as a graduate university, made plain his own judgment that undergraduates, hopelessly collegiate and sports-minded, were intolerable obstacles to the life of scholarship; he graded them all "C" and deprecated even, or perhaps especially, those few who admired him despite his contempt. (Veblen's sarcasm, at once bitter and witty, concerning "the higher learning" [Veblen, 1918] has greatly influenced nonconformist academic attitudes. See my critique [Riesman, 1953, chap. 4]; also Diggins, 1978, chap. 9.) After Johns Hopkins, Veblen taught at the University of Chicago in its early years, before being let go more for his open bohemianism than for his alleged failure to advertise the university or his seemingly intentional inadequacies as an undergraduate teacher. He would hardly have believed conceivable the college of the University of Chicago as it became shortly after his death in 1929, when it was virtually free of the situation that so outraged him, of shabby-genteel academics hired to provide a bit of polish, which could only add to the game-playing skills of the young barbarians of the sexual chase, of the athletic field, and of the induction into wasteful dissipation and consumption.

World War II Veterans

Veblen would have been even more surprised to discover after the end of the Second World War a large cohort of veterans crowding into the most selective universities and dispensing quickly with the collegiate in the rush to make up for lost time. (He might well have been dismayed, nonetheless, by their lack of what he termed idle curiosity, and if he could not have dismissed them as barbarians resembling earlier "collegiate" students, he might have considered their careerism an eagerness either to produce or to purchase useless vendibles, hardly less barbarian.) A number of these GIs had been moved around the United States, and some had been educated in V-12 programs at top-flight American universities. The GI Bill of Rights of that period enabled them to purchase the best education to which they could gain access, independent of tuition charges,[2] and thereby freed them to attend selective residential colleges, which included not only private ones but major out-of-state public universities, jumping the high-tuition surcharges that some states have maintained against out-of-state students.[3] Sometimes these surcharges as well as quotas were voted in due to a legislature's unreflective localism, as at the University of Massachusetts (recently, with enrollment declines from in-state, the quota has been raised); sometimes, as notably at the University of Wisconsin-Madison, because the major state university proved all too attractive for cosmopolitan students, often referred to as "New

[2] In part owing to a belief that some institutions exploited the Veterans Administration's beneficence by raising their tuition and in part because of the loss of cultural legitimacy and political influence by private higher education since World War II, the GI Bill for Vietnam veterans paid a fixed monthly stipend to every recipient out of which he was expected to cover tuition as well as other costs. Because the amount was too small to meet the costs of most private (and some out-of-state public) colleges and universities, attendance at local public institutions appeared far more advantageous to the great majority of students dependent on this source of educational financing. Finn (1978, chap. 1) gives a lucid account of the abuses of the World War II GI Bill and hence the shift to a more restricted policy.

[3] The chief exception to this rule that comes to mind is the type of subsidy given, for example, by the Southern Regional Education Board to attend, say, a school of veterinary medicine outside one's state but within one's region in order to minimize the proliferation of institutions for small numbers of students. Somewhat similar provisions operate in northern New England under the auspices of the New England Board of Higher Education. Another exception is the reciprocity agreement between Minnesota and Wisconsin that allows students to pay in-state tuition—a proviso chiefly made use of near the state border where commuters are nearer to a college or a particular program in the neighboring state than to a similar facility in their home state. For discussion of portable grants and other forms of state aid to students, see Carnegie Council on Policy Studies in Higher Education (1977).

Yorkers," seen (not always entirely unfairly) as "outside agitators" who corrupt even if they do not crowd the supposedly undefiled home-grown students.

The veterans did not subordinate themselves to the institutions into which they crowded. Their role in facilitating the academic revolution was, in the main, indirect. They did a great deal to rid the undergraduate colleges of their collegiate and juvenile elements; the veterans were mature, vocationally oriented, eager to get on with the delayed tasks of learning. Moreover, since they were part of a cohort, many of whom had been out of educational institutions for five or six years, they did not feel themselves to be insecure or inferior students; they knew they were in the same boat with others who had been equally delayed, and they benefited from the general social support provided for World War II veterans. Some had managed to escape the PX enclaves in which most overseas Americans disported themselves to avoid contact with indigenous populations; some had in the wartime Civil Affairs schools learned Japanese or German or other languages and wanted to continue study of the cultures to which the war had exposed them. (Unfortunately for them and for the country, the curriculum to which they were subjected remained provincially Western. The exceptions were the colleges that in the past had trained missionaries, and also some scholars, in Middle and Far Eastern history, language, and culture; a few black colleges—notably Lincoln in Pennsylvania and Howard in Washington, D.C.—had provided some instruction in African history and culture.)

Later, when the first waves of older students started to knock on college doors before the recent academic depression caused colleges to compete eagerly for them, many older students felt uncomfortable amid a crowd of eager-beaver teenagers. After the Second World War, in contrast, it was often the veterans who set the pace, not the students immediately out of high school. The veterans' experience, in fact, turned out to be a good omen for the later ideal of encouraging stopouts. Whether the veterans had had (as the British would say) "a good war," as many did, or a rough time of it, as some did (especially in boot camp, where they were persecuted as intellectuals by noncommissioned officers who envied them the opportunity to go to Officer Candidate School), they brought to the classroom a kind of sober realism that remained there when they secured their baccalaureates and, in a surprising number of cases, went on to further study. The war experience had given many veterans who returned alive and unmaimed a confidence that they could cope with unanticipated situations. Many would not have attended college had they not become GIs; a number sustained the confidence that aided them in believing they could profit from an academic career and even make a contribution. As veterans of a war generally considered "just," the GIs won support from concerned faculty members who helped waive requirements and otherwise provided moral and psychological support, while the GI Bill provided at least minimum, and in some situations relatively bounteous, financial support.

The GIs brought to many liberal arts colleges the institution's first experience of a heterogeneous student body, no longer drawn from a single social and geographic catchbasin, while on their side, the GIs had already cut loose from home base and did not have to justify against charges of elitism or local disloyalty attendance at prestigious institutions en route to becoming national.

Verne Stadtman, himself a World War II veteran who entered Berkeley for the 1947–48 academic year, when it was bursting with undergraduates, has commented that the veterans not only facilitated the academic revolution by dispensing with the collegiate but may in subtle ways have undermined that subordination of students to the hegemony of the faculty and the administration which had prevailed hitherto. *In loco parentis* made little sense for married veterans. As stated above, regulations were bent to make allowances for Veterans, and some younger faculty members (especially if they were not themselves veterans) may have been intimidated by them. In undermining the collegiate—not everywhere and uniformly, of course—the veterans also undermined traditions, even though the impact was diffuse and, at the time, unorganized by any active movements of protest.

In the light of hindsight, it is interesting to compare the lack of protest from either students or faculty members of that day over the crowded classrooms and dormitories and the extra demands often put on faculty members (for example, in 1946 I taught simultaneously a regular class, which had begun in the fall of 1945, and another course for veterans who were beginning in January 1946) with today's complaints by students, for example, at Harvard College, about what they regarded as overcrowding in the comparatively lavish residential Houses (partly the result of increased rents and food costs in Cambridge, which have led students away from the off-campus living many once eagerly sought) plus somewhat increased numbers to permit a larger proportion of women students, and the widespread complaint of faculty members forced by financial need to carry a somewhat heavier student load than in earlier, more flush times. It would not have occurred to most faculty members to complain about the inconveniences introduced by the veterans, who came from all social strata except the very bottom; compare the generally suppressed but occasionally public complaints of senior, scholarly faculty members coping with open admissions at the New York City Colleges, often dealing with Vietnam veterans and other students who have been much more intimidating (see Gross, 1980).

The Search for Students Goes National

Meanwhile, a number of major, selective private universities were moving in a similar direction for internal purposes.

The Example of Harvard. As already noted, Columbia College had lost its local elite, as had the college of the University of Chicago, the undergraduate college and, to a lesser degree, the Women's College of the University of Pennsylvania (Hopkins never did recruit from the Baltimore area's elite). But Harvard had and still has the loyalty of local and Atlantic Seaboard social elites, while drawing, even before the Second World War, from a wider social catch-basin.[4] At Harvard, provincialism and inbreeding were to some extent still prevalent in the faculty as well as in much of the recruitment of students. President James Bryant Conant, a distinguished research chemist, set out to change this. Before the Second World War he had already realized the provinciality of American natural science in general and that of his own institution in particular.

[4] For a discussion of the religious roots that in part may explain the divergent fates of the University of Pennsylvania and of Harvard College despite the metropolitan locations of both, see Baltzell (1979).

After the war, with the aid of Provost Paul Buck, he instituted the ad hoc committee system, by which all appointments to tenure had to be vetted by a visiting committee that included both people in the candidate's field from outside Harvard and people in neighboring fields inside Harvard, thus avoiding the temptation, to which inbred departments are prone, of slow or sometimes rapid declines into mediocrity. The charge to an ad hoc committee was to ask itself whether the candidates proposed by the department were the best who could be found anywhere and if not, why not. Knowing that they would have to run this gauntlet, the departments themselves began to anticipate ad hoc committee reactions and guide themselves accordingly.[5]

Similarly, Conant intensified the process that the College Entrance Examination Board had already made feasible—namely, national rather than Eastern Seaboard recruitment to Harvard College—by establishing the Harvard National Scholarships and appointing as dean of admissions an energetic man from Ohio, no Brahmin, Wilbur J. Bender. Bender encouraged his admissions recruiters and alumni to make the rounds of secondary schools in the areas where they lived, to bring into the Harvard applicant pool the widest possible diversity of applicants sufficiently well motivated and potentially academically adept to survive at Harvard—a kind of color-blind Affirmative Action. President Conant and Provost Paul Buck, their eyes on the diversity of high schools from which Harvard College would now be drawing its undergraduate student body, sponsored the faculty committee that prepared the famous "Red Book" (Committee on the Objectives of a General Education in a Free Society, 1945). One of the aims of the program proposed in this book was to give students coming from backgrounds not traditional to the college a basic introduction to Western civilization as well as to the natural sciences and their history and to the social sciences—a program of general education that, as worked out in practice, proved far less coherent than the established sequences of Columbia and Chicago. Conant also

[5] Like all reforms, the ad hoc committee system could be a mixed blessing, and much depended on the uses made of it by the president and the relevant deans. For a fuller discussion, see Riesman (1975a, pp. 308–314). See also, for an account of the spirited quality of Harvard College after World War II, Huntington (1969).

backed what had been in many cases a wartime imperative, namely, a three-year degree—not at all a new idea either at Harvard or elsewhere, but one useful to veterans eager to get through, and paving the way for the high school Advanced Placement program.

The United States as Catchbasin. As Trow (1961) has noted, rates of college attendance over the decades have paralleled the increase in the number of high school graduates. If the increasing proportion of the age cohort attended only locally available colleges, the consequences of numerical increase would not have produced institutions with a "critical mass" of able students. But in fact, there was a significant though small proportion of high school graduates who were prepared to be recruited nationally (rough estimates run between 10 and 20 percent). The advertising slogan promoted as a public service by the Advertising Council in the previous era, "Give to the college of your choice," stated implicitly to prospective students and their parents that one might attend the college of one's choice, that there was a choice, and that college-going was a good idea. Furthermore, as a few colleges and universities expanded national recruiting in order to widen their orbits of talent, whether talent for academic or artistic pursuits or for leadership, they joined another, much larger orbit of institutions that was already engaged in national recruiting of star high school athletes. Big-league state universities and some notable private ones could afford not only to field football teams (though in many cases to support the entire athletic program from the gate receipts and, later, television rights) but to send coaches and alumni scouting for high school prospects. I recall one instance some years ago in which Louisiana State University made a determined push for a football prospect graduating from Brownsville High School in Texas, bringing him and his family to Baton Rouge for dinner with the governor, introducing the student to faculty members who promised solicitude, and yet losing him in the end to the local pull so powerful in that imperium of a state, the University of Texas. And less affluent Catholic colleges, such as Providence College or St. John's University, could afford that urban sport invented by a YMCA instructor for the very reason that it could be played by a small number of players in a confined urban space. Moreover, since so many of the top high school basketball stars have been black, antijock faculty members and students could be appeased by the realization that racial integration—or at least the proper contingent of blacks that came to be expected in every self-regarding predominantly white institution—could often be most readily achieved by building a reputation for prowess in basketball.[6] Correspondingly, as colleges found their traditional catchbasins being invaded by raiding parties from elsewhere, they were in turn forced to expand their own orbits of recruitment if they were to maintain, let alone enhance, their prior standards of selectivity, whether in academic or athletic arenas.

The spread of national recruiting by what had once been more or less exclusive Ivy League–type colleges and universities was accompanied by the provision of scholarship aid and, as tuitions rose, price discounting of tuition on the basis of need rather than academic or other merit. (Two eminent institutions, Harvard and Rice University, have been wealthy enough in the past to accept a class on the basis of institutional definitions of merit, only later considering how to finance students who accepted the offer of admission. Whether any private institution can continue such a policy in the face of inflation and correspondingly rising tuition is uncertain.) Consequently, relatively unselective colleges, including a number of public "open admissions" institutions, which saw themselves suffering from a "brain drain" of able students and, along with them, their reputations and their attraction for scholarly faculty members, have begun to offer some scholarships based on

[6] Both black and white athletes were sometimes mismatched with the recruiting institutions by the poor judgment of coaches and cooperative admissions officers. In addition, some black athletes found themselves at odds with predominantly white coaching staffs whose Marine-drill-sergeant style was taken, rightly or wrongly, as a racial insult. (A few black athletes, such as Harry Edwards, or pro-black whites, such as John Scott, the radical former director of athletics at Oberlin College, made what they could of such incidents in order to create, on the whole without success, feelings of racial solidarity among black athletes—many of whom had so little solidarity of any sort as to justify the comment a black basketball player made to me a few years ago, "We dribble more than we pass," expressing his disappointment at the lack of team play among individual high school stars. But the mismatching was far more serious in the area of academic and cultural values; see, for example, Sowell, 1976b.)

It adds perspective to recall that ethnic succession had occurred much earlier in football (see Riesman and Denney, 1951), as it did later in boxing and other contests.

merit as well as financial aid packages primarily based on need.[7] For example, merit scholarships are now being offered at CCNY and Baruch Colleges of CUNY (Fiske, 1978, 1979c), as well as by several unselective colleges in the SUNY system.

Provincialism and Urbanity in College Choice. Yet, despite recruiting efforts and offers of financial aid, a substantial number of American students felt their choices to be in practice constrained by the loyalty of their families and often themselves to the colleges of a particular denomination. Thus, a college-bound child of Norwegian-American parents might have a choice between St. Olaf College in Northfield, Minnesota, and Decorah College in Luther, Iowa, based on family tradition, academic aptitude, distance from home and friends, and so on. Similarly, a graduate of a Jesuit high school could choose among a number of the twenty-eight Jesuit institutions, including the College of the Holy Cross, Georgetown University, and Boston College. (Those who preferred Notre Dame for the sake of science or football or other reasons were not discouraged, although it is administered by the Congregation of the Sacred Heart, not by the Society of Jesus.) There are also regional loyalties and regional aversions.

   Perhaps the Lone Star State student from Brownsville who could not be persuaded to consider LSU would have been, if suffi-

[7] Among the more reputable private colleges, there has in the past been an agreement to define "need" on the basis of the standard formulas set by the College Scholarship Service of the College Entrance Examination Board. These formulas determine how much of the cost of a student's education should be borne by the student and his or her family, taking into account income, siblings, and the student's ability to earn money in the summer, perhaps in a college work-study program. As applicant pools dry up and competition with other private colleges and the subsidized public sector intensifies, financial aid officers are understandably tempted to redefine "need" so as to bring in students who will pay at least enough to cover costs at the economic margin. If, as seems likely, such a practice has spread, the temptation of students and their parents (already in evidence among consumer-wise families) to bargain over financial aid has increased, resulting in a net loss of funds that families can furnish to the entire private sector. Two economists, Stephen P. Dresch of Yale and Kenneth M. Deitch of the staff of the Sloan Commission on Government and Higher Education, and an institutional researcher, Larry H. Litten, associate director of the Consortium on Financing Higher Education, have aided my understanding of these issues through their own writing, comments, and bibliographic leads. See, for a general overview, Bailey (1980).

ciently talented, quite happy to attend Rice University—like the University of Texas, a world-class institution. Conversely, students in the Northeast are often willing to consider Stanford—and Reed draws a quarter of its students from the East—but such students generally reject going to the South, with a partial exception made for Duke University; and Oberlin is about as far as they will travel to the vast terrain of the Middle West, though, as already indicated, they are willing to jump to the West Coast. Regional attractions or aversions do not arise for students who are unwilling, even if financially able, to go "too far"—undoubtedly the great majority. In an earlier era, women students particularly were confined in this way, by their own timidity and by parental protectiveness, but my research assistants and I have been turning up (in nonrandom but dispersed interviews) young men who seem not to desire adventure and who want to remain within what one might term "laundry range" of home base. (For a discussion of recent psychological studies concerning the apparently greater difficulty young people have in leaving home, protracting adolescence physically as well as symbolically, see Goleman, 1980; for historical perspective, see Kett, 1977.) These same interviews have uncovered an asymmetry that, since we have no sample, must remain speculative—namely, that young men are more apt to follow their girlfriends' college choice than vice versa. It is as if the young woman were more eager to break away from her local boyfriend and were less likely to attend a college because he was going there. This may be an as yet undocumented aspect of women's liberation.

Jewish Students and the Search for the "Best College." There was one numerically small but intellectually significant cadre of Americans who not only lacked religious or regional loyalties but wanted for themselves, as their families wanted for them, whatever was defined in an increasingly nationalized system of prestige as simply "the best." The very belief that, for any particular young person, any college could be defined as "the best" in some system of national rankings is both absurd and tenacious, as I have had any number of reasons to discover in talking to prospective students who have come to define Harvard College as "the best" even though it is evident from their interests and aptitudes and from

Harvard's own limitations that it not only is not "the best" for them as individuals but is potentially harmful. Consumers Union, in its *Guide* and *Reports*, will rarely state that a particular car, for example, is "the best" for all purposes and situations; it may list a number of cars as among the best, noting various tradeoffs that the purchaser should take into account. The idea that there is an all-purpose "best" college is like assuming that athletic contests, in which it is possible to say who can run a particular distance the fastest (who is, of course, not "the best" all-round runner for varying distances or hurdles), who can pole-vault the highest, and so on, could set a national trend that one can discover in every field a perennial "best." This is a mode of thought that advertising has helped spread. Hertz is Number One (although Avis has made a selling point out of "trying harder," as have a number of colleges and universities in local and national orbits), and various products are urged on consumers by similar selling techniques. However, that part of the population which regards itself as sophisticated believes it is relatively immune to aggressive advertising and salesmanship, often assuming, for example, that no cultivated reader would find a "best seller" anything but a bad book. The heavily overapplied "brand name" universities do not need to engage in egregious marketing, but they are nevertheless in competition with one another for the potentially most brilliant scholars and for scholar-athletes, and their alumni and alumnae are sufficiently distributed around the country to assist both in recruiting efforts and in making sure that, where there are multiple applications to highly selective institutions, acceptance by "their" college will in turn lead to acceptance of the offer by the student being courted. Yet, it is the fact of high selectivity that prevents dismissal of the academic "best sellers" as knowledgeable people are apt to dismiss not only the Emmy Awards but also the Pulitzer Prizes.

The interviews I have done or supervised with twelfth-graders and freshmen make clear the lure of what has been abstractly defined as "the best" and how little investigation frequently accompanies the decision whether the institution is optimal for the particular person; for a seventeen-year-old there is probably no one institution that can be defined as optimal except in rare cases of specialized interests and qualities. Certainly these students show no effort to discover more suitable alternatives comparable to their effort to win the grades and extracurricular accoutrements that are believed to enhance their chances of admission to "the best" college or perhaps a very small group of "the best."

The groups in American society who are best situated to search the whole country for "the best" have no firm denominational or regional ties or fervent alumni loyalties to link them to a particular locale or institution. (I am speaking here of liberal arts colleges, in contrast to institutions that attract people because of their specialized curricula—for example, an institute of technology or, at the graduate level, a school of veterinary medicine.) The search for a national, generalized "best" has occurred mainly among the children of relatively recent immigrants—Jews, Greeks, Armenians, Orientals, blacks who have migrated from South to North, and other, smaller ethnic groups—who have either not established attachments or, as in the case of the migrating blacks, have relinquished attachments to church-related black colleges or black public institutions to seek their fortunes at predominantly white institutions.[8]

The distinguished historian of higher education Laurence Veysey regards the arrival of refugees from Nazism in the 1930s as the time when the faculties of the major institutions were enriched with "the simultaneous appearance at the undergraduate level of ever-larger numbers of immigrant sons and grandsons whom internal discriminatory quotas could no longer effectively cordon.

---

[8] For a survey of the reasons native Mississippi blacks give for preferring predominantly black Mississippi colleges or predominantly white ones, see Cunnigen (1978). Today, in the secularized cities, only a few young blacks have preferred to attend black colleges rather than accept the lures offered by nationally known, predominantly white colleges and universities eager to recruit them. (Administrators of predominantly black private colleges in the South have said in conversation what I have myself observed on several visits: namely, the choice of some "city slicker" blacks from Northern cities to come South, partly because their families migrated from that locale, partly in the expectation of lording it over fellow students, coasting to an easy degree in competition with those they define as naive.) Furthermore, blacks traditionally, like Jews in the last several generations, have not discriminated against women. Indeed, in the traditional Negro colleges, women greatly outnumbered men, and whole kinship networks would pool resources to help a black student attend college with College Board scores as low as 300 on each half of the SAT—scores that until recently were a signal to white students that they were not "college material."

Especially to the extent that Jewish intellectual flair might prove catching among admiring Protestants and Catholics, the American university had thus gained a major new lever for change of emphasis away from football and fraternities" (Veysey, 1973b, p. 14). Thus, both directly via distinguished refugees and indirectly by making anti-Jewish prejudice impermissible, the Second World War opened the gates of the most selective colleges at the time when the children or grandchildren of the pre–World War I waves of Eastern European immigration had created a cohort of applicants, the largest number concentrated in New York City and its suburbs, whose parents had in many instances attended the free-tuition colleges there before the Second World War, creating loyalty to these colleges, particularly CCNY, but not such powerful loyalty as to lead alumni to pressure their own children to attend an altered CCNY (or, for women, Hunter College, now coeducational).

Similarly, although German Jews were among the first arrivals in San Francisco after the American Indians and Spaniards, and although much of the social elite of the Bay Area is quite happy when its children attend Berkeley as undergraduates, the proportion of Bay Area Jewish families whose children attend the University of California, according to Seymour Martin Lipset (in conversation), is quite small. They, too, want "the best," which may be Stanford or Reed or the Ivy League. Of course, at the postbaccalaureate level this situation changes, for at that point the university, mildly selective at the undergraduate level, becomes highly selective and of course has a world-class standing.

Generally, then, Jewish students are less homebound in college choice than the majority. The chief exceptions—here I speak on the basis of personal impressions—are in the South, where regional loyalties may overcome the ethnic patterns prevalent in the North, so that Jewish students from Charlotte may decide to attend the University of North Carolina, turning down Harvard or Duke, as Jewish students in Galveston may prefer the University of Texas to the Ivy League.

Even though the immigrant Jews who arrived in such large numbers in New York City and at other seaport points of entry and then spread throughout the United States, often as peddlers and

merchants, were poor, and even though many of the next generation were poor, a high proportion had an asset most useful in a
rapidly changing industrial society that places a high premium on
education—namely, literacy. This in turn makes possible a hunger
for further education. Although in the selective colleges one occasionally hears bemused talk about "Jewish American Princesses,"
one finds in these same colleges even today a number of Jewish
students whose families have remained in humble economic circumstances, students who have achieved their educational chance
through Merit Scholarships and often, like other financially hard-
pressed students, their own earnings and loans.

Thus, precisely when leading private colleges were expanding their networks of recruiting, large numbers of Jewish students were already knocking on the door. If, for example, they had
grown up in Omaha, no traditions of family loyalty or state pride
pointed them toward the University of Nebraska if they could get
into Stanford or Harvard, and of course no religious tradition
pointed them toward readily available (Jesuit) Creighton or Southern Methodist.[9] Furthermore, Jewish parents who had attained
some measure of affluence tended to be permissive toward their
children and thus prepared to see them leave home even at the risk
of losing them from the ethnic fold, while the young people themselves, often independently of their particular interests and talents,
generally cooperated with their parents in searching out the national "best sellers." Thomas Cottle (1978, chap. 1) has poignantly
described his own ambivalence about falling in with what he saw as
a vulgar striving for success in joining in a tacit alliance with his

[9] The single Jewish counterpart until the establishment of Brandeis University was
Yeshiva University, opened in New York in 1886, primarily for training in Hebrew
scholarship. A liberal arts branch for men began only in 1926, and for women in
1954—but 90 percent of those receiving the Yeshiva baccalaureate go on to graduate or professional school, at which point the search for the national "best" can
begin. When Brandeis University was founded in 1948, its driving entrepreneur-
founder, Abraham Sachar, moved it instantly into the national best-seller class by
attracting a faculty of distinction. Brandeis was also explicitly secular, not confining
its appeal to Jews and certainly not to the more or less Orthodox Hebraists for
whom Yeshiva had been created; it was therefore a possibility for those who wanted
an ethnic tie not to Judaism but to Jewishness without sacrificing what had become
defined as the model of the academically superior university college with a nationwide appeal.

father to seek admission to Harvard College; he did not want to be like the other apparently unabashed strivers around him.[10]

Jewish families in America are no more alike than families in other ethnic groups, and many Jewish parents feel great ambivalence about the danger of "losing" their children. Any Hillel rabbi on a secular campus can recount stories of Jewish parents who have become upset when their children started dating non-Jewish partners and moving toward marriage with them. One brave rabbi, besieged by such parental complaints, would reply that Jewish parents could not have it both ways: they could not claim to be a chosen and separate people and at the same time demand admission to colleges of a cosmopolitan nature where their children would have a good chance of meeting and marrying Gentiles.[11]

Impact of Sputnik

The Advanced Placement program, though adumbrated in the veteran rush in individual cases, was the result of a new development—the Russian launching of Sputnik in 1957, an event that gave educators the opportunity to make a case for the general inadequacy of the American educational scheme.

Sputnik made it legitimate for senior faculty members, especially in the natural sciences and mathematics, to enter an arena previously dominated by schools and departments of education and to develop a curriculum to improve the teaching of mathematics, physics, and biology in secondary schools, along with summer institutes (many of them sponsored by the National Science Foundation) to instruct high school teachers in the "new math" or new ways of teaching science as a process of discovery rather than as a conglomerate of facts and formulas. The cognitive psychologist Jerome Bruner was especially influential in guiding the thinking of those scientists who were experimenting both in schools and in universities with teaching ever more sophisticated subjects to ever-

[10] For descriptions of the types of pressures on the most selective colleges and the impact of these pressures on peers in secondary schools that prepare for such colleges, see Sacks (1978) and Wells (1978).

[11] For a vivid description of the ambivalence of Jewish mothers in a lower-middle-class community in Detroit toward releasing their sons to a secular university for the sake of the latters' "making it" in America, see Seidler and Ravitz (1955).

younger precollegiate students—enterprises also attempted with less support and self-confidence by some people in the social sciences and humanities.

The new pressures for high school improvements, proceeding simultaneously with increased pressures for entry into selective colleges (which in the private sector were not expanding their enrollments, except marginally, but were using their larger applicant pools to increase their powers of selection) were the kinds of pressures that would once have been confined to such special enclaves as Reed College or the college of the University of Chicago. However, they began to make themselves felt in a small but influential number of secondary schools. First, there were the private preparatory schools that had been accustomed to having all their students have their choice among Ivy League institutions but found that choice no longer open as national recruiting increased. There were also two kinds of public schools with similar ambitions: first, the national pacemakers in affluent suburban areas where a high proportion of parents were college-educated and often professional, such as New Trier in Evanston; and, second, those rare and currently threatened citywide high schools into which entry was by competitive examinations, such as the Bronx High School of Science, the High School of the Performing Arts, Stuyvesant High School, and, for young women, Hunter High School in New York City; Central High School in Philadelphia; Walnut Hill High School in Cincinnati; Boston Latin and Girls Latin high schools in Boston—all now abandoned or under pressure for the alleged sin of "elitism," which is a code word for racism or, vis-à-vis the single-sex schools, for sexism. (For a discussion of the advantages for many women of noncoeducation in junior high and high school and the harm done to women's verbal aptitudes—without any increase in their mathematical and scientific aptitudes—by coeducation in its present peer-dominated forms, see Riesman, 1978d.)

In some of these high schools, such as the Bronx High School of Science, there were, ready and waiting for able students, teachers who had obtained doctorates during the Depression years—when colleges were only slowly expanding their faculties, and many still discriminated against Jews—and had gone to teach in the secondary schools. Similarly, a number of the better private preparatory schools had been able to recruit scholarly teachers, some with but most without the doctorate, who did not have quite the status of masters in the leading English public schools or teachers at a French lycée (Jean-Paul Sartre and Simone de Beauvoir were both such teachers) but were the closest American analogue. And as much of society began to regard education as having greater importance for the sake of competition with the Russians, if for no better reasons, many distinguished colleges and universities instituted Master of Arts in Teaching programs whose focus was on subject matter, rather than on what many (frequently snobbish) liberal arts college graduates regarded as the "Mickey Mouse" materials concerning curriculum, techniques for teaching reading, or other subjects on which schools of education were concentrating in their efforts to establish their work as professional (Glazer, 1974a, 1974b). Many high school teachers rose to the opportunity they were given to offer college-level courses, which colleges were increasingly prepared to accept on the basis of the College Board's Advanced Placement examinations in spite of wounds to the vanity of college professors who found it hard to believe that any secondary school teacher could teach "their" subject in a way that a true scholar could regard as satisfactory.

Role of the College Board

It is important to note the double-edged role of the College Entrance Examination Board. On the one hand, the Educational Testing Service prepared examinations used by the College Board, which provided a certain degree of leverage for teachers in secondary schools that sent many of their students to selective colleges; if the students did not study, they were told they would not do well on the College Boards or, with somewhat lesser frequency and weight, the comparable examinations provided by the American College Testing Service. (Today, there is an analogous attempt by parents and some state school officials to require so-called competency examinations before one can receive a high school diploma— a pressure fiercely resisted by officials of the National Education Association, the most powerful teachers' union, for such examinations can of course be used as leverage against particular teachers and schools.) On the other hand, the College Board-sponsored

Scholastic Aptitude Test (SAT) freed secondary school students from personal subordination to the prejudices and college preferences of their teachers, counselors, and headmasters. For example, at a time when some Catholic parochial schools, unlike such distinguished ones as Portsmouth Priory, sought to make sure that their students would stay in the faith by sending them on to the top-flight Catholic colleges and universities and threatening individuals with negative letters of recommendation if they dared apply to selective secular colleges, the College Board test scores could often make this strategy plain to astute admissions officials and thus free high school students from subordination both in the classroom and in choice of college. (The Graduate Record Examination has served similarly to free students from subordination to particular faculty members in their undergraduate colleges.) I think, for example, of two brilliant Catholics from upstate New York, a young man and a young woman, who entered Harvard in the middle 1960s from parochial schools that wanted them to attend, on the one hand, either Fordham or Holy Cross and, on the other, either a local Catholic college or Manhattanville. The headmasters wrote scathing letters of disrecommendation for these students, but their SAT scores near the 800 ceiling were a tipoff to what was really happening. At Harvard, they flourished in an atmosphere where their intellectuality was respected and their reflective and critical Catholicism was strengthened (something that does not always happen). This liberating and partially destratifying potential of the College Boards is, in my judgment, tendentiously overlooked by such "revisionist" accounts as that of Schudson (1972).

With the development of the SAT as a complement of or, in many cases, a substitute for subject-matter tests, applicants were even freed in some measure from the limitations of course offerings at their particular high schools. Meanwhile, of course, colleges increasingly dropped requirements or substituted ones more easily met in wider echelons (modern foreign languages, for example, for the classical languages). Scores on the College Board exams made it possible for school officials to encourage particular students and their parents to widen the orbit of college choice by pointing to the demonstrated ability of the children; they also sometimes served to protect children against pressureful parents—the type who insisted on "the best"—by making clear that a particular child had a slim chance of being accepted at the most selective colleges or, if accepted, of emerging unscathed. Similarly, some students might be warned against their own grandiosity by doing less well on the SAT than they had expected, especially if their high school grades were also poor; they might recognize that, though hardly any colleges rely entirely on test scores in determining admissibility, the competition would be too tough in a college composed primarily of more-capable test takers; they might apply to colleges not requiring tests or, if not deflated in their ambitions, to those few institutions that ask students for a portfolio of accomplishments, such as examples of painting or poetry.

To be sure, school officials, whether headmasters, teachers, or guidance counselors, did not always use the tests in such individuated ways. They might have more concern for their institution's reputation for getting its students into the colleges of their first choice than for betting on a student with a less than idyllic record who nevertheless wanted a crack at the most selective colleges and who might possibly be admitted. Furthermore, perhaps especially in the lesser-known secondary schools, guidance officials were afraid that if the first student whose application they encouraged to Columbia or the University of Chicago should not do well, it would impair the chances of future students from the same high school to have a fair hearing at such a college. Since students in middle- or upper-middle-class secondary schools talked freely among themselves about where they were going to college, as most of them increasingly intended to do, such conflicts between the individual and the collectivity did not long remain hidden. Individuals discovered that school officials could not prevent them from taking the College Boards, even though doing so might run the risk of a negative recommendation from a counselor or principal whose advice had been disregarded. Some colleges even welcomed those defined as "troublemakers" in high school, supposing that such students had been bored in an inadequate high school and might thrive in a more cosmopolitan college. This surmise, like other exercises of judgment, might of course turn out to be incorrect. (I deal in a later section with the controversy over testing and especially the Educational Testing Service that has erupted in the last several years and become manifest in actual or pending legislation; for an excellent account of the controversy and its participants, see Lerner, 1980.)

Even a good showing on the College Boards, though often of great help, did not invariably make attendance at a distant college seem feasible either for low-income families or, where a daughter was concerned, relatively affluent ones—families who, though they would pay to send a son to Stanford, saw no point in "wasting" college expenses on a girl, who could work as a nurse on the basis of a degree from the local college or hospital until she married. Nor did it seem feasible for students who recognized that to attend a college more distant or more distinguished than the flagship campus of the local state university would mark them as snobs. The creation of the National Merit Scholarship Corporation and its increasingly widely diffused system of examinations served not only to make financial assistance possible for low-income students but also, for provincially rooted students, to legitimate leaving home base.

David Ricks (1961) describes how receiving one of the national awards legitimated his leaving a Mountain State area, largely Mormon, where his peers were all going to the local universities if going to college at all (Latter-day Saints, America's chief self-created "ethnic"-religious group, are notably high in college attendance[12]), to attend the University of Chicago. His own self-confidence, without such legitimation, would not have been enough to pry him loose. (See also Rever, 1978, and, emphasizing social-psychological factors, Katz, 1978, and references there cited. Katz believes that the highly qualified student has little freedom to choose a low-status, noncompetitive college, although recent evidence on the number of white males who are not attending college immediately after graduating from secondary school suggests that freedom of choice among moderately affluent students, including

[12] Another sizable "made in America" denomination, the Seventh-day Adventists, has ten colleges, and each member of that virtually indigenous denomination is said to be within a day's driving distance of one of them. In contrast, the Christian Scientists, another denomination that originated in this country, put only the most limited pressure on their young people to attend Principia College in Illinois, the single Christian Science college. It should be added that Mormons also can be found all over the place, from Stanford and the University of Southern California to MIT and Harvard.

those of high academic ability as measured by test scores, may be greater than a few years ago.)

Those who could almost never be pried loose in that era were the students who would have been better off entering the residential "Early College" at the end of the tenth grade.[13] (In college towns, such as Austin, Ann Arbor, or Berkeley, it is not uncommon for eleventh- and twelfth-grade students still living at home to be spending half or more of their class hours at the local state university.) Tiny Shimer College, which struggled for survival for years in the small town of Mount Carroll, Illinois (Jencks and Riesman, 1966), and to a lesser extent the University of Chicago, especially for the graduates of its own Laboratory School, were willing to accept students after the tenth grade, but the high schools and most parents were unwilling to let go of students who might seem intellectually precocious yet socially immature and on whom high schools counted to become their valedictorians, editors of the school paper, presidents of student government, or athletes. Today, certainly beginning by junior high if not earlier, young people are more sophisticated in nonintellectual ways; drugs, including alcohol, and sex are not a novelty for them by the tenth grade.

[13] For a discussion of Simon's Rock Early College in Great Barrington, Massachusetts, which has pioneered in providing a baccalaureate degree to students entering after the tenth grade, making clear the advantages for some students of this way of breaking the age-grading now prevailing, see Whitlock (1978). In 1980, Simon's Rock became affiliated with Bard College, not far away across the state line in Annandale-on-Hudson, New York, becoming in effect a junior college whose graduates would complete their baccalaureates at Bard.

3

The Rise of
Student Disaffection

Readers mindful of the role played by Jewish activists in the beginning of the period of protests in the 1960s may find it paradoxical
that in the immediate post-Sputnik era just such Jewish students
helped lead the way toward turning the undergraduate colleges—
in which they made up as much as a third of the student body—in
the direction in which Reed College or the college of the University
of Chicago had long since moved: namely, internalization of
faculty values (themselves increasingly carried by Jewish faculty
members, including distinguished emigrés who had no attachment
whatsoever to American collegiate traditions—see Veysey, 1973b).
Indeed, the more cosmopolitan Jewish students often pointed the
way for more provincial Jewish students from the South and West
and from smaller communities, just as they helped set the tone for
some student bodies, at least as far as publicly expressed opinion
went—often from positions of vantage as editors of the student
press or leaders of student government. (See Baltzell, 1976.)

With varying degrees of emphasis on the role of Jewish leadership (see especially Rothman, in press; Rothman and others,
1977), many student-watchers such as Kenneth Keniston, Richard
Flacks, Jeanne Bloch, and Stanley Rothman described in the late
1960s as "protest-prone" these students who came from affluent,
cosmopolitan, liberal, and occasionally radical families. Permissively reared and permissively treated in school and college, these
students at times appeared to act with a vehemence designed to

elicit some sort of reaction from authorities, who were seldom their own indulgent parents. (A minority of the activists, sometimes the most violent, were from conservative and even authoritarian families, traditionally Catholic or evangelical Protestant.) It takes a certain effort of the historical imagination to envisage these students as they were in the '50s and early '60s, but such imagination would be assisted by a photograph of the leaders of the Free Speech Movement at Berkeley in the fall of 1964, showing students whose dress and manner were by contemporary standards extremely "straight," who had been outstanding in their academic work, and who, as surveys showed, had only modest objections to the teaching they were receiving at what they chose—picking up Clark Kerr's term—to call pejoratively the multiversity (see Somers, 1965).

Many will recall, and others will have read of, the ways in which first the civil-rights movements (the original source behind the FSM at Berkeley and the major occasion, if not the source, behind the Columbia building occupations of the spring of 1968) and then the protests against the Vietnam war led to these students' becoming leaders, along with many faculty members of various ages, of the later efforts to "radicalize" the universities. But the usual accounts of this epoch leave a number of elements out of account, which are necessary if we are to understand the shift in the stances of leading students from pioneers of internalized subordination to faculty values to apparent subverters of those values. One element was the draft itself. Many dedicated and reflective students, happy to be attending universities, discovered an agonizing moral dilemma because such attendance provided a shelter from the draft which their egalitarianism led them to condemn as elitist. The moral dilemma might become especially evident when these students were driving ROTC chapters off their campuses, coercing both some less vocal students, who were not opposed to the war, and those for whom ROTC provided needed scholarship aid. There was in addition another group of involuntary students who entered college precisely to avoid the draft. This group included a number of alienated, anti-intellectual, yet often intelligent students who were forced to keep up their grades to maintain their deferment, yet were bitterly hostile to the captivity inside what they defined as a "total institution" brought about by their seizing its opportunity for shelter.

Although women in college were of course not directly affected by the draft, they were deeply involved with brothers and lovers who were, and a number sought to engage in antidraft activities as a kind of moral equivalent of a war that was not then directly theirs to fight (Thorne, 1972).

Meritocracy Defeats Itself

In addition, Gerald Grant and I have emphasized in earlier writings the extent to which the very accomplishments of selectivity and meritocracy in the post-Sputnik decade created a situation on the selective college campus where students were doing far more serious work than in an earlier, more relaxed era without achieving comparable academic recognition. We have already noted that selective universities did not substantially increase their enrollments when they attracted abler students. They became more selective at the point of admission but also more selective at the point of conferring honors and distinctions. In effect, students were doing more and better work for less "reward" in the very academic coin of the realm they had learned to value, not simply as making the grade, but as defining personal adequacy (Grant and Riesman, 1975, 1978, chap. 6).[1]

There is still another paradox in the antiuniversity protests of the late 1960s and later, latent in the fact that the protesters cared enough about universities to want them to act as ideal models of appropriate civic behavior. Loudly proclaiming their independence and their allergy to all constraints, some of the very ablest students (always in consort with their faculty allies, often students of a generation just before their own) were insisting that the university act as, in a way, ideal parents: compassionate yet fair-minded, creating within a larger market system a quasisocialist enclave that should not be guided by "mere" commercial or finan-

[1] In a review of Grant and Riesman (1978), the distinguished Israeli sociologist of science and of higher education Joseph Ben-David (1980) questions this judgment, citing the work of Somers mentioned earlier and asking what "hard" evidence there is for disaffection with the academic aspects of university life, at least once students had freed themselves from irksome requirements.

cial motives. The students who set the tone for their more rebellious and activist followers were, with the exception of stern
revolutionaries, extraordinarily tolerant toward other students
who were dealing in drugs on campus, often selling hard drugs
to teenagers, and then laundering their criminal gains by the
commerce of the counterculture, such as head shops, boutiques,
organic-food stores, and underground presses (see Goldsmith,
1973). But these same student activists insisted that the university
itself have an investment portfolio uncontaminated by even indirect connection with South African investments, weapons
manufacture, J. P. Stevens, the pharmaceutical industry, or whatever other villains were the targets of student idealism—a goal
almost unattainable in an interlocking world economy. As Verne
Stadtman has pointed out (personal correspondence), university
faculties helped provide students with the legitimacy that in turn
permitted student leaders to sit in judgment on the university as a
civic entity. Faculties did so by describing the student generation of
the early 1960s as not only the brightest, which test scores indicate
that they may well have been (scores rose fairly steadily; the now
widely heralded decline began in 1964), but also the most idealistic
—an assessment that often depended not on what students actually
did but on what they had learned to say (see Bennett and Delattre,
1978). They also put students on committees, even on boards
of trustees, as if willfulness and impetuousness and indeed self-
righteousness were the qualities most needed in university governance, as against such mere mechanical, humdrum requirements
as effectiveness, concern for financial stability, and experience of
life—qualities not often combined on any extant board.

     To put what has been said in other terms, many of the pro-
testing students, far from being hostile to the values of the university or seeing them as obstacles, like the medical students in *Boys
in White* or the undergraduates in *Making The Grade*, were imbued
with ultrauniversity values and were insisting that the university
live up to the ideals some of its most eloquent leaders proclaimed.
Supported by faculty members of similar outlook, they behaved
vis-à-vis the university as radical children behaved vis-à-vis liberal
and permissive parents, rejecting the pragmatism and sense of
limits that they saw inhibiting the parents. Protesters in the leading

universities were only rarely engaged in "oedipal" generational protests, nor was there a gap between themselves and their academic mentors: rather, they were living up to mandates instilled by parental or faculty adults in the vulnerable and permeable structures they found so easy to invade and to seek to "reconstruct." (See Decter, 1975.)

Western society, with increasing intensity since the time of Rousseau but beginning much earlier, has seen repeated attacks on hypocrisy and repeated efforts at establishing the code of plain-speaking candor. Many of the protesters were thus in a long tradition, going back to what Michael Walzer, speaking of the era of Cromwell, has termed "the revolution of the saints," a tradition with powerful roots in Puritan New England and in American literature. Judith Shklar describes this history brilliantly in "Let Us Not Be Hypocritical" (1979; see also Anderson, 1979) in an issue of *Daedalus* entitled "Hypocrisy, Illusion, and Evasion," illustrating the very different values of such a non-Western culture as that of Iran, in which hypocrisy is equated with tact and civility (Bateson, 1979). In renewing a crusade against hypocrisy that has recurrently been especially strong in the United States, the students who were most active in unmasking disparities from the ideal in the university and in society did not spare one another, one result being a constant shift to more extreme positions in order to avoid charges of selling out, compromise, and hypocrisy. At the same time, since students also could not live up to their own exalted ideals, disaffection grew not only with the university but with one another; distrust became generalized, and we live still with its legacies.

I must emphasize that the attack on hypocrisy is in no way novel. During my own time as an undergraduate, the "Christer"—often a student headed for the Protestant ministry, often working in a settlement house, clearly not "one of the boys" who enjoyed disobeying the Volstead Act or obeying the prevalent sexual double standard—was frequently attacked for hypocrisy. What differed in the period of protests was that the antihypocrites, who claimed to be radical, acquired a battery of potent slogans at the same time when the society was deeply compromised by the conduct of the war in Vietnam and its domestic consequences and when universities had become dependent on federal support or philanthropic support that could in turn be attacked as compromised. The "Christers" were no threat to a generally "collegiate" student culture. In contrast, the radicals could make use of all the devices of modern media technology to seem to represent the voice of students nationally and even internationally.

What has just been said is limited to the eminent universities whose undergraduate colleges have attracted a predominantly upper-middle-class and relatively sophisticated student body. It is in these institutions that faculty members joined students in the antiwar movement, as illustrated by the first teach-in in the United States, which occurred at the University of Michigan in 1965. It should be remembered also that, in the most selective of these institutions, the great majority of graduating seniors—as many as 80 percent or more—were planning on postbaccalaureate study. When that study was medicine, the faculty teaching the premedical courses retained throughout the period of protest a very large hegemony over the students for whom it has stood as gatekeepers. To a lesser extent, similar faculty control can be maintained over students who need recommendations for the leading law schools, schools of public policy and of management, and graduate schools of arts and sciences. This has remained so even though requirements have been relaxed (even in the great majority of highly selective institutions) and even though students are free to choose majors and courses with minimal formal constraints. The scarcity of desirable postbaccalaureate opportunities in relation to the swelling number of applicants brought about a competitive milieu, which many of these students hated. They were at best ambivalent about their own competitiveness; often they longed for camaraderie and were quite ready to assail the university for making them as competitive as they felt they had to become. There is a paradox in the fact that such a large proportion of these students sought out the massive universities, necessarily organized according to *Gesellschaft* principles, while demanding that they be reorganized in accordance with a longed-for *Gemeinschaft*.

Many books have been written about the impact of the political protests and the reforms in governance and in curriculum, including the introduction of such new subjects as ethnic studies and women's studies. I can only touch briefly on some of the ways

in which meritocracy was undermined—ways prophetically anticipated in Michael Young's ingenious social science fiction (1959;
Riesman, 1967a, 1975a).

Credit for Off-Campus Involvement. One route taken by many institutions was to find ways to provide academic credit for such off-
campus involvement as tutoring disadvantaged children or serving
as legislative interns in local, state, or federal government or in
similar posts in regulatory agencies. One often unfulfilled hope was
that students would become more pragmatic. As already noted,
Antioch College had, under Arthur Morgan's leadership, provided
students with regularly recurring off-campus terms, with an unevenly successful effort to link these both to the curriculum and to
potential careers, but the traditional Antioch required five years
to achieve the baccalaureate degree. Under the newer dispensa-
tions, it became possible for individual faculty members, in an
often quite unsupervised way, to give students academic credit for
any plausible off-campus effort. As a faculty member who has
supervised a fair amount of such off-campus effort and has observed its supervision by others, I have been aware of the dangers
of saturating small communities with student inquisitors, as well as
overloading government officials who lack time or experience or
both for careful supervision and evaluation of student work. (A
notable exception was the short-lived internship program called
"Tunbridge" run by Jan Rakoff, assistant professor of sociology at
the now defunct Lone Mountain College in San Francisco; Rakoff
created a network of carefully instructed advisers who were
screened for their capacity, as well as willingness, to assist students,
who were in turn carefully counseled as to what they might justly
expect from such volunteer supervisors.) Larry H. Litten (personal
correspondence) notes that some devotees of such internships have
insisted that there is too much writing in the college curriculum; he
and I are in agreement that there is usually not enough, at least for
current levels of literacy even among upper-middle-class students.
We have also shared the observation that many deans of students
and others working in the student services area have favored such
involvement, and I would add to them the many activist campus
ministers I have met; these individuals have chosen a nonacademic

career line and often harbor considerable resentments against
faculty members who regard them, if they notice them at all, with
scarcely concealed disdain.

In assessing the loosening of the curriculum that has permitted, and in some cases encouraged, off-campus work, the term
independent study has often turned out to mean neither "independence," if there is to be careful faculty supervision enforced by
some kind of overall quality control, nor "study," unless the off-
campus work is coupled with the requirement that the student
make some substantial written report on it either during the time
he or she is away from campus or on return.

The term *independent study* can also refer to any academic
work conducted on campus under the mentorship of a particular
faculty member, rather than under the auspices of a department.
In the 1960s a number of colleges offered such opportunities as a
lure for students, advertising in catalogues and brochures as well as
in various college guides. Many of the more traditional colleges
provided such an option, and for a time it was attractive to many
undergraduates who believed themselves capable of independent
work, a belief congruent with the characteristic American insistence that the task of socialization is in large part training for independence and that the latter can rarely come too soon. However,
the well-nigh universal belief that one should be independent is
contradicted by the actual behavior of many students who, as already noted, may prefer to stay close to home although they can
easily afford the costs of travel and other expenses of attending
college at a distance; indeed, we are all familiar with students and
other young people who manage to prolong their adolescence well
into their twenties. Neither the Educational Testing Service nor
any other agency is capable of providing reliable characterological
measures of the capacity of a particular student to work independently. Hence, the result for many students pursuing independent
study has been a letdown, a feeling of premature despair concerning their ability to pace themselves and to work with minimal and,
in fact, often perfunctory supervision.

In considering these issues, it is necessary to take account of
an institution's entire context and climate and not individual students with an abstract belief in curricular freedom on the one side

and individual faculty members on the other side who do not understand that the burdens of supervising independent study may
be much heavier than they had anticipated. For example, when
Worcester Polytechnic Institute, which had been a fairly traditional
engineering school with students subordinated to the various departments, whether in civil or electrical or other branches of engineering or in the natural sciences, drastically reshaped its curriculum and set up a Washington office for students who would
spend a term working, for example, for the Environmental Protection Agency or for the Office of Technology Assessment, the aim
was to give students a sense of the impacts of technology and the
larger society on each other. For the hard-working students at
WPI, mostly first-generation-in-college and traditionally recruited
from a hundred-mile radius of Worcester, the opportunity available to a minority to see something of the larger world could be
extremely valuable; resident faculty members, on leave from the
Worcester campus, were on hand to supervise the students and to
help the interchange of ideas among students working on different
projects for different agencies. Since the field of engineering provides ample internal constraints, monitored by the accrediting
processes of the engineering profession itself, the Washington
semester enriched, rather than diluted, the curriculum.

Independent study for academic credit must be distinguished
from stopouts or leaves of absence, which in my judgment have
proved their value in Harvard College, where (except during the
period of the Vietnam war draft) close to one fifth of the students
take a term or an entire year off, during which they have a chance
to decide whether they have started down a mistaken path to a
career or, having felt themselves previously too sheltered, expose
themselves to various sorts of jobs in "the real world." It is the
general experience that such students return with a surer sense of
themselves, particularly so in the many cases in which the institution further disrupts a student's self-esteem.

In the late 1960s, Harvard College made it possible for students who could put together an individuated sequence of courses
and an appropriate senior thesis at the end of the road to pursue
an independent major (termed in Harvard lingo a Special Concentration). I was one of the sponsors of this proposal, recognizing that

many students would discover that the program they wished to pursue could in fact be managed within one of the regular departments. Other students find that they cannot put together enough faculty sponsorship to guide a self-designed major and to undertake the always arduous tasks of supervising and responding to the senior thesis. Yet, there is always a small minority of students, perhaps fifteen each year, who create an interesting amalgam among departments for which they find adequate faculty support and the necessary approval of the committee supervising independent concentrations. Students who start down the road of a Special Concentration often discover the difficult tradeoff they must make, in a still high-pressure and competitive environment, between, on the one hand, freedom and the desire to create their own course of study and, on the other, subordination to departmental hegemony. Larry H. Litten, former director of institutional research and assistant professor of education at Carleton College, has put the matter well (personal correspondence):

> Special majors were quite popular for a while; they were all but dead when I left Carleton. Students began to realize, I believe, that what I tried to tell my advisees— what you gain in individual "freedom" and "creativity" you sacrifice often in access to faculty who are understandably more involved with students who are following the curriculum which they have worked long and hard to define and implement. The "major" represents the things that faculty are interested in and the problems that they believe are worth attending to; the student will be lucky if he can engage faculty equally on his personal project when there are other students who are willing to wrestle with those that the faculty have singled out as important. Autonomy comes with all its consequences. It is too bad that students can't understand or be introduced to the sociology of intellectual life, to realize that while they have legitimate claims on faculty as teachers, they do not have legitimate grounds for unilaterally defining intellectual fields of endeavor.

In interpreting Litten's remarks, context is again important. Many students who have been admitted to an Ivy League–type institution seek out Carleton College because they desire the close personal contact with faculty members that such top-flight and relatively small (1,600 students) colleges promise and provide; correspondingly, Carleton faculty members carry heavy teaching loads, in both formal and informal terms, compared with their counterparts at research universities. In contrast, at MIT, some senior faculty members, primarily researchers, will welcome the occasional undergraduate—talented to begin with, or he or she would not be at MIT—who seeks them out under the Undergraduate Research Opportunities Program. And when faculty members from different fields decide on their own initiative to join one another in examining some particular topic and invite undergraduates to study with them in their self-educating enterprise, students may find enclaves of a nondepartmental sort within a large university where they will be able to pursue a somewhat independent path under a faculty umbrella. For example, the Federated Learning Communities at the State University of New York in Stony Brook bring together, under the overall supervision of Professor Patrick J. Hill, different ad hoc combinations—for example, a chemist, an ecologist, and a social psychologist to study the practical and political issues involved in certain environmental issues. Each such faculty team is composed of senior faculty members who have tenure and are not threatened by partial absence from their departmental obligations; each team also includes someone termed the "Mentor," the faculty member whose task it is to attend all lectures and discussions and meet with students and individual faculty members to assess whether students are learning what the faculty members believe they are teaching. The faculty members return to their departments after a stint of such mutuality, and new cohorts are recruited in the same or other areas, depending on faculty interest and opportunity.

In the current era of budgetary restraint and retrenchment, such ventures are often the first to suffer if they cannot find outside foundation or similar support. Thus, a faculty committee reviewing Charles Muscatine's Collegiate Seminar Program ("Strawberry College"), which offered undergraduates opportunities for self-designed study at Berkeley, concluded that the program as then constituted was too loose and disorganized, recommending somewhat more formal and supervised arrangements (Hassitt and others, 1979); however, the faculty decided to eliminate the program entirely, particularly when Professor Muscatine objected to the committee's assessment (Muscatine, 1979). There are countless other cases in which faculty members have made efforts to create, in effect, new specialties in the interstices among departments, only to discover that students who had fought for such relaxations in the sixties were not the students of the seventies, so many of whom in the more competitive colleges are concerned with postbaccalaureate placement and do not wish to chance creating a transcript that appears in many ways irregular, especially if doing so requires just as much effort as a regular departmental major (or more).

Grade Inflation and Diploma Inflation. Readers are familiar with the phenomenon of grade inflation, in which a C became in effect a failing grade, and only a few institutions, such as the outstanding women's colleges and the college of the University of Chicago, maintained the older norms. In addition to grade inflation, there came into being what might be termed the sanitized transcript, from which all failing grades were erased if a student managed on repeated trials to pass a course; similarly, courses taken pass/no credit were simply eliminated if the student's performance did not meet the minimal requirement of a "pass." Occasionally, as with the Keller plan or other forms of programmed learning and computer-assisted instruction, the elimination of failure did not lead to grade inflation, but rather gave students the opportunity to proceed at their own pace so that the slow were not humiliated by the quick nor the adept held back by the less adept.

There are, moreover, a number of situations in which what is important is student mastery, not the time taken to achieve it. Indeed, in many instances, students who try and try again, those often termed "overachievers," exhibit a pertinacity that is important information for a postbaccalaureate academic institution or an employer, reflecting well on the student's capacities. For example, I have sometimes argued in my own department that, beyond a certain threshold of competence revealed by the Graduate Record Examination or similar tests of cognitive capacity, we should favor those students who have been long-distance runners or swimmers or who have mastered a difficult language or a difficult instrument—using these as unobtrusive measures of ability to endure frustration and to persist in the face of faculty rebuff and indifference or a student's own self-doubts. But there are also settings where we may want to know—for example, for a pilot or a surgeon—how fast the person learns as well as how much has eventually been learned. Mastery learning, which permits breaking up the traditional semester into modules relevant to the topic and to the varying speeds of learning, need not conceal either the number of trials or the amount of time taken to complete a certain module. Such concealment confuses the goals of pedagogy with those of credentialing—a confusion present in varying degrees in almost all academic settings where work is done for academic credit. There is thus no necessary connection between favoring mastery learning and opposition to the sanitized transcript and to grade inflation.

As an aspect of the effort of some of the more selective institutions to pull back from grade inflation, Berkeley has adopted the device of providing the student with a transcript that accompanies the grade received in a course with the average grade in the course, so that one can distinguish between an A earned in a course with a general grade level of B or C and an A earned in a course in which everyone else received a virtually similar award (Suslow, 1976). This system, proposed but not adopted at Harvard,[2] where an effort has been made to control grade inflation on a voluntary basis by furnishing individual faculty members with data allowing them to compare the grade distribution of their own courses with the pattern of other courses and with the grades received by their students in other courses, does handicap students in the type of mastery learning course just mentioned, in which all but the most

---

[2] Dean Whitla, director of institutional research in Harvard College, has reported that the percentage of Harvard students receiving A's, about 14 percent, has not changed since 1898; grade inflation has occurred in the large number of B's and B-pluses now given for work that would once have brought C's and D's (personal communication).

indolent or clearly inadequate students will eventually obtain an honor grade. The system also penalizes students in courses in which a faculty member is so evocative, yet at the same time demanding, that they extend themselves and do better than the campuswide average or their own work in other courses, but the transcript makes it look as if the course were just another "gut" (so called because students pass through it easily).

One might also speak of diploma inflation as a result of the pressure to give course credit for remedial work, first demanded by and on behalf of underprepared blacks and then by other nonwhites similarly handicapped by family background and the inadequacies of previous schooling. In the more selective institutions, this and similar demands have employed the rationale that the institutions themselves, by their unquestioned commitment to what were seen as narrowly cognitive and fiercely competitive white middle-class norms, needed to change their inherited and traditional orientations to take account of the different skills and talents of the enlarged cohorts of nonwhite matriculants. However, the expectation that the whole mind-set of a culture could be changed in more than minor ways seems misplaced. This is especially so because blacks are among the oldest nonindigenous Americans and, despite and because of oppression, had both absorbed American culture and contributed greatly to it in speech and music and many styles of life; subcultures so fundamentally American as those to be found among blacks generally paralleled white social stratifications and regional differences. No matter how separatist the ideology or how determined the search for forms of cultural expression (which did, indeed, exist) that could be traced to African or Afro-Caribbean sources, most blacks were enrolling in previously overwhelmingly white institutions, ambitious to succeed within the educational and occupational framework already in place. I recall from the late 1960s a number of emotionally charged discussions with black students, themselves exceptionally talented by the prevailing academic norms, who said that they had entered the most prestigious, predominantly white institutions, where they suffered from their visible and (as they believed, rightly or wrongly) stigmatized positions, in order to be able to influence from within the "white power structure" in favor of the less privileged fellow blacks with whom they sought identification.

Many strategies were devised for easing the transition. A number of the leading preparatory schools, such as Phillips Exeter, Baldwin, Putney, Sidwell Friends, and other schools founded by Quakers, recruited black students in settings where small classes and tutorial work could help them prepare for entry to selective colleges. Summer programs such as the many ABC (A Better Chance) programs were conducted, with the same aim, on the campuses of residential colleges. Brandeis University developed the Transitional Year Program for black students who had completed high school, not promising that after a year's work they would automatically be admitted to Brandeis itself, but that the program would attempt to place them in appropriate selective colleges. (Columbia, Yale, and Harvard created in the 1960s the Intensive Summer Studies Program, which brought blacks from the black colleges of the South, plus a handful of whites from relatively unselective Southern colleges, to the three institutions for one or two summers of a mix of tutoring and regular summer school courses to help prepare these students for entry to postbaccalaureate medical, legal, and doctoral programs. After a year or two of experience with this effort, the decision was made also to bring some faculty members from the black colleges to the three institutions for summer study, so that these professors would see the milieu in which students from their institutions had been working and could help them keep up the level and pace of work during their subsequent undergraduate years.)

If there had been many more such programs and much more experience among white faculty members in teaching black students with inadequate previous schooling, it might have been possible to avoid giving college-level credit for non-college-level work and to find the necessary subsidies to allow blacks, if necessary, to take more time to get a baccalaureate degree. However, the relatively sudden increase in numbers of blacks, especially in those selective, liberal colleges that could afford to recruit students irrespective of financial need (Wesleyan, Oberlin, the Ivy League, Stanford, and many others), meant that these colleges were faced with entering classes containing 8 to 10 percent or more blacks, and it proved impossible to resist the demands of the majority that they receive college-level credit for any work done in postsecondary institutions. These students believed that it would be humiliating to

do remedial noncredit work, not seeing the humiliation of a concession of a regular grade for work not previously regarded as
college-level.[3] Indeed, the presence of visibly ill-prepared nonwhites (as against the invisible equally unprepared whites scattered
in almost any classroom) led many guilty or intimidated white instructors to bestow passing or even honor grades on inadequate
work, judging the student by his or her own progress rather than
by previously established norms. And how could instructors then
give a low grade to a white student who performed at a higher
level? Thus, the entry of large and often organized cohorts of black
students (and, more recently, Spanish-speaking students) was one
factor in raising the general level of grades and in curbing the
previous reign of more or less meritocratic standards. Not only
were these standards fuzzy at the edges, but the whole structure of
college credits given, as it often seemed, simply for time served had
been built on tradition and tacit faculty norms. It did not take long
for the very term *standards* to become a term of abuse, like *elitism*.
Previously, the rationale for particular grades had been based on
tacit but widely agreed-on norms in a particular field. The norm
was frequently represented by a curve in which, for example, it was
assumed that in any particular classroom 10 or 15 percent of the
students would merit A's, and another 10 or 15 percent would

[3] Larry H. Litten (personal correspondence) comments on this statement as follows:
"To a certain extent, I think that some of the things we see as 'humiliation' of
'minorities' (for example, the acceptance of credits for remedial work) is really being
very savvy—that it will be credentials that get one into the starting gate, and the
political climate may well help keep one in the race combined with the proper
amount of skill at manipulating future situations. Also, in the early political con-
frontations, I think that many students were surprised that they obtained as much
concession as they did." Certainly, this last statement is correct; some of the students
who helped create the Harvard Afro-American Studies Department over earlier
faculty objections did not expect that Harvard would give in to their demands; yet,
in retrospect, some saw the concession itself—in the light of the department's relative lack of academic respectability—as perhaps unintentional humiliation of blacks.
And Litten is also right in other respects. When scholarly black faculty members
have raised the question of what a student can do with a degree in black or Afro-
American studies—a question black students themselves increasingly raise, since
most do not major in the area, but rather use it as a source of solidarity and
occasional "soft options"—I have responded that if one gets a degree in black
studies, one many continue in a program that will lead to teaching black studies or to
being recruited into academic administration in the often awkward position of a
spokesperson for but also to activist black undergraduates.

receive failing grades, with B's or C's (or numerical equivalents, which look more definitive than they generally could be) distributed to the bulk of the students. The number of credits a given course had been allowed to confer had also been based on norms not clearly spelled out—and at times quite inequitable where based on the number of class meetings but not counting, in science courses, time taken up by laboratory work. And because the rationales for grades and credits were so commonly based on prevailing and accepted conventions, adversary attitudes within the faculty and among the student body could, with varying degrees of ease, destroy the legitimacy of the structure.

One group of students who suffered from these developments was the hard-working and well-prepared blacks, some middle-class in origin and others aspiring to become middle-class, who complained to those who would listen that their grades and diplomas were being devalued—especially where grades had been completely abolished—and that they would be regarded as blacks who had got through by favor, when in fact they could do well without favor. The affluent "protest-prone" students described earlier did not suffer in the same way from grade inflation; they could do well on the Graduate Record Examination or the comparable admissions tests for entry into medical school or into selective schools of law and management; in the leading undergraduate colleges, such students could also count on letters of recommendation from well-known and widely connected professors.

Inroads of the Counterculture and Women's Liberation. After the enormous outpouring of demonstrations pursuant to the Cambodian invasion of 1970, with the side effects on universities that all such actions had, it seemed to many observers as if the campuses had suddenly become quiet. On the one hand, the protests helped engender a sense of disillusion because they appeared to have minimal impact on the war or on American foreign policy. On the other hand, the most potent stimulus to activism diminished when the draft ended and the withdrawal of troops from Vietnam began. Furthermore, at many institutions new presidents were inaugurated of a more conciliatory temper, as the starchier figures of an older generation withdrew (Grayson Kirk at Columbia, Nathan

Pusey at Harvard, and many others). However, my own visits to
and exchanges with less visible campuses made clear to me that
activism, like other phenomena that begin with the visible elites,
had not come to an end, but rather was socially mobile to new
strata: one could no longer tell where a demonstration would break
out by looking for the "protest-prone" students whom observers of
radical youth in the 1960s had identified. My impressions were
more than supported by a systematic study done by the American
Council on Education, which indicated that in places to which television cables did not run and at campuses of which the country had
never heard, campus revolts continued (Bayer and Astin, 1971).

Among the student activists of the 1960s, very few had unequivocally political and revolutionary aims, even though they
might use slogans with a revolutionary ring. They wanted freedom
from the pressures they were under; their cry was "liberation," by
which they meant personal liberation quite as much as cohort liberation (Pitts, 1969). At the outset, the counterculture, as it came to
be called, and political activism seemed to be allied: both movements sought freedom from the constraints of university life,
whether in the curriculum or in the extracurriculum (*in loco parentis*
vanished with astonishing speed, with the Catholic colleges not far
behind the secular ones—a tacit alignment between faculty and
students, convenient in freeing the former from disagreeable
supervisory tasks in dormitories or extracurricular life generally).
By the 1970s, especially in nonelite colleges and universities, it had
become clear that the counterculture, which promised liberation,
had a much more potent impact and longer staying power than
activism, which promised hard work and repeated frustrations. An
exception must be made here for the organized public-interest
research groups (PIRGs), supported by student fees and dominated by the crusading energies of Ralph Nader, for many of these
groups had batteries of lawyers who could take up what was regarded as a student cause, such as attacking the Educational Testing Service. (I shall come later to the reasons for my judgment that
this latter cause is not in the interest of most students.) Some of
these students spoke of "the long march through institutions" while
they were beginning their paralegal and legal careers.

Such concepts as "the long march" appealed to only a minority of pertinacious student activists who were prepared for the

patient organizing work and, in some instances, the readings in Marx, Lenin, and more contemporary revolutionary writers, from whose ideas these more revolutionary activists sought to develop strategies to cope with the obdurate inertia, if not hostility, of the great bulk of students and of the surrounding population. In the view of these radical activists, the counterculture was a seduction toward a socially irresponsible hedonism. However, most of the political activists had never been so solemn and dedicated; they might march in a demonstration or attend a mass meeting or teach-in, but these were sporadic occasions combining the attractions of sheer momentum with those of camaraderie. (It frequently occurred, and still on occasion occurs, that indifferent or politically conservative students will attend a demonstration for the sake of the "action"; if the leaders can maneuver matters so that police are called in and there is a confrontation, some of these often happenstance fellow travelers will make an ideological shift, minimizing dissonance by bringing their convictions in line with their actions and the sometimes untoward consequences that ensue.) For most of these sporadic and less committed radicals, liberation—sexual, parietal, pharmacological—was attractive. In the end, the counterculture won out and has made its way throughout the society, even to the "hardhats" underneath whose helmets long hair is often visible—which, in an earlier era, would have been an occasion for antagonism between the affluent in their blue jeans and the working class with its more conservative cultural values.

Here again, the American pattern of the downward mobility of fashion was in operation. There was also a certain amount of what might be called upward mobility from below, as lower-class black styles (and, to a far smaller degree, the various styles of Spanish-speaking and American Indian students) became popular among the elite and spread as musical fashions have—from the bottom of society to the top and then filtering down into the middle and lower-middle subcultures of youth (see Meyersohn and Katz, 1957). Today, only a trained eye can tell the blue jeans of the affluent from the blue jeans of students who are the first in their families to attend college. And while one group may listen to the lyrics of a Joan Baez or Bob Dylan song, all groups listened to the beat.

To put it a bit differently, political activism promised hard work, frustration, even possible arrest. Hard work and relatively low pay would await those activists who, eschewing passivity, entered law schools with the intent of becoming public-interest lawyers, or medical schools with the aim of practicing community medicine and reforming health care, or schools of journalism (or the equivalent apprenticeships) in the expectation of becoming investigative journalists or reviving an older, crusading style in what has come to be known as advocacy journalism. Some entered government service, especially in regulatory agencies at the state and federal levels; some became legislative assistants to liberal senators and congressmen or staffed the latter's subcommittees; a few even won elective office. Yet, on the whole, the victory went to the counterculture.

The victory has been won not only among many students, including students who have entered four-year or community colleges after a period of odd jobs, but unevenly among faculty members as well. I remember my astonishment at hearing the eulogy to the counterculture, Reich's *Greening of America* (1970), praised by many apparently serious intellectuals and academicians as a work of major significance. Older male faculty members took "liberation" to mean that they could shed the wives who had seen them through their doctorates, trade them in as obsolescent, and take up with younger women, including students; few faculty members were so square as to voice objection. Younger ones, drawn into the twin streams of political activism and the counterculture in the 1960s, continued the same division when they began teaching, as retrenchment set in, at unselective state and private colleges as well as at research institutions or top-flight liberal arts colleges. Some (in such fields as sociology, history, modern languages, and philosophy) maintained their radicalism and the elements of Puritanism, or at least work-mindedness, characteristic of scholarly Marxists. (The impact of increasing numbers of radical faculty members, especially in the social sciences, on upper-middle-class students has in general not produced a new generation of student activists; the students come to college having imbibed diluted radicalism from the media and some school history texts [see FitzGerald, 1980], yet their fears for the vocational future tend to lead them toward resignation [Mankoff, 1980].) Other faculty members adopted the permissiveness of the counterculture, rapping with their students, casual about turning in syllabuses or grade lists and meeting other requirements dismissed as stuffy and bureaucratic, counting on the students' own tolerance to allow them to get away with the alleged spontaneity of doing *their* own thing. When faculty members of radical persuasion encountered working-class students and attempted "consciousness raising," they sometimes made fools of themselves as students defended their own cultural norms (see London, 1978; but compare Birenbaum, 1971), but at other times they could damage students by demeaning the value of the curriculum in which they were enrolled (see Neumann and Riesman, 1980). When they took the other road, of hedonism and laissez faire, they frequently succeeded in winning student approbation, which might even lead, in a "teach or perish" setting, to their retention (see Grant and Riesman, 1978, chap. 9).

Berger and Berger (1971) had believed that, as the social elites succumbed to the counterculture, became less achievement-oriented, and drifted gently into downward social mobility, their places in the top echelons of the occupational structure would be taken by the working class, which would remain unaffected by the new hedonism. Undoubtedly, many working-class young people sought out vocational programs (rather than liberal arts transfer programs) in community colleges and then, if they felt that further education would be of benefit, moved from those programs to vocational programs in four-year institutions. They were after secure jobs, although they might use some of the money their work brought them in ways influenced by the counterculture. But the views of Berger and Berger left out of account the influence of the elite on some of the strivers among the nonelite who had also to combat peer pressure not to excel and now also found themselves deprived of expected faculty support in those institutions where scholarly standards had only minimal anchoring. Of course, in engineering schools and similar technical institutions, achievement motivation remained high throughout the 1960s and 1970s. Moreover, at the flagship campuses of major state universities, distribution requirements were generally retained (in part as a means of dividing up student traffic), so that undergraduates could not discover in the catalogues, which did not name instructors for particular courses, unequivocally "soft options" in the curriculum. But in much of the society, hedonism proved attractive at all social levels, though of course there are many exceptions to whom the Bergers' paradigm does apply, notably older women whose previous education has been truncated and who are now turning up in community colleges and four-year institutions with powerful motivation to secure the necessary credentials to pursue a full-time professional career.

Among the first groups to react negatively to the counterculture were various segments of the women's movements. During the era of political activism they had already suffered from consignment to subsidiary roles by both black and white "macho" radicals. Many also realized that sexual "liberation" meant that they were to be fair game, uninhibited by jealousy or a greater desire for stability and affective ties than many men had who were playing the field.

There is no single women's movement, but many movements with different objectives. Their combined impact on society seems to me far greater than that of either the activism of an earlier era[4] or the earlier stages of the counterculture, in which the leading gurus, both in their writing and in management of communes in a sometimes quasitotalitarian way, also have tended to be male. Some women actively competed in previously stag fields, such as engineering, medicine, the higher reaches of the law, management, and banking. Men who wished to have relationships with such women were asked to take more of a hand in housework and, where a child or two was born, in child care. Masculine ambition

---

[4] As this book goes to press (July 1980), campus-based protests against registration for the draft have given some student and faculty radicals, nostalgic for the demonstrations of the earlier period of campus growth and relative affluence, the hope of a revival of activism. But that seems to me hardly a radical cause. It is not an attack on militarism, since basic training and even military service of the average GI have in recent decades engendered, not the "military mind," but indifference and cynicism. Dependence on the volunteer, or mercenary, army recalls the Northern pattern in the Civil War of buying exemption from the draft. The absence of conventional forces that can reliably be counted on is one of many pressures against achieving any measure of arms control over the rapid increase in our nuclear weapons arsenals, since the conventional forces, with their rapid turnover and attrition and lack of high technical competence, can scarcely be counted on; see Riesman (1980b).

had to come to terms with understandably strident and newly awakened feminist ambition. But another wing of the women's movements sought to bring to the world of work dominated by men the softenings and personal concern traditionally more characteristic of nurturant women. (See Hochschild, 1975.)

The older women just mentioned, who returned to or began at college, commonly had to work part-time to support themselves and their not yet fully grown children. A large proportion of these enterprising women felt the need for additional earnings in the family to keep up with inflationary costs. But they, and others less hard-pressed financially, were also affected by the women's movements. In fact, the increasing number of women at work has been coterminous with the rise of an ideology to justify such work; and since a number of women who were coming to college either for the first time or to complete an unfinished education were catching up with their husbands educationally or even surpassing them, strains in the family produced increasing numbers of divorces, and the women had to go it alone on the basis of their new-found powers.

The women's liberation movements have also assisted a minority of ambitious younger women to develop their powers in opening entry to positions in such fields as management, banking, medicine, and government—fields whose high status has partly reflected the fact of male hegemony within them. (Medicine lacks the extraordinarily high status it has in the United States in other countries, such as the Soviet Union, where most practitioners are women.) Academically capable women who once might have become schoolteachers now find less hazardous work and higher-status careers in postsecondary education, law, and the fields just mentioned. After a brief flurry of interest in school reform on the part of both sexes, symbolized by the programs conferring a master of arts in teaching in the early 1960s, capable men did not step in to replace women as precollegiate teachers. Thus, while there is a surplus of teachers in many fields, there is a lack in perhaps the crucial one: the teaching of mathematics and science. Persons of both sexes equipped with knowledge of quantitative and high-technology subjects have far more lucrative and less stressful careers open to them than teaching school. The counterculture has served to strengthen the already powerful peer culture of the schools in resistance to the authority of teachers, and the adversarial movements for "children's rights" have intimidated teachers and principals alike. Furthermore, faced with arguments that single-sex schools are "unnatural" and in some fashion sexist, such excellent public secondary schools as Hunter High in New York or Girls Latin in Boston have become, like their once-male counterparts, coeducational; for economic and ideological reasons, the same phenomenon has occurred (with rare exceptions) in the independent schools. The congeries of current developments has had the shocking result that, although all College Board scores have declined in the last fifteen years, the most dramatic decline has been in women's verbal scores—a decline not matched by any increase in quantitative scores, where men continue to excel. For the first time in history, one can find colleges where the verbal scores of entering men are slightly above those of entering women. Many interpretations have been offered for this decline.

The College Entrance Examination Board appointed a panel chaired by Willard Wirtz to probe possible causes; the panel in turn commissioned a number of specialized studies, for example, comparing more traditional and more experimental high schools (where no substantial difference in score patterns was found). See College Entrance Examination Board (1977); for an additional hypothesis, see Riesman (1978d). Much attention was given to television viewing, but this seems to have approximately equal effects on boys and girls; one possible minor factor not considered was the impact of direct-dial long-distance telephoning on girls' letter writing, but such an impact is hardly established conclusively, since many fewer young women appear to keep diaries today than in an earlier era.

In adding my own interpretation to other causes thought relevant to this drop, I have speculated that the most likely cause is sexual activity: for girls this is generally more involving and also more cause for anxiety than it is for boys. Moreover, thanks to the loss of parental control and the general cultural permissiveness, girls in junior high and high school have become even more subject to the judgment of boys to whom they are now tied in sexual, drug-taking, and drinking activities. For, although some girls in school have always been aware that they must not be "too bright" if they were to be liked by both sexes, this imperative becomes more powerful still when one does not want to use a larger vocabulary or read more books than one's actual or would-be lover. Regrettably, the lovers have not introduced their girlfriends to their basement workshops and other activities that would provide a manual basis for quantitative and mathematical interests; in spite of the fact that a few women are becoming welders and truck drivers, and a larger number computer operators and even engineers, this is still a trickle. Furthermore, as several students of education have pointed out to me, something I should not have forgotten from my own boyhood as an avid follower of the batting averages of the two generally losing Philadelphia baseball teams of that era, following sports may make a not inconsiderable contribution to boys' comparative confidence in dealing with figures. As Larry H. Litten puts it (personal correspondence): "I am sure that following the sports pages has contributed significantly to the mathematical development of men (particularly with things like 'earned run averages,' 'batting averages,' 'won/lost percentages,' 'yardage penalties,' etc.). One might argue that cooking involves measurements, but I would submit that the range of mathematics is paltry by comparison. Furthermore, the mathematics in sports is an integral part of much conversation about sports . . . it may be a long time before women and their mothers 'talk sports' like boys and their fathers. It might help to have discussions of newspaper sports sections brought into elementary school classrooms."

"Learning for Its Own Sake"? The fall in women's test scores has had no visible effect on college attendance. However, with the disappearance of the draft and the desire of some young men to get started in the work force—young men whose ideology is still one of hating school—the proportion of white men has begun to fall, and at the same time the proportion of women has continued to rise.[5]

---

[5] A recent study has turned up evidence that I did not anticipate; namely, that women who have done well on the PSAT gain more support from their fathers than from their mothers if they wish to apply to selective colleges to which they are presumptively admissible—private colleges with high nominal tuitions (see Litten, Jahoda, and Morris, 1980; and Litten and others, 1980, pp. 8–13).

But for reasons suggested above, the women are not bringing to postsecondary studies the diligence and preparation in literacy previously more characteristic of women than of men. They have not in any considerable number studied foreign languages, read serious history, read and memorized poetry, or written poetry or fiction or experimented in other genres. Hence, it is rare to meet faculty members who were teaching in the period of the academic revolution who do not complain about the intellectual impoverishment of many students and of their inability to read difficult texts or to write lucid, let alone grammatical, prose.

Although it is easy to exaggerate the proportion of students who in any epoch enjoyed "learning for its own sake," both women and men today are often involuntary captives, needing a credential to go on to postbaccalaureate training and doing the necessary work grimly and anxiously rather than with any sense of pleasure in learning.

I have interviewed students in this situation at my own and other selective colleges who do find excitement in one of the sciences, which they have taken as much out of an initial interest in science as out of a decision to pursue a premedical program. The most frustrating experiences I have had are with black women who get genuinely engaged in a scientific subject but then conclude that there are "no jobs" for Ph.D.s and decide that they will pursue a career in medicine—sometimes, for idealistic reasons already indicated, in community medicine or family practice, sometimes in a specialty they intend to practice, but virtually never in research medicine. I must emphasize that I have in mind students from upper-middle-class families who would understand more readily than working-class parents, white or black, the decision to try to make a living in an academic specialty rather than the more familiar professions of law, medicine, or engineering. It is the students themselves, not their parents, who are understandably anxious about risks. In academic work, "too much" excitement in a particular scientific field threatens them because it may endanger their overall grade average. (Colorado College to some extent avoids this widespread phenomenon because, in its modular scheme, students commonly pursue a single subject at a time.) I never feel that it is justified to say to such students that there *are* jobs if one disaggregates by field and subspecialty and that as, so to speak, double minorities they have the benefit of affirmative action in securing such jobs—in fact, among some students of this high quality, it is a threat rather than an opportunity, since they fear that they will in fact receive jobs through affirmative action and will harbor the misgiving that they secured their positions on something other than merit. Some of these students have such a strong sense of social duty that pleasure in learning seems somehow "elitist," and it would be doubly "elitist"—a word always used pejoratively—to take account of the fact that they stand on the high platform of their selective undergraduate college, with recommendations from known scientists and mentors to help them in the first stages of their careers. One could argue that the call of social duty might instead impel a capable undergraduate to seek to become a role model for other minority-group members and/or women as a teacher, particularly in academic specialties previously dominated by white males. But the social imperatives also serve to justify avoidance of the risk, incurred in any academic calling, that one may not finish the course or do sufficiently distinguished work to earn a scarce tenure place in a top-flight institution—self-doubts that, despite the women's movements, continue to be stronger among women than among men of comparable potential.

Another illustration may clarify the issue, since social duty could be interpreted either in terms of attending law school or in terms of securing the doctorate in a policy-related field. I recall a very determined Chicana student, the eldest child in a family of migrant workers, one of the first Chicanas recruited to an Ivy League college. Although her parents spoke Spanish at home and a little English, they insisted that she learn standard English, and she herself began to express strong reservations about bilingual education, as mandated by federal courts, which brought students like herself under the auspices of teachers "illiterate in two languages." I told her that the other Chicana and many Chicano students were, like herself, planning to go to law school and that (although there were not enough lawyers of Mexican-American origin) I knew of no one engaged in a disinterested study of whether, in transitional settings, bilingualism could sometimes be helpful, especially if the family were recent immigrants from Mexico and had the not uncommon hope of eventually making enough money to return there; in such cases, the children might not want to lose their ties, linguistic or otherwise, to the ancestral culture. But in other cases, as many Mexican-American parents in Denver contend, court orders mandating desegregation and bilingual education have enabled "hustlers" who may be of Guatemalan or even Basque origin to replace reasonably competent white teachers. The Chicana student was half persuaded but then concluded that this enterprise would be self-indulgent and that she should go to work for MALDEF, the Mexican-American Legal Defense and Education Fund; self-confident as she had become, she probably also felt that this was a surer, quicker route than one that was of more intellectual interest to her and, she was inclined to agree, no less important for other Mexican-Americans.

Even faculty members who have a diligent student body, such as those who teach pre-meds in selective colleges, do not have a fully engaged one; the students are studying chemistry or biology because they have to as a prerequisite, not because they find excitement in the subject matter. (For an argument that medical schools could virtually abolish the pre-med syndrome and encourage premedical aspirants to study the classics, history, and other liberating arts, beyond the bare minimum of quantitative work, see Thomas, 1979, pp. 113–116.) We are back in the era of the studies at the University of Kansas, although in an altered atmosphere, recalling that the Kansas medical students saw the faculty as obstacles to their getting out into practice and paying off their debts; their immediate objective was not how to learn to become doctors but how to pass the hurdles of the medical school itself. On the undergraduate campus, the aim was to "make the grade," with maximum benefit to oneself and one's fraternity and with a minimum of personal involvement in the subject matter (Becker, Geer, and Hughes, 1968; Becker and others, 1961).

Lest readers think that, as an older faculty member, I am succumbing to nostalgia, I must emphasize that there has never been a time in my experience as a teacher when students have not been concerned about grades. But I have known many students who were prepared to put the quality of their education ahead of an unblemished grade record and to allow an interest in a particular subject to carry them far beyond what was required to do well in that subject even at the cost of doing slightly less well in their other subjects—an experience that is possible at Evergreen State College and at those institutions, most of them small and private, that operate on the contract system.

Premedical students in highly selective institutions, where there is a high proportion of such students, are notorious for their ruthless competition; they may spill or dilute their rivals' organic-chemistry compounds. And in all subjects, students increasingly steal books from the library, in spite of intensified security measures, or cut out and sequester journal articles required for examinations. Faculty members aware of such practices are hesitant to interfere, fearing "hassles"—the spread of this term is itself an unobtrusive measure of attitudes—and even litigation if they should accuse the student of stealing or of plagiarism; I have seen a number of instances in which students brazen out such conduct and intimidate faculty members who do not feel they have absolute proof or can convince a grievance committee, let alone a courtroom. In this way, even the most diligent students may contribute to undermining academic standards by their excessive competition, even while other students, once admitted to college, receive much the same kind of social promotion that has become characteristic of secondary schools (where it has led to the beginning of efforts at competence-based examinations to control the practice).

Impact of Increased Admission of Blacks

I have made a number of references to black students—for example, in their impact on grade inflation and, indirectly, on the outlooks of the counterculture. I now turn more directly to the consequences for the more selective colleges, which are also the more socially concerned, of recruiting black students not as individuals but to fill a quota, as high as 12 percent at Wesleyan and 10 percent at many other equally eminent institutions.

Although the phrase *black community* is constantly used, I habitually put the term in quotation marks to indicate recognition of the enormous diversity concealed within that easy phrase. Blacks from the Caribbean and from Africa are different from one another: Jamaican blacks differ from Trinidadian blacks, and both from blacks from Haiti or from the American Virgin Islands; English-speaking Ibo differ from Hausa or Hausa-Fulani, who have also learned English in Nigeria. Methodist blacks from Chapel Hill are likely to be different from evangelical blacks from northern Louisiana or Catholic blacks from Mobile or the southern Louisiana parishes. Urban-born children of Southern migrant, nonchurchgoing families (often the product of either inner-city or tumultuously desegregated urban schools) again are different from upper-middle-class blacks from families in which both parents are professionals working in metropolitan areas such as Washington, D.C., Los Angeles, Atlanta, or Chicago. These are distinctions rarely made by white administrators, faculty members, or upper-middle-class students—some of whom would often prefer to recruit "disadvantaged" blacks (either "authentic ghetto blacks," in a phrase often used, or unsophisticated blacks from the rural South) over well-educated blacks both of whose parents hold postbaccalaureate degrees. Partly because whites have lumped blacks together as just described, the rapid increase in the number of blacks on formerly predominantly white college campuses often produced a critical mass—indeed, from the institution's viewpoint, sometimes something more than that.

Reed College in 1968–69 provided an illustration all the more dramatic because of the scholarly qualities of Reed dwelt upon earlier in this book. Unlike Wesleyan and Oberlin at that time and Harvard then and now, Reed has always been close to the edge of financial extinction; it has had virtually no endowment; it has few alumni in lucrative professions. In its own locale of Portland, Oregon, it has often been regarded as the scene of political radicalism and cultural outrage. But the political and financial precariousness of an institution has rarely given pause to radical students and faculty. Few black students could believe (or declare a belief if they held it) that a white college, more affluent in the possessions its white students brought with them than these students' proletarian talk and dress could hide, could be threatened with bankruptcy by black demands. And black "nonnegotiable" demands had an escalating character; what was won at one campus became the norm at another, and the network fast spread the news of what had been gained elsewhere. Thus, if blacks at Harvard College, riding piggyback on SDS success in a situation of symbiotic mutual exploitation, could gain an Afro-American studies department where black undergraduates had de facto control of faculty recruitment, or black students at Cornell could emerge from a building occupation with guns and win the support of mass meetings and, as it seemed from afar, the blessing of former president James Perkins, why could blacks at Reed College not have whatever privileges they wanted also?

After making a set of demands for a separatist facility and program, the blacks packed their bags and threatened to leave Reed unless the demands were met. Those who spoke in their name (in effect holding captive more scholarly blacks of different outlook) said in effect to the Reed "community": "You need us more than we need you. As a liberal college, you cannot afford to be without black students, for it is this that attracts liberal white students and faculty members to Reed." The observation is not as crazy as it may now sound; white students (and white faculty members) at a liberal college wanted to be assured that there would be "authentic" blacks to attest to the idealism of the campus and to assure diversity (even though in fact there was minimal personal contact), much as in other, more collegiate circles, students wanted to be sure that physical education facilities would be adequate and that big-name bands would come to the campus as part of an active social life.

Such an analogy obviously puts matters too crudely: Reed students and faculty members include many idealists, guilty about their privileges and feeling a personal need, as it would have been put in old-time religion, to "testify" against racism and other social evils. But the complex and mixed motives of the whites did not alter the perception of the Reed College blacks (and many blacks who behaved in similar fashion elsewhere) that they were being recruited not as individuals for their own personal qualities, but as a kind of exhibit A, a living museum, a testimony at once to idealism and exoticism. Even so, I myself believe that the Reed College blacks made a mistake, for it is unlikely that they could have succeeded in mobilizing a boycott of the college by black students; hence they could have been replaced by other blacks had Reed College not given in to their threats and begged them to stay.

There is a general tendency of whites greatly to overestimate black solidarity and to accept at face value those orators who claim to speak for all blacks—misjudgments that, once made, become self-confirming. At the faculty level, where the numbers involved are relatively small, it is possible for blacks to boycott a particular institution, as scholarly American blacks in effect boycotted the Harvard Afro-American studies department, refusing to be put in a situation in which they would be chosen in part by undergraduates in a way not consonant with regular Harvard procedures.

Originally, the Harvard Faculty of Arts and Sciences had supported the proposal of a committee headed by Henry Rosovsky for an Afro-American studies program, similar to area studies programs already extant at Harvard and not organized as departments. However, after the occupation of University Hall and the ensuing disturbances in the spring of 1969, militant blacks in a rare act of cooperation with SDS and sympathetic white faculty members, with the added persuasive power of some militant blacks (one of whom carried a cleaver into the decisive faculty meeting), persuaded the faculty to reverse itself, to scrap the Rosovsky Report and to create a new department whose guiding committee would include black undergraduates. The argument was made that black students were uniquely situated, as presumptive insiders, not only to contribute suggestions and advice but also to help make actual decisions on recruitment. (I was asked to help recruit black faculty members for the new department and drew on networks of friends and acquaintances among black scholars in the United States without finding a single person of distinction willing even to consider coming to Harvard under such conditions. Later, when Orlando Patterson was recruited, a Jamaican trained in sociology at the London School of Economics who had been teaching at the University of the British West Indies, he was not yet thirty, and his location put him outside the network of black scholars in the United States. The distinguished anthropologist St. Clair Drake recruited him to teach summer school at Roosevelt University in the summer of 1969, and it was there that Talcott Parsons reached him and invited him to come to the new Harvard department. St. Clair Drake had left for Stanford just before Patterson's arrival and was therefore in no position to advise him; I myself sought to recruit St. Clair Drake for the new department, but he knew enough to decline without hesitation. Thus Patterson could not have imagined that Harvard College would create a program so unscholarly as the one he found on arrival, from which he sought release soon thereafter.)

Later, in conversation, some of the black student activists declared in confidence that they were humiliated by the outcome, since the program was widely recognized as of poor quality by black Harvard undergraduates as well as by black and white faculty members at other leading universities. They had never expected that their "nonnegotiable" demands would be acceded to, and they regarded their victory as a statement by the white faculty that nothing much could be expected of blacks anyway, so why not give them what they demanded? Harvard's black political scientist, Professor Martin Kilson, who had served on the committee Rosovsky headed and who opposed the faculty decision, believes that, if faculty members had been willing to admit that they were frightened, their judgment would have been less impaired, and they would not have needed to rationalize their decision on the ground that they could not make sensible judgments on behalf of so alien a group as blacks. (On the whole issue of who is an insider and who is an outsider, whether as defined by race, occupation, gender, or ethnicity, see, for example, Merton, 1972, and Rose, 1978.)

In metropolitan centers, black students and faculty members sometimes felt a certain guilt at their privileges in comparison with the impoverished ghetto blacks nearby. But the latter could also be mobilized to increase the intimidating power of protest, as happened so dramatically during the student-faculty strike at San Francisco State College in 1968–69 and in the demand at CCNY for open admissions of nonwhite students at a campus located in Harlem. Moreover, in these metropolitan settings black students at neighboring institutions could cooperate in protest activities.[6]

[6] Professor Wilson Record of Portland State University, Oregon, has made a systematic study of black-studies directors and the programs of which they were at least nominally in charge, carefully illustrating cross-pressures they were under, on the one hand, for scholarly respectability from their academic colleagues and, on the other hand, for "relevance" to local and national black issues from students and local black activists. See, for example, Record (1973, 1974); see also, for accounts of white condescension at Cornell University, Sowell (1972) and Strout and Grossvogel (1970).

For a careful study of the actual impact of open admissions at CUNY, see the tables and discussion in Lavin, Alba, and Silberstein (1979).

It would be a distortion to emphasize only the aspects of the introduction of less well-prepared nonwhite students and not the great care and idealism exhibited by many well-prepared students and faculty members, white and black, in remedial and supportive activities. Such work is often handicraft labor and invisible. Where it involves peer tutoring, it is especially unlikely to be noticed and hence will not serve as an open form of humiliation for sensitive black neophytes.

Furthermore, the entry of black students as a visible group whose dominant and defiantly visible values were different—for example, in being more likely to be night people—provided a certain freedom for many faculty members, permitting them to feel less guilty not only about their own changing "life-styles" but also about the hypocrisy of teaching in conformity with traditional academic values concerning which they had developed doubts. As already indicated, the counterculture freed them as well as students from some restraints, and the black students—as perceived in the ideology of whites—provided another form of alternative culture. (For a trenchant and haunting analysis of the various forms of romanticism in middle-class culture and the often damaging consequences for black and Hispanic students when offered benefits as "minorities" without reference to class and culture, see Rodriguez, 1978.)

Nevertheless, as Verne Stadtman has observed, "The existence of the counterculture in the backyard—sometimes in the front yard—of colleges and universities . . . challenged the claims of these institutions that they spoke *for* or in the *interests of* a unified society" (personal correspondence).

Results of the Backlash

Having studied the right wing during the McCarthy era and earlier, I had expected that the combination of political turmoil and countercultural flamboyance would bring about a far more powerful backlash against colleges and universities than actually occurred. In my judgment, the polls registered the backlash, for example, in facilitating the election of Nixon in 1968, in part by withdrawal of the radical left, which declined to vote for Humphrey (see Cottle, 1974, chap. 10; Rosenberg, Verba, and

Converse, 1970). Ronald Reagan was only the most prominent of politicians who campaigned in California against the turbulence at Berkeley and at the other University of California and state college campuses, notably San Francisco State College; S. I. Hayakawa, the histrionic president at San Francisco State, who helped quell the turbulence, won election to the Senate as a consequence. Yet I was premature in predicting a much sharper backlash by angry taxpayers antagonistic to professors who appeared not only to tolerate students who jeered at patriotism and other traditional values but actually to incite them, as well as professors who were commonly tolerant of, even when not advocates of, the seductions of the counterculture (Riesman, 1969a, 1971). One of the reasons I urged that students pay a larger share of the costs of their education through a national Educational Opportunity Bank or similar device was to minimize the resentment of adults at seeing reasonably well-to-do students at residential state universities who, as it was put by antagonistic black students at the State University of New York College at Old Westbury, were getting their degrees in "GG," or "grooving on the grass."

State universities' regents or trustees could on occasion respond to the public mood by dismissing the president, as when the regents of the University of California dismissed President Clark Kerr after Ronald Reagan became governor and ex officio chairman of the board of regents;[7] similarly, the regents of the University of Texas intermittently sought to interfere by changing president and even deans (see Dugger, 1974). But the academic revolution had gone much too far to allow similar intervention in departmental affairs and the general faculty control of appointments and curriculum. In major private universities, the trustees often sought more conciliatory presidents, sympathetic to vocal student and organized extramural demands. Liberal lawyers skilled in labor relations and arbitration became heads of a number of major universities: Kingman Brewster, Jr., at Yale; Derek Bok at Harvard; Rob-

---

[7] In California, paradoxically, Reagan's successor as governor, Jerry Brown, exhibited more anti-intellectual attitudes than his predecessor and was joined in this by an influential legislator, John Vasconcellos, who saw the university as too cognitively oriented, too highbrow. He had been influenced by Esalen, as Brown had been, and their attack voiced the outlook of the counterculture itself, not the offended traditionalists.

ben Fleming at Michigan; Robert O'Neil at Indiana, appointed in
1980 as president of the University of Wisconsin state system; and,
as we go to press, Michael Sovern at Columbia and Ira M. Heyman
at Berkeley. Nevertheless, in spite of changes at the top, the departments have remained as the building blocks of academia in all but a
few experimental institutions; the departments have proved capable of resisting interference from regents and trustees and their
supposed deputies, the college and university presidents (Veysey,
1973b).

What the backlash did do, facilitated by the end of the period
of growth and the beginning of retrenchment, was to support
legislative or state system mandates of increased faculty teaching
loads and increased accountability in terms of how faculty members spent their time. In the effort to enforce such regulations and
to minimize expensive duplication of resources by competing institutions within a state, systemwide managerial controls were instituted, giving state chancellors of higher education or similar
officers power to review requests for new capital expenditures and,
in some states, new postbaccalaureate programs.

Owing not only to the power of departments but also to
the difficulty of monitoring the actual, as against the reported,
behavior of faculty members (for example, the mandated "contact
hours" with students), controls have often proved ineffective. But
their existence and the paperwork they require[8] have led many
faculty members to see themselves as deprofessionalized, subject
to remote authority at the state capital, at a time when they have

---

[8] Many faculty members do not distinguish between paperwork that results from
the internal review processes of their own institutions, that stemming from state or
systemwide authorities, and the increasing amount required by the federal government. In the case of the federal requirements, there is sometimes a failure to
distinguish between paperwork required by uniform regulations concerning affirmative action or treatment of the handicapped or compliance with the provisions
of the Occupational Safety and Health Administration, on the one hand, and, on
the other, the paperwork demanded from researchers applying for grants or those
who have received grants and must periodically account in detail, as must the
institution itself, for how the funds are spent. For a full discussion of federal regulation and possible alternatives, see the report of the Sloan Commission on Government in Higher Education (1980), chap. 3; concerning state regulations (and also
the need to decentralize collective bargaining where it exists), see chap. 4 of the
report.

also come under pressure from student customers whose traffic would determine whether a department could grow or would remain static or even, in still relatively few but ominous cases, face actual retrenchment at the tenure level. What Martin Trow (1975a) has termed "private space," psychic and physical room for maneuver at the departmental or even institutional level, declined as statewide authority—and here, of course, I am talking of the dominant public sector—applied formula funding to individual educational units.

Faculty resistance to efforts at centralized state control took either the individual forms already implied, as when supervision of a single thesis or independent study project is registered as a course in order to appear to meet the required number of contact hours, or the more collective resistance of unionization. In addition to the belief that collective bargaining could raise faculty salaries, preserve tenure rights, and provide, through elaborate grievance procedures, a virtual right to automatic tenure, unionization could often be taken as a statement by the faculty that, since we are being treated as employees, we might as well have the collective bargaining privileges many states by law give to their own civil servants, and we too are civil servants. Correspondingly, we will promote by seniority, rather than by merit; we will see students only up to the limit of the required contact hours and no more; we will surrender our rights as members of the faculty senate to those who speak in our name as union activists and bargaining agents (although many faculty members were not aware that this would be a consequence of unionizing).[9]

Some student leaders, at least at the outset, supported faculty

[9] Correspondingly, some state college and university presidents (though not in public) welcomed the union, regarding it as easier to deal with a single bargaining agent than with an anarchic or clique-ridden faculty. The union official, rarely a scholar or productive researcher, might have in mind a financially generous package, which would help the particular union in competition in other states with rival union organizing drives. For this, he or she might be willing to sacrifice faculty sabbaticals, secretarial assistance, money for travel to professional meetings, and so on, much to the dismay of some previously prounion faculty members who had not calculated the potential costs to their scholarly concerns of a generous wage settlement. For a contrary view, cogently expressed by the president of the National Education Association, see Ryor (1978).

efforts to form a union. They thought this was a proper proletarian tactic; activist students have tended to be prounion partly out of a general prolabor outlook and partly won over by faculty members who paint the administration and trustees as the interfering, complicitous, and philistine enemy. It has taken a while for students to realize that unions, whatever the rhetoric, are generally not in their interest.[10] Frequently, unions provide the single forum on a democratized campus where faculty members can meet with one another while justifying the exclusion of students. In Florida, in California, and elsewhere, student lobbyists have asked for a seat at the bargaining table; it has generally been denied. Student lobbyists have certainly not automatically favored the demands of any particular faculty union. (Information from Layton Olson of the National Student Lobby, Washington, D.C.; see also Stark, 1977, pp. 25–27.) With greater sophistication, student lobbyists have learned how to work in harmony with, as well as in opposition to, faculty demands, depending on the context. (For discussion of efforts by students to sit in on collective bargaining sessions and otherwise to influence the bargaining process, how these issues vary from state to state, and what sorts of proposals student lobbies have brought forward, see Shark, Brouder, and Associates, 1976; these issues are also regularly covered in *National On-Campus Report.*) The salary raises won by the union must come from somewhere, and they are often at student expense, if not in reduced contact hours, then in higher tuition or in the elimination of supposed "frills," such as long library hours, counseling, and other student services.

There is a vast literature on unions and collective bargaining, and it is not my purpose here to review the now-familiar argu-

---

[10] Ryor (1978) makes a convincing case that in certain situations the restraints collective bargaining agreements put on the release of faculty members when student credit hours fall may protect students from the kind of faculty seductions discussed in detail later in this book. Even collegiality may be protected, Ryor argues, when it becomes difficult (although not quite impossible) to release tenured faculty members because they do not bring in student customers; to that degree, collegiality might even be served by unionization. Difficulties with this thesis arise in what I have observed in practice—namely, unions pressing for granting tenure to mediocre and marginally responsible teachers who are no service to their students nor stimulus to their colleagues.

ments. Rather, I am discussing unions in the context of the rise of student dissatisfaction and the delegitimation of traditional academic values. In part the unions represent a defense against dissatisfaction among the students and in the general society; in part they increase that discontent, as in Florida, where faculties hoped by statewide unionizing to increase their salaries, only to engender budget cuts because the legislature was angry with the union and its tactics.

Another way of looking at unionization is to see it as a measure of faculty discontent and alienation. It has occurred not only in public institutions but in substantial private ones, such as Boston University, Long Island University, and Fairleigh Dickinson University; Oberlin College came very close to being unionized, after many decades in which the faculty prided itself on faculty self-government. Furthermore, as I have pointed out in a short note in the journal *Comment,* unionization has been a way for faculty members, mostly white males, further to entrench, through seniority rights, those already on board, thus resisting affirmative action without appearing to be bigoted: I am inclined to believe that unionization was powerfully boosted at Florida State when the president declared his full support for affirmative action and on the Amherst campus of the University of Massachusetts when President Robert Wood likewise made his commitment clear not only by appointing a black chancellor for the campus and a woman vice-president of the university but by continual pressure on this theme at a time of relatively declining resources.

This faculty disaffection is potentially contagious. It is generally believed that the large movements of protest are for the most part over, and in the selective colleges there is great nostalgia for having missed out on the legendary great protests of the late 1960s, much as in earlier years people regretted having missed out on the "good war." But I would not conclude that campuses are invariably going to remain relatively quiet. Certainly, they have not been so in the major institutions on issues of divestiture of South African investments and general policy on "complicity" with antiunion companies such as J. P. Stevens or supposedly complicitous academicians who aided repressive regimes, whether in the Shah's Iran or in post-Allende Chile. In such cases, the loss of a sense of autonomy among the faculty carries over to students, but that is no guarantee against a future student mobilization, for the disaffection runs deep, and many are looking for the appropriate cause that will unite students in the way opposition to the Vietnam war did. (For an argument that a cause has already been found that has united many survivors of earlier protests along with younger recruits—the campaign against nuclear power—see Shattan, 1980.)

At the same time, unionization is a protection not only against what is regarded as the arbitrariness of particular presidents, trustees, or systemwide managers but also against being completely subject to the whims of the student marketplace—the theme to which I now turn.

4

College Marketing
and Student Customers

I deal in this chapter with two kinds of student impact on the curriculum, indeed, on the fate of whole institutions. By far the more important of these operates primarily through the market. Individual students decide, of course as part of general social developments, whether it makes sense to go to college or, if so, whether to attend a residential institution; and if that decision is made, what level of effort and what level of financial contribution a student (and, in the case of financial subsidy, his or her family) is prepared to make. Of course, while students are making these more or less individual choices, colleges are seeking in various ways to position themselves, in the best cases to try to influence student choices for the sake of the students themselves, and in many cases simply to respond to market forces by the various strategies colleges have found that will retain some members of their old clientele while inviting new ones to fill up the vacancies (Glenny, 1980, and sources there cited).

That a college adopts a marketing strategy is not necessarily a concession to crass commercialism for the sake of survival. It all depends on what the aims are and the means employed. At its best, college marketing can mean a careful survey of what distinctive segment of students a college is currently serving, whether it is adequately serving their needs as well as their wants, and whether there are enough such students likely to be available in the future so that the college can stay on course and maintain its traditional program. A marketing survey may discover that much recruiting effort is wasted; recruiters are sent to cities that are most unlikely to send students to the particular institution,[1] while other areas that remain untouched have grown more affluent and better-educated, to give one kind of example, and might now provide a constituency if, through high school visits and in other ways, potential students and their families could be made aware of the institution and what it offers specifically for individuals of this sort and level.

Presently, these issues arise primarily in private institutions. So far as I am aware, no public institution has closed, although several have been consolidated and others threatened with closing (as experimental Evergreen State College in Olympia, Washington, was for a time before receiving a stay of execution after a careful review by state authorities).

In the case of Southwest Minnesota State University, a former president (Catherine Tisinger) concluded that it should be closed. It was built—indeed, overbuilt—to serve a rural community, but it recruited a faculty regarded as radical in the community, unprepared to adapt to the community's judgments as to what was suitable education for its children. Local high schools declined to encourage their students to attend the institution. But the president's effort to close it as a drain on state resources met objections not only from faculty members but also from local business interests and local legislators, and this kind of support is something most public institutions have. A number of the Massachusetts state colleges have similarly protected themselves by recruiting, either as presidents or as faculty members, former state officials who are still influential politicians. They hope in this way to prevent what might be a rational use of state resources: namely, full support of the recently built community college network, and also of the University of Massachusetts, as enrollments—and along with them, any trace of selectivity—fall in most of the state colleges, which, as in

[1] An illustration comes from the effort of some of the small, denominational colleges in North Carolina to recruit students across the border in South Carolina, unaware that South Carolina has the most liberal policy for scholarship aid to indigenous students attending private colleges in the state to be found anywhere in the country: thus, South Carolina offers middle-income parents $2,000 in such aid, and its own small, liberal arts colleges naturally benefit at the expense of comparable ones in neighboring Georgia or North Carolina.

many other parts of the country, began as teacher's colleges and still turn out a large proportion of people with degrees in education who cannot find jobs in that field.

Marketing in the Private Sector

At the end of World War II, half the students in American colleges and universities were in privately controlled institutions. The research universities and the more selective liberal arts colleges chose not to expand enrollments in order to grow, leaving that to the enormously expanded public sector. However, the presidents of a number of private institutions, some of them begun since World War II, were just as entrepreneurial as any of the college boosters and founders whom Boorstin (1965) has celebrated in his account of college founding in the nineteenth century. In the growing northern suburbs of New Jersey, Peter Sammartino took a small college and turned it into the multicampus Fairleigh Dickinson University (Sammartino, 1977), one soon to suffer from public competition from Bergen County Community College and from Ramapo College of New Jersey (Grant and Riesman, 1978, chap. 9; Sammartino, 1978). New York University, with a variety of schools and several campuses, expanded at one point to 40,000 students (it has now shrunk to half that) to become the largest private university in America, a place now occupied by Northeastern University, with campuses in Boston and its suburbs and with its famous co-op program enrolling 35,000 students; here the entrepreneur was Asa Knowles, who recently retired as president, surely one of the most imaginative and least well known of American university executives.

But, despite such exceptions, private institutions could go only a short way to make up the steady loss, amounting to 1 percent a year, of the proportion of students enrolled in all institutions. Furthermore, major state universities, including Texas, Minnesota, Ohio State, and Penn State, all built branch campuses, sometimes two-year de facto community colleges with automatic transfer assured, but more commonly four-year institutions under a single board of regents. Few of the forty-three private colleges of Ohio, for example, could compete with the branches of the major land-

grant university or with the early-nineteenth-century state universities (Ohio University at Athens [1804] and Miami University in
Oxford [1809], which resembles the University of Virginia in having many of the qualities of a private college at public expense and
draws 20 percent of its students from out of state—the maximum
permitted). Nor could most of Ohio's private colleges compete
with the newly built state-controlled campuses, such as Cleveland
State University, with upgraded former teacher's colleges, such as
Bowling Green or Kent State, or with former municipal institutions
taken over by the state (Toledo, Cincinnati, and Akron).

Desperate for students who will bring in tuition, in part via
federal grants and loans, and in a few cases through state support
of scholarships at independent institutions, most unselective
private colleges have completely abandoned any requirements,
either at point of entry or at graduation, that would keep away
students who could possibly be attracted to matriculate and remain.
Research on changes in student choices done by Robert Blackburn
and his colleagues (1976; summarized in Levine, 1978) at
the Center for the Study of Higher Education indicates the losing
battle of faculty supporters of general education to maintain requirements in colleges that must cater to the student customer,
since any requirement is likely to turn away prospects. Distribution
requirements, which in many colleges allowed faculty members to
divide student traffic into agreed-on market shares, have given
way, in institutions with shrinking applicant pools, to a general
deliquescence of all requirements. The shift can be followed from
year to year by comparing what colleges and universities say about
themselves in successive editions of such guides as Cass and Birnbaum's *Comparative Guide to American Colleges.* One discovers, for
example, that such a once-Catholic college as the College of New
Rochelle is typical in stating that it has no requirements and that all
courses are elective (Cass and Birnbaum, 1977). However, it should
be added that not all efforts at survival result only in abject concessions to market forces. A good example is the branch campus of the
College of New Rochelle established for adults in the South Bronx,
where some students have not completed high school and have
been on welfare in one of the poorest metropolitan neighborhoods
in the country (Barbato, 1979).

The Flexible Fliers: Community Colleges. In many state universities, requirements have not been abolished. As noted earlier, faculty members have some protection because the catalogue does not give their names, and the departments divide up student traffic by market shares because, in the major public universities, the attraction of the institution is still sufficiently strong that students will put up with distribution requirements to get a degree from a flagship or other major state university campus. The departments at these state universities have traditionally been strong; there is no tradition, as in the community colleges, of presidential authority to shift faculty members around to meet the expectations of students— students must make their own peace with the system after the fashion described in *Making the Grade* (Becker, Geer, and Hughes, 1968).

In contrast, the community colleges have in many cases grown out of the high schools, having in the beginning been the de facto thirteenth and fourteenth grades of these schools. The faculties, although unionized, are more susceptible to presidential dictation, and the traditional arts and sciences departments, which form the bulwark of a traditional campus or research university, whether public or private, either are embryonic or lack independent existence. Correspondingly, it is widely recognized that by far the fastest-growing segment of postsecondary education in the last fifteen years has been the community colleges. The very term *community college* (in contrast to the earlier widespread use of *junior college*) indicates a commitment to serve educational and paraeducational needs of an area, as defined by the various constituencies within commuting distance. Today, as studies by the Higher Education Research Institute and the Carnegie Commission show, something like 42 percent of all students are in community colleges —but of course this does not mean 42 percent of all full-time students, since many in community colleges are working part-time, and some are even holding down full-time jobs and giving little commitment to the community college. This very lack of requirement for commitment is one of the attractions of the community college, not usually mentioned in discussions of stratification, which exhibit that the majority of students in community colleges come from the less privileged sections of the population, although this does not hold for some of the more eminent and attractive community colleges, such as Inver Hills outside the Twin Cities or Foothill College outside Palo Alto. Attending institutions such as these or Miami-Dade and other Florida community colleges (in a state where the majority of state institutions admit a restricted number of lower-division students, if any) involves no derogation of status. What is involved is a serious loss of the opportunities that residential colleges provide, including the experiential loss entailed in living in one's parents' home or one's own home and having minimal connection with the community college other than taking courses there. (For a succinct discussion based on the assumption that "value added" could be the same in all institutions if not for stratification between residential and nonresidential ones, see Astin, 1977b; Chickering, 1974.)

What the private colleges have shared with the community colleges, once the private institutions became aware of demographic realities, is a greater flexibility in pursuing undergraduates through aggressive recruitment in comparison with heavily tenured and unionized four-year state colleges[2] and a greater ability to retain students against the pull of attrition by continual salesmanship.

To illustrate again from the Ohio private colleges, which of course are not alone in this, some have handed over their admissions offices to professional agencies that promise to recruit students at so much a head. It is then up to the college to adapt its program to what the marketers are able to persuade students to buy. Then it is possible through the services of the College Board and the American College Testing Service to pinpoint students who have interests to which individual colleges can appeal by direct mailings, visits to high schools, attendance at local college fairs, and using fellow students as recruiters who are promised a reduction of tuition for each additional student they bring in.

---

[2] For a cogent argument that even unionized state colleges do not need to become heavily tenured if the president and a supportive board of trustees do not want this to happen, see Chait (1979), which includes a comparison of two simultaneously established New Jersey state colleges, one of which has 23 percent of its faculty on tenure, the other 85 percent.

Impact of "Overselling" on Students. Many if not all of these institutions are looking not only for students in general (because they cannot afford any selectivity) but also for a few able students to lend some academic luster to the campus and to sustain faculty and institutional morale. I have asked particularly bright students to collect for me all the literature they have received from colleges as a result of taking the College Board examinations; some have been in receipt of invitations from colleges so alien to their backgrounds as to seem a ridiculous waste of handsomely printed brochures. For example, a young woman with a high SAT in a metropolitan area of New York City will be sent a brochure from a small evangelical college in a Midwestern town, along with a hundred or more other mailings from institutions of modest to high selectivity. Students can become quite cynical because of all this, cynical about institutional integrity or a sense of coherence, and at the same time they are not especially helped by wise counseling to consider possible adventures outside the orbits of their high school and family friends. One recruiter told me of his experience of being one of fifty recruiters for two—yes, I mean two—midyear graduates of an Ohio high school. He spoke of his uncomfortable sense of how these students must feel, courted in an indiscriminate way by such a large contingent of disparate institutions. To be sure, although the great majority of students take SAT or ACT tests (sometimes both) before entering college, they apply only to a single college or perhaps to two, and 90 percent of all students are admitted to their first or only choice (see Hartnett and Feldmesser, 1980). But for that minority of students who are seeking appropriate challenges or entrance to the most selective institutions, one result of this barrage may be to engender a feeling of confusion, a sense that it really does not matter very much where one goes, and the choice is made for convenience rather than for an optimal match of student and institution. The fight conducted against attrition often means that students then will stay in institutions that they should leave— or, finding their course work either too hard or too easy, they may drop out.[3]

---

[3] In such matters, as in others, regional differences remain. That careful student of statistical data on college entrance and graduation rates, Alexander Astin, writes:

It is an interesting question why students who are so shrewd about buying a used car are on occasion so gullible about buying the far more important and useful tool of a college education. One reason is that many are insecure, and if a college goes after them hard, they take it, despite their cynicism, as evidence that they are really being courted. In spite of the deluge of promotional material they may have received, they prefer to believe that they have been selected, not that they are just one more body to be counted in a formula or for the student grants they can bring with them to help support a tuition-dependent private college. They have a vested interest in refusing to recognize their market power.

And, of course, not all apparent overselling results in a mismatch of student and institution. Many of the colleges recruiting nationally are using locator systems provided by brokerage services such as the College Board and the American College Testing Program to seek out students who might profit at that particular institution. Further, if the students come there in sufficient numbers, they can as a last resort help educate one another, whatever the institution's deficit in the area of faculty or library.

Nevertheless, as with advertising campaigns conducted by competing firms where there is a relatively inflexible demand curve, marketing increases the cost of education, but if one institution engages in it, the others must follow suit to retain or increase their market shares. Costs rise astronomically as more institutions—now including some underenrolled public institutions—enter the competition. Sometimes half of a student's tuition is expended in bringing him or her to the campus, and this slender margin will be lost if the student cannot be retained throughout the four or more years required to complete a regular baccalaureate program.

"One-Person Chess." A similar and quite understandable duplication of effort concerns "products" that are marketed in this increasingly

"My impression is that this is a uniquely California phenomenon: Even in our sophisticated multivariate analyses, living in California has always predicted dropping out of college even after we have controlled for ability, family background, type of college attended, and so forth. While this has always puzzled me somewhat, I now think I have some understanding of this isolated statistical fact" (personal communication, 1980). I have made the same observation in a less systematic way.

desperate fashion. Each director of admissions thinks his or her stratagem is unique, failing to realize that a hundred others, no less hungry and intelligent, will think of the identical device. For example, if it appears that students believe that a baccalaureate degree in business administration will bring them employment, it will not be long before a thousand colleges are offering such programs, recycling professors of economics or statistics, hiring adjunct faculty members, or simply relabeling old courses in order to make it appear that they have a program that teaches something about business management at the undergraduate level. Thus, fluctuations in the demand for certain kinds of preparation for undergraduates lead to building up programs that are obsolescent by the time of their creation. This pattern is reminiscent of quite different constellations during the period of the academic revolution, when a university trying to recruit a distinguished professor would equip an expensive laboratory or buy a formidable library of esoteric books that only such a professor would use; then the professor would accept an offer from another institution, and the campus that had recruited him would be left with its expensive equipment or books, possibly sold at a discount to the transient or, more likely, left as a monument to foiled ambitions. (College administrators are themselves sometimes gullible—and occasionally disingenuous—in purchasing, for example, elaborate computer-based information systems or internal broadcasting equipment such as video consoles, sometimes using transient faculty members to write the grant proposals that will bring aid under Title III of the federal higher education legislation, designed to aid so-called developing institutions. Often, this equipment will stand idle or perhaps be sold at a discount, the comparatively meager sums occasionally finding their way into administrators' pockets.)

Adult Education. During the last decade, all segments of higher education, with the community colleges perhaps in the lead, have made a special push for the adult market. Adult education was once the stepchild of the American university, greatly inferior in quality to the in-house education provided by many leading corporations for their employees. It was supposed to be a moneymaker, taught by faculty members from the regular program picking up a little extra money or by adjunct faculty members in talent-rich centers such as one finds in the major metropolitan areas. But when the demographic curve at long last began to make a dent on the euphoria of academic administrators, and it was realized that there would be no vast increase in the proportion of high school graduates attending college and that the majority of adult Americans had come of age at a time when college-going was the pursuit of a small minority, with an even smaller minority finishing the baccalaureate, there was an eager belief that recruiting adults for evening, weekend, or learning-at-a-distance programs would replace the eighteen- to twenty-four-year-old cohort.

In this field, some public institutions were as quick on the draw as the generally more flexible and desperate private ones. One of the most dramatic examples is provided by the work of David Sweet, former vice-chancellor of the Minnesota state college and university system, who became president of a new institution, then called Minnesota Metropolitan State College (now Metropolitan State University), which opened in 1971. It secured legislative authorization—which meant working out a treaty not to compete with the seven community colleges of the Twin Cities but to establish itself as an upper-division degree-granting institution that would give credit for previous academic work and also for certified competence in "life experience." Unfortunately, the legislature provided minimal initial funding ($300,000 for the first biennium), and David Sweet secured assistance from the Carnegie Corporation and other private sources in order to admit students in February 1972, using this seed money as a way to gain additional legislative support as part of the state system of Minnesota at a time when the University of Minnesota was under relatively unpopular leadership. I recall David Sweet declaring that there were 800,000 adults in the Twin Cities area who did not have a college degree—they were his potential clientele. The claim seemed to me exaggerated. By no means all those adults wanted a college degree. Among those who did, some might want particular skills or particular entertainment, which they might decide they could just as well secure at a nearby community college, another one of the state colleges, or, indeed, at the University of Minnesota and its branches, particularly its Twin Cities extension unit serving tens of thousands of those students each quarter. Minnesota Metropolitan, with its use of mentors and learning contracts tied to individuated experience, might in fact provide a better option, but not all potential clients would realize that. David Sweet sought to make clear that the new college did not give credit, as some institutions are now doing, simply for "life experience." Rather, credit was given for knowledge acquired from experiences not obtained in academic institutions but tested in terms of "competences" at Minnesota Metropolitan. For if students at the new institutions were to believe that their degrees meant something, then there would have to be ways of assessing credits for learning derived from life experience; if these seemed too lenient, students might come to feel that their brave new institution resembled the kind of club Groucho Marx would not join because, as he put it, any place that would take him couldn't be any good.

In fact, David Sweet attracted a faculty of self-proclaimed rebels against conventional academic credentialism, only to find that some of them turned out to be unhappy in their roles as mentors assessing credentials with an uncertain yardstick; such work requires unremitting craftsmanship, largely invisible to others. Understandably, some former rebels found that they missed the opportunities for showmanship provided by a classroom. Soon, Minnesota Metropolitan was in fact holding classes, only not giving them that name. It was establishing centers, something planned as soon as funds were available, although doing so meant surrendering the kind of publicity attained by operating a college out of an office above a drugstore in St. Paul. David Sweet brought national visibility to the new institution and sought to establish close ties to the local metropolitan areas and to turn part-time students into participative ones. He believed that the new enterprise could sustain itself financially if it became a four-year rather than an upper-division college—a hope denied by the chancellor of the state college and university system. This gave an advantage to other colleges in the Twin Cities, including private colleges on the edge of failure, which had entered the adult market but could also appeal to lower-division students. David Sweet sought to compensate for the loss of potential lower-division students by establishing liaisons with the seven community colleges in the area, to which he hoped also to spread the gospel of giving credit, not just for Carnegie units of time spent in the classroom, but for the ability to demonstrate what one had learned beyond college walls. However, these efforts to establish liaisons with the community colleges were only modestly successful. Sweet's educational ambition was to help students make use of all the resources of an area, believing that students who had done so, for example, by the use of Metropolitan State's large number of adjunct faculty members who held positions of importance in the Twin Cities, would continue their education long after receiving the desired credentials.

The Spread of "Learning at a Distance." In the last ten years, there has hardly been a major state without a public effort at a nonresidential degree-granting institution. In less populated areas, there have been occasional consortia, such as the University of Mid-America, whose headquarters is at the University of Nebraska in Lincoln and which serves the whole region through a consortium of eleven Midwestern state universities via television programs and correspondence courses. New York State has two quite separate programs. One is the External Degree Program of the Regents of the University of the State of New York, operating through the state education department—a program available not only to state residents but to people throughout the nation who come to New York State to secure credit by examination; members of the education department travel around the country counseling students. New York's other large public effort is Empire State College, whose headquarters is in Saratoga Springs. It prepares modules and sequences in great variety for students of all ages from just beyond high school to older adults. Empire State College has worked closely with the British Open University, which operates both by television and by modules handled through correspondence with mentors, and has discovered what one could have predicted: the level of British secondary schooling is such that many of the modules have proved too difficult for the average Empire State student and have required modification and some degree of dilution (Hassenger, 1979). Empire State College has centers located all around the state where students may meet with mentors, as well as a Center for Distance Learning, which maintains direct vicarious contact with students. Of course, many private institutions also offer external degrees, with greater or lesser ambiguities of quality control (Houle, 1973; Peterson and Associates, 1979).

In the funding formulas set up in the immediate post–World War II period of expansion and based on full-time equivalent students, no thought was given to the problems of additional expense imposed by adult part-time students who took perhaps only one course a term but cost as much to "process" and service as a full-time student; it might take four adult degree students to equal one FTE. And of course the same operates for private colleges, which have had to scale down tuition fees and charge their adult students by the credit hour rather than the term—and at rates that did not put them out of competition with the low-tuition public institutions, notably the community colleges.

In the marketing scramble, we have come full circle from the efforts of people like James Bryant Conant to extend the reach of formerly local universities to a nationwide clientele. In doing so, these universities invaded local catchbasins and forced local institutions also to recruit more widely if they were to maintain or increase their share of the student market. That was when students were plentiful. Now, when students of all ages are eagerly sought out, every institution, at least within geographic orbits, is in competition with almost every other. And the geographic orbits have been invaded by many institutions that have set up networks and off-campus centers, as Antioch College and Goddard College were among the first to do. As we shall see later in this book, the regional accrediting associations have had a hard time keeping up with such boundary-hopping forays.

Some Hazards of Student Consumerism for Students

Even the most shoddy, cut-rate, and cutthroat degrees are not necessarily frauds on the student consumer. They may, in fact, be examples of collusion between academic vendor and student buyer to secure a credential at some monetary cost but almost no cost in time or effort. At some community colleges and a few unselective four-year institutions, one finds academic deans and other administrators with an Ed.D. from institutions that demand some kind of thesis, such as Nova University, with its base in Florida and extension on Long Island, or the University of Sarasota or Walden University, also in Florida, which appear to demand virtually nothing. In a unionized setting that proceeds on the basis of seniority and formal credentials, egalitarianism dictates that one degree is as good as another. Unless an institution has been clearly defined as fraudulent—and some of the Florida and California degree mills are close to that point—its degree is as good as one from the University of Florida or Tulane. And a declaration of fraud will hardly be operative retroactively.

But there may be a secondary impact on the students who are taught by men and women who have not gone through the difficult, if at times ritualistic, work of earning a doctorate—perhaps individuals whose family situations did not permit them the luxury of even periodic residential education. It may follow that the students' own degrees will be devalued and their own judgments of academia made totally cynical. The holder of a doctorate secured at a distance—or with minimal attendance at perhaps a month-long seminar of people from a variety of fields pursuing a variety of degrees—is not likely to be a person to inspire students with a sense of the importance of the academic calling.

Is Marketing a Zero-Sum Game? The president and other members of the administration and some members of the board of trustees of a private college are more apt to see economic catastrophe ahead than are the faculty members. The latter, as I have often found in discussions, find it hard to believe that the institution to which they have devoted themselves is not so obviously deserving of support, both by student recruitment and by philanthropic donation, that if the president and development officer are any good, they would find ways to keep the place amply afloat. That is, faculty members recognize that the demographic cycle works against them in a generic way, but they cannot believe it will apply to their unique institution. A few years ago, President Merle Allshouse of Bloomfield College, a Presbyterian college in a Newark suburb, sought to get his faculty to relax the tenure requirements so as to make it possible to introduce new programs and curtail old ones. The faculty could not believe that Bloomfield College as it stood was no longer viable; it took a bankruptcy proceeding, which lasted for many years and provided funds for litigation, before Bloomfield College could re-emerge with a modest chance to survive. When the trustees of Wilson College, a United Presbyterian college for 230 women in southern Pennsylvania, decided along with the president that the institution should close while it was still afloat and not running a deficit, litigation by dissident factions on the board of trustees reopened the college; in the meantime, some faculty members had left, and the chances of survival as a single-sex institution in a relatively remote locale seem dim indeed. When Gail Thain Parker was president of Bennington College, she was asked by a committee of the board of trustees, who looked at budgets and enrollment prospects, to revise the curriculum so that Bennington would no longer run a deficit. She concluded that the language departments should be shut down and students be given the money to pay for Berlitz tuition if they wanted modern languages. In part because President Parker conducted herself with a kind of daring asperity, whatever chance she might have had to introduce realism into the faculty evaporated; because of her own conduct, her scathing account of faculty unrealism in her book *The Writing on the Wall* (1979) must be somewhat discounted. Against combined faculty and student protest, the trustees felt they could not protect her, and she was let go. Indeed, the turnover of presidents in such places is apt to be high, as faculty expectations fluctuate between the unduly euphoric and the unduly self-deprecating (on similar phenomena at New College in Sarasota, see Grant and Riesman, 1978, chap. 7).

As more and more private colleges have reached the point of unlikely return, there has been an increasing effort to make a case for federal support (see Breneman and Finn, 1978). Some modicum of support has been received indirectly, by raising the maximum family income beneath which a student is entitled to a Basic Educational Opportunity Grant—a program initially designed for the low-income student and now applicable also to a good many middle-income students. A top grant, $1,800 a year, will rarely pay half, or in some cases less than a third, of the stated tuition, not leaving anything for living expenses in a residential institution. A renewed effort at a tuition tax credit to aid private colleges seems unlikely; and the amount proposed when the effort was tried before, in 1978, of $250, was too small to do more than aid and pay tuition at a typical community college. Some states with large private sectors have been more responsive, though none have been as generous as South Carolina; thus, New York's so-called Bundy aid gives colleges a per capita grant for every baccalaureate, master's, or doctor's degree the institution confers (a temptation to keep students longer than might be optimal or justifiable). Pennsylvania has modified its once-generous scholarship aid from being wholly portable outside the state, so that half is portable, as against the whole amount available for in-state institutions. Indeed, most states with substantial private sectors have some form of scholarship aid on a per capita basis, but it is seldom sufficiently generous to pay costs of a high-tuition residential institution.

A number of presidents of large, urban private universities have argued that they would be prepared to educate students if provided with the per-student cost of education at state institutions, thus saving the state the expense of building new institutions. For example, when the University of Massachusetts decided to build a medical school, Boston University, Harvard, and Tufts offered to take all Massachusetts students who met their minimum requirements at the per capita cost of educating them in a state facility which would cost hundreds of millions of dollars to construct and which, as it turned out, at first lacked adequate hospital facilities for training students. On the whole, states have been unwilling to accept such a proposal, one also offered by New York University vis-à-vis expansion of the City University of New York. (In Massachusetts, the state institutions had going for them the cozy arrangement between architects, contractors, and politicians that is now being investigated by a commission headed by former President John William Ward of Amherst College.) There is a strong populist feeling that the state should have its own full slate of institutions even if the result is duplication and additional costs to the increasingly disgruntled taxpayers.[4]

---

[4] What is said in the text must be qualified by recognition that a number of public institutions have begun to suffer enrollment decline, but as made clear earlier, their costs do not go down proportionately with the decline of student enrollments, so that subsidizing students in private colleges in the state may obviate capital expendi-

But there have also been cases in which the private institutions have been slow to recognize the advantage of collaboration with publicly supported ones. For example, the chancellor of higher education for the state of Connecticut thought it would be helpful to the University of Bridgeport, a private institution whose future seems increasingly jeopardized by the underenrolled, overbuilt state colleges as well as by the state university and its branches, to use Housatonic Community College, which is publicly supported, as its lower division on the same campus and to offer easy transfer to the University of Bridgeport, which would retain only its upper-division level. But the university itself demurred; many members of its faculty were offended at the idea of association with a "mere" community college. Apparently, they have lost their chance for such an alliance, which, at least in my judgment, would have assured their survival and served the cause of higher education by an example of the possibilities of such cooperation.

Thus, one of the ways in which students suffer from the present market situation in postsecondary education is from the dilution of programs due to duplication, to overstaffing in some areas, and to understaffing in others that may be useful to students facing vocational insecurity.

Furthermore, the costs of recruiting students must eventually be paid by them in the form of increased tuition or decreased services—for example, in undermaintenance of the library or in curtailment of counseling services or remedial services (which are costly and invisible). Sometimes institutions will cut down the number of courses offered, at least in any one year, in order to provide more money for student procurement as well as for the other spiraling costs—of fuel, of meeting federal regulations—that all institutions must meet beyond the already ravaging costs of inflation. In liberal arts colleges with heavily tenured faculties, student/faculty ratios have grown, giving conscientious teachers

---

tures still being planned in some states but not reduce substantially costs of running the existing institutions, with heavily tenured faculties and excess plant and also sometimes dormitory space. To put it differently, much of the duplication between neighboring public and private institutions has already taken place, and one is not often allocating resources in a situation of a tide of new student applicants, but rather in many fields with excess tenured faculty, deciding more by clout than by calculation where the necessary cuts can be made.

more papers to read, more arguments with students, and eventually less contact with them as individuals. Yet since the very attraction of a liberal arts college is the accessibility of faculty members, such teachers are under very great pressures (see Cottle, 1978, chap. 4). As mentioned earlier, sabbaticals and money for travel to professional meetings tend to be eliminated, sometimes as a result of unionization and sometimes simply because there is not enough money. The federal law about to go into effect, requiring that retirement not be mandatory until age seventy, has thrown off calculations of many institutions that had built up retirement plans and opened vacancies for junior faculty members on the basis of arrangements for earlier retirement. It is not only in the experimental colleges but in many of these four-year institutions and some research universities as well, varying very much by discipline and department, that both administrators and faculty members speak of "burnout" of exhausted faculty members—generally those who have not been able to keep up their scholarly connections, though of course the great majority never did engage in active research. And, of course, the withdrawal of some professors into minimum performance throws a heavier burden on those who still try to carry the load of the demanding students and the need to expand catalogue offerings in order to create new marketing possibilities, as in the rapid expansion of undergraduate programs in business management, accounting, and computer science, as well as such fields of fluctuating popularity as environmental studies, ethnic studies, and women's studies.

A number of educational organizations and many consulting firms have established institutes and published articles and books on "faculty development" (*Change* magazine has been a leader in this field) to refresh faculty members and give them advice about their teaching and mutual support when faced with "impossible" expectations and also to prepare them for newer fields—for example, to prepare a professor of classics to teach accounting or an educational psychologist to teach business management. I have been led to skepticism about such devices by conversations with those who have participated in such institutes, candid comments by those who have directed them, the recognition that professors who take part are generally older and have a very hard time adjusting to the newest in their own fields, let alone a new field, and my own limited observations. Unquestionably, were it not for the tenure rules and their equivalent in union contracts, many institutions would prefer to recruit younger faculty members trained in some newly desired specialty who would cost less, would in today's market demand less, and would be better prepared than most of those who have gone through faculty development, however willingly or reluctantly.

The Onslaught on Standardized Testing. In a situation in which so much fraud is possible, it is natural that federal and state officials want to intervene to protect the student consumer. Their interest in doing so arises naturally from their positions as dispensers of funds or guardians of consumers against fraud. State attorneys general may also feel a similar sense of mission to protect state residents against abuse, whether in the selling of insurance or of educational institutions. These concerns have been heightened by some of the student lobbyists themselves, many of them following the model of the public-interest research groups that Ralph Nader helped organize on many university campuses, where student funds are used (sometimes subject to individual students' consent) to set up a monitoring agency, usually with a legal public-interest arm.

World history is full of examples of instances in which activists who have spoken in the name of a cohort—for example, in the name of "the workers"—have not served the cohort optimally. On a much smaller scale, one can find instances in which activist and articulate students attacking permeable institutions softened by guilt have succeeded in damaging students' academic futures. The paradigm I have in mind is the attack on the Educational Testing Service.

It seems possible that social and political reforms have had such a cyclical quality in our national life in part because of the large role played by lawyers, often drawn to the profession by, and trained by it in, adversary tactics; their forums, whether judicial or administrative, are commonly limited to "yes/no" rather than "more or less" cost/benefit modes of dealing with undoubted or alleged abuses. So it is with the adults who, moved by the abuses of children in the home, as well as far less clear-cut cases of abuse in educational institutions, have sought to create a bill of children's rights analogous to the Bill of Rights appended to the American Constitution, with a similar focus on due process. Christopher Lasch (1977) is one of several scholars who have recently emphasized the damage that advocates of children's rights, in an excess of zeal, may on occasion do to the family or the school. But closer to our concerns is the attack on educational testing in which Ralph Nader, acting as an advocate for students in their role as consumers, has had a leading hand.[5] He is joined here by "revisionist" psychologists, sociologists, and historians who interpret the College Boards without knowledge of their history as an attempt to stratify higher education. They seem never to have read a report of the marvelous exchange between Charles William Eliot, one of the sponsors of standardized testing, and the president of Lafayette College, who said that he would never allow any outside group of faculty members, such as those who composed the tests, to determine admission to Lafayette. Eliot replied that of course the College Board tests were advisory only, and if the president of Lafayette wanted to exclude all students who had done well on the College Boards, that was his privilege.

The current attack on the College Board tests assumes that the tests are widely used to restrict entry to college in an arbitrary and unfair way. But, as already noted, only a small proportion of students, 10 percent by rough estimate, attend colleges with sufficiently large applicant pools to practice any kind of selectivity—and it is these institutions (those in the Ivy League, Duke, Wesleyan, Amherst, Williams, and perhaps thirty others) that do not "go by the numbers" but take into account special talents, as in music or, unevenly, athletics or leadership; minority status; in varying degree, whether the applicant is the son or daughter of an alumnus or alumna—indeed, the many factors which make up the diverse mix that these truly selective colleges aim to recruit. Institutions ask applicants to take ETS or ACT tests, and applicants want to take

[5] For an account of the various lobbies organized against the Educational Testing Service, including the critical tabloid *Testing Digest*, see "Getting Testy" (1979); see also Nader and Nairn (1980). For a succinct account of the origin, uses, and limitations of intelligence tests, see Herrnstein (1980).

them for a variety of reasons, even though in fact they play little part—and, with the drop in the post–high school population, will play a declining part—in the actual admissions process. For one thing, as alluded to above in connection with Minnesota Metropolitan State University, there is what I call the Groucho Marx syndrome: students like to believe that they have been selected rather than admitted. For another, students want to test their adequacy so that they can make appropriate choices in that minority of instances in which they are not attending the local "available college." They want to know how they will stack up: will they be grossly overmatched by students of exceptional verbal and/or mathematical ability, or will they be insufficiently challenged? Such information is useful ammunition vis-à-vis either pressureful parents or careless or even bigoted guidance counselors. (In a clarifying essay already cited, Hartnett and Feldmesser, 1980, have discussed the literature—and the puzzles—in this whole area concerning why so many take tests and so little use is made of them for admissions purposes—although more use may be made for diagnostic reasons once the student is on campus.)

The tests used by the College Board have been under attack from a variety of angles beyond those of such antitechnocratic humanists as Jacques Barzun. Some scholars, including Banesh Hoffman, find ambiguities in particular questions; this is easy to do if one assumes that the examiner is seeking to trap the student by a particularly abstruse interpretation, leading to a choice of a more tortured rather than more obvious answer. Since every test contains trial runs of questions which are not counted in the score and which, if they prove ambiguous or nonconsonant with other questions of established reliability, will not be used, attack on the tests on technical grounds has in the past not been persuasive.[6]

---

[6] Since the foregoing was written, two psychologists at Harvard Medical School, Warner V. Slack and Douglas Porter, have published in the May 1980 *Harvard Educational Review* "The Scholastic Aptitude Test: A Critical Appraisal." Like other less technically sophisticated critics, they assume that the SAT plays a much more important part than it does in the whole admissions process, even in the small number of selective colleges (they act as if the showing on the SAT served to bar most students from college—an idea that would surprise all college admissions officials) and share the view that the Educational Testing Service (whose part in the whole national testing enterprise—including the huge role of the federal govern-

But it is not technical criticisms that have led to the passage of New York's so-called Truth in Testing law and the introduction of similar legislation in many state legislatures and in the Congress. Rather, it is the confluence of several powerful pressure groups with several ideological themes that are at once populist and, correspondingly, favored by a number of academics and intellectuals. The attack has the backing of the top officials and lobbyists of the National Education Association, much the largest and richest of the teachers' unions. (It is this group that held candidate Carter to his promise to create a new federal Department of Education, a measure that seemed to me and to many other observers of the Washington scene a risk, since it pulled education out of the strong combination that the Department of Health, Education, and Welfare provided, especially in ensuring the support of the AFL-CIO in going through the congressional committees that dealt jointly with education and labor). Many individual teachers want the

---

ment, which goes back to World War I—is small) hides the truth behind an "aura of secrecy" (p. 169), whereas in fact the Educational Testing Service, though naturally not wanting to reveal the answers it considers correct to tests that it may still want to use or is trying out, is unlike an industrial laboratory engaged in research and development on weapons and is quite accessible to scholars. But Slack and Porter make two arguably valid points. One is that, in some instances though not in all, students who have attended coaching schools do better on the tests. It is not clear, however, whether they do better because they have less test anxiety or because they are more highly motivated; students are also better off in high schools that encourage them to take the PSAT, the Preliminary Scholastic Aptitude Test, as most metropolitan high schools do (not all students bother), but a good many in rural areas and especially in the South do not—areas, in any case, often served not by ETS but by the American College Testing Program. Their other point, which I regard as having more validity, is that the SAT is not a test of aptitude but of achievement. In several senses, that is partly true. Students with large vocabularies, more at home with words, and those who are at ease with and not frightened by mathematical reasoning will do better on the test. Moreover, students who are motivated to achieve would be painstaking in taking the test; they would use the full time and not leave parts of the test unanswered, as many do, because they quit early or have misgauged their time. But the SAT *is* an aptitude test as well as an achievement test, since its focus is not on particular content but on verbal and mathematical ability to reason, to use analogies, and so on, apart from specific courses students may have had; in that sense, the SAT differs from the achievement tests also offered by ETS that students can take in a particular subject, both for purposes of college admission (although at least until the current grade inflation, admissions officers relied more on high school grades as evidence of achievement and of the pertinacity to continue to achieve in a classroom setting) and for purposes of placement in college.

leverage of tests as a way of encouraging potentially able students to finish high school and go on to postsecondary education. However, the leadership and some teachers have a double fear concerning the use of standardized tests. One is that standardized tests at the college and postbaccalaureate levels will continue to demonstrate the point made earlier in these pages: namely, that schoolteachers are drawn from the ranks of those who do poorly, in comparison with those entering other occupations, in tests of verbal and mathematical aptitude and accomplishment. Of course, one is talking about averages here, not about any individual teacher. The second fear arises out of the fast-spreading competence-testing movement in the states—a movement that runs the risk of judging teachers in terms of how well their pupils perform. Both kinds of tests have obvious liabilities in helping the often now highly critical school boards and wider publics judge the quality of performance of either particular teachers or, in the competence-based testing programs, particular schools. Other things being equal, one might assume that the more literate teachers, with greater competence in mathematics, will do better in the classroom, but other things are rarely equal, while measures of schoolteachers' classroom performance are no more reliable than our measures of faculty members' abilities as teachers for particular categories of students. In neither school nor college do such matters lie within a teacher's personal span of control.

The other major pressure group allied with the NEA is the consumer lobby, mobilized in this as in other instances by Ralph Nader and his junior associates, operating on the assumption that the colleges and the testing services are large and powerful organizations with interests antagonistic to those of students—making use of arbitrary and anxiety-creating instruments of selection. One ideological stream of protest, closely allied with the Nader view, regards the tests as culturally biased, noting the quite understandable but by no means complete correlation of test scores with family income; it would be astonishing if there were not some correlation, but it is far from perfect, with for example—according to one study—students from families with third-quartile incomes doing slightly less well on the tests than those from families in the fourth quartile. (Each quartile exhibits the full range of test scores—that is, from 200 to 800 in each of the two parts of the SAT, the verbal and the mathematical.) A number of black activists and their white supporters contend that the tests are racially biased (presumably irrespective of social class), serving to prevent blacks from attending colleges (which are assumed, as already noted, to be more selective than most are). Lists of questions are sometimes circulated that most middle-class whites cannot answer because they require knowledge of the street argot of some urban blacks—for example, "What is an LD?" (a Cadillac Eldorado).

I shall come to the question of cultural bias in a moment. My own view, one shared by many observant blacks, is that abolition of the tests—the real aim of many of the critics—would be a disservice to blacks. It would confirm the argument one often finds—namely, that blacks get admitted to college on the basis of color, not competence. Ralph Nader himself has suggested that interviews be used instead of tests, and this is an answer I have often found in pressing critics of tests for what alternative they would use for the small number of institutions that are at least in some part selective.[7] To require interviews would handicap those whose talents are not superficially evident and all who could not afford the cost and problems of scheduling interviews at a variety of widely scattered colleges. While doing badly on tests in comparison with the expectations of oneself, one's parents, and one's peers can be harsh, doing "badly" in an interview (concerning which students are at least as apprehensive as they are about tests, for which they at least have some practice from taking school examinations and the PSAT) often seems a more total verdict on the self. That is, if one does less well then expected on a test, one can say that one lacks cunning; if one "fails" an interview, one is likely to be haunted by doubts about a much larger fraction of the self. There are, to be sure, more and less perspicacious interviewers, but the general experience of admissions officials is that capable interviewers are rare and that the interview is far more unreliable than the combination of measures

---

[7] Recommendations from school principals and other officials are also sometimes suggested. This suggestion was made to me by a group of Japanese school officials and schoolteacher union leaders who complained against Japan's undeniably rigorous meritocracy and what has been termed by many—because so much hangs on the outcome—as "examination hell" (see Riesman and Riesman, 1967, pp. 335–336).

based on school performance, the essays students often write in applying to selective colleges, and the tests as a kind of outside measure of the range of students who are likely to succeed in a particular institution. It would be cruel and humiliating to admit students with low quantitative scores—and the tests of quantitative ability, not being primarily verbal, are relatively culture-free—to MIT or Rice or Cal Tech. The converse is also true: A student with little self-confidence or one whose guidance counselors and teachers have thought little of his or her ability may discover through the tests that these verdicts are biased—indeed, in some cases I have known, clearly racist. Such a student may then apply to the most selective institutions, against the advice of school officials. If the students' test scores are beyond the lower threshold indicating ability to do college-level work at that institution, in combination with high school grades (where these still have some probative value), the chances of admission are good. This is especially true if the student applies to a sufficient number of selective institutions, since so many other considerations come into play in choosing among students who are judged capable of doing the work (such as race, region, alumni or faculty parentage, musical talents, and so on) that admission to any one institution is something of a lottery and unpredictable.[8]

[8] An article by Barbara Lerner, "The War on Testing: David, Goliath, & Gallup" (1980), supports, on the basis of the work of someone who is both a psychologist at home in psychometrics and a lawyer, many of the foregoing judgments; Lerner's article is the most lucid I have read on the testing controversy. Furthermore, emphasizing the point that psychometricians generally make, that tests become less valid as predictors the closer one comes to the ceiling because one has already screened out most potential variance, she criticizes those major national law schools that use the Law School Admissions Test (LSAT) as the virtually exclusive device for admission. The procedure is understandable at Harvard Law School, which must process many thousands of applications, but, once a threshold is established, it is nevertheless an escape from judgment to use a few points on the LSAT near its top, where variance is inconsequential, as a way of deciding whom to admit. Yet "going by the numbers" even at this stratospheric tail, where their significance is minimal, is understandable. Interviews by amateurs are notoriously unreliable, and letters of recommendation, since the passage of the Buckley Amendment, have suffered from "letter inflation" akin to grade inflation. Furthermore, reliance on judgment would involve major national law schools in the increasing danger of litigation, as illustrated by the resort of DeFunis and Bakke to the federal courts. Although the Supreme Court ducked the former case as moot, and the latter case allowed discretion to individual institutions to take race into account (although not in terms of a

It has been a surprise to me that many black leaders joined in the attack on tests, rather than seeing that the most probable alternative to the tests is not likely to be massive interviewing, but rather an avid recruiting of students identified solely by color for what I have termed a "body count" to meet pressures for an appropriate number of disadvantaged students; correspondingly, the questioning of standards represented by the tests may also mislead some underprepared blacks themselves about where they would be best advised to pursue at least the first part of their postsecondary education.

In the ahistorical interpretation typified in an often-cited essay by Schudson (1972), the tests are regarded by "revisionist" critics as an effort by elites to hold onto their positions in an educational system that simply reproduces the prevailing social stratifications. However, it is clear from all the histories, published and unpublished, based on Eliot's private papers and on the work of Nicholas Murray Butler, executive secretary of what became the College Board, that the system was originally set up in order to avoid separate examinations by every major institution or the attempt of universities to accredit high schools. Nationalization of college attendance would not have been possible without the College Boards, now joined by the American College Testing Program. By eliminating Greek and Latin as prerequisites, the College Board made all subjects equal—French or Spanish was as good as Latin or Greek. Likewise, biology could be substituted for mathematics as a prerequisite. Hence all high schools could enter the competition. Although this move may have resulted in some dilution, it was the opposite of the effort to stratify that is put forth in Schudson's critique.

The Educational Testing Service is, in my observation, an open and indeed permeable institution, self-critical in the highest

---

quota), Bakke and other cases in the lower courts make clear the willingness of the federal courts to intervene with institutional autonomy even in areas where highly technical issues are involved. Dr. Lerner is well aware of this (p. 140). Of course, the "Public Interest" legal advocacy groups can pick and try to guide a particular federal judge, bringing along if needed a retinue of social science witnesses who share the litigants' values. (For a case study of a situation in which a class-action suit failed, to the great damage of those on whose presumed behalf it was brought, see Brill, 1971.)

degree. Its people would be the last to insist that the tests are infallible; they do insist that admission to college should depend on other information (including, of course, high school performance), not simply on test numbers. They are aware of test anxiety and encourage practice runs. In the field of mathematics, they encourage high schools to provide opportunities for students to review the content and concepts within regular high school programs, rather than attend private coaching schools, which vary widely in quality and which, in any event, because of their costs and locations, would at best minimally help the already advantaged.

I want to come now to the question of alleged cultural bias against minority students.[9] It is true that the verbal tests are difficult for those who cannot read standard English, and the new English composition test is difficult for those who cannot write standard English with reasonable proficiency. However, as we have seen, the tests are only one element in the decisions of the small number of selective colleges to eliminate students from consideration; elsewhere, the tests are used mainly—if required at all—as an aid to identify a small number of applicants who are quite unlikely to succeed and to identify students who may need special assistance to improve their skills. There has accumulated a good deal of evidence, especially from the work of the psychologist Julian Stanley (1967; Stanley and Porter, 1966), that the tests in many cases actually "overpredict" the college performance of blacks: their college grades are frequently lower than their test scores would suggest; a study of "minority" students, mostly black males, who have been in ABC (A Better Chance) in such selective secondary schools as Phillips Andover and Lawrenceville, makes clear that, for many of these students, high school grades, which indicate achievement, are better predictors than the SAT (Boyd, 1977). One interpretation of such findings is that, in gross comparisons that neglect individual qualities and look just at scores and grades, a number of blacks are "underachievers" in comparison with white students with similar

[9] For the judgment of the reflective black columnist of the *Washington Post* who writes frequently about education, William Raspberry, supporting the value of testing against a large majority of black activists, see Raspberry (1979). See also Patterson (1972); on labeling people as "minorities" in general, and Hispanics in particular, see Rodriguez (1978).

test scores. Hence, contrary to what is so often contended, the SAT may be an advantage to some blacks in gaining admission to selective institutions, although of course the eventual outcome of such admission for any particular student will vary greatly, depending on the student's own qualities and the ability of the institution to encourage students to live up to their potential.

I have already indicated that one great advantage of the tests for all who are likely to be discriminated against is precisely their neutrality as far as the high schools go. I have observed many cases in which guidance counselors and headmasters sought to prevent the admission of students to selective colleges and would have succeeded if they had been the only source of information, without the evidence of the College Board tests.

An outlook that has great appeal to many opponents of the Educational Testing Service is that it is a lucrative conspiracy against the interests of students and potential students. I have mentioned in an earlier footnote an issue on which reasonable people might disagree—namely, the extent to which the major national law schools should seek to differentiate among applicants already at extremely high levels of test performance on some basis other than their scores on the LSAT. And, as I mentioned in discussing the work of Slack and Porter, it appears arguable that more recognition should be given than the ample publicity ETS provides for potential test takers of the fact that the SAT cannot help measuring elements of achievement, not the pure abstraction of "aptitude" irrespective of one's previous history and one's habits of work-mindedness or sloppiness. Still, as I have indicated, I believe it is important to maintain the distinction between the SAT and the subject-matter tests—once the only ones used by the College Board—for the reason already adumbrated: the SAT goes a long distance toward freeing students from having to obey a particular division of labor in high school subjects—a division of labor often based on logrolling among various fields of study so that each teacher will get a certain amount of traffic. As a test of general intellectual ability without being completely content-free, the SAT helps students who, for idiosyncratic reasons, have not wanted to subordinate themselves to particular teachers in their high schools or who have been bored because of the slow pace of work or for other, less valorous reasons.

None of this is meant to deny what I have said to some officials of the Educational Testing Service and to psychologists concerned with testing: that it is important to develop tests of non-cognitive qualities—tests to be used for both diagnostic and admissions purposes. I want to know of students I am to teach to what extent they are pertinacious (are they the academic equivalent of long-distance runners?) and to what extent they are narcissistic (it will be hard to teach them anything if they already know everything). Understandably, ETS has refused to enter an area in which projective tests would be needed, whose demonstrated validity, to put it mildly, leaves much to be desired.

Student Involvement in the College Board. In 1977, on the premise that, since students were affected by College Entrance Examination Board decisions, they should have a say in management of the board, Kathleen Brouder, a professional student advocate, persuaded the College Board to create a committee on student involvement. I was a member of the committee, composed mainly of activist students, though joined by two officials of the College Board. The argument that appears in the report of that committee (Brouder, 1978) and turns up repeatedly in discussions of student membership on boards of trustees, faculty committees, and similar bodies is one of supposed symmetry. Since students are affected by what the College Board decides, it was argued, they should have equal representation on the board of trustees and equal say in the disposition of the money accumulated by the Educational Testing Service. This money is now used for research, but the assembled students could have found other ways of spending it—including additional ways, in the minds of some (for the majority of the student members were women, minorities, or both), of proving that the tests were racially and culturally biased.

The whole argument concerning "symmetry" is one that had become a common cry in the 1960s in order to delegitimate authority: we, the students, are affected by what you decide; hence we are entitled to have our say about it. But the fact is that we are all of us, every day of our lives, affected by decisions over which we have no control whatever. When the California Supreme Court decided the case of *Serrano* v. *Priest,* those involved with schools elsewhere in the country were affected, but they had no hearing before the court or any say based on alleged symmetry. When the United States decides to increase spending on weapons capable of a first strike, the destabilizing effects of such a decision affect people in Japan, Western Europe, the Soviet Union, and the United States itself—in fact, everyone living in the Northern Hemisphere and perhaps elsewhere. "Symmetry" does not dictate that the Congress or the Pentagon do more than at most listen with half an ear to voices from elsewhere, especially voices that carry no votes (of course they listen to voices within that claim to speak for voices outside).

I mention these larger, indeed global, issues to illustrate that the questions concerning the "polity" of the College Board are part of an ongoing dialectic concerning the relative priority of effectiveness in decision making and how to give hitherto unrepresented and genuinely voiceless individuals channels by which to influence, but not to paralyze, nontotalitarian decision makers. To the demand for "symmetry," the College Board and Educational Testing Service have responded in a conciliatory way, although without conceding the right of control of the testing process to nonprofessionals. Along with graduate, management, law school, and GRE representatives, they have issued proposed guidelines termed *Public Interest Principles for the Design and Use of Admissions Testing Programs,* declaring that, for example, the demand that test contents be published is justified where considerations of cost and the quality of the tests are not unduly jeopardized, and they have invited professionals outside the testing agencies to scrutinize their procedures and their data, while protecting the privacy of individual test takers (Educational Testing Service, 1980). Suggestions have also been made by ETS officials that an ombudsman be appointed by representatives of test takers to channel complaints and to oversee the implementation of the *Public Interest Principles.*

Indeed, in the case of the committee organized by Brouder, I could witness the occurrence of useful interchange between representatives of the College Board and the student activists, with the result of dispelling some misunderstandings. For example, an older black woman from one of the Chicago community colleges complained that minority students—all of whom she assumed to be "underprivileged"—could not afford the fees required to take the College Boards; she was not aware that these fees could be waived in appropriate cases. She also made the observation, seconded by others, that black parents were very reluctant to fill out the forms of the College Scholarship Service, perhaps fearing that the Internal Revenue Service or the welfare agency would discover that they had unreported income; here, too, the confidentiality of the College Board procedures could be clarified. More important, the difficulty many minority students have in getting their parents to go to the trouble of filling out the necessary forms was emphasized. Here also there is the possibility of assistance through College Board offices, which will help parents fill out the forms if they are at all willing to and which will assist students where parents entirely refuse to cooperate.

As a consequence of this and later meetings, the concept of "symmetry" was not conceded, which would have required putting equal numbers of students on the College Board as the representatives of the colleges themselves; but every effort was made to show a sense of responsibility of the College Board and of the Educational Testing Service, on which it relies for the College Board tests but which, as a nonprofit corporation, provides tests—and studies of the testing process—for many other clients. Certainly, both the board and the much larger ETS have been sensitive to the dangers of cultural or sexist bias; both work with colleges to make plain the limited usefulness of tests as one of a number of items to be taken account of where admissions are truly selective, as they so obviously are for medical schools and the leading schools of law and management. ETS has proposed to unselective colleges that they administer the tests, or others constructed specifically for diagnostic purposes, after students have matriculated, although it is not clear to me that this would satisfy the interest of students in knowing where they stand or, among the minority who make multiple applications, what general levels of ability they will find among their peers. It is this latter use of tests by students, coupled with general moderately accurate knowledge about standards of well-known institutions, that makes it possible for Reed College, the college of the University of Chicago, St. John's College, and a number of other liberal arts colleges to maintain a high average level of College Board scores even in the absence of a large applicant pool.

Efforts at clarification and conciliation did not prevent the passage in New York State of so-called Truth in Testing legislation, which requires testing agencies to publish tests and the correct answers to those tests within a stated time after administering the tests. I believe this is one of a number of instances in which efforts at consumer protection (like some of the laws passed and regulations adopted to protect the rights of mental patients or the rights of children) are actually harmful to those who are supposedly being protected. Testing agencies (ETS and ACT primarily) are compelled to design more tests than their professional staffs are capable of inventing. Test construction is difficult. If the answers to former tests are publicly available, then, for example, handicapped students or those who for religious reasons cannot take their tests on a Saturday or others who missed a particular testing session will not quickly have access to new tests, because the new tests must not repeat any questions on former tests. The Association of American Medical Colleges initially decided to discontinue administering the Medical College Admissions Test (MCAT) in New York State, but later the association obtained temporary exclusion from the provisions of the law through proceedings in federal court. Since New York has the largest contingent of medical students of any state, the students would have been seriously handicapped by withdrawal of the MCAT, an action that is still possible if permanent relief is not granted. Many other students have been inconvenienced by the withdrawal of some twenty small admissions testing programs in health fields (none of them administered by ETS), by changes in scheduling and fees, and by reduced opportunities for special or makeup testing in major programs.

Expanding the Curriculum Through Pressures from Students and Their Advocates

So far, we have discussed students as more or less autonomous units, exercising their power through the market, by choosing to attend one college and not another, to stay or to drop out or to transfer. I would like to turn now to alterations, largely expansions, of the curriculum on behalf of students and, in recent years, as the result of their direct intervention.

During the period prior to the Civil War, American entrepreneurial energies, fueled by denominational rivalry, started many colleges that did not survive. Some state universities, such as Michigan, which we now think of as one of the early great state universities, had periods of very hard times and low enrollment; they were, after all, "godless." After the Civil War, enrollments actually declined as population grew. With the defeat of the South, the business of America really *was* business; as Veysey (1965) and Rudolph (1962) have pointed out in their histories, there was no great clamor for "relevant" colleges from businessmen seeking technically trained employees nor from the still very large rural population for colleges to serve their interests and educate their children.

The Land-Grant Colleges. The passage of the Land-Grant College Act in 1862 did make it possible for new programs to be introduced to serve the upward mobility of a son who could be spared from farm work or a daughter who might be given a liberal arts education or trained in home economics (presumably, also, until married, as a teacher). Soon the institutions set up under the Morrill Act and those that became in part land-grant colleges, such as Massachusetts Institute of Technology, required liberal arts components so that they could offer programs similar to those at the state universities that were not simultaneously land-grant institutions. Conversely, the more traditional liberal arts colleges and universities, public and private, sometimes followed the lead of what was in fact a rather diverse set of land-grant models: they brought in architecture, which also made room for engineering; they did not discard the classical curriculum as yet, but added new subjects in the hope of attracting new clienteles. These students, attracted to land-grant institutions and others that might lead to careers in agricultural extension, food processing, and later pharmaceuticals and so on, were scorned by the traditionalists. Had no students attended, the colleges would have died. But students did come, and they managed to pay the minimal tuitions and the costs (often greater) of residential living with some combination of parental support, part-time work, and years out to work in order to save the money for further education. The coming of these students validated the land-grant idea, no matter how much the land-grants moved toward becoming multipurpose institutions.

Adult education had gone on in the United States for a long time, through mechanics institutes and the Chautauqua circuits and lyceums and museums in many cities. But adult education as part of a university came later, notably in the University of Chicago when it opened in 1892 and was nicknamed for its president "Harper's Bazaar." Adults were also expected to pay their own way—indeed, only quite recently has this changed even in subsidized state colleges and universities. This new adult clientele wanted a variety of educational fare, both vocational and of amateur and hobby or civic interest. Adult clients' influence on the curriculum for youth just out of high school has been minimal— again, until quite recently, when their presence in the classrooms of many community and other "open door" colleges has added a seriousness of purpose so notable in the many older women returning to continue education interrupted by marriage or by low-level and low-paying jobs.

Women's Studies. The serious adult women just mentioned have been one of the sources of student market pressure, and on many campuses political pressure also, for separate women's studies departments and programs. When I last looked, it was reported that there were such departments or substantial programs at a thousand institutions. My assessment of this development is ambivalent. I believe that many girls and women profit from single-sex schools (which have almost entirely disappeared) and from women's colleges, which are, with some notable exceptions, an endangered species. In the absence of such institutions, women on campus, both the younger immediately postsecondary students and the often self-mistrustful older women who are not sure that they can prove themselves adequate in an academic setting, need the support groups that women have often formed for themselves informally since the rise of the women's movements. There has been a spectacular flowering of research in the previously neglected history of women and attention to roles of women in other cultures, enriching history, literature, and anthropology and other social sciences. Scholarly journals, such as *Signs, Women's Studies,* or the *Psychology of Women Quarterly,* multiply. Institutes for research on the history of women and facilities for such research, such as

Radcliffe's Schlesinger Library, have also greatly expanded; so have centers for research on contemporary women, such as the newly established Stone Center at Wellesley College. Some contemporary scholars, notably Alice Rossi (1980), have been investigating the intricate interplay between societal and physiological elements in women's development or, as Eleanor Maccoby has, sex differences from birth onward (for example, the slightly greater aural acuity of most girl babies and the greater spatial acuity of most boy babies), and there is much research on cultural sex stereotyping in what has been a primarily patriarchal society (see Maccoby and Jacklin, 1974). All this has been to the great benefit of historical, literary, and social-scientific scholarship as well as of our whole culture.

The difficulty I see in the label "women's studies" in a college catalogue is that it is off-putting to men. I believe that boys and men need women's studies even more than many women today do, thanks to the enlightenment now often shared among women. I have discussed this issue with a number of leaders in women's studies without finding a label that is generally acceptable. "Gender studies" does not sound quite right, and neither does "dimorphism studies," proposed by Elise Boulding (personal correspondence); "family-life studies" or any label that seems to establish a particular form of relationship as the norm would be rejected by many feminists as well as uncloseted homosexuals. The now widely established label "women's studies" has an attraction for some women faculty members as a way to appeal to feminist students as a cohort to assure themselves of retention and tenure and (despite affirmative action) to reject other women scholars who do not share a particular feminist credo—for example, a belief that society should move as far as possible toward androgyny.

Hence, I would prefer to see support groups established for women in an extracurricular way, while all fields, from medicine and related sciences to, let us say, Islamic studies, would be enriched by focusing on the roles of both sexes as well as by further scholarship on women's contributions at all social levels. When it comes to scholarship, men have not been driven out of the field, though there is a certain temptation and danger that this will occur as places for women in higher education become scarcer with the general shrinkage of academic opportunity, despite continuing pressures for affirmative action. Senior scholarly historians, such as Carl Degler and William Chafe, continue to write about women's roles. The sociologist Robert S. Weiss, in *Going It Alone* (1979), discusses primarily the plight of single women, often left alone with children, struggling against psychological isolation and economic hardship. I myself continue to write, as I have for a number of years, about the advantage of women's schools and colleges for certain kinds of women at certain points in the life cycle, and of course I am particularly concerned with the situation girls and women face in contemporary schooling. In the younger generation, there are enough "liberated" men to work jointly with women on research projects that involve both problems peculiar to women and those shared by both sexes, as so poignantly in pressures on two-career families where the two careers are given equal weight and may need different locales for their pursuit and where institutions are adapting only slowly, if at all, to the needs of such families.

Black, Ethnic, and "Third World" Studies. In the wake of the civil-rights movements, predominantly white colleges and universities active in the movement, such as Oberlin, Stanford, Harvard, Amherst, and Columbia, began actively to recruit black students who were not outstanding athletes (or at least not recruited as athletes) and to offer financial aid to the many who came from nonaffluent backgrounds. During the same period, public institutions could take little part in recruiting at a distance because, though their tuitions might be low, they lacked funds to pay the costs of students' subsistence and travel. But public institutions in urban settings either were the most available colleges for blacks in the area or actively recruited blacks, as did Wayne State University in Detroit, San Francisco State College, state-supported Temple University in Philadelphia, Cleveland State University, and others. Various remedial programs were begun for the less academically well-prepared of these students, such as Brandeis' Transitional Year Program; the Cadbury Program at Haverford College, which provided for a year of postbaccalaureate, premedical study; the SEEK (Search for Education, Enlightenment, and Knowledge) program in the New York City Colleges before the adoption of open admissions; and ever so many outreach programs of tutoring in high schools. I have already referred to ABC (A Better Chance)—summer programs for students on predominantly white college and preparatory school campuses; and there are many Upward Bound programs, as well as others independently started in various parts of the country.

Simultaneously, with uneven success, efforts were made to recruit black instructors, in many cases at the cost of a "brain drain" of the faculties of the Southern and border-state black colleges, much as able black students were drawn away from the more academically notable of the same group of colleges. There were also efforts to recruit more black faculty members in graduate schools, as well as to encourage students from the black colleges to attend selective graduate schools. Carnegie-Mellon University ran a summer program in American history for faculty members at black colleges—of course, not all such faculty members are black.

These efforts, going back in a few cases to the late 1950s and in many more to the early 1960s, did not alter the curriculum. The effort was to help the students through the existing curriculum. But the expansion of the black-power movement in a rush, with the assassination of Martin Luther King, Jr., brought on both tumultuous expansion of recruitment of black students and a demand to expand the curriculum to include black studies or Afro-American studies. This demand was echoed by many white students. Some of these were liberal, like one Stanford freshman I talked with in 1968 who was one of a group that succeeded in terminating Stanford's required Western Civilization course, which had been popular for years (and has now been restored); the student scoffed that it was simply "whitey's bag." Other whites were radicals seeking to form a political coalition with blacks, as in the case of the famous student-initiated course at Berkeley taught by Eldridge Cleaver, or the radical whites at San Francisco State College, or those in the Harvard chapter of Students for a Democratic Society who worked with activist blacks to establish an Afro-American studies department, whose staffing would be in part in the hands of black undergraduates themselves. There was also, as in the Stanford instance just mentioned, an effort by whites to discredit the supposedly all-Western, and hence all-white, "heritage" courses of the traditional liberal arts curriculum: in part, a rejection of curricular restraints; in part, a search for immediate relevance; and in part, liberal middle-class self-contempt.

A loss of pride in and dedication to the intellectual heritage of the Western world—a heritage eagerly devoured by many individual writers and intellectuals throughout the rest of the planet—is perhaps one reason predominantly liberal white faculties and student bodies so readily accepted the spokespersons who came forth who claimed to speak on behalf of all nonwhite students and who, picking up a convenient shorthand used in previous political discourse, gave themselves such names as the "Third World Coalition Front." For example, at San Francisco State College, where there was a sizable contingent of Chicano and Chicana students, as well as students of Asian background (this latter group rarely got involved in demonstrations), the term *Third World* came into wide use—a term that, when used as a slogan rather than a shortcut, homogenizes the most incredible diversity of peoples and cultures. The use of the term also permitted students and their faculty supporters to link American military imperialism in Vietnam and CIA efforts in Latin America and elsewhere to the cause of expanding the curriculum. Efforts to create "Third World colleges" sprang up especially in California, where there is such a concentration of both blacks and people of Mexican-American origin. There were efforts at the University of California at San Diego to establish "Lumumba-Zapata College" as the third of the colleges being created at that expanding institution; there was a similar effort at the University of California at Santa Cruz. Such efforts languished because of the paucity of Mexican-American faculty members with the doctorate, leading to the appointment of scholars from Latin America or persons trained at the University of Puerto Rico or, as at the State University of New York College at Old Westbury, which was one of the leaders in seeking to establish a multiracial campus at every level, the appointment as academic vice-president of a woman of Basque origin.

The genuine scarcity of Hispanic professors, especially of Mexican-American background, in contrast to the (only relative) availability of black professors, is, among other things, testimony to the hundred-year existence of black colleges; until very recently there has not been a single college run by and for Hispanic Americans. However, there are now enough colleges with substantial numbers of students of Hispanic origin so as to lead to a demand for Chicano studies programs in Southwestern institutions as well as in cities with increasing numbers of students from Mexican-American background. Similarly, Puerto Rican students in the New York metropolitan area have asked for Boricuan studies (this being the indigenous term for Puerto Rican, as *Chicano* was originally a slang appellation for Mexican-Americans). There are of course a great many other Americans who have come from the Spanish-speaking Caribbean or from Guatemala or other Central and South American countries; some of these, like Francophone Haitians and Lusitanians from the Cape Verde Islands and elsewhere, have also wanted heritage programs where there is a sufficient concentration to make such a demand feasible. (So far as I know, the Cuban refugees, at least until the most recent 1980 migration, have generally followed the traditional immigrant path of wanting assimilation to the prevailing scholarly and curricular patterns.)

In contrast, either programs or departments of black or Afro-American studies have been introduced into a very large proportion of the major colleges and universities in the country, the University of Chicago being one of the few major institutions without an Afro-American studies department.[10] The establishing in the predominantly white universities (as well as in the black ones mentioned in footnote 10) of black or Afro-American studies departments has been easier than maintaining them with substantial enrollments. Most black students have sought academic fields that had a clear vocational outcome; to major in black studies prepared one only to teach black studies or perhaps to work in a poverty program, to the extent that black studies involved such questions as

---

[10] Only a minority of black colleges have either possessed the resources or thought it desirable to mount black studies programs: as faculty members in such institutions have said, often with active student agreement, "Everything we teach is related to black studies, for example in American history; we live in a black environment; we do not need black studies." Still, such leading black institutions as Howard, Florida A&M, Morgan State University in Baltimore, all public, and Tougaloo, Tuskegee, Lincoln in Pennsylvania, and Morehouse offer a bachelor's degree in black or Afro-American studies.

discrimination in housing and other urban issues (also, of course, dealt with in extant courses in sociology or political science).

But many wanted to have the black presence recognized on the campus in the regular curricular offerings, pointing out, not incorrectly, that there was already room for East Asian studies, Middle Eastern studies (sometimes focused on Jewish concerns, sometimes more ecumenical), and an increasing number of ethnic groups that brought their own money in order to establish chairs, such as the Armenian chair at Pennsylvania or the Chair in Polish Literature and several Ukrainian chairs at Harvard. Why should black students not have the legitimacy of similar recognition? Why not, indeed? What Clark Kerr terms the multiversity had expanded to include an enormous variety of subjects desired by some class of customers; why should these new customers not also be entitled to their share of the academic offerings?

Furthermore, the presence of a black or Afro-American studies department on a campus provided a social, if not an academic, base for students whose majors were in a regular academic discipline. The black studies departments and cultural centers served many black students as decompression chambers where they could find like-minded people and work to counter patronizing, if not bigoted, attitudes on the larger campus. These enclaves allowed them to venture forth into the wider university with the support, sometimes including the academic "soft options," provided by even peripheral involvement in the black studies departments or programs.

Yet many problems were created for scholarly black students and black faculty members in already established departments by the rapid and uneven staffing of black and Afro-American studies departments. Wilson Record (1974) has described the ambivalent situation of the directors of programs and of those who chair black or Afro-American studies departments, on the one side seeking academic respectability, on the other side seeking to be responsive to the more nationalist separatist black students and, where available, blacks in the surrounding metropolis. Record has noted the frequent turnover among blacks running such programs and departments and the preference of some to move toward joint appointments. Sometimes black students are pressured, occasionally by liberal whites, including faculty members, or by fellow blacks, to fill up the roster of the program, quite apart from individual desire. The difficulty in a number of the new departments lies in the narrowness or provincialism that arises from a belief that blacks should study only subjects clearly labeled "black"—a paradoxically perverse form of racism. Blacks under this dispensation are not credited with empathy, with the ability to imagine the relevance to their lives of topics not labeled "black topics" (see Merton, 1972). Some years ago the Yale economist James Tobin (1966) made the cogent observation that it might be more important for blacks to understand the balance of payments and the role at that time of General de Gaulle in influencing that balance than to make one more study of, let us say, redlining in the city, discrimination in the suburbs, or other more obviously "black" topics. But it is just at this point that many people in the field of black studies are narrow and literal-minded. I have heard of instances in which all books by whites are banned from the program, and in the initial years at Harvard, white students felt themselves de facto excluded. Yet, just as most men need women's studies more than most women, most whites could profit from black studies far more than most blacks raised in predominantly black milieus do—however, the labels tend to be off-putting.

Herman Blake, a black sociologist who is now the senior provost of the University of California at Santa Cruz, has insisted that Oakes College, which he heads and which has a multiracial student body and faculty, demonstrate the competence of nonwhites in every field of scholarship. He is supportive of faculty members whose interests are not in topics deemed "relevant"—for example, one black professor who taught Sanskrit—and Blake shared with me the hope we both have of drawing more blacks and Chicanos into the sciences and advanced technology. He has also said (personal communications) that he must spend more time with white students and faculty members at Oakes College in helping them adjust to a predominantly nonwhite milieu than with nonwhite students, and he is critical of white instructors who give nonwhite students inflated evaluations (Santa Cruz does not have grades, except in premedical courses).

Both women's studies and black studies programs have broadened the curriculum in many previously ethnocentric or male-centered institutions. For example, white historians have been encouraged to expand their understanding of slavery both in the United States and in cross-cultural perspective, and many, including such a distinguished historian of the South as C. Vann Woodward, have made efforts to encourage able black graduate students to pursue topics that have greatly altered and enriched our knowledge of the past and hence our understanding of the present. The same phenomenon is especially clear for women's studies.

Much as women's studies has helped to deprovincialize scholarship in history, in psychology, and in a number of other fields, a marked deprovincialization of scholarship has occurred with the support of an emphasis on black and Afro-American studies. Older historians of the South have for many years encouraged both white and black scholars in this field. David Brion Davis, William Chafe (who has used oral history to study the impact of the first sit-in at Greensboro, North Carolina, and trace its consequences), Eugene Genovese, Herbert Gutman, Robert Fogel, and many other whites have studied slavery and its consequences, often in comparative perspective, and have encouraged students as well. Well-established black scholars, such as John Hope Franklin, Harold Cruse, Tobe Johnson, Martin Kilson, and Elliott Skinner, have expanded the reach of Afro-American studies in history and into African anthropology.[11] In institutions where Afro-American studies departments embrace African studies, one result, spurred by other developments in contemporary affairs, has been a change in the abysmal ignorance of the many worlds of Islam within Africa and in an arc stretching from Spain and Mauritania to Indonesia and the Philippines (although the majority Filipino culture has been Catholic rather than Moslem).

---

[11] For a still useful symposium, see Robinson, Foster, and Ogilvie (1969): David Brion Davis in his concluding "Reflections" makes clear the difficulty for the university in its role as custodian, "presented by the blacks' demand for practicality and utility" (p. 220), while his essay and the whole volume suggest the ferment and vitality brought to Yale by this multifaceted discussion in which literary intellectuals, such as Harold Cruse and the psychiatrist Dr. Alvin Poussaint took part, as well as Sidney W. Mintz, an anthropologist who has studied Caribbean cultures; the appendix contains plans for the Afro-American studies major at Yale, which, according to widespread opinion, has been the most effective one in the United States.

The immense disparity among different countries and peoples within countries who adhere to one or another form of Islamic religion and give it a more or less central place in their scheme of life illustrates why I regard the term *Third World* as misleading. It is important to emphasize the enormous differences among peoples in the rest of the world and the necessity for Americans to learn more about these differences through anthropological, historical, archeological, and literary and linguistic studies, as well as comparative study of religions. In a time of shrinkage of academic places for subjects deemed esoteric, which is at the same time a period of desperation for the black underclass in our metropolitan centers, it is difficult for centers and programs that use the term *Third World* to be more than meeting grounds in which an attempt is made to reconcile under a single banner such activist students as can be mobilized from the more experienced blacks, the less experienced Hispanic Americans, and the relative newcomers of Asian origin. Each of these groups is divided within itself along class and regional and many other fissures, not to speak of the enormous differences in stage of mobilization and of scholarly attainment among all the diverse groups "Third World" coalitions seek to include. It is damaging to scholarship to overaggregate areas of investigation and teaching in this fashion, when what we really need in universities, especially during a period of retrenchment, is what Donald T. Campbell (1979–80) terms "novel narrowness": a series of specialties at the margins of the existing academic departments, which are all the more likely to become tight compartments as individuals feel less free to take chances in fields in which it is harder and harder to find new academic positions with secure tenure within an institution that is itself secure.

The civil-rights movements provided the élan, the tactics, and the models for later movements, including some segments of the women's movements and the diverse movements of Spanish Americans (again including a variety of subgroups—in the East, not only Borinqueños from Puerto Rico but many other groups from Latin America, as well as Lusitanian groups from the Cape Verde Islands and Francophone Haitians). In addition, a number of white ethnic groups were stimulated to mobilize along analogous lines. Sometimes this took the form of backlash. Italians established Verrazano

College in upstate New York, only to see it fail when the founding of private colleges coincided with the foundering of many. (Greek Orthodox Americans have maintained Hellenic College in the Boston area as a small, though viable, college whose chief mission is to train Greek Orthodox priests.) Many previously secularized Jews became interested in Hebrew, a characteristically American effort at revival with the additional impetus coming from concern for the State of Israel. Jewish studies and many Holocaust studies appeared in catalogues of institutions with heavy concentrations of Jewish students.

There has also been a group of intellectuals and political leaders—they cannot as yet be termed a movement—who have emphasized that America is a pluralistic society, praised the American mosaic as against cultural standardization, and sought to retain the sympathy of newly self-conscious white ethnic groups for the black Americans who began the process of separatism, as against the more traditional belief, if not in the melting pot, then at least in a unified national culture with a common language and destiny. The *Novak Report on the New Ethnicity,* edited by Michael Novak, who in recent years began emphasizing Slovak "roots" and who sings the praises of the general concern with finding roots in the face of tendencies toward what he would see as homogenization, has been a leader in this development. Ethnic studies within the United States, including Hawaii, along with comparative studies of ethnic groups in other societies (Canada, Yugoslavia, various African states, South and Southeast Asia, and the Soviet Union) have also helped broaden the curriculum and led to scholarly efforts such as the *Ethnic Encyclopedia* now under preparation by the Harvard University Press. (For a view that the "ethnic revival" is primarily symbolic, a way in which working-class Americans can identify themselves in a fairly peripheral style, see Gans, 1979.)

I would like to sum up this section with the proposition that some students from backgrounds to which college has previously been alien (for black students, this means predominantly white colleges and universities) may find such programs useful as a transitional stage en route to greater universalism. This position is accepted by the black sociologist Orlando Patterson (1978), who nevertheless believes that the dangers of fragmentation may be greater than the advantages of temporary solace.

The Arts. The movements I have been describing, whose results have left their legacies in the curriculum of many colleges where there are, or at one time were, powerful political and ideological pressures to expand the curriculum, all have their starting point in the civil-rights movements and in the growth of black nationalism. There are many small, private liberal arts colleges in rural areas which make desperate efforts to recruit black students. One can read in their self-descriptions that they have black studies programs, a black cultural center, special remedial work available to students; yet they manage to recruit only a tiny number of blacks, sometimes 1 percent. And I watch many such colleges struggle to find black faculty members against the competition of major universities and distinguished liberal arts colleges, fighting against the handicap of rural locations in parts of the country where, since there is no black middle class, faculty members would fear to be isolated. (In a number of cases with which I am familiar, such colleges have recruited blacks on a moonlighting basis, so busy with their other work that they have been little help in enriching the curriculum and serving the interests of the overwhelmingly white students and the few blacks the institution has managed to attract.)

All the other movements of protest dealt with in the foregoing pages are, directly or indirectly, derivative of the civil-rights movements by and on behalf of blacks; even some Asian-American students have now become active as a cohort, although most do not benefit from affirmative action since they are among the most scholarly and studious of any young people and outperform whites in mathematical and quantitative areas and often in verbal skills as well (if not suffering from handicaps of language, as among recent immigrants from Southeast Asia). But the student pressures to expand work in the arts have, so far as I know, never been accomplished by demonstrations or protest. Rather, students of colleges with minuscule or limited offerings in the arts have flooded into the area, so that it has been intrainstitutional market power, coupled with faculty recognition of the importance many students attach to this area—and, of course, some faculty members also— that has led to expansion. Obviously, this not a new area—Syracuse University was strong in the arts from its inception over 100 years ago. Experimental women's colleges, such as Bennington and Sarah Lawrence, as well as Scripps College in the Claremont group, have made clear the interest that at least one cohort of students has had in this field, and the more experimental coeducational colleges, such as Hampshire, have followed this lead in their heavy emphasis on the arts.

But in many Ivy League institutions, the arts remained extramural until quite recently and even now have not always found a secure place within the curriculum. Here I can draw once again on my own experience. A number of years ago I served on one of the committees that led to the creation of the new Harvard College concentration in visual and environmental studies. I was influenced by the observation I had made as an undergraduate that those students who concentrated in architecture seemed among the happiest and most self-confident of any students in college. It seemed to me that they were able not only to work academically and intellectually—for example, in architectural and art history—but to use their hands and make things. They could draw; they could design. They found within the curriculum an arena for physical dexterity similar to what other students found in sports or in extracurricular musical performance. The new program in visual and environmental studies included design (although not architecture as such, long ago made an exclusively postbaccalaureate subject); an additional outcome was an efflorescence of work of high quality in photography and film. Animated films and documentaries produced by undergraduates have been (and continue to be) shown on the Public Broadcasting Service, and many graduates of the program have gone on to do distinguished work in film.

It is hard for traditional faculty members or alumni to grasp the fact that these can be serious subjects pursued in a determined and disciplined way. For example, when Diana Trilling, who had concentrated in art history as a Radcliffe undergraduate, revisited Radcliffe and lived in one of the dormitories, she began her major essay "We Must March My Darlings" (1977) by recounting her conversation with a student who, as it seemed to her, was fooling around with film—and I confess that I myself have in a jocular way sometimes referred to film as the narcotic of the semitalented. But what Trilling did not fully grasp was that what this student was doing was not undisciplined work, nor was it any kind of soft option; many courses in the Department of Visual and Environmental Studies are heavily oversubscribed, and students must show portfolios of capable work to secure admission. It is hard to find any students who work with greater ardor and zest: it is not unusual for them to work around the clock, planning a photographic show while completing a film and matching it with music, perhaps written by a student in composition at Harvard to fit the film in an imaginative way.

Students voted with their feet and with this intensity of effort to enter the courses offered by the new Department of Visual and Environmental Studies. They were not aware that their eagerness supported the faculty reformers, for the permission to work for credit in any particular art or craft was not a "cause" that appealed to a large and vocal student lobby. And of course students who came later, after the initial debates, were wholly unaware of their importance as customers to support what had previously been regarded as a dilettantish and nonacademic area. Ironically, the very seriousness with which students pursued these subjects led to objections both from faculty members and from some fellow students— namely, that the work had become too professionalized, driving out amateur students and going too far to prepare people for immediate postbaccalaureate vocations.[12]

---

[12] Such arguments led, in fact, to considerable student objection when Harvard recruited Robert Brustein and his American Repertory Theatre from Yale. When, in 1979–80, Professor Brustein proposed to offer some courses for credit that would combine, for example, performing a Shakespeare play with the study of Shakespeare's language, the objections voiced by some members of the English Department echoed, for quite different motives, these student complaints, especially from students themselves active in theater who believed that they could not compete with the professional repertory company Brustein brought with him. (One member of the English department, himself a playwright, William Alfred, insisted that one could understand Shakespeare far better if one performed his plays rather than simply read them.) The contention had also been voiced by students that, at a highly competitive university college, work in the arts should be, like athletics, a leisure-time activity, not for credit but rather a break from driving academic routines. At the faculty meeting that considered Brustein's modest and limited proposals, I argued that this view, which might have made sense in an earlier day, ignores the needs of students who are working part-time to earn their way or have to fulfill demanding premedical requirements or have other reasons for needing to be paid in the coin of academic credit if they are to have an opportunity for work in the arts. Without such credit, many students, lacking time for extracurricular pursuits, would be excluded altogether.

The objections from members of the English department were foreseeable;

The faculty members who, in my observation, have generally made such arguments have come from the humanities and are not aware that they are applying a two-edged sword, which can as easily spear them. A professor of English is not necessarily teaching one of the liberal arts to expand student horizons, curiosities, and aliveness; he—it is usually a male—may be preparing students to teach English as he has taught English in the past. What could be more vocational or professionalized? One cannot tell from content alone what is or is not an excessively professional subject. And what, in my judgment, matters most for student consumers is to find a proper balance between work they can do in college, which they can employ immediately on graduation, so that they will at least feel confident that they will know what to do on their first Monday at work, and studies that have a far longer horizon in time and place and add to the fund of curiosity and depth of historical and cross-cultural knowledge that make living in the modern world less mysterious and less likely to lead to student withdrawal out of cynicism or despair that one cannot possibly know enough to have an intelligent opinion.

In the arts, then, as in ethnic and women's studies, student customers have increased opportunities, no doubt at some cost to university budgets but also of some benefit to university coverage. However, it is necessary to add that, since the pressure for ethnic and women's studies has come from students and their politicized faculty supporters rather than from within the growth of the academic disciplines themselves, which would have moved at a much slower pace, there is the drawback evident in so many of the ethnic studies programs that the demand for faculty has far exceeded the

---

earlier they had led to the departure of Daniel Seltzer, who taught courses in drama, for Princeton, as in the 1920s they had led to the departure of George Pierce Baker and his work in drama for Yale. Harvey Mansfield, Jr., Professor of Government, raised an objection in principle that work in drama was per se unacademic and had no place in a university setting. It seemed to me that his view would mean that laboratory work would also have no place; much of it is mechanical and depends on dexterity quite as much as musical performance does. Certainly, there are institutions so unintellectual and antiacademic that one would want to side with Mansfield's judgment, but Harvard College, with its still primarily cognitive and analytic orientation, is not one of them. Brustein's proposal did secure faculty approval, subject to a review in four years to see whether it deserved to continue to receive the imprimatur of credit.

supply of qualified candidates (provided one does not follow the stratagem assumed by some proponents of affirmative action: to interpret *qualified* as meaning the level of ability of the least adequate white male with tenure on the campus—hardly a formula to invite much academic sympathy; some federal courts have interpreted *qualified* to mean no more than possessing the doctorate in the appropriate field).

The "Brain Drain" of Women and Minorities away from Ph.D. Programs. Indeed, in my experience with nonwhite students and with women of all ethnic and racial groups, the ablest, if they can do science, head for medical school (just as most of the ablest white males do), and those who cannot are inclined to go to law school (with only an occasional recruit, though a growing number, to schools of business). The very same students who seek "role models" in all fields and at all levels of faculty refuse to enter Ph.D. programs in which they might become such role models themselves. And although it would be racist or sexist to expect that, because they belong to a certain racial or sexual group, they should follow any particular track that is not in their own interest, the fact is that many of these students are deeply engaged in their academic pursuits and enter law or medicine precisely because they are convinced that they must help "their people"—and quickly, whether in community medicine or some form of public-interest law. Unwilling to take advantage of affirmative action themselves (and generally, in the cases I speak of, not needing to, because they are in expanding fields and are exceptionally talented), though willing enough in most cases to support affirmative action for the less gifted, they are nevertheless sufficiently subject to peer pressure to conclude that an interest in eighteenth-century French literature (as in the case of a young Bryn Mawr graduate who ended up in law school) or in ethology (a young black woman at Harvard who also went to law school) is too remote from the alleged needs of black people or of women to justify the luxury of their pursuing it. Blacks are in fact the first quasi-immigrant group to be asked in the first generation to behave with noblesse oblige toward their fellows, an issue of career choice that W. E. B. DuBois did not face when he began his career. He did, however, concentrate his work on blacks, later extended to Africa. Similarly, many black scholars of a generation ago, such as E. Franklin Frazier or John Hope Franklin (who remains active), chose to study subjects of obvious reference to blacks, and black novelists and poets have tended to deal with "black" topics—but this was a self-imposed mandate rather than one imposed from outside, and many have used subject matter drawn from the whole wide world as talent and interest have impelled them.

But even if one is thinking in the narrowest ethnic and provincial terms, it seems important for nonwhites (as for women) to have representatives of high quality on the faculty in fields not defined as "black" or as "Hispanic" or as "women's studies"; quite possibly, the more esoteric the field, the more important the model—an issue discussed earlier in connection with the efforts of Herman Blake at the University of California at Santa Cruz (see Dreyfuss, 1979).

Another sort of "brain drain" away from faculty positions has come about through the pressure to promote minority and women faculty members to administrative positions. These pressures sometimes come from outside the institution, through either affirmative action requirements or community pressures, sometimes from within—including the value for public-relations purposes of being the first major state university to appoint a black or a woman as president or chancellor. Sometimes, as in the appointment of the distinguished black from the Rockefeller Foundation, Clifton Wharton, as president of Michigan State University, the candidate has qualifications that could operate in the absence of affirmative action, although such pressure makes such appointments easier in those fast-disappearing enclaves in which overt bigotry can still be expressed. I am especially sensitive to the instances in which scientists have been promoted into administrative positions who are female or black or both and therefore are especially valuable as symbols, as much for white male faculty members and students as for blacks or women, because both groups have tended to concentrate in the "talk trades." It should be clear that I do not have in mind any simple concept of "role models." Not only is it fallacious to assume that there is necessarily a correlation between gender or skin color and ability to help particular subcultures among a heterogeneous group of students, but it is no less fallacious and also condescending to conclude that students have no capacity for the vicarious, for finding qualities to value from people of a different sex or race or, for that matter, historical period. No doubt, black students will sometimes feel more comfortable in the presence of black teachers or counselors, especially if there are not sharp differences of class and hence of subculture. However, in conveying the basic skills of reading and writing in successful remedial programs, whites who are capable of being compassionate without being condescending have often been effective. (There is a similar fallacy in the belief that black interviewers always get more truthful statements from blacks, or women from women—they may simply get the party line, given to someone the respondent might run into anywhere. Concerning interviewing on sensitive issues across lines of race and gender, see Robins, 1979.)

Of course, anyone who prefers an administrative to a faculty position is entitled to make that choice as an individual. And many individuals who have made that choice have told me they believe that, with administrative leverage, they can be of more use because of their gender or their race or both. But there is now a more ample supply, though still relatively small, of black and female administrators than of black and female individual teachers in the fields of science, high technology, and engineering. Hence, I feel a personal sense of regret when I witness the career of Jewell Cobb, who started as a biology teacher, became dean of Connecticut College and then of Douglass College, and was recently runner-up for the presidency of Hunter College—she will almost undoubtedly become a university president. Similarly, Randolph Bromery, when I first met him as a faculty member at the University of Massachusetts at Amherst, was said to be the one black in America with a Ph.D. degree in geology; the then new, liberal, and public-relations-conscious administration of Robert Wood appointed him as chancellor—and later another black as vice-chancellor. During Bromery's tenure, his qualities as a scientist were subordinate to his situation as the top administrator of the flagship campus of the University of Massachusetts.

I could go through a whole list of black scientists who have moved into administration. And in some of these instances, I wonder whether they have not been put under pressure by boards of trustees and other responsible, predominantly white male officials who wanted them in such positions, in part for reasons of public relations and affirmative action, and also out of the exploitative but often mistaken judgment that black administrators will be more effective in resisting academically dubious demands from mobilized black cadres. There are many examples to the contrary: The appointment of a black president or chancellor is often a signal to the nationalist blacks on campus to test the new appointee to see whether he or she is "Negro" or "black." Similar tests are applied by activist wings of the women's movements on campus, to see whether a woman administrator is sufficiently aggressively feminist.

Ethnic and Religious Colleges as Decompression Chambers

Likewise, black colleges seem to me to serve an extremely useful purpose in facilitating a transitional ethnicity as well as in assisting students who would feel humiliated by the more demanding competition at many predominantly white institutions—especially those major white institutions sufficiently affluent to compete with one another to recruit what is regarded as a sufficient cohort of blacks, if need be, through full-ride scholarships. That is why the move, originally spearheaded by an NAACP lawsuit in New Orleans (*Adams* v. *Morgan*, later *Adams* v. *Califano*), to merge the public black colleges with neighboring white counterparts in an integrated system has been so bitterly fought by these institutions' devoted alumni, faculties, and student bodies, who can see submergence in most mergers. This is yet another case, comparable to the fight against the Educational Testing Service, in which spokespersons have claimed to be acting in the interest of student customers. Those who brought the suit, members of the Legal Defense and Education Fund of the NAACP, were overwhelmingly Yankees, white and black; those who have pressed it in the Office of Civil Rights and in what used to be HEW, like former Secretary Califano himself, have been almost without exception Yankees. Southern blacks were no more consulted than in the instance of the Atlanta school desegregation case, where the Atlanta head of the local NAACP chapter was dismissed by the national office for accepting a compromise plan that minimized the busing and further white flight from what had become a black-dominated metropolis. Meantime, before and since the New Orleans lawsuit, black students have voted with their feet to attend the public black colleges. One black scientist who had attended such a college spoke for a number when he said to me a few years ago that he was glad he had attended college before the predominantly white universities started to recruit blacks, for he almost certainly would have been lured to such an institution. As it was, he was not ashamed to fail in some of his first efforts to do science, and to try again; there was no public humiliation before whites who at least half-expected blacks to fail in such a field. Once he had his baccalaureate, he could go on to a major Northern university for his doctorate, having found his academic footing in a less stressful milieu.

Many religious colleges serve a similar purpose for various ethnic groups. Denominational affiliation has often been a "cover" for ethnicity. For example, the largest single category of private institutions in America and overwhelmingly the largest number of women's colleges were set up to serve Catholic populations that were in fact ethnic—originally predominantly Irish, as in most of the urban Jesuit institutions, but in other locales variously French-Canadian or German. Among these institutions in a particular community there is often an ethnic division of labor, so that, for example, among the women's Catholic colleges in Detroit (now nominally coeducational), Mercy College, the largest and oldest, catered originally to Irish Catholics; Marygrove to Polish Catholics; Madonna to Italian Catholics in a Detroit suburb. Mercy and Marygrove have a large proportion of black students—20 percent in both cases—a number of whom are graduates of the parochial schools, to which predominantly Protestant blacks send their children if they can afford to in order to avoid the violence, vandalism, and general inadequacy of the majority of the public schools.[13]

---

[13] Many black students desirous of an education undistracted by either black nationalism or the counterculture are attracted to the evangelical Protestant colleges discussed in the next chapter. One of the highest proportions of black students at any private liberal arts college other than black colleges—30 percent—is at Pepperdine University, primarily on the Los Angeles campus. The college is a conservative institution created by the Church of Christ, a college that "wishes to be known as a Christian college, emphasizing the standards and the concerns of the Christian

Similarly, Catholic colleges in the Southwest attract, as well as blacks, many Chicano students who are devout Catholics and prefer a Catholic institution, despite the considerable differences between the Catholicism of the Mexican peasantry, from whom so many Chicano families have descended, and the Catholicism of the American Roman Catholic Church, which in doctrine and often in personnel has tended to be dominated by Irish-Americans. However, ethnicity among whites is far less powerful on the West Coast than in the East and Middle West. The Irish in California do not think of themselves as having come originally from County Cork, but from Boston or Queens or Chicago, and the whole spirit of the state of California is one of tolerance for ethnic as for other differences, so that individuals have less occasion for ethnic defensiveness.

It is Norwegian allegiance that attracts excellent students to St. Olaf College in Northfield, Minnesota, or to Decorah College in Luther, Iowa, not the fact that these colleges are American Lutheran. Gustavus Adolphus College in St. Peter, Minnesota, also Lutheran, attracts many students of Swedish-American background. Concordia College in Moorhead, Minnesota, is also American Lutheran; it is attractive to Germans, while Concordia College in Bronxville, New York, a small institution, not founded until 1969, offers a refuge for the more conservative Missouri Synod Lutherans, who are also commonly German. Other Missouri Synod Lutherans of German ancestry in the Midwest have available Valparaiso University and its law school in Indiana as well as several teacher's colleges in Illinois and Nebraska—for the Missouri Synod Lutherans conduct a number of parochial schools.

The private black colleges are primarily religious founda-

---

faith" (Cass and Birnbaum, 1977, p. 492). Chapel attendance is required; there is a curfew; neither alcohol nor visitors of the opposite sex are permitted in dormitories. I am told that Los Angeles blacks who have despaired of the public schools and have when possible sent their children to parochial schools have chosen Pepperdine (whose downtown campus is geographically accessible) in preference to the state colleges or UCLA; they assume that the public colleges will turn out to resemble the public schools as too disorderly to permit serious learning. The Catholic colleges of the Los Angeles area, such as Loyola-Marymount, can probably offer neither the financial aid that wealthy Pepperdine can provide nor the assurance of moral coherence.

tions, either the result of white philanthropy through the American Missionary Association and other such groups or under black religious auspices.

Among whites in the Southeast, religion did not generally serve as a cover for ethnicity, because most people regarded themselves, whether of English or of Scotch-Irish descent, as simply white, Protestant Americans, and their choices were based on religious rather than ethnic affiliations.

Many of the once devoutly religious colleges in California have shed their denominational ties. The University of Redlands in Southern California was long associated with the American Baptist Church but now is independent; it created in the late sixties the highly experimental Johnston College and, in a characteristic move to recruit adults, the Alfred North Whitehead College of Liberal Arts and Career Studies for a "new constituency of older students" (Cass and Birnbaum, 1977, p. 511). Evangelical LaVerne College, once tied closely to the Church of the Brethren, also in Southern California, again is independent, and it has established branches in different parts of the country, on army bases and elsewhere, to recruit new constituencies. Whittier College, established by Quakers and also in Southern California, is now independent, with 28 percent Catholic students; so is Westmont College in Santa Barbara, once fervently evangelical.

In all these colleges and many others, including Protestant colleges that have retained their evangelical character (to be discussed in Chapter Five), students may be sent by their parents, though of course with their own consent, but the decision how long to stay, once they have made the partial break from home, lies largely in their own hands. Hence, in colleges of high academic and intellectual quality, such as St. Olaf, one finds 84 percent of the students staying on to graduate and 26 percent going on to postbaccalaureate studies; but in other institutions, attrition can reach as high as 50 percent as students decide that they want a wider world (and no doubt also a broader range of academic programs than many of the smaller institutions provide), having satisfied themselves and their parents with a transitional ethnicity that is in part religious.

The Public/Private Option

So much has been written about the declining role of the private colleges (by me among many others; Riesman, 1975b) that there seems no point in repeating the discussion at length here. Many of the great state universities have been open admissions institutions since their inception, often required by law to accept all high school graduates; community colleges have opened their doors to students of a certain age whether or not they have completed high school. With the general decline of religious faith except among the evangelical denominations, private institutions had to offer something special to attract students away from the great variety of public institutions with negligible tuition—a spread that has increased markedly since the Second World War, especially as many state universities have kept tuition artificially low by not indexing it to inflation.

"Open admissions" in the great state universities, however, has often had a de jure rather than a de facto existence. High school guidance counselors would warn students away from attending, for example, the University of Illinois at Urbana, suggesting instead less academically competitive institutions, such as the many regional state colleges and universities in Illinois. Furthermore, except for the Universities of Washington and Minnesota and UCLA, the great state universities have been located in small towns, and therefore students had to pay the costs of residence and often to live in locales where jobs were few. To be sure, the great public universities located in metropolises have attracted students from elsewhere, notably at the postbaccalaureate level, but there are also undergraduates who either prefer not to commute or live beyond commuting range. UCLA, Washington, and Minnesota have all built dormitories, as well as depending on the local rental housing market for noncommuters.

The term *open admissions* applies to the institution as a whole, not to particular programs. In generally unselective private and public commuter universities, programs requiring mathematical aptitudes or above-average facility with languages will not admit students whose graduation from high school is the result of social promotion rather than evidence of all-round literacy and numeracy. One consequence is that many students from low-

income backgrounds and with an inadequate high school preparation have been channeled into majoring in education, thus landing
in one of the most oversupplied baccalaureate fields today. (Even
so, studies show that black males with a college degree do far better
in earnings, regardless of the field of the degree, in comparison with
those without a degree than do white males; degrees in education
have long been useful for black females.) Such considerations have
recently impelled the board of regents of the state of Georgia to
initiate competency tests for minimal literacy, on the ground that
standard English usage is necessary for most jobs and that both
black and white students without minimal literacy defeat their
parents' hopes that higher education will serve their children both
for social mobility and for wider horizons (Watters, 1969). In a
recent decision reported by Lerner (1980), *Deborah P.* v. *Turlington,* a
federal district court in Florida knocked out a similar competency
test in that state on the ground that its impact would be "racist,"
since more black than white students would fail the test; the consequence of this judicial interference is in effect to compel the high
schools to hand out diplomas irrespective of students' ability, thus
avoiding the responsibility of both students and schools to see that
the former acquire the basic tools needed to do more than un-
skilled labor in an industrial society.

5

The Limits of Student Choice: The Evangelical Colleges

The one category of institution where the academic revolution made least headway in the earlier era—namely, the Protestant evangelical colleges—remains the arena in which students subordinate themselves, with greater or lesser willingness, to the authority of the institution and its faculty. This authority is not purely academic, but moral or spiritual.

The "deviant case" of the evangelical colleges dramatically illustrates the limits of sovereignty based on students' market power: most of these colleges are tuition-dependent, and yet they retain nearly complete institutional authority. In some measure, depending on the degree of church control and administrative hierarchy, faculty members have caught up with the academic revolution and are still seeking to assimilate it into a holistic undergraduate curriculum. The weakness of departments and of the academic disciplines on some of these campuses, which makes for greater flexibility in adopting such innovations as computer-assisted instruction or in meeting student interest, whether in the arts or in courses on management, reflects in many cases the influence of the president and other academic leaders, which overbalances the departmentalism that hedges faculty autonomy in major secular institutions.

The evangelical institutions differ very much from one another, though they are often stereotyped as academic and cultural backwaters by students and faculty members at cosmopolitan institutions who (whatever their private idolatries) regard religion as superstition. Brigham Young University, with its students drawn from all over the world (though, as students said to me on a visit, it does not follow that the institution is "cosmopolitan"), is very different in tone from Oral Roberts University or Oklahoma Christian College. In general, in many curricular matters, these institutions are flexible—in part, as Verne Stadtman has observed on the basis of visits, because they know what they are trying to do and hence are not threatened; in part because of colleaguial cohesiveness; and in some cases, as indicated earlier, because the president and trustees exercise more authority over the faculty than has been true where the academic revolution has fully triumphed. For example, Oklahoma Christian goes in for new instructional technology with more freedom than has been possible in many secular institutions.

Some students seek out the evangelical colleges with the support and under the influence of parents who do not explicitly direct the children to those colleges, but tell them that they can go to college and receive support wherever they like—but the parents are themselves often graduates of these same institutions or have other ties to them and to the sponsoring denominations. The choice contains both negative and positive elements. There is an explicit decision to avoid secular, cosmopolitan institutions, especially in large urban conglomerations, for these students—along with their parents—are in revolt against modernity and what passes for sophistication in the national culture and the national media.[1] But there is also a positive element, an attraction to an institution known to make demands; in many cases, work programs are coupled with academic programs. The most famous instance is Berea College, a nondenominational Christian institution that developed in part out of the antislavery movement before the Civil

---

[1] For a reflective discussion of the shopping tours carried on by educated, homeless, egocentric, alienated selves in the contemporary world, see Morgenthau and Person (1978), stressing the attractions of the movements that emphasize "not the ascendancy of the self, but its obliteration, for example, by the cult of eastern religions and the self-designated 'Jesus freaks' " (p. 346).

War and was unsegregated until forced by the Kentucky Jim Crow laws to establish, for a time, a separate college for Negroes; its work program has been exemplary, symbolically illustrated by the fact that the list of faculty members and administrators at the back of its catalogue is headed "Commissioned Workers and Special Staff Members." Berea College continues to emphasize its strong commitment to service, to the kind of cooperativeness at odds with the modern emphasis on what Quentin Anderson has termed, in a book of that title, "the imperial self."

Someone observing on a brief visit the almost "un-American" obedience to rules and civility of student behavior at residential evangelical colleges would suppose that individuality is lacking among these students. Such outsiders are apt to be deceived by their ethnocentrism. Secularists for the most part, they will be unaware of theological differences, certainly among the faculty and often among the students. Furthermore, deviations are not flaunted, although even this may not be universal: students at Southern Baptist Wake Forest University have held "dance-ins." And I recall the reflective and quietly protesting students I met in the middle 1960s at Furman University, also Southern Baptist, who wondered why, if the denomination was drawing the line between church and state so severely as not to accept a science building offered through federal funds, it permitted an ROTC chapter to exist on campus.

A number of years ago, the sociologist James A. Davis described the campus as a "frog pond" (Davis, 1966), arguing that students used one another as a reference group and that many students were better off to be, in effect, big frogs in a smaller, inconspicuous campus than little frogs at a major university college. As the reputations of institutions become more a matter of national knowledge, at least in student grapevines, students in one frog pond are apt to compare themselves not only with one another but with their imagination of frog ponds elsewhere, and they may even want to test their adequacy, for example by spending a semester or summer school term at a larger campus, a bigger pond. Still, the smaller campuses undoubtedly provide more personal attention and dedicated teaching than do the lower-division classes at world-class state universities such as the University of Texas at Austin or the University of California at Berkeley. I sometimes think that, for many students, two years at a small college (or a women's college for shy women or a black college for self-mistrustful blacks) followed by two years at a major university would be optimal, even though for the smaller institutions the attrition would look bad on their records, deprive faculty members of the opportunity to teach advanced courses, and deprive the freshman and sophomore students of the advantages of tutoring and other help from able, upper-division students.

At any rate, if one judges according to "value added," some of the residential evangelical institutions have redoubtable records, for they accept students with SAT total scores as low as 700 and rarely as high as the national median of around 900; yet as many as a third of their students or even more go on to graduate or professional study—an extraordinarily high figure, considering the tested aptitude of the students at intake. (I am speaking of the predominantly white colleges, not of the Southern church-related private black colleges, although some of the best of these latter colleges also send many students on to further education.) I recognize that this is an inadequate measure of "value added" in the overall sense; in fact, many graduates of the black colleges are avidly recruited by large, national corporations directly from college, and I am not expressing simply an academic self-interest in using the proportion of postbaccalaureate students as one potential, but inadequate, index for "value added." It means something, and it can be measured, but like other items that can easily be measured, it of course does not mean everything.

Profiles of Representative Colleges

Mars Hill College, in Mars Hill, North Carolina, is a Southern Baptist institution enrolling 700 men and 800 women. It accepts 94 percent of its applicants; two thirds enroll, having average freshman SAT scores of 395 verbal and 410 mathematical. Class attendance is required and freshman seminars are mandatory as part of a core curriculum developed in recent years by some intelligent and inventive faculty members. All students must take a course in religion/philosophy. There are no coed dormitories,[2] and intervisitation is limited in ways long since abandoned, for example, by virtually all the country's Catholic colleges. Tuition and fees are kept under $2,000. Though Mars Hill is not overapplied, its faculty has, with support from the Fund for the Improvement of Postsecondary Education, sought to develop a competence-based program in the liberal arts and sciences, focused on the outcomes sought rather than the courses or credit hours that make up the usual curriculum. Only a dedicated faculty would be prepared to submit itself to the demands of such an overarching and intricate mandate—whose novelty is not advertised in the immediate catchbasin from which Mars Hill draws its students in the Appalachian South, lest the place be thought faddish and hence no longer a "safe" college. A sixth of the graduates go on immediately to further study. At Berea College, whose test scores are considerably higher and which is about the same size, a larger proportion—29 percent—pursue graduate work, commonly with the aim of returning to the Appalachian region to put their talents to use locally.

More dramatic still, in terms of average test scores, is the record of Erskine College in South Carolina, a Presbyterian college with average test scores of 439 verbal and 494 mathematical for men; for women, 481 verbal and 467 mathematical. (I have the impression that, in the South, women's verbal scores are still considerably higher than men's in comparison with the closer approximation in the rest of the country.) Erskine graduates 75 percent of its entering freshmen, 32 percent of whom continue to graduate and professional schools, including medical schools, dental schools, law schools, and business schools. But, as the vice-president and dean of the college, Jimmy Aldon Knight, pointed out to me, these

[2] In current coresidential living arrangements, sexual pressures on students are sometimes thought to be moderated by what has been termed the "incest taboo," in which students who share corridors or entries do not want to sleep together because of the awkwardness they would feel if the relationship should terminate while they were still having to see each other in the "liberated" bathrooms and at meals. The only study of the issue I know of (DeLamater, 1974) suggests that the "incest taboo" exists where women unite to enforce it; where they do not, a male prefers the convenience of going next door to the trouble of finding women in other residences. DeLamater's study was done in a major state university; to understand all the varieties of what Lamont (1979) terms "campus shock," one would need much more detailed investigation of particular institutions and of enclaves within them.

low average scores include a wide range; six National Merit finalists entered as freshman in 1979—indeed, the faculty faces the problem of teaching a student body, as in any virtually open admissions institution, in which one might find the full range of academic ability. Erskine is attractive to a number of talented students in part because there are Erskine Scholars who have more freedom than other students in their curricular choices, although on the extra-curricular side, Erskine provides traditional dormitories and declares, "Erskine is a church-related institution and seeks 'to provide a liberal arts education in a Christian environment.' " Also advantageous is South Carolina's newly liberal scholarship aid to South Carolina students attending private in-state institutions, amounting to as much as $2,000 and available to families of well above average income.

Test scores are higher still (476 verbal, 479 mathematical) at Berry College in Mount Berry, Georgia, a nondenominational Christian institution that requires seven quarters of religion and philosophy, expects class attendance, has no fraternities, sororities, or coed dormitories, and of course allows no drinking on campus. Twenty-two percent of Berry College students go on to graduate work—and this figure must be compared with those at institutions of much higher average initial test scores where 10 percent or fewer go on to further study, as is the case at many of the comprehensive state colleges and universities that draw most of their students from the surrounding region.

Interviews with Luster D. Mathis, vice-president and dean of Berry College, and with other people at the college make clear that a number of students who would have been admissible to the University of Georgia, to Auburn University across the state line in Alabama, or to Florida State had chosen Berry College because of its Christian environment and its small scale. One of the women students had visited Meredith College in Raleigh, North Carolina, a women's college of 1,300 students, Southern Baptist and described by student leaders as "providing quality Christian education for the women who will be mothers, teachers, lawyers, doctors, and community leaders in the future." But Meredith College draws a more sophisticated student body, including some capable horse-women. Students play an active part in the college's self-regulation.

Since the campus is on the outskirts of Raleigh, it is not far from the land-grant university, North Carolina State, nor indeed from Duke or Chapel Hill. Its students, therefore, have an opportunity to be around the more "collegiate" atmospheres—a good illustration of the fact that the "frog pond" notion is limited by awareness of other colleges as groups by which to judge one's own institution and hence the quality of one's own academic performance and the restraints imposed on one by one's home base. (For a critique of the frog-pond theory in terms of the awareness of students that the judgments of their own institutions have to be weighed against the judgments of other institutions as learned through contact, grapevine, or even mythology, see Bassis, 1977.) It seems clear that students in the evangelical colleges are aware in greater or lesser degree of the differences in standards of conduct in the collegiate worlds, often not only in their immediate environs, but on a national basis. For example, the Berry College student who had visited Meredith had been attracted to the program it offers in fashion design, whereas at Berry the best she could manage was to combine several courses in business administration with a home-economics major. However, Berry College fitted her view of an appropriate college style of life, a frog pond of the proper moral temperature, even though the college was less suitable for her vocational aims.

In England, the evangelical sects that grew out of the Puritan revolution are often termed "nonconformist" because their members refuse to conform to the established Anglican church. The students at these evangelical colleges, though part of a culture at odds with, and in that sense nonconformist vis-à-vis, the prevailing secularism, are deeply engaged in vocational preparation for primarily secular callings; only in minimal degree are these colleges training ministers for the groups of sects they represent. The students who attend these colleges are from close-knit but rarely well-to-do families; for example, at Elon College, a Church of Christ college near Greensboro, North Carolina, two thirds of the students are the first generation of their families to attend college. They know that they must make a living, and "academics" itself may be one road to that end, although many of these institutions are seeking to shift traditional liberal arts faculties to vocational programs—to return to Elon College, nearly a quarter of its students get their baccalaureates in business and management.

Berry College lies on the edge of a forest preserve seventy miles northwest of Atlanta, and students praise the beauty and serenity of the campus, which is spotlessly maintained. But unlike Dartmouth College students, who belong to the Outing Club and, depending on the season, go camping, skiing, or canoeing, half the Berry College students go home for weekends; the same kinship networks that led them to Berry College in the first place keep them close to their families of origin. One first-year student reports that he feels he has to go home every Friday afternoon to cut his mother's lawn, since the older children have all grown and flown the nest. Like most students who attend colleges near home, these students wanted to go away to college but not too far away, although a few students interviewed at Berry had applied (despite low scores that made their chances seem slim) to Vanderbilt University.

But not all evangelical colleges are rural. Birmingham-Southern College, which is United Methodist, regards itself as Christian in a way that, for example, Ohio Wesleyan, which was begun by Methodists, no longer does. It considered moving to the suburbs of Birmingham but decided to stay in the city. It aims for a recruitment of 8 percent black students, and its new president, Neal Berte, the energetic former dean of the experimental New College of the University of Alabama at Tuscaloosa, is seeking to liberalize both the curriculum and the prevalent parietal restrictions—hoping, as all such innovators must hope, that it will be possible to acquire new constituencies without losing traditional ones. As is true of many small liberal arts colleges in the Middle West and South, a Washington Semester is offered for students who want to experience a larger and quite different environment. Apparently, this strategy has paid off, for in a period of generally declining private college enrollments, Birmingham-Southern has grown from 727 students in 1975 to 1,405 in 1979.

A much more famously strict evangelical college, Oral Roberts University in Tulsa, is larger than those just described, with 3,000 students and, like Birmingham-Southern, SAT scores comfortably above the 1,000 level. Admission requires not only the

SAT but also a pastor's recommendation. Oral Roberts is described in Cass and Birnbaum (1977, p. 477) as "a 'Christ-centered' institution; it makes some religious demands on students; eight hours of theology, attendance at two chapel services each week, Sunday worship off-campus required of all students." There are neither coed dormitories nor fraternities or sororities. Again tuition is remarkably low, $1,400, and the further comment is made that "some scholarships [are] awarded on the basis of academic merit alone."

I have already mentioned the worldwide recruitment of Brigham Young University, which has over 20,000 students; here again, admission requires an interview by an ecclesiastical authority. (However, some 2 percent of BYU students are non-Mormons, attracted by its program, its reputation for friendliness despite its size, and its general moral atmosphere.) A number of years ago, most of the male students had served abroad or within the United States on the two-year mission that is required of all Mormon families who can afford it, a program now extended to young women. (One of its latent functions appeared to be to cement the faith of the evangelists, despite frequent failure to convert "godless" Dutchmen, secular Japanese, skeptical Vermonters, or inhabitants of wherever else the mission might take one.) Class attendance is required; so are courses in religion; so is obedience to the well-known Latter-day Saint prohibitions against all stimulants. Students themselves enforce a Code of Student Conduct far stricter than that observed by the fellow Mormons who form the majority at the University of Utah in Salt Lake City and at Utah State in Logan.

The Catholic Church combines a congeries of traditions, stretching back nearly 2,000 years, so that various versions of Catholicism are available both to different ethnic and national groups and to different social and intellectual strata. There is no comparable flexibility in Latter-day Saint theology, even though rigidity has been somewhat attenuated, notably by the existence of a heretical journal, *Dialogue: The Journal of Mormon Thought,* published at Stanford, which circulates widely among faculty and students on the Brigham Young campus. It is the largest campus I have visited that maintains an intense cooperative esprit de corps. In general, the Mormons take care of one another, as they notably

did during the Great Depression, and yet they are successful competitors in the country at large. Utah shares with California the
honor of sending more students on to college than any other state.
Twenty-six percent of Brigham Young students go on for further
education after BYU; they come to major university centers, including many of the leading medical schools, and join the network
of voluntary, church- and "ethnic"-related organizations that offer
some shelter against the ridicule they often receive, including until
recently what were, if aimed at individuals, unfair charges of racial
bigotry.

Because of its size and wealth and the dedication of many who
have entered academic life in service to the group, BYU has been
able to attract an superior faculty even while the Mormons occupy
places of distinction in universities throughout the United States
and overseas. And, despite intense pressures from HEW, it has
continued to resist federal intervention when this would jeopardize
its autonomy.

Maintaining religious distinctiveness can involve complex
moral issues. This was true for the Latter-day Saints during the
period when blacks were permitted to be members (and sometimes
were, especially in Africa) but not to occupy any of the graded
series of offices in the church hierarchy—a prohibition now removed by a revelation to the president of the church. Davidson
College faced a situation of ambiguity a few years ago when it
recruited a Jewish professor and asked him to sign its standard
contract, which requires faculty members to abide by the Christian
spirit of the college—a contract other Jewish faculty members had
been willing to accept. This academician sent the contract back with
a note that he accepted the conditions but wanted to warn the
college that he would seek to change the college so that such conditions—that is, of devout Christianity—would no longer prevail. At
this point, the institution, after much inner travail, decided that the
contract had been rejected despite nominal acceptance, and when
the issue became public, the college was embarrassed by what
seemed to me unfair charges of anti-Semitism. Jews can hardly be
said to be a group discriminated against or stigmatized in academic
life today. The situation would be different if Davidson College
had refused to accept Christian black professors or Jews suffi-

ciently ecumenical (or, indeed, Christian in religion) to adhere to Davidson's tenets.

"Safe" Colleges as Halfway Houses

The future of these evangelical colleges is assured for the time being, not only because parents are willing to sacrifice to keep their children away from worldly contamination but also because in these circles theological differences are regarded with a fierceness whose closest analogue at secular universities may be the divisions among various splinter groups of radicals, each "more radical than thou." Conservative Free Methodists do not want the Southern Baptists to capture their young; they maintain both their churches and their colleges in a struggle among denominations, each of which is evangelical in a different way—a pattern much more familiar in the eras of the great religious revivals of the eighteenth and early nineteenth centuries.

But it must be pointed out that theological conservatism or Biblical literalism is by no means necessarily accompanied by political conservatism, let alone reaction (although there are a good many evangelical preachers, notably with wide television audiences, who do espouse a reactionary, patrioteering politics and are eager to support politicians whose evidence of being "born again" lies in their right-wing outlook, rather than in their Christian devotion). For example, some of the smallest sects, such as the Mennonites and Mennonite Brethren, which between them sponsor half a dozen colleges, all of them tiny, are pacifist, as is the Church of the Brethren, at one time controlling seven colleges, several of which, such as LaVerne in California, have become independent of the church and have reached out for adult constituencies, running extension programs on army bases and elsewhere in order to remain afloat without altering the fundamental character of the undergraduate sectarian college. I have mentioned the Seventh-day Adventist colleges in the previous chapter; all are rather small, except for Loma Linda University, which runs one of the better medical schools in Southern California. Similarly, although Christian Reformed Calvin College in Kalamazoo is more conservative (in what I have referred to metaphorically as "colonial" fashion) than any church found in the Netherlands, many of its faculty members in the home town of Gerald Ford were active supporters of George McGovern.

The evangelical colleges have sought to maintain a traditional curriculum or, as at Mars Hill, to change the curriculum in order to maintain traditional values in new scientific and cultural settings; still, other evangelical colleges have, as already mentioned, been quite experimental. For example, the arts have a large place at Oral Roberts University, larger than in most of the traditional liberal arts colleges and universities. I have also mentioned experiments with self-paced learning at Oklahoma Christian College, founded by the Church of Christ and requiring not only a course in Bible each trimester, but daily chapel services; like many of these colleges, Oklahoma Christian College is unselective, and virtually all applicants are accepted.

Although there are considerable variations, attrition at the evangelical colleges is about at the national norm of 50 percent, and this very fact seems to me one of the virtues of these institutions, like other specialized institutions (for example, black colleges and women's colleges): they can serve as decompression chambers that make the passage from home to the larger world less traumatic for the shy or the provincial. I have talked with students attending evangelical colleges who are quite self-conscious about their choice of institution. I think, for example, of a student from a small town in the Northwest whose parents wanted her to attend Seattle Pacific University, which defines itself (Cass and Birnbaum, 1977, p. 574) as a Free Methodist "church-related university whose primary purpose 'is to serve the educational needs of the evangelical Christian community.'" She persuaded her parents to let her attend Wheaton College in Illinois, academically superior and no less evangelical, but near the metropolis of Chicago. She had, however, to contend with her high school guidance counselor, who could not see why the local institution was not good enough for her and who succeeded in talking her sister, who had been admitted to both Wheaton and Stanford, out of attending either.

Students who have never been far from home either geographically or metaphorically often find after a year or two that they can navigate in larger waters. They also may want a greater diversity of programs than most of the small evangelical colleges offer; if they are extremely bright, they are apt to "run out of school" even though increasing efforts are made to retain them not only for the sake of their tuitions but also because attrition, as guidance counselors and admissions recruiters invariably declare, looks bad on a college's record. Students will sometimes also attend such a college to please their parents and, having done so for a time, feel free to move into a larger academic universe.

Students often joke about the restrictions to which they are subjected in the denominational colleges, and I have mentioned a "dance-in" at Southern Baptist Wake Forest. But at Berry College, for example, students chafed less at the restrictions imposed by the institution itself than at being harried by crusading zealots among their fellow students who regarded them as insufficiently devout and kept after them to become born-again Christians—a kind of perpetual revivalism that created frictions in a college one of whose appeals lay in its promise of cooperative harmony. Of course, on a campus as large as Brigham Young University, conflicts between the substantial minority of political liberals and even radicals among the faculty and students and the tendency in recent decades to turn the church in a right-wing direction under the influence of such leaders as Ezra Taft Benson could not be submerged and indeed served to diminish the warmth of the campus without violating the campuswide norms of civility and gentleness.

As the Amish and the Hutterites recognized, there is really no such thing as a "safe" college in America. All the dozens of sects that have established their own colleges were creating what might be thought of as halfway houses that at once try to keep young people in the fold and make them sufficiently *au courant* with contemporary scientific knowledge and changing esthetic conventions so that they will not leave the fold altogether to attend secular colleges. Even today, as if the battle over Darwin and evolution were still a vital one, many faculty members in secular institutions (in a manner reminiscent of H. L. Mencken or the less frequently read writings of Mark Twain or Thorstein Veblen) enjoy ridiculing what Veblen termed "devout observances."[3]

[3] In conversations over many years with devout students at Harvard and Radcliffe, I have been repeatedly struck by the intrusive cruelty of roommates and other fellow students whose vaunted tolerance does not extend to those who do not share their

It would be as absurd to contend that the evangelical colleges are invariably the "safe" colleges they appear to be as to claim that priests invariably adhere to their vows of chastity, poverty, and obedience. Even though honor codes, when they work, are probably the most effective devices for policing campus conduct (as they seem to be at the University of Virginia) that exist in American academia, I know of one campus with intense moral cohesion where several women students refused to testify before a student-faculty honor court against a popular black student where the penalty would have been automatic dismissal. (The student in question, after the current fashion, brought his lawyer to the hearing; in an unusual move, the institution's president dismissed the court, saying that it would have to bear an unfair responsibility and that he would personally recommend to the board of trustees that the student be dismissed. The story has a happy ending: the young man returned after a year's probation to pay his own tuition in order to be able to graduate, and he was grateful in the end that he had not been granted "most favored nation" treatment.)

Secularization of the Once-Catholic Colleges

The college just mentioned is Catholic, and it does have a certain cohesion, but many readers will have noted, I would imagine, that up to this point I have not mentioned Catholic colleges as among those maintaining not only overt student deference but internalized student acquiescence in Christian campus norms. In fact, I do not know a single Catholic college of which this can today be said. It would not be too farfetched to suggest that a kind of Protestant Reformation has occurred within Catholicism in the Western world and that, as more and more religious have "kicked the habit" and laicized the institutions, one cannot speak of a truly Catholic college

---

own moral relativism. I have also been appalled by the way professors, especially in an earlier day, would give lectures on American history ridiculing the "excesses" of revivalistic movements and describing such indigenous denominations as Mormonism in a spirit of hilarious debunking, wholly insensitive to Mormons in their audience—professors who would be preternaturally sensitive about any derogatory comments concerning black students and (today) meticulous in their use of such nonsexist neologisms as *chairperson*. Among Harvard professors and some New England students, these attitudes may represent a residue of anti–Irish Catholic intolerance.

in the way that one can speak, say, of a Mennonite college or a Southern Baptist college. In 1964, when Father Theodore Hesburgh, president of the University of Notre Dame, addressed the National Catholic Education Association at its annual meeting in Atlantic City, he was regarded by many of the priests and sisters in his audience as a heretic. But in the fall of the same year, when Monsignor Ivan Illich was one of the leaders of a meeting of the Sister Formation Movement held at Marquette University, Illich was regarded, in all his charisma, as something of a hero, and many of the sisters who heard him journeyed to his center at Cuernavaca for study with him and his group. Only a few years after the Catholic colleges and universities had been attacked for their anti-intellectualism and their backwardness when compared with their secular counterparts by John Courtney Murray, S.J., Thomas O'Dea, Monsignor John Tracy Ellis, Philip Gleason, Robert Hassenger, James Trent, and many other Catholic intellectuals, a number of the Catholic colleges moved into the very forefront of what was then the academic avant-garde.

Elizabeth Sewell's Bensalem College at Fordham University (Sewell, 1973) was perhaps the most poignant illustration of the lengths to which Catholics were prepared to go to shed traditions regarded as academically insulating and confining (see Jerome, 1970). As I once put it, Fordham University moved so quickly as to leave behind its well-to-do Papal Legate–type Catholic donors before it was in a position to compete with more obviously secular institutions for cosmopolitan donors of all faiths; its president, Leo McLaughlin, S.J., was let go to be replaced by the more prudent and managerially adept former president of Boston College, Michael Shea, S.J. (In a move characteristic of many religious at the time, Father McLaughlin went to teach writing at predominantly black Johnson C. Smith University in Charlotte and in turn left there to run the tutorial program at a state college, Ramapo College in New Jersey, having in the meantime, like so many others, left the order.)

Indeed, although the evangelical impulse within Catholicism has not created any new Catholic colleges or even maintained on an even keel such pioneering innovations as Sister Jacqueline Grennan's Webster College, which took the lead in science education, or the other college run by the Sisters of Loretto (Loretto Heights College in Denver), evangelical ex-religious are to be found in many of the more experimental secular institutions today, just as one finds a divinity degree in the background of many of the reformers in the more innovative once-Protestant or public liberal arts colleges. No wonder that every year in its annual education issue the intellectual Catholic weekly, *Commonweal*, carries an article with a title such as "What Is Catholic About the Catholic College?" In one case, in a conservative archdiocese headed by Cardinal McIntyre in Los Angeles, the Sisters of the Immaculate Heart of Mary turned Immaculate Heart College into one of the most avant-garde institutions in the country, most noted perhaps for the work of the graphic artist Sister Corita. The college's combination of political and countercultural radicalism so offended the cardinal that, with the aid of the Vatican, he got the order suspended from the church, so that the remaining religious formed themselves into a lay sisterhood in order to maintain their separate identity.

The only new sects apt to be formed by Catholicism are the ultratraditionalist ones, such as that formed in Cambridge, Massachusetts, some years ago by Father Feeney, who was defrocked for insisting that there was no salvation outside the Catholic Church. Still, there are several small Catholic colleges that are struggling to revive traditions not very different from those of the two St. John's Colleges; tiny St. Thomas Aquinas College, which has a core curriculum and systematic devotions but is not yet accredited, is an example. The diocesan University of Dallas, a small institution with high standards that started as a graduate school, is a conservative institution in a relatively conservative area, with required class attendance and a fairly structured curriculum, but no religion courses are required. Furthermore, since it exists in a major metropolitan center and half the students commute, it cannot achieve the cohesion of an institution such as Mars Hill or Berry College. Correspondingly, the ambitions of its students, like those at most Catholic colleges, are primarily vocational and secondarily academic. Few Catholic colleges can be classified as "collegiate" in the Clark-Trow typology: virtually none permit fraternities or sororities—and only a handful, such as IHC (as Immaculate Heart College prefers to be known) or Manhattanville, offer lures to the nonconformist.

If we return, then, to our focus on the question whether in these more or less religious institutions the academic revolution has subordinated the student body to internalization of faculty values, the answer would seem generally to be in the affirmative for the evangelical Protestant colleges and in the negative for the once-Catholic colleges. But the former groups subordinated the students to an ethos that combines religious values with the ethical neutrality traditional in the American campus culture; these transcendent norms dictate the nature of the curriculum, within the limits imposed by vocational and academic aspirations. And although these colleges cannot in fact provide the safety or insurance they appear to promise, what they can do is to give moral aid and comfort to students who on cosmopolitan campuses would feel like misfits. What seems hypocrisy to many is an effort to validate consensual norms even while recognizing that they will sometimes be violated in practice. The evangelical colleges offer a partial and temporary escape from freedom—an enclave that is neither total nor totalitarian.

6

Student Power in the Public Community Colleges

Community colleges have always offered students what many see as a virtue—namely, minimal commitment. (An exception is transfer students, who may have to meet certain minimal requirements at four-year institutions—a diminishing constraint as the four-year institutions become more and more eager for students, any students.) This is the very opposite of the subordination demanded by institutions that experienced the academic revolution or maintained the combination of the academic and the religious found in evangelical colleges. Virtually all community colleges depend on the automobile and suit their schedules to part-time students, generally older (the average age at one Boston institution is 27.4) and often married.

The public community colleges have been the fastest-growing segment of American postsecondary education and have, in a time of retrenchment, maintained until recently the highest morale and—like the evangelical colleges, but for different reasons—enormous flexibility. They differ almost as much from one another as four-year state colleges do; what they have in common is that they began with an orientation to serve the community. (All but a few of them illustrated this by changing their names from "junior" to "community" colleges.) The faculties have not lost hegemony, because they never had it. They were from the beginning subject to two sources of authority: first, the administration, often headed by hard-driving, entrepreneurial presidents, and, second, an increasingly far-flung network of students of all ages and virtually every conceivable interest whom the faculty was hired to serve.

Clark Kerr speaks of the "multiversity" as a bazaar, and many have spoken of the academic supermarket, referring to large, comprehensive state and undistinguished private universities. But there are limits to what the multiversity will offer, limits tested, for example, in the battles over black studies and over credit for the arts, discussed in Chapter Four. Increasingly, though there is dispute in major institutions, credit is given for "experiential learning," especially when some analytic framework can be found for describing and testing this (see Commission on Non-Traditional Study, 1973). Learning at a distance, as in the new Center for Distance Learning of New York State's Empire State College or in the University of Mid-America (see Chapter Four), is increasingly recognized for credit in transferring into major universities. In general, there is an effort to test in nontraditional ways in assessing nontraditional student bodies (Carnegie Council on Policy Studies in Higher Education, 1979b; Cross, 1971, 1976). We shall see in the chapters that follow that, with increasing market power in the hands of students even at the great research universities, the line has become blurred between the market power of the customer in the multiversity and in the community colleges, where it is assumed that, whatever any seven persons want, the college will find someone to teach it to them. When this happens at the multiversity, traditional faculty members are resistant and resentful; they feel that they did not enter academic life to teach basket weaving or to be part of an institution where basket weaving earns as many credits as physical chemistry. The community college, however, never set such limits on what is appropriate: defining its mission as service to the community, it was there to supply whatever was demanded and to create demand by imaginative supply. And here there was no bashfulness about advertising—a bashfulness quickly being shed by four-year institutions as well (Fiske, 1979c).

In many states, such as California, the community colleges grew directly out of the high schools and drew much of their original faculty from the high schools, being in effect the thirteenth and fourteenth grades of the local school system—differing from the K through 12 grades in that attendance was voluntary. As it is sometimes put by self-derogatory students themselves, community colleges were "high schools with ashtrays." Correspondingly, the president had much of the authority of a superintendent of schools or a local principal. In the transfer or liberal arts programs faculty members might have master's degrees, as they might also have in some of the terminal vocational programs—but high school teachers too might have these in states that require more schooling for teacher certification than a baccalaureate, as in California, where a postbaccalaureate year is required if one is to teach in the public schools. But hardly any Ph.D.s taught in community colleges (some hid their Ph.D.s lest they appear "overqualified"); generally, the president and sometimes the dean have held the Ed.D., just as the superintendent of schools in a major school district might.

And, like the public schools, the community colleges were among the first where unionization took hold—in part as protection against arbitrary discharge by presidents believed to be tyrannical, in part because there never was the ethos of academic professionalism that made the union movement seem not wholly appropriate. In other words, community college faculty members experienced only at considerable remove the victory of the faculty that Jencks and I termed the "academic revolution"; if they achieved through unionization some independence from the local authorities, they might feel that they had a bit more control over their local union representative (if not over the national union— generally, the National Education Association) than over their president or the state community college system. Since many community college teachers do not identify closely with the academic disciplines from which those came who teach the liberal arts and sciences, and very few are connected with the national disciplines either through attending meetings or through writing for the refereed journals, community college teachers did not experience the academic revolution in the form of a victory of departmentalized faculty members over administrative and outside controls. Correspondingly, since many community college teachers have in only modest degree come to regard themselves as independent professionals, linked through their academic goals to similar professionals everywhere, they felt little loss of prestige from the student protest movements of the 1960s, although as individuals they may, like faculty members everywhere, suffer from the exercise of student market power.

Like any generalizations, the foregoing are subject to many qualifications; one must disaggregate among community colleges. Some relatively new community colleges have acquired quite independent-minded faculty members. While it lasted, Staten Island Community College, which was part of CUNY, was a place of radical ferment under the presidency of William Birenbaum, who became president of a dying Antioch College network when the community college was merged with Richmond College to become the four-year College of Staten Island (Birenbaum, 1971). Inver Hills Community College in a suburb of the Twin Cities has a faculty probably of greater independence than in near-bankrupt private institutions, because it is relatively new, attractive, and growing. And, within community colleges, faculty members in technical programs of restricted entry, such as nursing or occupational therapy, have power as gatekeepers that those in the liberal arts segments of the same college lack. The prevalent notion among critics of community colleges who see them only as ways of "reproducing" social structure (in terms borrowed from the French scholar Pierre Bourdieu) is that the transfer programs are the partly open door to upward mobility, and the vocational programs are a form of "tracking" that puts a ceiling on further advance and keeps the poor in their place (Karabel, 1972). Whatever may have been the case in an earlier day, the technical programs are today often those most overapplied because of their ready vocational utility; transfer from the technical programs of a community college to similar programs in four-year institutions appears to be no more difficult than transfer from the community college liberal arts programs to the upper division in comprehensive state or private institutions (see Lavin, Alba, and Silberstein, 1979). In fact, transfer into the Bachelor of Technology degree program at the University of Connecticut is likely to be easier from technical community colleges than from the regular, larger chain of community colleges, although qualified graduates of both the technical colleges and the regional community colleges may transfer to Central Connecticut State College and in two years usually complete the requirements for a bachelor's degree in industrial technology. The dean of engineering at the University of Connecticut writes: "Community college graduates are much less likely to ever be admitted to our engineering program compared to technical college graduates" (personal communications from Peter W. McFadden, Dean of Engineering, University of Connecticut; Donald H. Winandy, Coordinator of Planning and Academic Affairs, Connecticut Board of Higher Education). Similarly, Springfield Technical College in Massachusetts probably has the highest standing of any of the state's community colleges, and its students are courted by the public and private institutions in western Massachusetts (information from interviews by William Neumann and discussions with state education officials, 1976–1980).

A sense of the great diversity among community colleges is enhanced by a visit to the three campuses of Miami-Dade Community College in Florida, which an informal survey (Johnson, 1979) showed to be the ideal toward which many community colleges strive: Miami-Dade, under the energetic presidency of Peter Masiko, Jr., has 55,000 students; it clearly has more appeal than a great many four-year institutions, public and private, and it is so huge that it is unlikely that the president can oversee every action of the faculty, even through a chain of academic-bureaucratic command. The faculty may feel a certain security, and in Florida, where some major baccalaureate institutions have no lower division, it is taken as a matter of course that the majority of postsecondary students will enter a community college and then after two years, if they have taken the proper courses and wish to do so, will transfer to one of the regional upper-division state universities or to one of the state universities that recruit, with greater or lesser selectivity, a generally restricted number of freshmen and sophomores. But it does not follow that students at the college at Santa Fe, in the Gainesville area, which sends many of its students on to the University of Florida but is small and undistinguished, or students at Manatee Junior College in Bradenton, north of Sarasota, who can continue at the Sarasota or St. Petersburg branch of the University of South Florida, feel as self-confident as typical students at Miami-Dade.

Community colleges have outreach programs resembling programs for adult education in many high schools whose buildings are used afternoons and evenings. It has become a major part of the mission not only of the community colleges but also of many four-year institutions to provide evening and weekend courses for adults. Moreover, some of the best educational television is now being produced by community colleges that prepare programs for a national audience, programs aired during hours of little commercial value in the early morning.

Transfer Students and Terminal Students

Statewide Problems of Articulation. In an earlier day and to some extent still at present, students intending to transfer have faced the question of how many of their community college credits would prove acceptable at a four-year institution. In some states, such as Georgia, Florida, and California, articulation is almost guaranteed; Florida has the same course-numbering system for community colleges and upper-division and four-year institutions. Georgia has a compact requiring the state university and other four-year institutions to give full credit for courses passed at whatever level, designated as appropriate for transfer, in a community or unselective four-year institution.

Since the implication is that students will need only two years of further college-level work before securing their baccalaureates, the squeeze on the institution to which they have transferred can be intense—especially when, as in Florida, the legislature has mandated the possibility of a three-year degree, in part as a money-saving measure for the state and in part as a presumed option for the students.[1] These difficulties were evident to me on visiting the first upper-division university in the United States, Florida Atlantic University in Boca Raton, in 1964, shortly after it opened. A number of faculty members with "good" degrees had been recruited on the promise that they would teach only upper-division students and master's candidates; presumably a doctoral program lay in the offing. But what they found was that students who had taken a smattering of liberal arts courses in a community college were turn-

[1] The Florida legislature declared its indebtedness to the monograph of the Carnegie Commission on Higher Education (1971) entitled *Less Time, More Options,* which plugged the three-year degree but hardly expected it to be applied to such instances of excessive compression.

ing up with a desire to study political science, for example, without having had any courses in history or in other fields that the political scientists would regard as appropriate preparation. Faculty members discovered that they had, as it were, to let down ladders to give these students a rudimentary background—and then somehow manage to squeeze in a major in their field in the allotted two-year span. At the University of Georgia in Athens, similar problems arise with transfers from community colleges who wish to major in music or in the plastic arts. Departmental requirements include ability to perform on an instrument for entry into the major in music and a portfolio or other work for entry into the plastic arts. Transfer students may arrive having taken courses designated as suitable for transfer but not meeting these requirements. The present situation is reported to be a stalemate, with the registrar at Athens occasionally finding ways to avoid any direct confrontation with the statewide compact on transfers.

The "Cooling Out" Thesis. Twenty years ago, when researchers in California (Burton Clark, Leland Medsker, Arthur Cohen) were studying community colleges, the spotlight was on the transfer students. In that state, community colleges were seen as a kind of moat built by the Master Plan of 1960 (designed in part by Clark Kerr) around the University of California, protecting it from having to take inept students in as freshmen. The Master Plan allowed the community colleges to screen students, often giving them better instruction than they would have received at the lower-division level of state four-year colleges and universities, and permitting transfer to the University of California if they had taken appropriate liberal arts courses and maintained a certain grade-point average—formerly B, now reduced to C.

Burton Clark's well-known essay "The 'Cooling Out' Function in Higher Education" (1960a) borrowed a phrase from Erving Goffman's use of the con-man argot of "cooling out the mark" (that is, the sucker). Clark described community college counselors and faculty members as skilled in convincing the lower socioeconomic strata that they had had a crack at higher education while gently persuading them that they were not "college material." When this essay was published, presumably based mostly on Clark's experience in California, it was the transfer program that had status in the community colleges, not the terminal vocational programs. I recall a dedicated professor of English in one of the Los Angeles community colleges who reported a number of years ago that, if one should tell a black student who was eighteen years old and hence entitled to attend but who had received a fourth-grade education in Louisiana that he really was not suitable for the transfer program but might do well in ceramics, given the need for people in this field and his manual dexterity, the student would react with charges of racism and threats to bring the NAACP into a case against the condescending, if kindly, professor. This attitude then prevalent among black students represented a traditional attitude, characteristic of the black education of the Negro colleges of the South and border states—namely, that blacks wanted a "real college," not some "junior" substitute. If they entered a community college, therefore, it was only en route to a "real" four-year institution. No wonder that Clark (1960b) described the open door as commonly becoming a revolving door. (See Medsker, 1960; but compare Clark, 1980.)

But London's (1978) participant-observation study of a community college (overwhelmingly white) in Boston suggests that the high attrition characteristic of transfer programs in community colleges reflects not so much the "cooling out" effort by counselors and faculty members (who, on the contrary, often struggle in vain to retain students, whether out of interest in the students' fates or interest in their own financial security) as the experimental and tentative way in which these students approach the community college in the first instance: They will give it a try, but, having already learned to dislike school and to mistrust themselves as scholars, they are ready to take flight at the first sign of difficulty or defeat. Often, they leave without notice to anyone, picking up their last Veterans Administration or other state or federal grant before taking off. Many return to postsecondary education, perhaps at another community college, perhaps at a four-year college. (This statement is based on a limited study of transcripts of students in public postsecondary institutions in Massachusetts, where a record of stopping out and stopping in may turn up five institutions in the course of a student's eventually securing a bachelor's degree.)

From "Cooling Out" to "Cultural Reproduction." Varying among states and institutions, the whole tilt of community college programs in the 1970s was away from preoccupation with transfer students and toward students securing a terminal degree with immediate prospects for employment. As already indicated, it is at this point that many community colleges become selective. Fields of relatively ready employment and those requiring elaborate equipment and skilled instruction are heavily oversubscribed, while the transfer programs may serve as holding stations for those students who have been denied entry to programs in electronics, health care, occupational therapy, and many other fields. Indeed, these same vocational programs are now sought after by students one might term "reverse transfers," who have completed a liberal arts baccalaureate that they find unmarketable and then have turned to the community colleges for programs that promise them immediate vocational payoff (Riesman, 1978b). In all such cases, the community college does serve as an open door, even as a second-chance institution, contrary to the assessment made by radical critics who, going well beyond the descriptive accounts by Clark or Medsker cited earlier, see community colleges as part of a tacit conspiracy by the capitalist elite to reserve places in status-conferring institutions for their own offspring while giving the relatively deprived the illusion of equality of opportunity through colleges that impose a ceiling on aspiration and, at best, offer through their terminal programs a road to dead-end jobs (Karabel, 1972; Tinto, 1977).

The belief that these programs impose a ceiling on students and make later transfer unlikely is consistent with the judgment that students who in high school are "tracked" into vocational programs are also condemned to dead-end jobs and have no chance for careers—*career* being defined in terms of major professional and managerial advancement, as well as constituting a retrospective judgment on a series of positions an individual has held which may not have been part of an original plan but add up to some kind of personal commitment, no matter what degree of alienation the individual may feel. However valid this picture may have been in an earlier era, limited probings at present indicate its overaggregated extravagance. Many people do not graduate from technical programs because they get jobs after a year or so, sometimes in co-op arrangements. Attrition, though seen by critics and often by the institution as a bad sign, may thus in fact be a success story: A student has landed a job without having to acquire all the credentials. In many cases, the employer will see to any further (generally part-time) education, either in intramural courses or in later subsidized return for further education, often at the baccalaureate and postbaccalaureate levels. The same is true of those who graduate from technical colleges, as noted above.

In the Northeast, perhaps especially New England, where private higher education has long had hegemony and ethnic defensiveness has been endemic, it is clear that entry into a community college often does signify a willingness to accept a ceiling on aspiration. But it is equally true that many such entrants are testing higher education rather than being tested by it; very little is at stake in the student's sense of adequacy. Indeed, many students feel so inadequate that they are threatened by a serious test and do not want to risk it. Others are equally threatened by the possibility of success, which would remove them from their families, neighborhoods, and peer groups. Recall in this connection the scorn for the "college boys" that the author of *Street Corner Society* himself, William F. Whyte, Jr. (1943), though a Harvard Junior Fellow, shared with the "corner boys." Often these students respond to their feelings of insecurity by showing their contempt for the institution through their behavior in class, as in the giggling and insolent behavior of women students in the secretarial sciences program—even though these students were diligent enough in their actual secretarial exercises—reported in London (1978).

Undoubtedly, at the community college described by London, the faculty is in charge for the most part only in the terminal programs. But even in such programs, as in secretarial science class or in police science and fire science, the students take charge, and instructors are in the position of supplicants begging for a modicum of order and attention—again an extension of high school to the thirteenth and fourteenth grades. To this judgment, the older women returning to community colleges for further education are a distinct exception; they are highly motivated and serious students, often disgusted by what they see as the still-adolescent behavior of the majority of students, who act as if, in

Paul Goodman's famous phrase, growing up were indeed absurd, and they hoped to put if off as long as possible.

As Howard London observes on the basis of informal conversations and interviews with students, and as I have myself in a less systematic way found in discussion with students at the same institution, many of them described themselves as having "messed up" in high school: they were periodically truant; they engaged in a considerable amount of vandalism; on leaving high school, the young men took mainly blue-collar jobs, and they sometimes declared how there also they had "messed up," one boasting that he had been fired from six jobs for failure to show up or other dereliction. A sizable number, now slowly diminishing, entered the armed services or the merchant marine, and their attendance at the local community college recently built in their neighborhood was motivated in considerable part by the bribe offered for college attendance; as a few students said to Howard London, "It beats working."[2]

It is clear from London's interviews, as well as from the few my research assistants have conducted, that these students, while they were in high school, were not considered, and did not consider themselves, "college material." As one student told London, "All during high school, college was the furthest thing from my mind. . . . When I graduated, I didn't want to work. . . . I didn't do anything except swim during the summer, and then I heard about this place. So I wound up here through nobody's fault except my own." Or as another student remarked, though he was offered a scholarship at a local university, going to college then "wasn't in my plans. No one else in my family went to college. . . . I found out about here. I used to think I was lucky because I used to think I didn't have to go to college" (1978, p. 16).

Twenty-five years earlier, Kahl (1953) had studied Boston public school senior boys of relatively high intelligence from working-class families of sufficient income so as not to need to

---

[2] Grant (1972b) commented apropos of the much-praised Higher Education Act amendments of 1972, which provided federal grants for college attendance by students from low-income families, that students were in effect being bribed to support postsecondary education while being given no equivalent support for learning a skilled trade, let alone starting a small business.

have their sons start working immediately for purposes of family support. Matching boys whose fathers supported their college attendance with those whose fathers in effect said, "Do you think you're better than me?," Kahl concluded that boys did not attend college when it would have indicated a rejection of their fathers, a statement that "the old man" was not worth much. But that was an era when the "capital" that fathers possessed was often the power to locate their sons in construction jobs or other skilled trades and when blue-collar work was not so widely seen as demeaning or, in current parlance, as "dead end" or "meaningless" work.

Kahl's study was done at a time when only a minority of students in working-class high schools went on to any sort of college and when graduation from high school was not automatic, but required at least a certain modicum of motivation to learn. The curriculum was already considerably diluted as a consequence of the "Life Adjustment" school of thought, but still, by today's standards, schools were orderly and relatively free of violence.

In the last quarter-century, with the vast expansion of both high school graduation and college attendance, the aspirations of young people have greatly expanded. However, neither the level of effort many young people are willing to exert in public school nor the effort and ability of their teachers has risen to meet these aspirations; rather, both have fallen, and the quality of public school education has declined, as highlighted by the falling test scores. (See, for example, College Entrance Examination Board, 1977, particularly pt. 4; also National Academy of Education, 1978.) Nevertheless, white students coming from family backgrounds such as those studied by Kahl are today inclined to attend college: they fear that their fathers and uncles can no longer place them in the construction trades, in part because of affirmative action requirements, and their parents have urged them to attend college in a society where the whole neighborhood—in terms used by realtors—has been tipped toward college and it is easier to attend than not to. As already stated, whites now attend college with test scores that once would have signaled them to stay away from college, although blacks with such scores have been attending Negro colleges for generations; open admissions has brought more moderately able and moderately well-to-do whites into CUNY than the nonwhites for whom the arrangements were originally made (Lavin, Alba, and Silberstein, 1979).

At the denominational colleges discussed in Chapter Four, students with such levels of tested aptitude are often "overachievers," diligently working to compensate for their academic liabilities. In contrast, London's ethnography describes the way students in a public community college put severe peer pressure on one another to punish "rate busters," or "DARs" (Damned Average Raisers). They preferred to humiliate the teacher by disorderly conduct and refusal to attend class regularly, let alone to do the required readings, to the risk of making a real effort that might turn out to be worthless and thus prove the inadequacy that was an underlying source of anxiety for them; they behaved like those few students in selective colleges who unconsciously fail to set the alarm clock and oversleep an examination that, they fear, might reveal their incompetence.

These problems were least acute for faculty members in vocational programs who did not come from liberal arts backgrounds, but were themselves craftsmen, teaching such subjects as television repair or such middle-class skills as accounting or computer programming. As the shift from the older term *junior college* to the prevailing one, *community college*, implies, these institutions and their leadership were oriented not to higher education and its traditional values and standards but to the community at large, which they were serving both by preparing students for the labor force and by postponing their entry into it, by providing adult education both for credit and for recreational purposes, and often by their open accessibility as community centers for all kinds of voluntary activities.

Morale and Momentum in the Community Colleges

Some community college presidents have taken precautions lest faculty members in the liberal arts and transfer programs should have an opportunity to feel any superiority of status over those without academic degrees who are teaching in the vocational and technical areas. For example, in the St. Louis community college district, under the leadership of President Joseph Cosand, later chairman of the American Council on Education and director of

the University of Michigan Center for the Study of Higher Education, the faculty was split up in such a way as to avoid the formation
of departmental cliques: thus a teacher of literature would have an
office next to a shop instructor. In the present academic market,
when community colleges have been continuing to expand and
Ph.D.s from leading universities have sought positions teaching in
them, community college presidents have been wary about these
candidates as "overqualified" and as likely to be dissatisfied.[3] When
they have been recruited, they have been told in so many words,
"This isn't Harvard," which is a declaration of anti-intellectualism:
any faculty member who tries to teach as if this were an Ivy League
college will not last long.[4] In effect, the new faculty member is
being warned that any attempt greatly to raise the level of instruction will prove both unsuccessful and frustrating.

Like the evangelical colleges, community colleges are *sui
generis*. Since the academic revolution scarcely touched them, the
academic counterrevolution had only marginal consequences. Student disaffection may be slightly greater now than earlier because
of the general rise of permissiveness in the society, particularly in
the secondary schools. It is especially in the transfer programs,
which focus on liberal arts, rather than in the overapplied technical
ones, that community college students are apt to see themselves as
"back in school," with all the hostility toward teacher and dislike of
study acquired in school, through both personal experience and
peer-group outlook. Only as more and more teachers unable to get
positions in four-year institutions gravitate to community colleges
will there develop among faculty members the feelings of victimiza-
tion that we shall find in subsequent sections to be endemic at

---

[3] In this respect, as in so many others, community colleges are not identical. I recall
visiting Cape Cod Community College in Hyannis, Massachusetts, in 1969, when it
occupied an old high school and was preparing to move to a handsome new campus
being built outside the town; I remarked to the president that it seemed to me he
had a remarkable number of Ph.D.s on the faculty, and did this not lead to resentment among some of these faculty members? He replied that a number of them had
held tenured positions in universities, including one professor from Boston University, and had moved to Hyannis, on Cape Cod, as a pleasant place to live and to
bring up children, and some of these men and women were among the most committed of the faculty members.

[4] For a statistical portrait of community college faculties, see Cohen and Brawer
(1977); for a critique, see Birenbaum (1971).

underapplied four-year institutions. Such faculty members may vent on the community colleges their resentment at having to cater to students' desire to be entertained and to be passed on through social promotion—resentment they would feel quite as much in many four-year institutions.

All this is not to suggest that community college administrators feel superior to their counterparts in four-year institutions. In spite of their immense growth, with the doubling of numbers and the quintupling of students in the 1960s, there is still an edge of defensiveness to be seen in issues of the monthly put out by the American Association of Community and Junior Colleges, *Community and Junior College Journal.* And at the annual meeting of the association in Atlanta in April 1978, it seemed apparent that the institutional representatives wanted to hear the praise they received from the leading figures who served as speakers, such as Ernest Boyer, then United States Commissioner of Education; they were still sufficiently on the defensive to need to be told what a marvelous job they were doing.

Furthermore, Proposition 13 in California, which hit at the property tax from which California community colleges derive much of their revenue, has dampened the sense of expansion and momentum that the community colleges have held while four-year institutions have been in a period of stagnation or even decline. With enrollments threatened by the gas shortage in some institutions and funds jeopardized by taxpayer revolts in others, the community colleges may lose their sense of independence from the general fate of academia—whatever ambivalence their administrators may feel toward that independence and whatever wish they may have to be considered a substantial segment of the entire post-secondary educational enterprise.[5]

As the older generation of former high school teachers dies out and community college faculty members are increasingly people with M.A.s (who often have their baccalaureates from excellent liberal arts colleges), the relative insulation of the community colleges from the problems facing four-year institutions begins to diminish. By no means are all teachers in the community colleges

[5] For the reaction of a community college president and his associates to the hegemony of student "consumers," see Vaughan, Elosser, and Flynn (1976).

simply jobholders, themselves commuters, doing the minimum at work that demands fewer hours than high school teaching, allows them to be called "Professor," and pays somewhat higher salaries. There are also many in the liberal arts programs who are devoted to redeeming the potential which they believe, in their egalitarian zeal, to lie concealed in every student and which they have managed to uncover in some previously unmotivated students. Such faculty members want to introduce their students to a world of wider horizons and even to high culture, as in the case of one English professor at a community college who bought tickets to the local theater for her students—and found that many did not show at the appointed place and hour.

The way such efforts can miscarry is graphically illustrated in London's (1978) account. One quotation (pp. 69–70) is typical; London is talking in the student lounge with Steve and Jan, two students in the fire science program:

> We talk about hockey for a while, and the bell rings. They decide to skip Ashley's class. After a few more minutes I ask what they thought of Ashley [a social science teacher].
>
> Jan: "The first week of classes she told us about her background, how she taught at some exclusive private school. It seems the whole semester she's been talking down to us like she was on some kind of platform. I know a lot of guys don't like that. You can bet your ass that's why we're not in class right now."
>
> Steve agrees.

Or again (pp. 75–76):

> Costello [the teacher of a law-enforcement class] begins by saying that he wants to discuss a short newspaper article on the death penalty. He reads the article and says, "It would be interesting to discuss the death penalty, wouldn't it?" Three students say, "No," rather loudly, look at each other, and smile. Costello begins discussing the death penalty as if he had not heard their remarks.

Those instructors fare no better who seek to identify themselves with the students as working-class, regarding them as victims of a system of purposeful educational stratification and seeking to "radicalize" them. These efforts readily boomerang, as in the case of an English teacher who uses crane operators to illustrate a low-status working-class occupation and is responded to by a male student who says defiantly, " 'In my neighborhood, construction workers have high status.' A number of students cheer. The students resent the anti-American remarks made by the teacher, and the class gets out of hand" (pp. 78–79).

In the interviewing my research assistants and I have done with community college faculty members and counselors, we have found a number who started out with idealistic hopes and a sense of mission, some of them rejecting other opportunities and choosing to teach in the community college in order to work with students who in the past had had less opportunity and who generally came from working-class backgrounds. Many of these faculty idealists, to employ again a phrase often used, were "burned out." They had found that their idealism was exhausting even when not misplaced. It brought them few rewards in terms of student response; more experienced colleagues regarded them as naive and occasionally as irritants. "Burnout" is certainly not confined to community colleges: it is endemic in a great variety of academic settings. (It is, for example, quite common at the more experimental colleges, where faculty members become exhausted by the constant demands of omnivorous students and by the meetings occasioned because of the fluidity of the curriculum and the initial belief in participatory democracy; see Grant and Riesman, 1978, pp. 103–104, 324–325.)

If one studies the catalogues of community colleges, it is evident that a large number of their presidents have a doctorate in education, with a specialty in the administration of higher education, from one of the great state or land-grant universities or occasionally from a private institution such as Teachers College of Columbia or the Stanford or Harvard Graduate School of Education. Quite a few, however, do have their degrees in a discipline, which is the characteristic route for other segments of postsecondary education, where presidents climb the academic ladder within a field, perhaps become heads of departments, then academic deans or vice-presidents for academic affairs, and then are chosen, often by another institution, in a presidential search. As I have emphasized, the ethos of many community college presidents is that they are there to serve the community's wants as the community defines these; if there is demand for a course in how to play bridge, it is of no consequence to them that such a course would not be deemed appropriately "academic" in most four-year institutions. But in this as in other matters, there are exceptions, and occasional community college presidents have placed limits on what they consider appropriate work for credit, and to the extent that the market allows, they share the outlook of many faculty members who have come from arts and sciences backgrounds and who seek to maintain as best they can the standards instilled in them in their own student days. Still, it remains true in general that student sovereignty has been exercised through the administration's ability to change the inventory rapidly, as some "product lines" appear to sell more quickly while others move slowly or not at all. And, as we have seen, the very growth of community colleges has provided momentum, if not a clear and well-defined sense of mission. Along with growth, tenure has been almost automatic for faculty members who have proved themselves at least moderately flexible and adaptable. (As in the public schools, the probationary period is generally short, often no more than two years.)

In a number of states, the decline of enrollments seems to have been most severe in the unselective four-year state colleges (many of them former teacher's colleges and unprepared for the dramatic drop in the demand for schoolteachers) and similar unselective and undistinctive private four-year colleges. In some states even now, virtually the entire student population could find room in the community colleges, plus the major flagship and land-grant state universities. One result is to blur the distinction between community and four-year colleges, as the latter scramble to institute their own vocational programs, adapt themselves to part-time students who can come to class only in the late afternoon, evenings, and weekends, and vigorously pursue the market for returning adults. It is time to turn to the consequences of student hegemony in these four-year institutions, the ones that in greater or lesser degree are in the position of having experienced an academic revolution and are now faced with the counterrevolution.

7

The Free Market, "Marginal Differentiation," and Restrictions on Diversity

In the preceding pages, I trust I have indicated that, at both the two-year and four-year levels, American postsecondary education is extraordinarily diverse in terms of institutions and even more so in terms of programs and enclaves within institutions. However, the more competitive the market situation becomes, the more likely is the development of what economists call "marginal differentiation," in which institutions will not take the risk of departing radically from what appear to be consumer wants, but will only offer slight divergencies from the standard brands in order to have a basis for advertising and to claim a share of the mass market.

In an essay on consumer behavior, a collaborator and I described the ways in which consumers also do not want to get too far out of line, to seem too outré, so that in their purchases they are inclined to make relatively minor variations on the standard package (Riesman and Roseborough, 1955). There are contrary trends, efforts to select a portion of the market for a specialized appeal, just as there are consumers in search of novelty in educational and other "products." The rise of specialized magazines indicates the desire of some advertisers to appeal to a narrow segment of the market, but on the whole the massiveness of the mass media inclines marketers to appeal to as wide a segment as possible and therefore to remain within the restrictions of marginal differentiation.

An era of combined recession and inflation and of chancy postbaccalaureate opportunity is not one in which students will be inclined to seek out academic options radically different from the great majority, among whom either isomorphism or marginal differentiation appears to be the most secure strategy. That is why, paradoxically, the very competitiveness of the market situation I have been describing diminishes the educational options among institutions, even though moderately venturesome students can find a variety of optional paths through the curriculum within particular institutions. To illustrate: The unusual student who seeks a coherent undergraduate curriculum, a genuine core, that will be shared with fellow students so that extracurricular contacts can be refreshed by sharing common conversational coin has few places among which to choose. It is true that St. John's College in Santa Fe is somewhat underenrolled, but the number of students with money for tuition and travel and a desire for that particular kind of near-total coherence is small. Similarly, Shimer College sought against tremendous odds to maintain a sequential curriculum devoted mainly to interdisciplinary general-education courses, but because of its location and its refusal to introduce any obviously vocational curriculum, it hovers near extinction. Even the relatively small (2,400 students) college of the University of Chicago, which no longer has a wholly required program but does emphasize general education, has had for some years actively to recruit students from smaller communities all over the country to provide an applicant pool with both the high academic aptitude the college requires and the self-confidence to live in a cosmopolitan, racially mixed neighborhood at an institution that resolutely puts students on their own in all extracurricular matters. (In the last few years, the college has made considerable efforts to overcome the high attrition among students for whom the competitive academic milieu and the metropolitan environment proved overwhelming; see Spady, 1967.) Until the 1960s, greatly overapplied and academically eminent Amherst College had an almost totally required freshman year, with notoriously demanding programs in mathematics and the natural sciences, in English literature, in American studies. Recently, President John William Ward (who has since resigned) sought to restore a somewhat similar program, but, as has happened elsewhere, faculty members have been reluctant; while discussion proceeds, Amherst students still have considerable lee-way, made even greater by the Five-College Consortium in the area, which allows them to take courses at neighboring institutions, as well as by provisions for independent study with faculty ap-proval (Select Committee on the Curriculum, 1978). The greatly overapplied University of Notre Dame has a freshman year that is almost entirely required—and, thanks not only to careful selection among applicants but also to an intensive program of orientation and advising for entering students, the university loses virtually no students on academic grounds, but pulls them all through the re-quired freshman program.[1]

The reader has probably observed that every one of the institutions mentioned is private and primarily residential. The national appeal of these colleges and universities is inevitably limited by virtue of their location, the high academic demands they put on students, their high tuition (even when ample financial aid is available), or in Notre Dame's case, the Catholic auspices, no matter how liberal and ecumenical the institution is in fact. Where is the student to turn who would like a coherent program in the public sector with subsidized tuition and an academically more hetero-geneous student body? Although colleges in the public sector com-pete with one another as well as with institutions in the private sector for students and for faculty, they are rarely given the entrepreneurial leeway that the private sector makes available in principle, even if rarely in practice. They are subject to an increas-ingly tight system of statewide controls which limit the programs they can offer and which, since they base funding on head-count formulas, tend to discourage innovation. Their freedom of maneuver is also limited by a far greater prevalence of collective bargaining in the public than in the private institutions. Further-more, colleges that depend heavily on commuter students feel that they must offer the fullest possible range for students tied by resi-dence, job, or marriage to particular localities.

[1] Cardinal Newman College in St. Louis is a recent, quite small, and not yet ac-credited institution whose very name implies its "back to basics" orientation. Its viability, like that of some of the Protestant evangelical colleges discussed earlier, is not assured.

In an earlier era, a few major state and land-grant universities did require entering students, whatever their prospective undergraduate school or major, to pursue an integrated general-education program for the first two years. This was true at the University of Minnesota and, until quite recently, the overapplied University of Florida. Often these programs disappeared not because of student resistance but because they resulted in a de facto two-class faculty, and fewer people could be found who wanted to teach general-education courses rather than specialized departmental courses.

For a number of years I have sought to persuade faculty members and administrators that their hierarchies are dysfunctional in assigning the newest faculty members to introductory courses rather than assigning these neophytes to the specialized courses that will enable them to continue publishable work in their specialties; senior faculty members should be recruited to teach lower-division students. In some institutions, this does happen. Some major Berkeley scientists, including Nobel Prize winners, such as Owen Chamberlain, have taught introductory courses, as have Edwin Purcell and Stephen Weinberg, the Harvard physicists who are Nobel laureates. But it is certainly not the prevailing practice in research universities or institutions seeking to become such. (See Grant and Riesman, 1978, chap. 10.)

I have already referred to Donald Campbell's observation that, especially in a period of retrenchment, nontenured faculty members feel under pressure to seek the security of work along the lines that are central to their own home-base departments, rather than taking the risks of working at the border with other departments where some of their colleagues will not be voting members of the central cohort that will decide on their retention and promotion to tenure. In this way, Campbell maintains, there will be less opportunity for universities to cultivate what he terms "novel narrowness"—that is, the beginnings of a new specialty in the interstices among departments. And this risk-averse behavior will be duplicated by upwardly mobile institutions, using the current surplus of capable faculty members in order to recruit people regarded, in a judgment by the senior eminences of these fields, as central to the fields as they are now constituted (Campbell, 1979–80; see also Geertz, 1980).

Quite apart from the risk-averse behavior that is understandable in the face of the current stasis and retrenchment in academia, a further factor may be at work in the disappearance of novel offerings, whether in the form of general education or in the form of embryonic new specialties—namely, the probability that during the period of great expansion of academia in the 1960s, many faculty members were recruited who neither came from cultivated home backgrounds nor had overcome not doing so through pre-collegiate schooling. (Public and even private schools were increasingly lax.) Such persons would not be capable of teaching either general education courses or the novel narrowness recommended by Campbell, owing to a lack of sufficient cultural background to scan the horizon beyond their immediate disciplines; rather, they live, like most Americans, on a plane of flat and localized contemporaneity.

Homogenization by Decree

Some federal legislation as interpreted in regulations and court decisions also tends to force colleges toward isomorphism. For example, the one-sentence statute forbidding discrimination against handicapped students has been interpreted as if it declared that colleges could not form consortia in which some institutions specialized in assisting blind students; others, deaf students; still others, the wheelchair-bound. (Strictly enforced, this last provision could put out of business a nonaffluent private college such as Mary Baldwin College in Staunton, Virginia, which enrolls 600 young women at a campus built on a steep hillside.)

The Southern Regional Education Board has been notable for its willingness to defray the cost of attending an appropriate college in another state within the board's purview in such scarce and expensive fields as veterinary medicine or nuclear engineering. Although in the secondary schools bilingual education, as mandated by Title VII of the Elementary and Secondary Education Act, has often had the unhappy consequence of maintaining separatism desired neither by Spanish-speaking parents nor by their children (see, for example, Thernstrom, 1980), education in languages other than English, so that people become truly bilingual or multilingual, would seem an admirable aim for colleges and universities. And where students desire courses taught in relatively esoteric languages for which not many institutions have adequate staff, there should be (and in some cases there are) provisions for transfer to permit academic institutions to concentrate on certain languages while ignoring others. This may be difficult in California and some Southwestern states where bilingualism has come to mean, not the command of another language in addition to standard English, but the right to be taught all subjects in Spanish—not mandated for colleges by Title VII, but likely to be insisted on through political pressure from Mexican-American lobbyists and their "Anglo" allies. Similarly, before the passage of affirmative action legislation and regulations, when a number of institutions, mainly private and prestigious, were starting active recruitment of minority (especially black) students to their undergraduate colleges and graduate and professional schools, one could have imagined such recruiting accompanied by efforts at a division of labor among institutions. This would have meant more systematic and less frantic efforts to recruit minority faculty and staff members, including admissions and financial aid officers. It seemed to me at the time that, for example, Cornell could have concentrated on medical students and on graduate students in certain specialized fields; meantime, the University of Pennsylvania could have made special efforts in the Wharton School and in veterinary medicine; Harvard could have emphasized recruitment of blacks for the largest of the major national law schools, leaving the recruitment of students in engineering to cooperative efforts with MIT. It was a quixotic notion. In fact, each major institution competitively recruited in each area, whether or not it had adequate support services in that area or an adequate applicant pool. The combination of the lack of any tradition of genuine interinstitutional cooperation and the internal pressures within each educational unit of a multiversity made the idea seem unrealistic long before federal and state regulations and judicial decisions added their weight toward uniformity. Thus, in many institutions black faculty and staff members were too few to protect themselves from the pressures of being thought of as go-betweens or representatives or tokens, while students were often placed in situations of intense academic competition for which their prior education had not prepared them and without adequate provision for remedial measures that might have enabled them to catch up with their peers.

This proposal of a division of labor does not carry the implication that individual black students, who of course can be as capable and as able to look out for themselvès as any white person, should be excluded from the choice of a particular institution; such applicants should have every conceivable choice open to them. Rather, the argument is that active recruiting could better be handled by means of an academic division of labor, and this would improve the lot of most disadvantaged students, of whatever ethnic group, who would have the opportunity to attend educational units within large universities that had made a special effort to prepare remedial and social support services for them.

I recall discussions with founders of some pedagogically experimental colleges in the middle and late 1960s that were planning to create an individualized curriculum, perhaps based on independent study and negotiated contracts. One presidential planñer remarked: "Of course we must make an active effort to recruit black students." I responded that well-prepared black students would generally prefer not to take a chance on a new and untried institution, whereas less well-prepared blacks would not be well served by an unstructured one, bound to appeal to white countercultural students (and faculty members), especially in a rural setting with virtually no neighboring black population. I proposed instead that, if the institution was concerned with blacks, it should make a serious effort to tutor blacks in the nearest cities with minority populations—blacks who could be prepared to attend appropriate colleges, which would not generally be the college engaged in such tutorial work. And I pointed in vain to nearby white populations of recent ethnic immigration, where very few twelfth-graders attended any postsecondary institutions other than those provided by the army or the nearest community colleges— but of course such "invisible" students held no appeal for liberal and guilty whites.

In some institutions in the early 1960s, active recruitment of black students seemed courageous because of the conservative nature of the community surrounding the college. However, *within* the college, it would have taken courage, as well as knowledge and imagination about social-class and cultural differences among black students of both sexes, to refuse to make special efforts for underprepared blacks. (It should be clear that I am not speaking here about upper- and upper-middle-class blacks.) For example, New College in Sarasota (now New College of the University of South Florida) made considerable efforts to recruit blacks from Sarasota. A tiny number did come. They generally found themselves disoriented in the offbeat, unstructured environment—as poignantly illustrated by the instance of one local black from a poor family who was given LSD by a white student experimenter and suffered a psychotic episode. Although faculty members sought to help the black students as best they could, only one succeeded in graduating.

Title IX of the Higher Education Act amendments does not require traditionally single-sex colleges to become coeducational. I have been told of the case of Kings College, once a Catholic college for men, which was apparently instructed by governmental authorities, quite illegally, that it had to become coeducational if it was to continue receiving essential governmental scholarship funds for its students; it had had a cooperative relationship with College Misericordia (and still does), also in the Wilkes-Barre area, which now recruits a handful of men. So far as I know, the only all-male colleges still extant are Washington & Lee in Virginia and formerly Presbyterian Wabash College in Indiana.

Just recently, Haverford College has decided to become coeducational and recruit women, in spite of its close relations with neighboring Bryn Mawr College, which permitted students the option of coresidential living on either of the two campuses or of single-sex living and offered, with some limitations, the opportunity not only to take courses but to major at the other institution. Similarly, Amherst College decided to become coeducational beginning in 1975, in the face of the argument that the nearby high-quality women's colleges, Smith and Mount Holyoke, as well as coeducational Hampshire College and the University of Massachusetts in Amherst, provided ample opportunity for classroom as well as out-of-class contacts with women. It is widely recognized that there is an asymmetry of status, so that formerly all-male colleges, which in recent years almost everywhere have become coeducational, have had no difficulty in attracting women of equivalent or higher academic capacity, whereas the women's colleges that out of panic in the late sixties began to seek men students have had far greater difficulty—even such well-known colleges as Vassar, Connecticut College, Sarah Lawrence, Bennington, Pitzer (in the Claremont group, where again there were men in the other colleges of the consortium), and a number of the more eminent Catholic women's colleges, such as Manhattanville. Vassar, Connecticut College, and Elmira College are among a small number of former women's colleges that have recruited substantial numbers of men (though still a minority), with test scores equal or superior to the women's and of comparable quality in other respects.

In a way, the situation resembles the effort of the black colleges to recruit white students, which cannot compare with the ability of predominantly white institutions to set in motion a "brain drain" of able black students who might once have attended the black colleges. The only exceptions are such institutions as West Virginia State College at Charleston, which, owing to its availability as a commuter institution for neighboring whites, now has a day population of predominantly white students, though retaining a residential population of blacks; the situation is similar at Lincoln University in Jefferson City, Missouri.

Diversity by Design Within the University

What public universities can do, particularly the stronger and more attractive ones, is to create voluntary islands of coherence offered as an option. Under the leadership of President John Hannah, Michigan State University (which had also had a general-education curriculum, since abandoned) began to experiment with subcolleges, each with its coherent program and geared to a specific area, that would carry undergraduates through their four-year trajectory. Thus, Justin Morrill College was set up with an international focus, requiring acquisition of fluency in French or another foreign language; Lyman Briggs College had the mandate of a focus on the natural sciences; James Madison College emphasized the social sciences. The 400 to 600 students in each of these colleges were housed together in hopes of providing, on a cancerously large campus of over 47,000 students, some sense of mutuality among both students and faculty. At the same time, the wider campus offered opportunities to take specialized electives—in fact, seductive opportunities, which drew many (particularly male) students away from the subcolleges toward majors in job-related fields such as engineering or straight economics.

In 1958 Monteith College was set up as a subcollege of Wayne

State University in Detroit (with the aid of a large grant from a foundation) with a virtually required program in the University of Chicago manner. After serving as a model for other institutions, Monteith College was abolished as a separate entity in 1976, in part as a supposed way to save scarce resources, but also reflecting a continuing antagonism from other colleges at Wayne, as well as schisms within Monteith itself. (It should be noted that Wayne State is almost entirely a commuter urban university, making any attempt at curricular and personal coherence more difficult than in residential institutions.)

These examples do not begin to suggest the range of subcolleges within state universities. In Michigan alone, in addition to the examples just given, the University of Michigan has created an experimental Residential College; Oakland University, originally an offshoot of Michigan State, has experimented with subcolleges; the Grand Valley State Colleges indicate by their very name their adherence to a collegiate plan.

The State University of New York campus at Brockport, with the assistance of a Carnegie Corporation grant, has created the Alternate College, which makes it possible for students entering as freshmen or in some cases as sophomores to get their baccalaureates in three years through an integrated program of general education. Wisely, in my judgment, the Alternate College has no faculty of its own, but manages to persuade departments to lend it teachers temporarily for interdisciplinary courses—and it is careful that these be senior faculty members, not threatened in their disciplinary attachments by a stint in the Alternate College. The college enrolls some 500 students and is wholly unselective in admission requirements, though, inevitably, the more highly motivated and, on the whole, better-prepared students are the ones who choose it.

The Federated Learning Communities of the State University of New York at Stony Brook proceed on a somewhat different principle. Under the leadership of Professor Patrick J. Hill, and depending upon the availability and interest and capacity of senior faculty members, nucleations are created, bringing together, for example, a biologist, a philosopher, and a social psychologist to provide for a student's entire program in environmental studies. One of the unusual features of the program is that one faculty member is designated as the Mentor, whose task it is to attend all the lectures given by individual faculty members, talk with students, and convey back to the faculty members what has been actually learned, in contrast to what they may have thought they had taught. The Mentor, of course, also receives an education through the program, so that the Federated Learning Communities may be regarded as a congeries of enterprises in faculty development.

When John Silber was dean of the College of Arts and Sciences at the University of Texas, he established Plan Two, a voluntary program of general and comparative studies "open to selected students of high ability" (Cass and Birnbaum, 1977, p. 630). The University of Virginia is considering a program entitled Curriculum II, for which it hopes able students will apply—not simply an honor or an honors college, but a wholly required curriculum for volunteers. The experience with such a voluntary program in a small private college for women, Hollins College in Virginia, has not so far been encouraging. Hollins created a Liberal Studies College that offered cohesiveness, weekly luncheon colloquia, and a more intellectual milieu than the college as a whole; however, it required students to take courses in philosophy, mathematics, classics, art, history, English, and economics. According to admissions officials, hardly any students were attracted to Hollins College by this opportunity. Furthermore, the number enrolling in and staying with the program has been minuscule: out of twenty-eight entrants in the fall of 1977, four remain as full-time, four as affiliate members.[2] Those concerned with a liberal studies option at Hollins College have not given up. They hope to bring the program up to "critical mass" by actively recruiting students interested in the option.

Similarly, at Bowling Green State University in Ohio, the philosopher Gary Woditch has directed a competence-based liberal education program, which has been marginal and insecure, not attracting a large student contingent.

[2] I am indebted to Arthur R. Poskocil, associate professor of sociology at Hollins College, for a detailed account of the experiment (personal correspondence, 1978), including the characteristics of those students, of higher intellectuality, wider reading, and greater academic aptitude, who at least expressed interest in the Liberal Studies College and who often joined it at the beginning, only to leak away to less demanding programs—for example, to avoid the requirements in quantitative fields.

Since its opening in 1965, the most luminous illustration of the subcollege option in public higher education has been the University of California at Santa Cruz. Its original design, developed when Clark Kerr was president of the University of California system, contemplated building a series of colleges of about 600 students each. The colleges would be residentially self-contained under the leadership of a provost; a group of a few senior faculty members would develop collegewide curricula with different foci, which would in turn be compatible with different styles of noncollegiate life in each of the colleges. One college was to be built every year until the campus reached the ceiling of 27,500 students that President Kerr had succeeded in imposing on both Berkeley and UCLA—already well beyond what he regarded as the optimal scale for a good research university, between 10,000 and 15,000 students. In order to maintain academic standards at levels appropriate to the University of California system, each field of study was to be organized by a Board of Studies, comparable to a department except that it had to share appointive power and half the budget for appointments with the several colleges.

For each of the new colleges, a separate firm of architects was engaged, thus going outside the pattern common in state systems of a single, official campuswide architect. It is hard to think of any university constructed with such close attention to the relation between architectural forms and collegiate life, whether in the dining facilities of the colleges or in their residential arrangements.[3]

[3] In this area also, John Hannah at Michigan State had been something of a pioneer, constructing what were termed "living-learning units"—that is, dormitories with classroom space and faculty offices—none of them, in my view, architectural masterpieces, and apparently not terribly successful in pedagogic terms. (On the general question of the importance of architecture, often neglected by verbally acute but visually unalive teachers and students, see Trow, 1968.) The University of Wisconsin at Green Bay, opening in 1968 as a four-year campus dedicated primarily to the environment, under the chancellorship of Edward Weidner, who had been at Michigan State under John Hannah, was housed in a campus that sought to emphasize student/faculty interaction through, for example, its "people pockets," sheltered outdoor enclaves where small groups could meet for seminars or talk if weather permitted. Hampshire College, which opened in the fall of 1970, sought to be architecturally as well as pedagogically innovative, making provisions even on a relatively modest budget for different styles of student life and teaching. For a discussion of architectural innovation at two New Jersey state colleges, Stockton State and Ramapo College, which opened in 1971 with the benefit of distinguished

The animating ideas of Santa Cruz, including architectural and scenic magnificence, served at the outset to attract some eminent senior faculty members from leading universities in the United Kingdom and the United States, as well as younger ones with their degrees from the most eminent research universities. And for a time it was the most sought-after campus in the University of California system. However, a full-scale university campus never did develop; graduate programs were introduced in only a few fields, and there was no engineering school to help alter the image Santa Cruz soon acquired of being tilted heavily toward the humanities and of having a certain academic softness, implicit in the system of evaluations rather than grades.

Chancellor Robert Sinsheimer and many faculty members recently concluded that the absence of grades in an altered vocational and educational atmosphere was the reason Santa Cruz was losing students both through heavy attrition and through nonenrollment (currently, a number of students are "redirects" who applied to Berkeley or UCLA and are promised that after two years they can transfer there). Urged on by such considerations, the faculty voted to allow students the option of grades or evaluations. There was a passionate reaction from students and some faculty members, who held that what made Santa Cruz distinctive was the absence of grades and that, if they were available as an alternative, an atmosphere of competitiveness would set in—and Santa Cruz would not necessarily recruit more students, because it would lose one of the features, indeed perhaps the chief symbol, that made it distinctive in the University of California system. Correspondingly, the faculty reversed itself. However, according to Alan Hershfield, vice-president for planning in the overall University of California, studies are underway to see whether the students' assessment is correct or, rather, whether the absence of grades is one of the prime reasons that Santa Cruz, along with Riverside, is the most

architectural planning, see Grant and Riesman (1978, pp. 301–302, 327–328, 414, n. 6). Evergreen State College in Olympia, Washington, should be added to the roster of new public institutions whose construction took account of the still poorly understood relations between architecture and learning—an understanding that is inevitably plagued by changes in users' values and tastes and in the constraints imposed by the larger society, such as the unexpected rise in the cost of air conditioning and other uses of energy.

underenrolled campus in the university system—indeed, for a time, threatened with closing. If students prove to be turned away from Santa Cruz by the need for grades, either on entrance or after entrance, the issue will be reconsidered.

The original coherence of the several colleges at Santa Cruz has diminished for several reasons. In many instances, the core curriculum organized in a college disintegrated as both students and professors preferred to follow their own bents; the cohesion of the colleges was further weakened because many students preferred to live off campus. Furthermore, attrition and stopout rates were high. As the number of faculty members increased, the Boards of Studies naturally grew larger, and as the founder-provost gave way in many cases to less powerful or charismatic successors, many faculty members oriented primarily to the colleges came to believe that the Boards of Studies—and hence the general academic evil, as they saw it, of departmentalism—were creeping into the Garden of Eden. (In contrast, a number of the more scholarly faculty members at Santa Cruz long ago concluded that tenure had been granted too readily to teachers with insufficient scholarly concerns, attracted to Santa Cruz by the advertised "free" life-styles, including sexual swinging, identified with Esalen and other California—but now national—seductions. Scholarly faculty members pressed for what came to be called "reaggregation," in which the colleges would be coterminous with Boards of Studies and people would choose or be assigned to colleges on the basis of academic concerns rather than life-styles.)

Limits on Student Choice

Given the potential power of students and its frequent use by individual students for their own reasons, without full awareness of its collective impact (see Schelling, 1971), we must return to the question of what prevents students from making full use of their market power. In other words, why, from the point of view of students, is the free market not as free as it might appear?

Partial Oligopolies in the Academic Marketplace. In commerce and industry, markets are of course not free in conditions of oligopoly, in which a small number of sellers (however limited by the antitrust laws and the Federal Trade Commission) confront unorganized potential customers who lack countervailing market power or lack the information to use the power they have. However, informed customers can limit oligopolistic control by finding foreign suppliers or substitutes for the product. Moreover, if sufficiently informed and organized, they can bring political and economic pressure against oligopolistic pricing, as has often happened when American steel companies' pricing practices have been thwarted by presidential "jawboning" or by the fact or threat of antitrust suits.

However, in the academic marketplace, the closest analogue in postsecondary education to an oligopoly is in the field of medical education. The number of schools and the number of places within schools have expanded notably, and yet there remains a large pool of applicants who possess the requisite scientific skills and can at least appear to present appropriate qualities of character, including pertinacity and scrupulousness. Medical education in the United States, with its science-based and clinical components, is so fearsomely expensive that the presidents of private universities that possess—or are possessed by—a medical school and its affiliated hospitals often joke among themselves about the bankruptcy they fear as a result of the mounting costs of such a school. Federal and state governments moved some years ago to increase the number of places by helping fund development of new medical schools and expansion of existing ones, as well as by funding support for medical students (including ample loans). From society's point of view, there is evidence of maldistribution of doctors, notably surgeons, but it is not clear that, in comparison with other social needs, the country is numerically undersupplied with physicians. Even so, one small group of would-be student customers and their parents were able to bring persistent pressure on Congress to put through a short-lived mandate that medical schools receiving federal subsidy must include in their final two-year clinical programs appropriately prepared American applicants who had attended non-American medical schools—a few of which, as in Guadalajara, have depended heavily on American dollars from students who were (or whose parents were) prepared to pay large sums to provide what is, for the time being, the financial safe harbor of an M.D.

But in almost no other field is there a comparable situation. Programs in veterinary medicine are even harder of access than medical school, but dental schools are, on the whole, not overapplied. (In the present climate of the women's movements, I have found it impossible to suggest to a young woman contemplating a two-career marriage and children that pediatric dentistry would offer her the opportunity to practice at home, to use her manual dexterity and nurturant skills, and to do very well financially—for such women, only medicine is good enough. Furthermore, the Jews who were once denied places in medical school because of quotas and then went to dental school as a second choice can now usually enter medical school. Consequently, one finds dentistry as a career of choice among ethnically oriented Chinese, for example, who want to serve their communities and at the same time do well financially, or among Armenians, or among those social strata not influenced by the prejudices of the elite about what constitutes a proper calling.) Doctoral programs in clinical psychology exist in considerable number, but those approved by the American Psychological Association for training as a licensed therapist have in the past been overapplied.

It is true that there are a small number of heavily overapplied undergraduate colleges that have attained a kind of national brand-name status, comparable to celebrity or best-seller status; but just as best sellers are not the only books for serious reading, so the overapplied institutions are by no means the only ones having first-rate faculties and facilities for undergraduate education. As discussed in Chapter Two, a brand-name institution may be far from optimal for any particular student (just as it may not be optimal for many of the faculty members who hold or seek to hold positions in it).

To many eager students at selective undergraduates colleges, it appears as if there were also a shortage of places in law schools. But this is true only if one has in mind a relatively small number of national law schools, again with brand-name reputations. Almost any student who can graduate from college can find a law school, even an accredited law school, somewhere.

When it comes to Ph.D. programs, the supply is far greater than the demand—an imbalance going well beyond that at the baccalaureate level, since in the 1950s and 1960s so many institutions sought to embark on Ph.D. programs as symbols of academic respectability and status. This drive to become an institution that grants the doctorate continued (and is even now continuing) well beyond the time when it had already become clear that, with the demographic shift, academic jobs for holders of the doctorate in most fields would be far fewer. And by their very nature, the highly specialized Ph.D. programs that prepare people in esoteric fields—for example, Syriac at the University of Pennsylvania or Ukrainian at Harvard—are not overapplied even in major universities, because there appear to be no potential academic positions, making pursuit of the doctorate a worthwhile risk only for those wholly committed to the field as a calling, irrespective of vocational opportunities.

Viscosity in Student Attitudes. Although high school students among the well-to-do do not always wisely exercise the choices available to them, they are almost invariably aware that they have a choice, though this may be constricted by parental veto or stinginess. Much of the stratification in American higher education comes about because young people from noncollege families, notably minority students, but not only they, find the very idea of choice unsettling; they lack motivation or stimulation to search for possibilities that are in fact available and thus fail to make use of their market power.[4]

When Barry Munitz (now chancellor of the University of Houston) was a staff associate of the Carnegie Commission on Higher Education in 1968–69, he was asked to do a quick survey of the attitudes of twelfth-grade blacks in inner-city high schools toward the concept of a national Educational Opportunity Bank (see Chapter Eleven). In talking with blacks in Newark, in Brooklyn, and elsewhere, Munitz discovered that they could not believe such

[4] For a breezy and lucid effort to spread widely information concerning what colleges offer, how to determine their costs, how to decide whether to attend, and how to go about choosing a college, see the eight-page brochure in newspaper format published by the College Entrance Examination Board (1977–78), made available to counselors, students, parents, and others. Among other bits of advice, it urges high school juniors to begin planning for "after high school what?" and not to wait until their last high school year.

a scheme was not just another subtle or sophisticated "ripoff": surely the federal government would not just give them money that was not a loan, not a mortgage, and that would not lead to repossession of their television set or car or other appurtenances. Barry Munitz counseled the Carnegie Commission that it was clear that such individuals would have to be persuaded to attend college for one or two years before they could even recognize that such largesse was not a loan or mortgage but a form of postponed tuition and other educational costs, to be repaid only to the extent that they could afford to do so by virtue of postcollege earnings.

According to a great many studies of the reasons for the increases in college attendance among children of families whose income is below the median for the United States, the low cost and geographic accessibility of a college are primary factors. Perhaps two thirds of all freshmen with no prior college attendance apply to what is, in their social and cultural orbit, the "available college," which often means the nearest community college or four-year regional state college. Some do not even apply; yet they appear and are admitted—many community colleges compete with proprietary institutions in having the ever-open door of rolling admissions. Students go where their siblings and friends have gone; unless they have distinguished themselves in some fashion, they are not apt to be sought after by roving recruiters from national institutions or picked out by teachers, coaches, or harried guidance counselors in order to provide them with a wider range of options.

Brokerage services free of charge are increasingly available, such as the educational opportunity centers to be found in many major cities, which act as switchboards with respect to college choice, as the Educational Testing Service and the College Board will also do. But there operates what might be regarded as a sumptuary "law." In an earlier age, the aristocracy imposed restrictions on people of lower social status to limit what clothes they might wear or what other marks of ostentation they might possess, dependent on the station in life to which they were consigned. Today, sumptuary restraints are more apt to emerge from the judgments of one's peers, parents, or counselors (themselves often graduates of local institutions), who, in effect, say to a student who has aspirations transcending his or her milieu: "Who do you think you are?"

"You may be college material, but are you Stanford material?" As noted in Chapter Two, one of the great benefits of the National Merit Scholarship competition and like awards is that they have helped legitimize the raising of aspirations among recipients and runners-up, encouraging them to escape self-imposed obeisance to the sumptuary customs of their milieu as well as their own misgivings about the institutions where they would feel academically if not always socially comfortable.

The funding formulas of public institutions, based on credit hours or full-time equivalent students, lead today to a particularly strenuous campaign to woo middle- and upper-middle-class full-time students to institutions in the public sector. The entire funding system is weighted against those who must work part-time or even full-time in order to get through school, since one needs three or four of these students to have comparable leverage on the state system, and processing these students is itself costly. Thus, the persuasions to attend an in-state public college or university full-time are intensified.

When students are asked about their choice or lack of choice of college, they often give financial reasons: they are attending the local college because that is all they can afford, or they are attending College A rather than College B, which they might have preferred, because College A offered them a better financial aid package. But inquiries can often reveal that a student did not attend a "College Night" where he or she might have discovered College C, which would offer still more money. Or perhaps the student did attend but hesitated to ask questions that might seem stupid or might offend a college representative—the student being unaware that the college representative is even more eager for the student than vice versa. It is easier to say that one does not have (or has not been offered) the money than to say that one is afraid one would be out of one's economic or social class in a given college. (Such a college might in fact be optimal for the particular student, provided it offered enough orientation to create a feeling of academic and social habituation, though not to the point of comfort, as that would be not wholly desirable in an already hedonistic population.) Furthermore, students often interpret financial aid offers as if they were statements about their own value—the higher the offer, the more the college wants them. And students are apt to believe that many more colleges are selective than in fact are, especially in the private sector, where the vast majority of colleges are today wholly unselective.

Another limit on college choice is that students from low-income backgrounds are apt to think of a price difference of $300 between College X and College Y as significant. They do not look far enough ahead to realize that, amortized over a lifetime in inflated dollars, the difference is negligible. Thus, they head to one college rather than another for reasons that might lead them or their parents to buy one car rather than another because it costs a few hundred dollars less for starters, though the difference may be more than amortized over the life of the vehicle. To a student from a poor home, $1,000 seems a tremendous sum and $5,000 "out of sight," but the difference over a twenty-five-year period of continuing inflation vanishes—indeed, reverses—if an education that costs $5,000 more will allow one to earn, at ten years out of college, $500 more per year in steadier work.[5]

Yet another factor limiting college choice (not only what college one goes to but whether one goes at all) is youthful indifference about one's future. This unconcern is not confined to students from low-income families. I have in mind a young woman from a middle-income family who had attended a suburban high school and who said of herself what many might say: "I didn't have any plans at age eighteen. At age eighteen you don't think too much of the future." Her remark suggests that social scientists can no longer separate the lower from the higher social strata by noting that the

---

[5] Barry Munitz provides an appropriate anecdote from an occasion on which he was the commencement speaker at one of the top minority high schools in Houston, one with many black and Mexican-American students. During the commencement ceremony, the highlight was the announcement by the principal to the full audience of students, parents, and other family members of the top ten scholarship winners in the class by total dollar amount. The audience was ecstatic at the large amounts being given out, some of them academic, others athletic. At first offended by what had the quality of a daytime television quiz show, Munitz later reflected that, given this particular high school and its constituency, the emphasis on linkage between successful competition for college admission and acquisition of substantial financial support provided a balance to the widespread fear that collège was inevitably costly rather than remunerative, especially in dealing with students whose life experience did not justify or give opportunity for thinking in terms of lifetime plans.

former are more apt to live on a day-to-day basis (see, for example, Banfield, 1970), while the middle and upper classes have the power and habit of thinking and planning in long-run terms. With the spread of affluence in the post–World War II era, along with egalitarian ideals, attitudes once characteristic of lower-class young people have filtered upward, and reasonably well-to-do young people who would once have been thinking about career contingencies in junior high will now be found among those who have not bothered to take the PSAT as high school juniors in order to be able to think sensibly about college choice in the fall of their senior year, as well as to give themselves the advantage of a trial run. (I am inclined to think that, despite the women's liberation movements, women are less apt than men to think ahead, except in the topmost social and professional strata. For an imaginative argument that women in general, as a still-oppressed group, behave like the lower class and are unable to plan ahead, see Steinem, 1980.)

In fact, more and more students in the nonselective and generally nonresidential institutions where we have interviewed have worked after high school or "messed around," as some will say, and then returned to college in their middle or late twenties, often on a part-time basis.[6] Such delayed return is currently, in my judgment, given extravagant praise in the propaganda on behalf of "lifelong learning." Certainly, no person who cares about the continual development of human faculties can be opposed to the ideal of such learning, but in the United States it seems unwise to suggest to the high school population that, since college will always be available, it does not much matter whether they attend immediately after high school or not. Such a prospect would not pose a problem in such countries as Japan, where one can count on precollegiate education

---

[6] The Carnegie Council (1979b) has recently prepared a cogent discussion of alternatives to college and, indeed, of the whole problem of transition from school to work at differing ages and under alternative structures of opportunity. One such widely backed structure is a national volunteer service, a kind of Peace Corps/VISTA/ACTION program available to everyone. On the basis of my experience with the Peace Corps and other volunteer agencies, I have opposed anything more than some small-scale experiments in this direction, for I am convinced that we do not now have available a cohort of people who can put other people to work productively and who will regard themselves and be regarded as authoritative but not authoritarian: our situation is very different from what it was during the era of the Civilian Conservation Corps, which is often taken as a model.

to provide an adequate grounding in mathematics and foreign languages, both of which are most easily learned when one is young. But in the United States, where one can have little confidence that even good English usage is acquired in secondary school, one may be cut off from certain kinds of lifelong learning by the difficulty of starting virtually from scratch in such fields in one's adult years. This is in marked contrast to fields such as my own, where, apart from understanding of quantitative issues such as demography—and that is a large exception—I am sometimes inclined to feel it should not be studied until one has had a good deal of experience of life. As it is, in many social strata it would be pointless to make much of when or where one begins college— after all, one can always drop out or transfer. One plays it cool.

Such casualness, whether at age eighteen or later, is cultural light-years removed from the tense anxieties among the small but salient competitive minority who apply to a dozen of the most selective institutions and, with their friends and families, tensely await what Sacks (1978) calls "Bloody Monday"—the day the announcements come from Princeton, Harvard, Amherst, Oberlin, and Pomona.

Special Problems of Foreign Students. In comparison with the situation in most of the world, the varieties of American higher education are bewildering to foreigners. A dramatic example is the case of a Barbadian student who had passed his A and O level examinations, which would entitle him to enter the university system of the United Kingdom. He applied to Harvard and Cornell. When he was asked to take the SAT, a requirement that he misinterpreted as a racial slur, he decided not to pursue that further. Since he assumed that other institutions were at comparable levels with Harvard and Cornell, and since he was not only academically talented (the Barbadians are known, not always charitably, as the schoolmasters of the Caribbean) but a fine basketball player, he was recruited by the coach of a Florida community college; from there he transferred to a local state university. But this was a disaster. He was bitter when he discovered how academically inferior the place was. For instance, he had to correct the teacher of English literature—this would hardly endear the college to him or vice versa. He had found one faculty member who appreciated his gifts, but he had really "run out of school" before he entered. Since the place is called a university and gives master's degrees, even someone from as nearby as Barbados might have trouble understanding the connotations of *college* and *university* in the private and public sectors of American postsecondary education.

The case is extreme, because of the student's being already fluent in English and because, unlike the overwhelming majority of non-American students, he did not come to the United States for training in science, engineering, or technology.

Apart from academic mismatching, if there is any group of students that is likely to end up in a situation of cultural isolation, it is foreign students.[7] Richard L. Hopkins, director of the School for International Training of the Experiment in International Living in Brattleboro, Vermont, has written me:

> To recruit students from radically different cultures to come to our institutions and then to leave them to fend for themselves without any provision being made for assisting them to develop adaptive behaviors is, in my opinion, irresponsible. . . . It's a concrete, daily problem. Foreign students become depressed, disoriented, angry—and they have no place to go except to each other. I am convinced that the larger universities, the Michigan States, impersonal and bureaucratic as they may be, nonetheless are better places for foreign students to be, if only because in such places they can enjoy the benefits of this ghetto. Foreign student offices are, in many institutions, run by failed academics (often

[7] Foreign students also face the problem of securing recognition of non-brand-name American diplomas in their own countries. For instance, some years ago, a graduate of Bennington College married to an English official in the Ministry of Education and Science had great difficulty securing a license to teach in secondary school because English authorities had never heard of Bennington and had only a relatively short list of American colleges and universities whose degrees could be approved as reasonably comparable to those from a British college of teacher education. Of course, this phenomenon also leads to mismatching, as foreign students with limited linguistic preparation apply to and sometimes succeed in entering highly competitive American colleges, in which they can fare as badly as indigenous Americans who are equally ill prepared.

teachers of foreign languages) who have only a dim
sense of the cultural perspective from which many of
their clients are operating. Even when the personnel are
sensitive and aggressive, they have little money and no
status. One of the most unfortunate aspects of this condition is the prospective learning that is lost both by
foreign students and Americans, through the failure of
the institution to foster learning from the intercultural
goings-on when the stranger meets those more embed-
ded in the community.

Mr. Hopkins continues by observing that many of these students
(as I have also seen them at technical institutes and universities) are
not only uncomfortable in human and cultural terms but also insufficiently absorbed into American culture to understand the em-
beddedness of our technology in our social fabric. Studies initiated
after the Second World War by the anthropologists John Bennett,
John and Ruth Useem, and Kurt Wolff indicate that, when these
students return home, they are in a sense again displaced persons,
not having learned quite enough about American culture to appreciate in advance the difficulty of applying its science and technology to their home cultures.

It does not help that the Immigration and Naturalization
Service has a not entirely undeserved reputation for punitiveness
in dealing with foreign students. I have most recently observed this
in attempts to protect Iranian students from the vindictiveness
visited upon some of them by ethnocentric Americans angry at the
seizure of American hostages and then treating these students,
whatever their personal outlook, as in effect hostages. The INS,
in ferreting out Iranian students and for a time (now at least
temporarily eased) forcing them either to return to Iran or to ask
for political asylum, has operated with what seems to the outsider
callous disregard of the plight of these students, many of whom
fear their families would be harmed if they asked for asylum and in
fact would like to return to Iran if conditions there become less
unstable.

One difficulty with the "ghettos" in which foreign students
are apt to live on the larger campuses is that the view formed of the
United States by earlier arrivals is handed ready-made to the new-

comers and is often politically tendentious, if not hostile to the United States. This can create a vicious circle in which the foreign student quickly becomes critical of the United States and in a sense so objective about it, after the fashion of Alfred Schutz's stranger, as to be off-putting for the average American, who is apt to assume that the foreigner should be grateful.

In an earlier era, when American academic institutions were not desperately hungry for the tuitions foreign students might bring with them, Columbia, the University of Chicago, and other universities set up International Houses where non-American students could meet one another and sympathetic and interested Americans. And there would be "trade routes," established by missionaries in foreign lands, often teaching in English-language schools in India or Africa, and encouraging their best students to attend an American college of their own denomination.[8] (Many Americans are aware that some of the first leaders of independence movements in African countries were educated at Lincoln University and other Negro colleges in the United States.) Yale and Harvard established connections with China; Amherst still maintains long-standing ties with Doshisha University in Kyoto, which has Amherst House as part of its own campus, and there is some two-way student exchange—now handicapped on the American side by the lowered purchasing power of the dollar as against the yen.

More recently, some of the small liberal arts colleges have been among the worst offenders in the recruitment of foreign students. Windham College in Putney, Vermont, is a classic case. In its effort to keep going in its last desperate years, it sent the I-20 forms abroad through a New York broker; no effort was made to check the English-language proficiency of the foreign students recruited to a small and failing college in rural Vermont. When it went bankrupt in the middle of the academic year, it left 75 foreign students stranded.

---

[8] Larry Litten, formerly director of institutional research at Carleton College, has pointed out that many of these missionaries sent their own children to colleges such as Carleton and Oberlin, with which they were familiar even if they were not graduates and even if the college did not adhere to their own denomination. The network spread to other Americans abroad, such as embassy officials or businessmen, looking for academically first-rate colleges "back in the States" for their children.

On the whole, however, benevolent innocence rather than rapacity marks the recruitment and treatment of foreign students. But the innocence is not really excusable. It rests on the same kind of overaggregated assumptions that operate vis-à-vis native Americans who appear in some way different, such as black students or students from Spanish-speaking backgrounds. For example, there is a tendency to treat all students from Islamic countries as if they were alike, despite the enormous differences within each country and among the different Arab- and non-Arab-speaking countries.

Of course, American institutions are often in a quandary when trying to interpret the linguistic capability and academic aptitude of foreign applicants—a problem also at the postbaccalaureate level for graduate and professional students. (The Educational Testing Service has recently prepared a new test of English as a foreign language, which uses a tape recorder to assess the performance of foreign students. It is now undergoing preliminary trials. See "New Exams to Assess English Skills," 1980.) There are surely American colleges whose admissions officials would not be aware, for example, that a high proportion of applicants from Lebanon would be reasonably fluent in French, and interpreting the previous work of an applicant from India can be extremely difficult even where facility in English is not a serious problem, as the heterogeneity of India's academic institutions almost rivals that of the United States.

It is generally assumed that foreign students are well-to-do. But many from African countries are desperately poor. Sometimes they are lumped with American blacks, and in fact not a few study at Howard and the University of the District of Columbia, but relations between American blacks and Africans are often cool on both sides. Some Latin American students are quite well-to-do and cosmopolitan and have no more problems of adjustment than most students from Western Europe, but again, others are poor and isolated. To recruit Kuwaiti or Saudi-Arabian students is generally a financial bonus to an institution and the surrounding community, but these students may have been brought up in strict Sunni Moslem modes, perhaps especially the young women, who will not be comfortable—and in some places not especially well treated by fellow students—on a cosmopolitan campus where even American students from evangelical homes often feel out of place. Western

Michigan University has recruited a number of such students in what seems a reasonably good matching in both academic and cultural terms. One graduate student tells me that some students from the wealthier desert kingdoms are pursuing further education, especially in technological fields, at Houston, which might seem a natural link for an oil-rich country—except that these students seem to have come on the assumption that Houston was hot and dry rather than hot and humid; many might be better off at Texas Technological University in Lubbock, but how would they hear of it? As Vietnamese students begin to trickle into our postsecondary institutions, they may in some of the more avant-garde ones face hostility comparable to that faced at these same institutions by Vietnam veterans who were treated as war criminals by many of the usually nonxenophobic and antiracist liberal-left students.

I am putting such emphasis on these problems because just as there has been a great expansion of the search for older and returning students and laying on of external degree programs of varying academic scrupulousness, so there is now in many institutions a hungry search for paying customers from other countries. Many colleges entering this pursuit have not had the experience of the research universities that have established campuses abroad. In addition, a number of universities, through their schools of education, have contracts for organizing and developing new indigenous institutions overseas and thus have ties to particular countries, such as the ties Florida State University has established with South Korea and with several Latin American countries.

Some of the smaller liberal arts colleges, knowing that they have no resources to provide a vestibule for the entry of foreign students, wisely refuse to accept them. Conceivably, the regional accrediting agencies could police the recruiting of foreign students as part of their assessment in accrediting a particular college or university—indeed, the Commission on Institutions of Higher Education of the New England Association of Schools and Colleges was aware that Windham College was failing, but because it feared litigation if it moved before it had solid evidence, it could not protect the foreign students eventually marooned there. But this may be an area in which voluntary policing by the regional accrediting associations may prove ineffective and national action by the Council on Postsecondary Accreditation may not be efficacious either. Since I am opposed to extensive consumer-protection legislation and federal regulation where voluntary private action and state action can manage reasonably well (a position developed later in this book), I should point out that I believe in the case of overseas students federal action may be needed to protect both potential "consumers" of education and the institutions recruiting them.

Federal action may not be necessary even there, for it is possible that a mobilization of voluntary agencies and organizations can be accomplished that will oversee the recruiting of foreign students, and there is the sanction available of withdrawing regional accreditation from institutions that can be shown to operate unscrupulously overseas. But within the large domestic arena of the United States, I want in the concluding chapters to examine in detail what can be done to reduce the state tariffs and viscosities that prevent the free market from being still more free and also what can be done by a great variety of individuals in different locales—counselors, accrediting associations, the College Entrance Examination Board, and other voluntary agencies—to achieve better matches between students and institutions. It would have been relatively easy during the period of great expansion of postsecondary education in the 1950s and 1960s to establish on a solid foundation the agencies of appropriate voluntary guidance for students and restraints on mischievous institutional self-promotion when institutional ambitions were focused on upward academic mobility and only rarely on sheer survival. But we Americans, as citizens of a country or as members of institutions, are not very good at thinking ahead, and countercyclical measures are seldom in place at the moment we need them. Correspondingly, we are faced with the question of providing better information for student choice in an era of cynical consumerism among prospective students and of desperate marketing by all but a tiny number of overapplied institutions. (For a lucid account of the ways similar problems of marketing and fierce competition for students—as well as greatly intensified competition for government funds and for renown—are occurring in the United Kingdom, see Klein, 1979; for the way students seek to protect themselves as consumers, by publishing in the magazine *Which* what Klein terms "anti-prospectuses," see Klein, 1979, pp. 317–318.)

8

Providing Information to Guide Student Choice

As noted in Chapter Seven, a market becomes more nearly free when consumers gain information about the products competing for their choice. In the higher education market, even while colleges have been engaging in the most aggressive marketing procedures to recruit students, considerable thought has been given to how to improve information students receive about colleges and hence to improve the matching, now so often happenstance, between a particular student and a particular institution.

On assignment from a federal agency, the American Institutes for Research (1977) did a study of how much information was made available to students and what the practices were in such areas as refund of tuition or time at which one could withdraw; as might be expected, it discovered there were wide disparities. However, colleges are not the only sources of such information. The AIR has itself prepared cassettes for the use of students, alerting them to the traps for the unwary that may lie in marketing oversell by some colleges (Bailey, 1980; Litten, 1980). These cassettes warn students that they should not give themselves to the "college of their choice" without carefully inquiring into specified features of the institution—tapes which guidance counselors can have available and which speak directly to the student in his or her role as potential producer/consumer. Furthermore, the educational opportunity centers, whose number is spreading in major cities, have available a great amount of computerized information, so that a student who wants to know what colleges are suitable can feed into the computer information on financial need, potential vocational or straight academic interests, geographic limits, test scores, and so on and be given a list of institutions that are within range. The College Board itself provides a great deal of information of this sort, just as the American College Testing Service does, seeking to make better matches between students and institutions.

The fact is that much more information is available to students, counselors, parents, and others who have a stake in or hand in students' college choices than is currently made use of. To be sure, catalogues ought to state what tuition refund policies are, make clear when students can withdraw from a course without having to pay for it, and give other information of this sort that is generally included in the catalogues of reputable institutions. Yet in all these considerations, we must bear in mind that we are dealing with a small minority of students who make an active choice of college—from 10 to 25 percent by the estimates of Alexander Astin and other students of the subject—with an additional small number who, having started at the local "available college," transfer to an institution more suitable to their developing skills and aspirations.

Guidance Counselors: Whose Side Are They On?

Efforts at matching are, of course, among the duties of high school guidance counselors. It is customary for many in higher education, as well as in secondary schools, to look down on counselors as individuals who have not been able to make the grade as teachers—much like the snobbery toward administrators—and, indeed, as people awaiting their chance for an administrative post. Nina McCain (1977, p. 54), former education editor of the *Boston Globe*, quotes the comment of an admissions director in a Boston-area college "that he very rarely gets hard questions about the college from students, parents, or high school guidance counselors. Until quite recently, students and counselors worried more about getting into colleges than about what colleges could offer once they got there."

The caricatures of guidance counselors, like any stereotypes, convey a portion of the truth: many are antiacademic individuals, perhaps biased about race, sex, and social class, too indolent to be teachers, too old and incompetent to be coaches. But it has been my good fortune to meet over a period of years a number of quite exceptional counselors, facing almost impossible loads and dilemmas. Indeed, one of the anxieties created by the present funding crises in the public schools (highlighted by the situation in Cleveland and other Ohio cities and by Proposition 13 in California) is that guidance counselors will be seen as luxuries who will have to be dispensed with in order to meet teachers' salaries and to make sure that teachers teach "the basics," which may also eliminate art, athletics, and other vital elements of the school program. In fact, students' accomplishments in these so-called nonessential areas provide counselors and colleges with additional information in the task of matching. (I need hardly say that I am all for teaching "the basics." But my definition of what is "basic" is wider than that of many taxpayers.)

There is tremendous variation in the quality of high school counselors and in the extent of their duties and how thin their resources are spread, both in terms of numbers of students they serve and in terms of the problems they are asked to face. If they have to handle cases of truancy and other discipline problems, they may contaminate their relations to students so that students are unlikely to seek them out for disinterested advice on whether to attend college and, if so, which college.

The conscientious counselor faces moral and practical dilemmas that vary with the school in which she or he works and with the intellectual abilities of the students and the orbits of the colleges they and their parents consider, as the counselor can, within narrow limits, extend or modify these. In the superior prep schools and top-flight suburban high schools, many of whose students seek to attend the most selective colleges (and whose parents press in the same direction), guidance counselors, wanting to keep a good record for the school at the most selective institutions, may discourage applications from "high risk" candidates, even if realistically they have no need to worry that recommending one or two such candidates would seriously lower the school's credibility.

Guidance counselors are now tremendously handicapped, in my judgment, by the Buckley Amendment, which was intended to control bias in letters of recommendation; both they and college

professors suffer from the general decline in the confidentiality of
records and from people's supposed right to see whatever anyone
writes about them. The result is that, in self-protection, guidance
officials write blandly praising letters, which are discarded as
worthless. Even before the amendment, students and others
gained the right or unscrupulously filched the files to see what was
said about them and their friends. Given the number of narcissistic
people in the general population, not to mention the paranoids
who soon enough develop real enemies, it is my experience that
even generally favorable letters of recommendation, when read by
the person recommended, may not seem favorable enough. If they
were more favorable still, however, they would lose all credibility,
much like the recommendations that come in from some progres-
sive schools that do not give grades, reporting—this is only a touch
of caricature—that "Johnny has learned to relate better to people"
or that "Mary is beginning to find herself."

Most guidance counselors, of course, do not have the opportunity for even this sort of report: they have too many students to
permit any effort at individuation. Nor do they have time or sufficient resources to individuate among institutions, let alone keep up
with the rapid changes that occur in institutions. A good deal can
be learned without a visit, both by getting information from students one knows who have attended a particular institution and by
such vicarious evidence as is provided by a proper discounting
of the college paper, by careful study of the catalogue and other
promotional and informational material, and by following the
institution over the years in the college guides, such as Cass
and Birnbaum and the *College Handbook*, published by the College
Entrance Examination Board, which come out virtually annually
and try to keep up to date. Still, the counselor, like the student
making a serious choice, will find that a visit is superior if done with
good questions to ask and a good eye for unobtrusive measures,
such as seeing who is in the library at night, what is on the bulletin
boards, who is in the student pubs and hangouts, what books other
than texts and best sellers are carried in the student bookstore.
(Managers of on-campus and also of off-campus bookstores increasingly report that students are now buying only texts; they
agree with many professors of literature that there has been a
general decline in nonobligatory reading. When I meet students

and ask them whether they have any "secret books," which are not recommended to them by professors but are read on their own—the way for several years the books of Carlos Castañeda were on the campus bookstore best-seller lists—the students are apt to say that they do not have such favorites.)

In a residential institution, staying overnight may provide a sample of the extent of noise, sexual and pharmacological mores, the messiness of dormitory rooms and public space, and the precautions students either are required to take or do in fact take against crime and vandalism. To be sure, not only can a single night in a single residential unit be a biased sample and be misinterpreted (for example, because of discussions with students), but bareness of decor and messiness of rooms may represent, as seems often to be so at Harvard College, a quasi-ideological statement that one is not an esthete or, worse still, an "elitist" who worries about mere appearances—even though students on whose walls hang only a few old posters are quite likely to possess elaborate hi-fi equipment and a large record collection.

According to guidance counselors with whom I have recently spoken, however, money for travel to distant colleges is just not available today. As one discerning counselor from a Midwestern public school put it: "Colleges desperate for students will invite us to visit and lay on a show for us. But we don't have the money to go on our own and mosey around." Another guidance official commented that, at any one time, perhaps 10 to 15 percent of colleges are rapidly changing; so that a visit to them or a sense of them as they were a few years ago is not sufficient to provide contemporary advice, even though the majority of institutions do not change so rapidly.[1]

---

[1] The Ivy League institutions and comparable ones (Stanford, Duke, Chicago, Wesleyan) may change their academic programs only slowly, but the applicants' imagery concerning them may change quite rapidly, thus altering the quality and type of students and hence the experience particular students are likely to have, owing to an altered mix of peers. To illustrate: Brown University was a few years ago the first choice of some students but a second choice for others who were turned down by Harvard or Yale, whereas currently many students choose Brown in preference to once more favored institutions. Brown has changed somewhat—for example, abandoning its formerly separate women's college (Pembroke) and in the freedom of its curriculum—but more important is the decision of some highly able students to choose an institution of less than overwhelming size, near Boston but not metropolitan and not as crime-ridden as Harvard has been.

To give a concrete example, I was told about a guidance counselor at one of the Eastern prep schools who, in wisely seeking to get some of her students to consider private selective colleges outside the Northeast quadrant, regularly recommended Macalester College. She was unaware that the DeWitt Wallace family, of *Reader's Digest* fame, was no longer lavishly supporting Macalester, so that the college's remarkably large number of Merit Scholars had dropped drastically, and though it was still an institution of superior quality, it was far from being as selective or as able to offer financial aid as had been true a few years earlier.

Every year, the alumni magazines of leading prep schools state where the just-graduated seniors are going to college—and virtually all of them are going immediately or after a year's delay for postponed admission. The shifts in destination in recent years are a striking indication of the democratizing of American higher education. A Merit Scholar from Baldwin School in 1979 goes, along with several classmates, to Colgate, an excellent institution but deviant from the choices of the other Merit Finalists, who are headed for Ivy League universities; only two students choose Bryn Mawr, for which Baldwin was once a feeder school; students spread out from Catholic and relatively unselective Villanova to Colorado College and the University of Washington. The South is generally avoided, except for non-Southern Miami and one student going to Duke. The reports from Phillips Exeter or Phillips Andover are quite similar, as against an earlier era when Exeter would have sent a hundred students to Harvard, and Andover a hundred to Yale and sixty to Harvard. (On the basis of hunch and no evidence at all, I have the impression that some admissions officials of the Ivy League and other highly overapplied institutions have only a single bias—namely, a prejudice against prep school graduates from "good families" with excellent but not superlative test scores, a record of useful volunteer activities: students who might provide a kind of social cement for the institution but who are in no way flamboyant or eccentric. A Radcliffe student who felt sure she would not be admitted to my undergraduate course because she was "uninteresting" was therefore not wholly paranoid, although she had applied a speculative and at best partial truth to a situation in which such judgments were inapplicable, since I had made clear that I would use a lottery if the course was overapplied.) [2]

In many parts of the country and in some strata everywhere, there has in the past been a strong ideological current against sending one's children away to boarding school or in some cases to any private schools other than the parochial ones. To some extent, this reflects the belief that citizens should support the public schools, but more important is the fear of appearing elitist or snobbish. Today, especially in metropolitan areas, these attitudes are changing as parents who can afford to, including many upper-income black parents, flee the inner-city public schools where learning is made difficult by violence (and the fear of violence and vandalism) and the fact that the teacher has to spend most of the available time keeping order and also looking after the special needs of handicapped children under the "mainstreaming" provisions of state and federal laws and as evidence of the intellectual inadequacy or sheer incompetence of many public school teachers piles up. A number of parents have concluded that, if family resources are limited, money spent on their children's precollegiate education in a good day school or boarding school is more important than money spent for attendance at private colleges. Well-known boarding schools (such as Pomfret in Connecticut) that a few years ago considered closing are now flourishing—and some of the graduates are saving money by attending state flagship campuses, which can often promise them smaller classes for honors students, access to faculty members, and in-state scholarship support. (That the problem of price discounting beyond ascertained family need is beginning to operate among the weaker private schools, as it already has

[2] What remains astonishing is the willingness of alumni, with whatever degree of grumbling, to accept the fact that their children will be turned down by "their" colleges in very considerable number and be replaced by students not necessarily of more evident academic potential coming from families of more recent immigration from Eastern or Southern Europe, Latin America, or the American South. Furthermore, as once-stag colleges have become coeducational, the sons of alumni are often turned down, and it is not always sufficient compensation that daughters may be admitted as numbers of men shrink somewhat to allow the recruitment of women, for in many traditional families, the college "inheritance" of a son is taken as more important than that of a daughter. For an ingenious study of the prospective financial consequences for Harvard College of admitting women on what is called a sex-blind basis, see Luke (1979).

among the weaker colleges, is discussed in an analysis of private schools' financial aid by Kenneth Deitch, an economist formerly with the Sloan Commission on the Financing of Higher Education [Deitch, 1980].) It is no wonder that the teachers' unions, both the National Education Association and the American Federation of Teachers, are opposed to the idea of vouchers, which would give parents freedom of choice, limited only by the requirement that schools accept a certain number of "disadvantaged" children and not just skim off the ablest students now attending the public schools. Indeed, already the most eminent private schools have actively recruited considerable numbers of nonwhite students, although they have had a great deal of difficulty in recruiting black or Hispanic faculty members, an area in which they are in competition with colleges and universities, which by no means always require the doctorate in their eagerness to recruit such faculty members.

In working with students on college choice, guidance counselors are sometimes under regional constraints in private schools, as they may also be even in well-to-do suburban neighborhoods. There is certainly one breed of guidance counselors who base their judgments on a combination of envy and local pride: "Don't you think the great University of Texas [and indeed it is great] is good enough for you?" There is a tendency to limit the geographic and academic orbits for able women more than for comparable men, though this seems to be changing fast.

As was noted earlier in discussing the work of Joseph Kahl, many working-class neighborhoods have been tipped in the direction of college attendance, so that the spread of the college-going rates of the rich and poor was substantially decreased between 1967 and 1976 (Glenny, 1980, pp. 366–367). However, no one seems to have made a study of the proportionately small but numerically sizable group of students from well-to-do families who are not attending college (many of whom were involuntary students during the Vietnam war draft). While there have been many studies devoted to the lower-income students who, even if they graduate from high school, do not attend college and how to encourage their attendance, as of course federal financial aid policy has sought to do, I know of no studies of this group of talented and reasonably affluent young men who do not attend college. There are more of them than would appear to be accounted for by those who attend conservatories or join communes and who may detest ambition and competition and prefer an (often gently cushioned) downward social mobility. Loss of their talents to society and to themselves, to the degree that college might enlarge their potential, seems not to worry policy makers, although it is certainly a source of anxiety to the private colleges that depend mainly on such students, who can afford to pay at least a substantial part of their college-going costs. For the first time in history, the number of women entering college now exceeds the number of men, although women are less likely to go on for the baccalaureate, and many drop out or stop out after two years.

Although a surprising number of students, including many blacks, attend college with family incomes of $5,000 or less, the largest shift in college attendance is among lower-middle-class and working-class families. There also, more women than men are likely to attend college—in part reflecting the fact that men can earn more than women in most blue-collar jobs. To suggest some of the consequences, one can note that, in a predominantly white Massachusetts state college, women with verbal SAT scores between 350 and 399 make up over a quarter of the student body, and 15 percent of the women have scores between 250 and 349. This was a college that as late as 1969 had few students, certainly few women, with verbal SATs under 500. Test-score data from a New Jersey state college, also predominantly white, show a similar distribution. Indeed, when I was asked by Father Timothy Healy, S.J., then vice-chancellor of the City University of New York, what I thought would be the outcome of open admissions in the CUNY system, my response was that many more moderately able and moderately well-to-do whites would take advantage of the then zero-tuition opportunity than the poorly prepared nonwhites at whom the open admissions program was aimed—a prediction that turned out, taking the system as a whole, to be correct (see Lavin, Alba, and Silberstein, 1979, p. 74).

Inner-City Black Students. One special category of guidance officers who have been faced with the fiercest sort of pressures and dilemmas is those who work in predominantly black inner-city schools. Long before affirmative action, however unevenly, became judicial and executive policy, the selective private colleges and some of the great state universities began actively recruiting black undergraduates. I recall a black guidance official at Cass Technical High School in Detroit saying (around 1960) that, after being neglected for decades, his school was suddenly swarming with recruiters from all over, asking him to trot out blacks for recruitment. It was bewildering; he himself did not know enough to advise the students, whose heads were often turned by the sudden wave of interest—and this was not only interest in athletes or in blacks of evident academic potential, but often in those who, in the lingo so condescendingly used, were thought to be "authentic ghetto blacks." Simultaneously, without any division of labor as to fields of study or areas of recruitment, a number of the most eminent predominantly white institutions, with Wesleyan and later Oberlin (which had admitted women and blacks since 1833) in the forefront, were seeking to move from perhaps 2 percent nonwhite enrollment to 10, 12, or (at Oberlin under the leadership of President Fuller) 25 percent.

To return to the case of Cass Technical High School in Detroit: Wayne State University had from the beginning been an urban university (in fact, under municipal auspices before becoming part of the state system), attracting blacks not only to its undergraduate colleges but also, under the Cadbury Program (which took blacks for a postbaccalaureate premedical year to a special program of premedical preparation at Haverford College), to its graduate and professional schools. The University of Michigan and Michigan State entered the competition; the new Oakland University, set up with high academic standards in 1958, was not in the running. Its faculty had rejected everything "collegiate," including intercollegiate athletics; they were not going to be a jock school. The chancellor thought this unwise in its own terms and was able to bring academically oriented professors around to accepting athletics by showing that only through hiring a black basketball coach would the image of Oakland as a place of total academic seriousness be sufficiently altered so that it would be possible to recruit blacks. He got the coach, and he did get, in part through active recruiting by faculty members themselves, a sizable proportion of blacks from the Detroit and Pontiac areas.

In these pacesetter schools, target goals and de facto quotas rapidly became institutionalized, though difficult of attainment; thus, although the University of Michigan promised the Black Action Movement a few years ago that it would recruit 10 percent blacks, it has had difficulty meeting that quota, just as Oberlin, even with the help of the congressional Black Caucus, has come nowhere close to the 25 percent goal its former President Fuller had publicly set. Still, these institutions have built-in networks of black recruiters, both full-time and student volunteers; students have established "trade routes" back to their own high schools and regions; black administrators and concerned whites police the degree to which the quotas are annually met, as does the student paper.

When the federal government (and some state governments as well) entered the scene, through the courts and HEW, pressures on guidance counselors in inner-city black high schools were of course intensified, for the efforts to increase the graduation of blacks from high school were not comparably forceful, nor were the often valiant efforts successful to provide those blacks graduated through "social promotion" with the basic skills needed at college. I recently met an older black woman of ferocious energy and passion who is a guidance counselor at an inner-city all-black high school in the Middle West. She spoke of the false lures held out by predominantly white colleges in their competitive recruiting of black students—and the lures that most troubled her were not those of ample financial aid, black studies programs, or anything of the sort, but the promise of provision of remedial skills for students of whose academic deficiencies she was well aware. In following up her students, she often found that the remedial programs were badly run, even corrupt, quite apart from the difficulty of persuading black students to undergo the seeming humiliation of enrolling in basic-skills courses. She believed that some of her protégés would be better off starting in a black college, under less competitive pressure, or in a predominantly white local community college, and later possibly transferring to a more selective institution after they had found their academic footing. But her attempts to persuade them to do so could not compete with the promises held out, sometimes disingenuously and sometimes sincerely, by the avid recruiters.

It is interesting in the light of what has just been said that a recent survey showed that blacks in college placed more trust in their high school guidance counselors than white students did— perhaps in part because more of the blacks came from families whose members, not having attended college, could be of no help at all. The same reliance on black counselors has turned up in interviews by William Neumann among black students at all levels of institution, from predominantly black Albany State College in Georgia to blacks studying in a Syracuse University external degree program.

It would be comforting to conclude that the indiscriminate recruiting of black students is a transitional phase, which can boast of some successes as well as a number of scarred victims, but that as blacks become better educated and more knowledgeable and pre- dominantly white institutions more accustomed to dealing with black students, more realistic transitional programs will be created within the colleges, and blacks may become more wary of the promises held out to them by recruiters.[3] I have heard, for example, black Harvard seniors, angry at what they consider the condescension shown blacks who are humiliated by often being given better grades than they deserve by guilty, liberal white in- structors, declare that they will no longer recruit for Harvard College in the home-town (or, rather, home-city) high school. More recently, several Chicana students, who were among the first recruited to Harvard from truly impoverished (migrant worker) backgrounds, have also refused to recruit for an institution they found disorienting. But one or two such refusals do not alter the angry accounts in the Harvard *Crimson* or complaints by affirmative action officers if the black applicant pool shrinks or the number of those who are admitted but who decline admission rises. Charges of "institutional racism" are easily made and, given

---

[3] In "Stages in the Response of White Colleges and Universities to Black Students," Gamson, Peterson, and Blackburn (1980) comment that in many cases forced re- trenchment had set in before predominantly white colleges and universities had learned how to accommodate to the massive black student influx that preceded official affirmative action programs and also before black students themselves, and often hastily recruited black staff and faculty members, had learned what could realistically be expected, rather than rhetorically demanded. Their study shows how various the reactions and responses could be at institutions of different size, selectiv- ity, and public or private control.

the vagueness of the charge and the guilty consciences of those accused, are difficult to rebut.

In my experience, deans and admissions officials in predominantly white private liberal arts colleges that have been in the forefront of recruiting "high risk" students (and my own institution is one of these) are apt to be amateurs, loyal alumni who have stayed on or returned to serve their alma mater. They are rarely familiar with institutional research, but prefer to fasten, in a kind of anecdotage, on a particular rough diamond who was clearly a "high risk" and has now gone on to glory and distinction in the all-American way. They do not follow up the students who quietly drop out or those who stick it out in bitterness and humiliation, refusing the "counterfeit nurturance" of remedial programs[4] and sometimes, to take an analogy from the military, "fleeing forward" to be able to boast about taking advanced courses—for example, taking courses in the natural sciences without ever having mastered mathematics.

The study by Gamson, Peterson, and Blackburn (1980) indicates that even now there is great variability among the predominantly white institutions that have recruited substantial numbers of nonwhite students. In some, the students have created garrisons of solidarity, often with support from nonwhite faculty and staff, in an effort to protect gains already made. These garrisons can have mixed effects on the students themselves, permitting mutual help and the support of the transitional ethnic base but also serving to imprison black students who would like to live in a more integrated fashion without being labeled "oreos," a term often used deprecatingly for people with dark skins but supposedly white middle-class aspirations. Unfortunately, whites are unaware of the wish of many blacks for greater interracial contact and are often too timid to make the necessary overtures or too tactless to know how.

Hispanic Americans. Spanish-surnamed Americans arrived later than American blacks as objects of compensatory concern. They do

---

[4] I have borrowed the term *counterfeit nurturance* from Lifton (1967), who used it in dealing with the attitude of many Japanese A-bomb victims toward the American physicians who were seeking to care for them.

not form a single entity—neither, of course, do American blacks—
but include Cubans, political refugees from Latin America,
Mexican-Americans in the Southwest, Puerto Rican and other
Caribbean migrants in the Northeast and Midwest. Many have the
advantage of being Catholic, able to rely on an organized church
that seeks to be ethnically ecumenical (a salvation also for some
of the most beleaguered Vietnamese refugees). However, many
suffer from a grave language barrier, one that is often intensified
rather than ameliorated by provisions for bilingual education.[5]
And although there are a hundred colleges and universities
founded primarily for blacks, those under Spanish-speaking control are but a recent handful: Hostos Community College in the
City University of New York system; Los Medanos College in
California; New Mexico Highlands University, only in recent years
having Spanish-speaking administrators; and some community colleges and segments of state colleges in the southern parts of Texas,
Colorado, and California. Black North Americans are used to
equal or even superior treatment for black women, who long made
up the majority of students and a large proportion of the faculty in
the Negro colleges; in contrast, there is no similar tradition in
Spanish-speaking groups. (I am reminded of the president of a
Mountain States college who believed he would satisfy the demands
of his Spanish-speaking students when he appointed a Chicana as
dean—only to have a violent outbreak because this was seen as a
slur on the "macho" spirit of the Chicanos.)

In interviews with Chicana and Chicano students and in
studies they have reported to me of surveys done in predominantly

---

[5] Bilingual education has created problems for many immigrant groups, including
Chinese recently coming from the Far East, but the problems are especially grave
when, on the one hand, the parents are determined that their children learn standard English and, on the other hand, there are dialects that are greatly different—
as in the cases of Haitians and French-Canadians in the Northeast and of the many
different Spanish-speaking groups. And leaving aside the arguments by William
Labov and other linguists that "black English" is a separate language and not simply
a dialect, it would seem that most black parents would like their children to learn
standard English, while not being humiliated at the hands of insensitive teachers—
black as well as white—who do not appreciate the grammatical differences between
black English and supposedly standard English, which is constantly changing and,
among other things, incorporating slang and other expressions borrowed from
blacks.

white institutions, it is clear that they have really no guidance at all in leaving home base, as many of their parents strongly object to their doing, and traveling, let us say, from the Imperial Valley of California to Brown or Harvard, Carleton or Amherst. Furthermore, although support structures have been built up in the major universities for Puerto Ricans, Cubans, Guatemalans, and other migrants from Central and South America, these people come from very different backgrounds—dramatically, of course, the Cubans—than the average Chicano or Chicana student, now being sought after as another recognized minority.

Guidance Counselor's Constituencies. I have gone into some detail about the situation of guidance counselors in predominantly or overwhelmingly black secondary schools, with passing reference to the much more difficult situation of Chicano students, even though the former group makes up less than an eighth of the public school population and the latter is even smaller (but growing). In fact, I have sought to help counter a widespread belief that guidance counselors, taken en masse, deal only with the children of the well-to-do and seek to get them into their preferred colleges. Actually, guidance counselors are often in the same position as teachers: devoting the bulk of their attention to a small minority of students in trouble in one way or another—including the paradoxical "trouble" of being overwhelmed by solicitations. But I have also wanted to make clear that there is tremendous diversity among guidance counselors, within schools and among them, in the cadres to whom they are forced to pay attention or about whom they have personal concern and interest.

When students can afford it, they are encouraged to visit colleges, including residential colleges at a distance from home, but like other tourists, they are uninformed about how to make the most of such a visit. Time and again, I have seen students decide against a college that in my judgment or a counselor's judgment would be a good match for the individual because the admissions interviewer and the student did not hit it off. My assistant, William Neumann, interviewing high school seniors and college freshmen at my instigation in order better to understand processes of college choice, spoke with a Boston College freshman who had been put off by an Antioch College recruiter who, by the student's account, seemed high on drugs at the time. Since the student was a square, athletic, academically able Irish Catholic, the admissions official from Antioch at least served as a warning signal in a way not entirely discrepant with Antioch as it has been, if not Antioch as it may want to become under its new administration. Conversely, an attractive admissions interviewer or recruiter coming to a high school can give an exceedingly misleading picture of an institution. Stephens College in Columbia, Missouri, whose recruiters' salaries depended on their effectiveness, also required them to visit the campus six months after those they had recruited had arrived, in order to see what errors in judgment they had made, to learn of new developments on campus, and to be cautioned against the overselling that was nevertheless a virtual imperative for a private women's college, especially outside the East Coast.

Auditing College Catalogues

In 1976 the Fund for the Improvement of Postsecondary Education helped support the creation of the National Task Force on Better Information for Student Choice, a group at first headed by Robert Corcoran of the Education Commission of the States. One aim of this group has been to increase the veracity and clarity of information in college catalogues, the ideal being a catalogue certified by an independent auditor as containing accurate information on such matters as tuition throughout a four-year sequence (and refund policy in case of withdrawal), the kinds of programs offered by the college, rates of attrition, the jobs and postbaccalaureate education pursued by graduates, and the range of test scores. I have been involved with this movement in a peripheral way and have studied the audited catalogue already produced at Barat College, a straightforward document, and the similar document of the University of California at Irvine, the work of former Vice-President John C. Hoy.

The search for greater candor and clarity in catalogue copy is undoubtedly useful to an institution's administrators and faculty members. For example, faculty members in a particular orbit may have little awareness of institutionwide stopping-out and attrition rates. Or in a private college such as Barat, they may not be aware of the extent to which the Illinois in-state scholarship program, which has helped some students to attend private colleges in the state, has led admissions officers to concentrate more on recruiting from within the state, thus increasing the provincialism of their students. And to declare, as the Barat catalogue does, that the college is not recommended for students who want to pursue certain specialized programs, whose main aim, for example, is to attend medical school, is a model departure from the temptation of many underenrolled, perhaps especially private colleges that claim to offer almost anything to anybody.

Who Reads Catalogues? The process of preparing an audited catalogue may well be useful to an institution, but it is far less clear to what extent students and even guidance counselors will even look at it and, if they do, will properly interpret such data as the figures on attrition, the number of Ph.D.s on the faculty, clues to the rapidity of faculty turnover, or the number of books in the library, where it may be that what matters is the degree to which the institution can afford to maintain the library and continue the serial subscriptions to increasingly expensive journals. In discussions with guidance counselors, I have found that most keep a stack of catalogues on hand or can refer students to nearby sources of ample catalogues and other promotional material. But there is widespread agreement that students do not study catalogues, and that is what one discovers in interviewing students accepted at most selective colleges. Even there, one often finds students attracted to a college by its reputation or by the fact that their friends are going there, all of which blocks out the potential knowledge that, in the field of their particular interest, even a great university may be deficient. They are often surprised, for example, to discover that Harvard College has only limited offerings in Sanskrit and Indian studies and, until the recent recruitment of Robert Brustein, discussed earlier, virtually no work in theater for academic credit (Yale, Princeton, or the University of Illinois, to name just three, would be far better for students with a primary interest in theater, or the University of Chicago or Pennsylvania for South Asian studies). My inquiries to Irvine officials about the extent to which students in fact made use of their carefully audited catalogue turned up statements by counselors that they knew of only two instances in which the catalogue had been a factor in recruitment or decision.

Furthermore, the prose in the catalogue may be audited, but not the photographs—and, like the figures on attrition, they are easily misinterpreted. For example, the Irvine catalogue has a cover photograph of a young woman gazing out at the water, implying that the Irvine campus is on the ocean, whereas it is only near it. Most catalogues of the larger and more selective colleges seem to include what affirmative action officials might decide was a "disproportionately" high number of photographs of attractive blacks, both on the faculty and among the students, not representative of the actual number.

Helen Astin, professor of higher education at UCLA, made use not only of statistical data but of catalogues in a report prepared for HEW on sex discrimination in access to postsecondary education (Astin, Harway, and McNamara, 1976). She counted a number of instances in which women were seen in passive and men in active roles (for example, a man astride a bicycle chatting with a woman sitting on a bench), but this may in fact represent a true picture of sex preferences, which do not necessarily mean that women are passive and men active—a picture easily, if unofficially, censored by an American version of "socialist realism" in which women are invariably shown in reversals of traditional sex roles. Such reversals would actually falsify the catalogue by implying that women were moving toward androgyny on that campus.

Institutional academic competition, of course, also leads to imitation of prevailing fashions in methods of instruction and contents and to jazzing up of course titles without necessarily changing course content (except possibly diluting it). Careful study of *The Yellow Pages of Undergraduate Innovations* (1974) indicates to those knowledgeable about particular institutions the enormous diversity of programs that pass themselves off as "innovative." Of course, this guide was intended primarily for professors and administrators looking for programs that are in use elsewhere so that they themselves do not have to start *de novo,* but individual entries could well be misleading to students who knew nothing about the institutions listed.

What are almost nowhere to be found are guides to the microclimates of subdepartments. In the smaller residential colleges—let us say, 2,000 students and under—the grapevine will convey the reputations of what are likely to be rather small departments, and faculty members themselves are likely to be relatively accessible and at least in some measure knowledgeable about their colleagues. Even so, knowledge of this sort deteriorates rapidly: It could not keep up with the rapid mobility of faculty in the brisk market of an earlier day, nor can it keep up with the nonretention of nontenured faculty in the slow or retrenching market of the present. As in the American Council on Education rankings of graduate programs, reputation even in a small institution tends to lag behind reality.

Misusing Data on Attrition. Colleges are sometimes required, either by their own standards or by various plans for student-consumer protection, to state their figures on attrition. It seems to me from conversations with high school guidance counselors that the colleges are correct in believing that in the eyes of the public high attrition rate can virtually never be satisfactorily explained as a potentially benign "social indicator." The small private, often denominational liberal arts colleges are the worst sufferers from the near unanimity of the verdict that attrition beyond, say, 20 percent will be taken as a negative sign by students and parents. Few people are aware that the national average is about 50 percent. (The unusual ability of such colleges to serve as decompression chambers is not well understood by prospective entering students, though they may understand it well enough if they seek out a community college with the initial intention of transferring to a larger or more demanding institution.)

Conversely, I have yet to find counselors or prospective students and their families who understand that Harvard's practically zero attrition (Cass and Birnbaum say that it is zero, and they are almost correct) is a definite warning signal. For no initial matching of college and student can be so idyllic as to make the milieu optimal even for a single year, let alone four. But in two decades of talking with students who are being harmed by Harvard for any number of reasons having to do with the student's own qualities, the luck of the draw of courses and majors, residential settings, and the vicious cycles that all of us can get into, I have succeeded in persuading only a tiny number of such students even to consider leaving Harvard. Because of the syndrome (discussed in Chapter Two) of a national ranking of what is "the best," students believe that leaving Harvard will stigmatize them, and they misjudge their ability to enter other, equally good—for them undoubtedly superior—liberal arts colleges or universities that have higher attrition and would welcome transfers; they feel it an ineradicable defeat to give up the Harvard guerdon, an irremediable failure. The situation is somewhat alleviated by Harvard's wise and generous policy of permitting stopouts, made use of by as many as a fifth of the student body, who often return from "real life" with a better sense of direction even if there has been no planning of the Antioch College sort as to what they might do in their time away from Harvard. (Harvard College, however, does not as a general rule give credit for study at another institution, although it is possible to cross-register at MIT. It lacks the facilities for study abroad that many institutions provide. A few years ago I proposed the possibility of a freshman year abroad for those students of reasonably cosmopolitan background who could profit from concentrated study in another culture, with courses given principally in the local language and in a setting where there would not be, as in Paris, many other Americans to whom to turn to avoid immersion in the indigenous culture. I also believed that in such a setting one could have a structured curriculum developed by the combination of local and Harvard faculty members recruited for the enterprise. The idea, which preceded development of a core curriculum, was not taken seriously. However, Leon Botstein, the president of Bard College, hopes to institute such a voluntary program shortly.)

In going over attrition data in successive years from the same institutions, I have noticed in many a secular diminution of attrition, which is especially troubling in colleges where able students would "run out of school" in the first few years. Plainly, the faculty is devoting great efforts to retain these students for their tuition, to fill its own upper-division classes, and to avert the misinterpretation of the public record that will occur if the college's attrition, now often held down to 20 percent where earlier it was 40 percent, begins to rise.

Misinformation on Doctoral Programs. Then there is widespread mis-information among those who plan to go on for further education. To illustrate from my own field and experience, undergraduates today who get interested in sociology as a field of further study are likely to overaggregate the generally shrinking market for Ph.D.s, just as writers about higher education do, and to assume that there are no jobs in sociology for college teachers. They also tend to have little knowledge of opportunities for work in applied fields (other than as probation officers or social workers). The possibility of work in market research, in the booming field of evaluation, or in all sorts of government jobs available to people in applied social science is seldom recognized—or, if recognized, is regarded as not intellectually or morally legitimate. Furthermore, students fre-quently apply aggregate figures to themselves, not taking account of their own special talents or, in selective colleges, the high plat-forms on which they already stand (Riesman, 1978a).

And then there is the further misjudgment that, in order to be accepted in a top-flight graduate department of sociology, one must have done substantial work in the field as an undergraduate, if not majored in it. Undergraduates may not be disabused of this judgment by their professors, eager for majors and perhaps no better informed themselves. Yet faculty members in many major graduate departments of sociology, aware that as an undergradu-ate subject sociology is often regarded, with some justification, as a "soft option," are more likely to respond positively to a candidate who has done outstanding work in a clearly difficult area, such as mathematics, philosophy, the natural sciences, or European or Far Eastern history (with some command of a difficult foreign lan-guage). They recognize that sociology is not a field, like mathemat-ics (or music or languages), in which an early start is both feasible and generally desirable and that in any case a study of the field is not likely to be rewarding for seven or eight consecutive years.

A reader might quarrel with this judgment on the ground that a student ought to do a fair amount of sociology as an under-graduate in order to discover whether he or she has aptitude for and liking for the field. In this domain, I prefer the British usage, in which students say they are going to "read" sociology or history, rather than "take" the subject. The faculty at any particular institu-tion with whom a student comes into contact may be a quite diver-

gent and unrepresentative sample of the field, no more enlighten-
ing than the Strong Vocational Interest Inventory, which many
people take to discover whether their interests jibe with those of
people currently in a field, without asking whether the field is
changing and without dreaming that they themselves might help
change it. An internship in a market-research or survey-research
agency might serve students better than some courses, and a reading list of half a dozen sociological classics could be undertaken
with minimal faculty guidance.

Then, although a few graduate departments of sociology may
be influenced in admission decisions by undergraduate work in the
field, the leading ones are surely influenced by the reputation of
the undergraduate college itself. Correspondingly, a student at a
small, unknown college hoping to attend a major graduate department will find it advantageous to have had contact with a sociology
professor who has his or her degree from a major research university and who can use connections thus established to pave
the way for particularly talented undergraduates. The Buckley
Amendment, though intended to protect students, has in fact resulted in protecting only the well-connected whose sponsors can
pick up the telephone, and in fact the Buckley Amendment is a
disaster for the unconnected. Thus, a student at a small college
may want at least to take a course with a faculty member who has
this kind of telephone contact to get around the loss of credibility
of letters due to the loss of privacy.

In sociology and anthropology, the professional associations
publish guides to graduate study, listing all universities giving postbaccalaureate degrees and stating who the faculty are, their subjects, where they got their own degrees, how many master's or
doctoral candidates are in residence, how many degrees were
granted the previous year, and where people who received these
degrees are currently employed. I find it astonishing that applicants to graduate schools in sociology and anthropology often do
not make use of these guides, but go by the brand names of the
university, ignoring, for example, the very high attrition at some
institutions, which should be a warning signal raising the question
in the student's mind whether he or she has the pertinacity to
complete the program when so many fall by the wayside. Similarly,
many students apply to do graduate work in sociology at Harvard

without realizing that our department is a small one, not prepared to train all-round sociologists in the way that Michigan or Wisconsin would be, but superb, for example, for someone who wants to combine sociology with East Asian studies or who has an interest in the sociology of art and culture or in other subspecialties that Harvard offers. (I might also add that we lose some students we accept to schools that offer them more money than our graduate school concludes they actually need when scarce funds are divided on the basis of equity and need, rather than merit. Interviews suggest that these students, like undergraduates, are lured away by what in the long run are relatively small bribes—money interpreted at times as statements of the institution's interest in them as individual candidates.)

Student Consumer Research on Colleges

Just as there are some student-edited guides to colleges, such as the Yale students' *Insiders' Guide to Colleges* (*Yale Daily News*, 1978), so students for a long time have been preparing course evaluations of greater or lesser discrimination and cogency. At their best, especially when they have used differentiated questions—for example, concerning quality and lucidity of lectures, amount and quality of reading, presumed fairness and general level of grading, and amount of effort needed to earn a top grade—these can be useful. When carefully done, they can provide feedback to the instructor,[6] although, as we shall see, this kind of market research has its dangers.

During the last several years at Harvard College, in addition to the well-known *Crimson's Confidential Guide to Courses,* which is based on sporadically collected ballots and a reasonably fair-minded if frequently witty and whimsical write-up by *Crimson* staff members, the student-faculty Committee on Undergraduate Education has published a booklet of more conventional evaluations of the larger lower-division courses, with the useful differentiations just mentioned concerning clarity of lectures, amount of reading,

---

[6] For a penetrating discussion of how course examinations, when carefully designed with this purpose in mind, can give an instructor a differentiated sense of what students have learned and what mistakes in teaching can be corrected, see Schelling (1963); also Cahn (1978).

and interest of the reading. The CUE Guide also permits instructors to make a statement about the aims of their courses.

Seldom have I seen anything quite so biting as a course guide prepared some years ago at the University of Illinois, which was as savage as if the authors were already prepared for careers as "New York intellectuals," literary critics, or adversary journalists! In this "multiversity," a strain of vindictiveness ran through the comments. One admirable guide with which I am familiar is the Barnard-Columbia Guide, which includes observant discussions of departments (now begun in a small way at Harvard by the *Crimson*'s "Confi Guide") as well as extremely careful course evaluation. (Some subsidy was provided by the university for this serious effort.)

More than three decades ago, Lyman Bryson wrote an essay, "Notes on a Theory of Advice," ([1948] 1964) which dealt with the question of advice for whom and for what—an issue in all these forms of advice that aggregate conclusions (the overall summary figures are rarely disaggregated by the grades particular "voters" received in the course they are evaluating). Students reading advice or listening to the grapevine are often insufficiently familiar with their own idiosyncrasies and follow the crowd, so that course evaluations tend to become self-confirming prophecies. I would prefer that students ponder what their own particular cognitive styles are or what their vitamin and other deficiencies are; in college they have perhaps their last chance to repair these deficiencies with relative safety from severe penalty and only moderate risks of humiliation before an audience most of whose members they will never see again.

Furthermore, the very bounteousness of options that is the result in many institutions of recent deliquescence of requirements[7] is bewildering, especially to entering students who accept advice from fellow students or from harried and often ignorant advisers in the absence of clear curricular guidelines. Earlier I

[7] One of the senior figures in the field of the history of American higher education (Rudolph, 1977) demonstrates in a recent book that cycles of relaxation and constraint in the curriculum did not begin with Charles W. Eliot's elective system at Harvard (which proved a model for some but by no means all institutions), but have a long and fascinating history.

mentioned the comparison of requirements between 1960 and 1975 in the essay prepared by Robert Blackburn and his University of Michigan colleagues (1976) for the Carnegie Council on Policy Studies in Higher Education. Blackburn not only examined formal requirements but analyzed actual student transcripts—something I have also done in a nonsystematic way. Transcripts are especially useful in illustrating avoidances, such as that of the science major who avoids courses he or she regards as "cultural bull." Far more common in colleges and universities that recruit primarily children of those who have themselves attended college, pre-meds excepted, are students who avoid any quantitative work; if there is still a science requirement, they discover which courses have the least science in them—perhaps "Physics for Poets"; in some places, geology; in others, evolution; in still others, the history or sociology of science; none of these are what scientists themselves, perhaps with undue narrowness, would call "doing science." Blackburn's study is discussed in a summary also prepared for the Carnegie Council by Martin Trow (1976a).

So far, I have been discussing primarily student-initiated course guides on the assumption that they might mislead particular students to flock to the courses of well-favored and frequently "easy" instructors, whether or not such behavior is optimal for them as individuals. What I have not yet discussed is the increasing danger that student evaluations of instructors will be manipulated by individual faculty members, faculty cliques, and student-faculty cadres in a situation in which retention and the rare chance for tenure become increasingly precarious with the dramatic fall in enrollments. Like most of us, professors almost invariably want to be liked (some do not, because it brings them too much traffic, and others who are members of major research-oriented colleague groups believe that to become popular is disreputable); whatever their personal tastes, many may have to court the student vote. But I know of no study that has done the detective work required to see how tendentiously or fraudulently this can be done. There is a fairly general awareness of those faculty members who give virtually everyone an A as a way of ensuring that they will have customers and who demand almost nothing in the way of work. In the softer areas (which in some colleges now, surprisingly, include psychol-

ogy) one may seek to win a student audience by "rapping" or running encounter groups in which the seamier aspects of life experience are regarded as the "real me," as of course happens also in
many settings outside academia.

In discussing black studies departments, I referred to non-
scholarly black faculty members who seek to maintain their precarious hold on academic life by building up a cadre of militant followers, threatening to charge the institution with racism if it releases
them. Spanish-surnamed faculty members have less commonly
been able to make use of such tactics, simply because there are
fewer of them, although in the Southwest and in the New York
area, there have been such instances. The greatest gains from
building a cohort have gone to women, both through building up
women's studies as a way of collecting a student following—an
enterprise that is often scholarly and worthwhile but should not be
confined to women—and through litigation on grounds of sex discrimination. Furthermore, in predominantly white colleges and
universities, there are apt to be more women than black males or
Chicanos on the faculty and of course in the student body (where in
many private and public institutions, women have outnumbered
men even before the recent changes in the ratio of women to men
at the point of college entry); hence, as some affirmative action
officers have said to me, white women have made more substantial
gains than nonwhite minorities through litigation or the threat of
it.

The threat of litigation has commonly led universities to settle
out of court, since their administrations prefer to avoid both the
immense costs in money and time of a lawsuit dragged through all
stages of appeal and the adverse publicity resulting from charges of
sexism. Some cases of this sort appear absurd on their face, as when
a woman sociologist already on tenure sued Simmons College, a
women's college in Boston, for sex discrimination when not
granted a full professorship by a senior departmental faculty composed entirely of women. The college, fearing the financial and
public-relations costs of a trial, awarded the plaintiff the professorship—and lost two capable women sociologists, who immediately
resigned. Similarly, I was asked by several women activists acting in
concert to testify on behalf of a plaintiff concerning the "old-boy

network" in a sex-discrimination case brought against Smith College; the pressures on me were such that it seemed as if the "old-boy network" had been succeeded by the "activist women's network," which could resort to pressureful tactics because it still felt itself, no doubt correctly, to be entitled to the privileges of acting as an aggrieved minority. But the fact is that Smith College, like other women's colleges, has given positions to women when they were grossly discriminated against by the major stag and coed research universities. One consequence is that, to a small degree, the women's colleges have suffered a "brain drain" of talented women faculty members to high-prestige research universities that also pay larger salaries, much as the black colleges have suffered in a similar way.

In the past, women have sometimes lost those suits that came to trial, especially when the institution could show that it followed correct procedures, advertising widely; courts have been somewhat reluctant to interfere with a department's judgment in such cases. However, a recent consent decree entered into by the University of Minnesota may mark a drastic change of the tendency toward such forbearance (see Broad, 1980). In that case, a woman chemist (who has since become an attorney) brought suit charging sex discrimination by the chemistry department, which had apparently made no serious efforts to recruit from the concededly small pool of women research chemists and at least one of whose members in internal correspondence had made a plainly sexist comment. The decree covers not only the offending department but the entire university, which for nearly a decade is to have its entire affirmative action procedures monitored by the Master appointed by the federal district court.

The way faculty members conduct themselves to gain renewals of contracts and tenure may deeply affect the morale of an institution, and such elements are unlikely to get into catalogues or counselors' notebooks. Prospective-student visitors may learn about such matters from the grapevine, but many will not understand the long-run consequences. So far as I know, there is no survey (which might not even be possible with anonymous questionnaires, but would require a detective) to discover the extent to which instructors use not only guile but actual fraud to circumvent the evaluation process. Just as episodes are reported in the press or gossiped about among pre-meds concerning students who destroy other students' materials for determining an "unknown" in an organic-chemistry class or knife out of an irreplaceable journal an essential reading for a course, so some faculty members may hear stories of instructors who not only forge their own evaluations and eliminate negative ones when they have an opportunity to collect student assessments but also manage to destroy any favorable evaluations of their competitors.

Some faculty members, aware that such practices exist or are rumored to exist, would like to dispense with student evaluation of teaching and substitute peer evaluation based on visits to classes. Yet apart from the fact that the presence of the colleague-observer may itself disturb the class being scrutinized or may represent the entry of an opposing faction protecting the fate of other candidates, there are many situations in which the remedy for forgery and other cheating is better policing of the way student evaluations are conducted, not their elimination. Consider the following constellation, described for me by a small number of presidents of unionized public institutions in states whose "sunshine laws" require that all documents involving the public business be accessible, much as in the federal Freedom of Information Act. These presidents, and some of their more scholarly faculty members, would like to elevate both the scholarly and the teaching qualities of the faculty by review of tenure cases on more than a pro forma basis. If someone who comes up for tenure is a notoriously poor teacher and no scholar either, faculty members asked to write letters of recommendation recognize that the person may well receive tenure and will see everything written about himself or herself in the files; hence, they write only what is favorable, thus avoiding trouble for themselves in personal terms or in the possibility of a prolonged grievance proceeding under the collective bargaining agreement and perhaps an eventual lawsuit. Privately, they tell the dean and the president that the person is worthless, but the only evidence in the record that is other than glowing comes from student evaluations. These may be, in spite of their unreliability, evidence or at least a warning signal that the faculty member in question is not the superb teacher his or her colleagues claim publicly that he or she is.

Evaluations are surely not the best evidence, these presidents agree, but they are the only evidence on which one might possibly deny tenure, if the student complaints are emphatic and sufficiently sustained and uniform. The students at least have the protection of anonymity; the colleague group does not.

Students tend to underestimate their influence where it is not associated with formal decision-making power. Even where they do possess formal power, as in the many cases in which students serve on committees with faculty and administration, even including committees deciding on promotion and tenure, in my observation students often do not believe they possess as much influence or power as they in fact do. This is especially but not only true of black students, who on the one hand have convinced themselves by their own rhetoric of the racism of their adversaries and on the other hand feel insecure concerning their legitimacy in a particular academic milieu, and thus they have frequently been surprised by how many concessions they have obtained. Students in general, even where they serve on boards of trustees, are not satisfied to have a forum in which to raise issues and to heighten sensibilities, since this does not give them the assurance of their own full acceptance. As Larry H. Litten writes (personal correspondence): "Young adults will always require more confirmation of their legitimacy than people who have experienced a greater share of success and compromise—and when they can convince themselves and others that their causes embrace or correspond to the causes of groups that are more widely acknowledged as disadvantaged, their tolerance for anything less than victory is understandably low. Victory, i.e., visible change, is the only evidence of power that they can claim."

I have observed incidents at my own institution in which a public demonstration is held on behalf of a junior faculty member who has been denied tenure and who is black or assertively feminist or politically radical (for example, a self-proclaimed Marxist) or all three. The majority of students who have worked with this person have handed in anonymous evaluations of a negative sort or commented informally to faculty members concerning the teacher's incompetence or tendency to play favorites and behave in an arbitrary fashion. These students are, for obvious reasons, silent when the demonstration occurs. If the demonstration does not succeed, a great majority of students will be confirmed in their belief that they have made no visible change in what they call "the system," whereas in fact they have contributed to a change by means of representative, rather than open participatory, forms. At any rate, student power and influence are likely to increase as sunshine laws and collective bargaining spread, especially in the public sector.[8]

One theme has increasingly forced itself on my attention as I have watched faculty members try to conform to what they and the colleagues who advise them conclude are majority student tastes on their campus: a consequence may be that an excessive homogeneity of teaching styles is developed that appears to please the majority but, since no single all-purpose style is satisfactory for all students, is sure to be dysfunctional for a substantial minority—often not even a minority but the majority who are less vocal or active.

For example, there are some departments in which the standard and approved performance is a lecture beamed at the supposed average—that is, a moderately half-awake and passive member of the student body—a lecture in which the speaker first says what he or she is going to say, then says it, and then summarizes what has been said. Sometimes, depending on the department or the institution, there will be the paraphernalia of overhead transparencies or multimedia presentations. The main characteristic of such performances is that they are slick and palatable; the students have no difficulty taking notes—the instructor may even have notes to hand out in class and will specify what students will be held for on the examination. The students are passive receptacles; nothing is asked of them in the way of active listening, let alone

---

[8] A useful source for keeping in touch with student litigation and lobbying is the *National On-Campus Report:* a national information service on the contemporary campus scene, published monthly at Madison, Wisconsin, and reporting, for example, on student lawsuits brought by public-interest research groups (the Naderite groups formed on many campuses through dues checkoffs from student fees) and on lobbying on behalf of Title IX vis-à-vis student athletics—a move that will not necessarily benefit women athletes if pressure and litigation result in a decision that equal amounts be spent on athletics for both sexes when it is big-time sports that supports the athletic programs for both sexes and when, to my regret, fewer women than men are active in sports. For a comprehensive account, see Kellams (1975).

active vocal participation and questioning. The lecture is so polished that it has no rough edges to invite further questioning about
its concepts. The professor may post office hours when students
may come and ask questions, but they are apt to be of the sort:
"Can I take an Incomplete?" (A recent study at Harvard shows the
very rapid rise in the number of medical excuses, which are the
only reason permitted for an Incomplete in the undergraduate
college—an increase that falls off dramatically to almost nothing in
the second term of the senior year.)

But then there are other institutions where the going style is
almost an aggressive "hang loose" or "laid back" approach; no faculty member would dare to wear a tie and jacket or to stand up and
hold forth; the class is a rap session, and everything is related to the
personal experience of students. This is not necessarily bad, any
more than the lucid lecture is necessarily bad—I am talking here
about homogeneity, not about quality or modes of cognition. The
"rap session" style may not even be thin in content, although it
often is; it may be quite evocative, helping students become more
curious about their own lives and the lives and scenes around them,
making them participant-observers who are actively relating the
books they read to wider orbits beyond their own immediate
frames of reference. But the point again is that what is useful for
the single faculty member in ensuring that he or she is retained is
harmful from the point of view of the department and the institution in that there is no way of protecting other styles that would
satisfy divergent tastes.

While both style and language are moving toward homogenization, there is no possibility of content becoming homogenized
in quite the same way. We would not expect a department of
history to offer only post–Civil War American history or only
Balkan history; there would be some division of labor, some sense
of coverage. (To be sure, there are departments in low-consensus
fields, such as sociology, where the courses are slanted according to
a particular political mode, and there may be a few professors who
are in effect frozen out by the near unanimity that selection and
self-selection have accomplished.) But to the degree that everything depends on student evaluations of teaching, only tenured
faculty members would dare experiment with either innovative

content or methods that might fail. Moreover, even they might fear to lose student customers to other departments in the ebb and flow of student traffic—where again it is the majority that is counted.

The nearest parallel I can think of comes from the single-member district in which only the majority counts, as against proportional representation—and I am suggesting that a faculty member in a department without formal requirements is impelled to act in self-protection as if he or she were running in a winner-take-all election.

Even faculty development programs, which are coming into increasing use to help anxious faculty members become less incompetent as teachers, may also give rise to a uniform style. At one liberal arts college, I observed a series of videotapes of junior faculty members who had been through a program of learning at an instructional center how to become better teachers. They were shown in "before" and "after" settings. In the "before" tapes, many were somewhat stiff and reserved, wearing coats and ties, standing up and using intricate vocabulary—then sometimes writing long words on the board while they lost eye contact with the students. After sufficient induction into what might be, perhaps unfairly, termed "Rogerian" techniques, the same faculty members would be sitting with students who were nearly indistinguishable from them, using the same vernacular speech with which students are themselves fully at home and thus not stretching student vocabularies, apostles of what Gamson (1967) termed "personalism." To be sure, a number of obvious pedagogic errors had been noted and corrected (such as speaking inaudibly while writing on the blackboard); instructors were more aware of their students but not necessarily less shy, especially if they had made the effort to alter their own personal styles in the interest of illusory mutual comfort. The overall result for the students is an impoverishment of available models. And the premise that students do not need to learn from teachers they consider "bad" caters to their passivity and lack of participation in their own education.

In this era in which students have become more sovereign in all but the small number of institutions where they are so eager to come that they will put up with almost anything and where, once in the gates, they are running scared to secure admission to favored postbaccalaureate education or employment, we are witnessing a rise of organized consumerism that seems to me to ride too much with the current tide, rather than in opposition to it.

Inadequacies of the Advising Process

Organized student movements and lobbies are beginning on both the state and national levels. One of the most illuminating such efforts is described in the final report of the research project on students and collective bargaining undertaken by the National Student Educational Fund (Shark, Brouder, and Associates, 1976; also Stark, 1977). In the case studies reported in that volume, students have sought to sit at the bargaining table along with faculty union representatives. They have realized that they have a stake in the collective bargaining contract as it affects, for example, the number of contact hours required of faculty members. When resources are scarce, as they inevitably are, students also have a stake in faculty salary levels because it often happens that an organized faculty has the power to increase its own compensation at the cost of, for example, student services of at least equivalent value for undergraduates.[9]

[9] As this book goes to press, the Supreme Court has just handed down its decision in the Yeshiva University case. By a slim five-to-four majority, the Court concluded what seems obvious: In most cases, college or university faculty members *are* "management." It is they who decide the content of their courses; collectively, they decide on the curriculum; with minor exceptions, they select their own colleague group; they are the masters of their classrooms, and the decisions they make on grading are primarily their own personal decisions. The Yeshiva University case covers only private institutions; public ones are often subject to state employee bargaining regulation and legislation. And the Yeshiva case has left some issues undecided. For example, it raises a question about untenured faculty members, although in most departments they are or could be as fully in charge of their own courses as anyone else, and from among them will come some of the senior faculty—that is, they are "management trainees," and in many departments they may and do vote and certainly have a say in the appointment process. How far an interpretation by a government agency can go beyond any sensible, conceivable intent of the original National Labor Relations Board, which was created to enforce Section 7a of the Wagner Labor Relations Act passed under Franklin Roosevelt and designed to assist efforts to reorganize America's basic industries, is illustrated by those cases in which department chairs and even deans have been included as "labor," with only the president and the board of trustees defined as "management." Most presidents could only dream of such a possibility, and few would want to be as autocratic as this legal fiction assumes—but I have met a few presidents who feel that they are better off dealing with a union bargaining agent, whose eye may be on future union competi-

A student service that comes to mind, although it cannot be found in the index to the book just cited, is the role of advising. Given what has been said so far in this discussion, it would seem that, if there is a tradeoff between faculty time spent in formal teaching and faculty time spent in advising students on their intracollege programs and their future careers, the latter is of about equal value. Faculty advising of students, including entering freshmen and those transfer students who are in effect freshmen twice, is at most large institutions, including my own, at best an embarrassment, at worst a disgrace. To illustrate from Harvard College, entering students are advised by resident proctor/advisers who live in the same or adjoining sections within dormitories in the freshman Yard. Many of these individuals are graduate students, including law or medical or business school students, who are naturally extremely preoccupied with their own studies and whose knowledge of what Harvard College offers either in curriculum or in support services is often not impressive. Indeed, if they are graduates of Harvard College, they may be no better, because they may have acquired a set of now-outdated prejudices about fields of study, prejudices that carry undue weight because they have been through it themselves, whereas someone coming to Harvard from a very different institution may be more diffident about curricular advice and equally generous with the personal advice that is often half-consciously sought under the guise of academic advice. When students as sophomores enter the Houses, they have already declared a field of concentration (major). They come under the jurisdiction of the tutor in that field assigned to the House if there are enough concentrators in the House; if not, an extramural tutor. But often they are not yet fully committed to the field, and for

tion in a neighboring state, as against dealing with anarchic departments and individual faculty members.

In a decision concerning the dismissal of three professors at Philander Smith College, a private, predominantly black college in Arkansas, Committee A on Academic Freedom and Tenure of the AAUP decided that the Yeshiva University case did not apply, since it was clear that the college's president, not the faculty, held virtually all "management" prerogatives. An administrative-law judge, under the National Labor Relations Board, stated that "unlike the situation in *Yeshiva*, the faculty at Philander Smith had no part in fixing let alone recommending salaries, or in the hiring, firing, or promoting of faculty. Authority over salaries and faculty hiring, firing, and promotion is concentrated in the college president" (American Association of University Professors, 1980).

personal advice they are more apt to return to their freshman proctor than to seek out someone whose main concern is with his or her junior or senior students who are considering writing an honors essay or are planning on postbaccalaureate study or employment and hence depend on their tutor for direct and immediate response.

Things are hardly better in the majority of state universities where counseling is in the hands of student-services personnel, who may not come under the collective bargaining contract and hence may be curtailed. Such individuals hear so many stories of casualties and sarcastic or indifferent professors that they can easily become antiacademic, if not anti-intellectual, and seek to protect students against the curricular pressures that for some of them are overwhelming but for others merely usefully discomforting.

And in neither instance do the faculty members who are doing the teaching get much direct feedback about the consequences of their actions—for example, how cutting their sarcasm can be or how a student's whole career can be affected by a single letter grade, as I have often seen happen, for example, with a student who has come to a major research university with the expectation of becoming a physicist, only to find that on his first examination he fails to receive a solid A (all too often, it is a male, since women are still ensconced, in spite of women's liberation and in part because of it, in what I have come to term the "talk trades"), and too readily concludes that he is not qualified to become a physicist, although by international norms he may be one of the ablest potential physicists in a field that needs very diverse types of individuals for its development.

My own general conclusion is that advising is the weakest link in the whole undergraduate process. Faculty advisers can at least learn how to become switchboards to those who can be more helpful, rather than assuming that they are necessarily bad advisers because they do not know enough and have had no special training in counseling.

Counseling Community College Students

For the growing number of students for whom the nearby community college appears optimal, there is no thought for matching student to institution. The community college is the unquestioned choice, not only in its negligible tuition and easy opportunity for financial aid, in its closeness to home or work, but also in the minimal commitment it requires from students (London, 1978). But some of these students in metropolitan areas have more choices than they realize among nearby community colleges and often gain little information on tradeoffs between, for example, a slightly longer commute to one institution and the superior programs it offers in the area of their interests. There are undoubtedly students who enter community colleges, particularly in the Northeast, because they are convinced that the four-year private institutions are too demanding and that they would be out of place there. This is perhaps especially true for older women, who are shy about returning to school and anxious about all they have missed since they were last in school and yet are highly motivated and, given proper support, could do well at certain kinds of private colleges— for example, at Alverno in Milwaukee or at Simmons in Boston; or, in a few cases, even at Wellesley, which has a center whose aim is to provide support and counseling for older women (see Riesman, 1979a).

For those who have always assumed they would go to college, it is extraordinarily difficult to imagine how forbidding the very title "College" or "University" can be to insecure prospective students. I have come across students who have decided to attend the local public university but cannot find their way to their first class; they feel stupid and are hesitant to ask where the class meets because they assume that "everyone" would know this and it is a dumb question. If the buildings are not clearly labeled, if the class has been shifted to another building without clear description of how to get there, if its time has been changed, the attachment of such prospective students to the institution is so slender, their insecurities so great, that they may slip away altogether. A recent immigrant to an urban area from Haiti, for example, fluent in French but awkward in English, may not yet have had the chance to meet a counselor—and may not be able to meet a Francophone one at all—with whom he or she would feel comfortable in describing what would appear to most people an insignificant obstacle. Yet it is just such students, once given proper support, who may make optimal use of a local institution, their commitment deepening as their insecurities diminish.

But once students are at a community college, the question arises of what advice they get concerning the courses to take that would make transfer to a four-year institution easy, even if at that point the student believes that an Associate of Arts degree will suffice. In fact, interviews we have done at community colleges in eastern Massachusetts reveal that counselors make a tremendous difference in the extent to which entering students can plan a program that makes transfer to a more or less selective private college or university in the area something to consider.

Experiments in Encouraging Transfers. The program and financial support to facilitate such transfers was pioneered by Humphrey Doermann, president of the Bush Foundation in St. Paul, who encouraged four-year private colleges in Minnesota, especially in the Twin Cities and nearby, to recruit from the local community colleges to fill places in their own upper divisions made available by attrition. For example, the College of St. Catherine, conducted by the Sisters of St. Joseph of Carondelet in central St. Paul, could recruit transfers for its vocational baccalaureate programs in business administration, library science, nursing, social work, and similar areas with the help of Bush Foundation grants. Similarly, United Methodist Hamline University, actually a small college with just over a thousand full-time students and fairly high average test scores, also located in St. Paul, was successful in recruiting transfers. However, the Bush program was minimally successful for residential colleges outside easy commuting range, clearly nonvocational in their academic programs; thus, Carleton College in nearby Northfield, which actively recruits black students to its entering class and makes elaborate provision for the desire many of these students have for separate social facilities, was no more successful in recruiting transfers than neighboring St. Olaf or the College of St. Benedict/St. John's University, the coordinate Benedictine institutions that are also nearby. It appears easier to persuade a black high school senior, who has perhaps had a summer at Carleton's remedial ABC (A Better Chance) program or another one like it, to enter this institution as a freshman than to recruit a community college student as a transfer, who is generally older and probably has a clearer vocational aim.

The Bush Foundation model was adopted by the Permanent

Charity Fund of Boston to see whether similar possibilities could be obtained by the use of financial assistance in the Boston metropolitan area. Some of the Boston donor group appear to have assumed that it was primarily financial barriers that stood in the way of pursuing a baccalaureate at a private, more or less selective institution, after one had got schooling in a community college. And there was something to be said for providing students with an alternative to Boston State College or Salem State—many could not consider attending the University of Massachusetts at Amherst, which was as much out of their league academically as it was distant geographically; moreover, in some four-year private institutions, of which there are many in the Boston area and throughout the state, more attention could be paid to individual students than in many of the state colleges or, in general, at the commuter University of Massachusetts in Boston.

But, as students of the several ethnic and regional subcultures could have predicted, what worked reasonably well in Minnesota worked much less well in eastern Massachusetts. For example, at some of the seven community colleges in the Twin Cities area there are students, often from fairly affluent families, who are prepared to finance the upper two years of education themselves at a private four-year institution or at the University of Minnesota, which would seem too formidable as a point of entry for some of them. No social stigma is attached to attending suburban community colleges, any more than it is in comparable community colleges in California, Washington, or Florida. It is, rather, a matter of saving money and of deciding on the degree of one's motivation and the direction of one's interests. Thus, the Bush Foundation did not have to do much to persuade students in Minnesota of the feasibility of such transfers, once the subsidy became available; the idea is already there. But in Massachusetts, there are old, entrenched patterns of ethnic and social-class defensiveness to contend with (see Sennett and Cobb, 1972).

Of course, it is not only in Massachusetts that community college students find it difficult to make any commitment, either about finishing or about planning ahead for transfer to four-year institutions, although this latter is easier to do where it is, so to speak, built into the system, as in California and Florida, or for the two upper-division universities of Illinois, Sangamon State and Governors State, built in the sixties to accommodate transfers. (The City University of New York is also something of a special case, providing as it does the opportunity for low-income and relatively unprepared students to choose among entering a community college, a relatively low-prestige four-year college, or one of the more traditionally demanding colleges of the system, such as Queens, Hunter, Brooklyn, or CCNY.)

We can almost watch these processes operate in slow motion in Massachusetts, thanks to Howard London's study (1978, 1980) of the first year at Bunker Hill Community College, in the overwhelmingly white Charlestown area of Boston. As we saw in Chapter Six, London describes how tentative was the involvement many students, especially male, had in making a try at continuing their schooling. Many of the students London approached at Bunker Hill Community College were threatened by the fear of failure. However, academic success could be almost as threatening: these students, who spent much time in peer-group sociability, were ambivalent about being regarded as "rate busters" whose attention to their teachers' expectations would be viewed as a threat by their friends. They preferred to limit their opportunities for social mobility, which, like promotion from laborer to foreman, might not be worth the social penalties attached. This constellation of fear both of failure and of success led them to take college lightly—certainly to pretend to—thus minimizing the risks to a shaky academic security and to peer solidarity.

Much in successful transfers depends on the receiving institutions and the degree to which they recognize the problems of transfer students and make arrangements for special counseling for them. The Permanent Charity Fund may have expected too many in numbers, too much in the way of applications to the most selective institutions; like most foundations, it hoped to start a self-renewing chain reaction among the institutions themselves, but in my judgment it withdrew support too soon in a period of general academic retrenchment. (It should be recognized that the Permanent Charity Fund had allotted an unusually large portion of its limited funds to the program, and it was impossible to guarantee that, had the program been continued two or three more years, impressive numbers of transfers would be aided. Qualitative analysis of the "success stories" could not be completed until after the program had already been terminated.)

It is easier to understand the attitudes of community college students once it is realized that private higher education has retained in New England, especially in Massachusetts, a hegemony unmatched elsewhere. When Christopher Jencks and I twenty years ago studied what was then the only campus of the University of Massachusetts—the land-grant and flagship campus at Amherst—many students shared with faculty members the attitude that, if they were really bright and capable, they would be attending Dartmouth or Harvard, or, in the same area, Amherst, Smith, or Mount Holyoke (Jencks and Riesman, 1962, pp. 133–147). This was in spite of the fact that at that time one applicant in four was admitted to the University of Massachusetts and the College Board scores were higher than in all but the most highly competitive private institutions; the university had achieved distinction in a number of academic areas, indicated by the graduate students it attracted and the faculty it recruited in these fields. If this was the attitude toward the flagship campus, which many people in the state still looked upon as the "cow college" because of its land-grant origins, one can imagine the lack of self-esteem of many who studied and taught in the four-year state colleges, slowly outgrowing their teacher's college origins, and in the more recently built network of public community colleges. (To be sure, such status hierarchies operate everywhere within higher education, as in other spheres of our national life. Michigan State University fought for years against the opposition of the University of Michigan to become a member of the cluster of the most distinguished research universities, the Association of American Universities. Florida State University continues to vie with the flagship and land-grant University of Florida, if not for parity in all fields, then for superiority in some and parity in others [Grant and others, 1979, pp. 366–369, 396–397].)

Geographic separation, as well as clear delineation of mission, sometimes minimizes the invidiousness of these academic pyramids, so that, for example, in California, the community colleges do not feel themselves to be in competition with the University of

California, nor do the more isolated state colleges, such as Stanislaus, Humboldt, or Chico, whereas many faculty members at San Francisco State University resent the fact that they cannot offer the doctorate except in cooperation with the Berkeley or San Francisco campus of the University of California. Similarly, major private institutions in the Boston metropolitan area, such as Boston University, Tufts, and Boston College, feel crowded by what I have sometimes termed the "Harvard-MIT fallout syndrome." In contrast, having a different mission, most faculty members at Northeastern University do not feel such resentment, although in the liberal arts and sciences some who have their doctorates from major research universities and either cannot or do not want to leave the area do resent teaching at an institution of whose accomplishments most faculty members at elite private colleges in the area are unaware. Faculty members at the University of Massachusetts in Boston, despite all the talk of the virtues of the urban university (Riesman, 1967b, 1974), feel similarly defensive both vis-à-vis the major private universities of the area and vis-à-vis the flagship campus at Amherst.

Transfer Students as Freshmen Twice. Good counseling for community college students may be crucial in making clear to them the alternatives that still lie ahead, notably today when so many colleges that once seemed formidable are underenrolled and eager to fill their ranks, especially in the upper division. But this also means that the transfer counselors at the community colleges must guard against the same kinds of rapacity of which high school counselors must be wary. Simultaneously, the receiving institutions need to recognize that transfer students are freshmen twice, often even more uneasy and insecure than first-time freshmen. (This fact is often concealed by transfers from other four-year institutions who, having cased one academic joint, are expert at casing another. For instance, one student who had transferred from Harvard to Hampshire and back again remarked that one could understand neither institution without having been at the other—a highly self-sufficient young man who made use of the college network to find philosophy courses at Mount Holyoke when he could not find what he wanted at Hampshire.) The act of transferring sometimes spurs students on, giving them new life. For example, notably at Harvard College, though many students reject student government as sandbox stuff and put behind them their trophies of leadership, their high school pennants and class rings, transfer students often turn out to have a great deal of school spirit and to be among the class leaders by the end of their two-year hegira. (However, having virtually no attrition, Harvard takes very few transfers, and because it has used the transfer process to increase its number of women students, there are almost no male transfers. Harvard has good public-relations reasons, which would operate in a larger fashion were there more spaces for transfers, for accepting students it believes can make the grade from Massachusetts public institutions.)

For such students, the community college has indeed been an open door, a step up the ladder of academic and social mobility—the only available door at the time in psychological and often financial terms. As already mentioned, a number of these students are now planning postbaccalaureate study, having gained self-esteem from the double victory—first over the community college and then over the second institution. Realistic plans for further study are often more common for them than for students who have never left the four-year institutions they entered but have been led on by faculty grade inflation and, in some cases, by their narcissism to believe that they are capable of advanced graduate work when in fact they lack the basic skills necessary for any serious further study.

But it should also be made clear that community college students can fall between stools: they can miss out on counseling at the institution of first entry, perhaps not using opportunities made available, such as college fairs held by four-year institutions, because to do so would mean missing a working day. Or transfer counselors may have been cut back in order to avoid having to let tenured faculty members go in a budgetary squeeze. Or students may miss out for all the reasons of bad luck that mark the fate of most of us. For example, a young woman who had transferred from one of the less demanding public institutions in Massachusetts had had a straight-A record, and on the basis of this the department she entered gave her full credit for previous work, demanded no further preparatory work, and assured her that she could easily graduate in two years. But she was neither prepared for the new level of effort demanded of her at Harvard nor willing to muster the necessary energy. She was bitter that an A at her first institution, which was almost automatic, carried little weight at Harvard when she ran into difficulty, did not hand in papers on time, and in fact lacked the skills for writing and organizing papers. She was embittered toward Harvard for having given her what she interpreted as assurances. What her case illustrates is that the judgment of transfers has to be at least as skillful as the judgment of entering freshmen. The additional two years' college record is not necessarily beneficial in making that assessment and may be misleading. It may simply mean that one has coasted for two more years, through the thirteenth and fourteenth grades, and is for that reason even less prepared for serious academic work than badly prepared entering freshmen.

Some Strategies for Improvement in Providing Guidance for Students

The considerations just outlined lead one in the direction of looking for state and federal, as well as local, philanthropic efforts toward improving and upgrading the work of counselors, lessening their turnover, and alleviating the understandable frustrations of having to deal with too many students on too many issues as well as offering guidance and advice—and this is true at the college level as well as in high schools.

In contrast, the improvement of catalogues is a limited remedy. And, as noted earlier, students rarely read them. Our interviews show us what common sense would tell us: student choices, in the minority of instances when there really are choices, are commonly based on what students tell each other or what alumni say or what recruiters say in private—and none of this can be monitored.

If students would pay attention to them, catalogues can be extremely illuminating even when they are not as elaborate as those prepared under the auspices of the National Task Force on Better Information for Student Choice. In most state universities and in large, unselective private ones, catalogues do not attach the names of professors to particular courses, whereas in selective institutions, the course is the property of the professor, and if it is not to be given, the course is bracketed or omitted. In a large state university, in contrast, the assumption is made that, if a course is listed, someone will be found somehow who will be dragooned into teaching it—perhaps a teaching assistant (Jung and others, 1976). This has the advantage that students will not be deprived of a course because of the absence of a faculty member; the drawback is that the course will not necessarily be a specialty of the person giving it. Students need to learn this about catalogues, but it is not always true. For example, the University of Indiana does not attach the names of professors to its courses, and yet in many fields it is more distinguished than most private institutions, and to take potluck there or to shop around, where that is feasible, to find the professors in a particular field in which Indiana is outstanding (say, linguistics or music) is probably a better bet than taking courses with named but otherwise unknown professors at a small liberal arts college.

Among the decisions for which students need counsel is, of course, whether to go to college at all. During the several years in which this book was in preparation, the Carnegie Council has itself turned its attention to alternative routes to work and to life in general other than college—apprenticeship, the military or alternative service, and postponed but lifelong or recurrent education (Carnegie Council on Policy Studies in Higher Education, 1979b).

In fact, Richard Freeman's study *The Overeducated American* (1976b) shows a close correlation between labor-market opportunities and college attendance. Thus, four years of college are exceedingly profitable for black males (whereas attendance at college without a baccalaureate counts for very little), but for white males, belonging to a strong labor union is a better predictor of income than possessing a college degree. Freeman does succeed in showing that, *in the aggregate*, demographic and economic data are better predictors of college enrollments than many educators would suppose who emphasize the social benefits of college (see Bowen, 1977; Hyman, Wright, and Reed, 1975) or the status-conferring benefits of college dealt with in quite different fashion in two books by Jencks and his collaborators (1972, 1979).

Viewed from the perspective of the higher education lobbies, colleges and universities have been exceptionally successful in pressing claims in state legislatures to subsidize education for the affluent as well as for the impoverished by keeping tuitions low at public institutions, in many states not even indexed to inflation (although there has been a slow rise, chronicled by Allan Ostar in the monthly publications of the American Association of State Colleges and Universities), while at the federal level, the amount of money spent on grants that students take with them to the colleges they choose or wander into has increased markedly in recent years. To avoid the regressive-tax precedent of tuition tax credits, the Carter Administration in the fall of 1978 greatly liberalized the range of family income that, under certain circumstances, could permit the subsidy of children by Basic Educational Opportunity Grants or other federal aid, including guaranteed loans. Soon after the passage of the Higher Education Act amendments of 1972, where this generosity to students—as against grants to institutions—really got started (apart from the veterans' programs), Gerald Grant (1972b) observed, as noted earlier, that students were being bribed to attend college. Young people are not given grants to learn a craft or start a small business, and CETA and other job-training programs have had less holding power in the form of congressional support—although perhaps not much less power in the sense of holding onto their clienteles—than the college-oriented programs.

Yet, granted all that Caroline Bird and Richard Freeman contend, and granted that a sizable number of affluent white males of high ability are concluding that college is not something they want, a strong case can be made for college on economic grounds, quite apart from the social and personal benefits. There is no doubt that not going to college allows one to get started earlier in the labor market, assuming that one is highly motivated, is serious about one's work, and shows up Mondays; it is also likely that one will marry earlier and have children earlier; pinched by inflation and drawn by the desire for better consumer goods, both parents may go to work. The difficulty comes if the trade that the young person has entered—or the trades that the two young persons have entered—is displaced by economic change, including international competition, or if the region of the country is itself subject to economic dislocation or recession. The college graduate comes into his or her own over a lifetime of wider horizons that make possible the efforts at reeducation or retraining that may be necessary in an altered economic setting. Moreover, attending college, even the local college, draws people away from home to some extent—and the worst off in a period of recession are those who are stay-at-homes, afraid to leave the West Virginia mines for Houston and the oil business or to take advantage of the enormously high wages being paid until recently in Alaska. The college-educated person is more likely to be aware of such possibilities and, especially if he or she has gone beyond the local community college, more ready to take advantage of the opportunities of new careers. Today, we simply do not have sufficient time-series data to disprove Richard Freeman's case. But we do know that college-educated people, on the average, enjoy their work more, although they also demand more of it, and that they live somewhat longer. They are more aware of the dangers of jobs in an asbestos factory, for example, and possibly more aware of the long-run hazards of smoking, although when it comes to drugs there may not be serious differences any more between the social classes. There is a slight tendency of college to make a person "healthy, wealthy, and wise," and it is one of the tasks of high school counselors, along with recruiters, to make these benefits clear without overselling college to involuntary captives of the college mythologies.

9

Student Consumerism and Educational Change

In contrast with the traditional careers of community college faculty members and administrators, a large proportion of those at four-year institutions began their careers with the aim, if not of advancing their discipline, at least of transmitting it. Such persons do not want to regard themselves as marketers of a product line, whether at the institutional, departmental, or individual level. Thus, many look with dismay on the low level of skills of their entering students, whom they are required to admit either by state funding formulas or because, in the private institutions, the applicant pool has shrunk. Many faculty members share the belief that too many concessions were made to student sovereignty in the previous decade, to the disadvantage of the students and also with the result of ruthless competition for student favor among faculty and departments.

To realize what attitudes prevailed in elite institutions and in the national media during the late 1960s, it is helpful to examine the huge shelf of books written by and about students during what was termed, with characteristic exaggeration, the era of protest. Consider, for example, the titles of two books by Harvard undergraduates: *The Whole World Is Watching* (Gerzon, 1969) and *The Right to Say "We"* (Zorza, 1970). These are among a number of titles that indicate the way flattery of the students by a combination of attention from faculty and administration, the mass media, and what might be thought of as the internationale of protest movements helped turn the heads of many activist students and their followers. To illustrate how far such self-aggrandizement went, I recall a mass meeting immediately after the Cambodian invasion and the killings at Kent State and Jackson State universities, held in Harvard's largest auditorium, Sanders Theater, where one of my more distinguished colleagues told the students that it was possible for them that very fall to unseat every congressman up for reelection and to elect a whole new Congress that would end the war in Vietnam, bring about racial justice, and do other marvelous things.

Concessions once made tend to become institutionalized, and there is perhaps nothing so traditional in academic life as a frozen experiment, whose devotees continue to need to uphold it, in part to justify having sacrificed their visibility as research scholars in order to throw themselves into the often unexpected intricacies of educational reform—sometimes even having dissolved their ties (as teachers as well as scholars) to their original academic discipline.

What is said here may seem inconsistent with the conclusions of the eminent historian of higher education Frederick Rudolph of Williams College, who in a recent book (1977) portrays the innumerable shifts and swings of fashion in calendars, grading patterns, appropriate subjects for credit, and other areas over the three centuries of American higher education. I have also referred earlier to Laurence Veysey's description (1973b) of fluctuations in all these supposedly standard curricular features between 1900 and the 1960s. Both these historians think in cyclical terms, and if one's time span is long enough, one can conceive of a distant epoch when faculty power over students and over the choices students make might recur. It is also important to note that the disciplines change incrementally and internally without faculty members' even thinking that anything so grandiose as "innovation" is underway. Thus, students can shop among fields but can only in limited degree resuscitate areas that no longer interest academic men and women, because of shifts in the structure of knowledge itself.

Veysey (1973b) emphasizes the stability of the department as the basic structural unit; so does Martin Trow (1977). This stability is the main reason that even the most highly selective colleges and universities, which could demand requirements and still be overapplied, have been so notably unsuccessful in making dramatic curricular changes. This was evident in *Study of Education at Stanford* (Stanford University, 1968), an elaborate series of recommendations for change that the faculty refused to accept (see Riesman, 1969b). The "Bressler Commission," appointed by Princeton's president, developed a good proposal for undergraduate coherence in 1971–1973, but it was defeated; a highly regarded Yale Committee chaired by Robert Dahl produced an admirable report, but this too was defeated by faculty vote. However, the Yale catalogue does contain guidelines suggesting the kind of general education toward which students should aim, and a number of students find these guidelines useful even though they are not mandatory.

Harvard's much-advertised core curriculum may be thought of as an exception, but this is not entirely true. An original plan for such a curriculum, drawn up by a faculty-student committee chaired by Professor James Q. Wilson, produced a plan for mandatory courses in a limited number of modes of inquiry. But by the time the elected Faculty Council and the faculty itself, over vocal student and some faculty protest, modified the original proposal, the outcome was a "core" of some ninety courses, some of them reworked departmental courses. Under the persuasive pressures of Dean Henry Rosovsky, the relatively autonomous departments were prepared to accept compromises that left their powers largely unimpaired, and there was no real agreement on a limited curriculum with which well-educated persons should be familiar.[1]

Student Influence in Governance and on Curriculum

One of the reasons it is difficult to reverse concessions once granted has to do with the democratization of internal governance that has

[1] There is a large literature on the core curriculum, much of it critical because of the understandable discrepancy between the image conveyed by the term *core* and the reality that a number of departmental courses of wide appeal to undergraduates have, with modifications, been included in the core. Such criticism underestimates the value of involving faculty members of a research-oriented university in discussion concerning undergraduate education—discussion more feasible when graduate enrollments in many areas are shrinking. Dean Rosovsky has the hope of involving senior faculty members in teaching courses given the imprimatur of the various subcommittees now implementing the general faculty vote supporting the concept of a core curriculum.

proceeded more or less parallel with the reforms themselves. Apart from particular views expressed by, for example, junior faculty members or activist students, the mere fact that the number of constituencies involved in making a decision has increased means almost inevitably that even the most minor decision takes a great deal of time and may entail adversary and combative discussions, which some faculty members find distasteful. Scholarly and thoughtful individuals tend to withdraw from all levels of the decision-making process when it involves politics and battles; hence, the achievement of curricular coherence is rendered less likely. Furthermore, as the number of those involved increases, and as they are self-selected or are chosen less on the basis of what they can contribute to the issue than as representing various constituencies (blacks, Hispanic Americans, women), it becomes harder for individuals to speak frankly or to submit written recommendations with assurance of confidentiality. Apart from leaks, which have always occurred on occasion but now are almost routine, "sunshine laws" in states like Florida and California are interpreted to mean that all such discussions must be public, open to the press and any interested person.

In such a situation, it is an error to speak of constituencies being "represented." There have been a number of situations in which students have not wanted to be put in a position of having to speak on behalf of "the students"; at Stockton State College, this led to a decision that student representatives on the College Council be chosen by lot, and of course even such a method of choice does not free the students who are chosen from the onus of being considered "co-opted" if they take a position with which other, vocal students disagree.[2]

Especially in the late 1960s and to a modest extent even today, there have been students whose undergraduate career consisted mainly of what I have a bit facetiously called a cocurriculum—that is, the politics of student activism sometimes combined with student journalism, management of rallies, and attendance at committee

[2] Hodgkinson (1974, especially p. 82) describes the Stockton State College procedures and many others; the president at that time, Richard Bjork, disagreed with Hodgkinson's evaluation. For discussion, see Grant and Riesman (1978, pp. 345–346).

meetings, demonstrations, and so forth. To the extent that these students turned attention to the curriculum, their desire in general, as already indicated, was to abolish constraints and restraints and to some degree also to make room for new cadres (more black students, women or more women, and so on) and for one or another curriculum believed appropriate for such students.

But there have also been a substantial number of students with a serious interest in curricular reform sufficient to lead them into inquiry about reforms at other times and places (Levine, 1978, chaps. 11, 13). One of the most outstanding examples is the work of Ira Magaziner and several student colleagues at Brown University, who published a report supporting a more serious curriculum in which entering students would have to take a series of "Modes of Inquiry" courses to acquaint them with a variety of cognitive styles and prepare them for further work. The proposals were supported by a magisterial document, discussing what was being done elsewhere. Magaziner and several of his fellow students worked very hard to persuade faculty members to support their view of what would have been, as many now at Brown recognize, a superior educational program. Unhappily, the majority of the students who had originally supported Magaziner decided in the end that they wanted to be rid of existing curricular restraints, thus becoming de facto allies of faculty members who feared the demands that a curriculum of the sort Magaziner proposed would place on them. The result was that at Brown, as elsewhere, after a short experiment with Modes of Inquiry courses and seminars, requirements were relaxed, and in that sense the reforms proved transitory.

Two former Brandeis students also belong in the category of educational reformers who "did their homework." Though unsuccessful on their home campus, they produced a book (Levine and Weingart, 1973) that deals with issues of concern to the small number of indefatigable and dedicated student educational reformers of the last decade.

With notable exceptions such as Ira Magaziner, those more vocal individuals whom faculty members and administrators have accepted as "the voice of the students" have tended to be those who are more likely to oppose curricular requirements. Often, the most significant voice is that expressed by the influential editors of the student paper or, in a few cases, several papers. Those attracted to student journalism, at least in colleges where they are not also journalism majors, tend to be more energetic and more academically capable than the average student. Their temptation, especially strong in an era of advocacy and exposé journalism, is at once anarchic and adversarial. They feel they do not need requirements, and since they are often doing at least two full-time jobs—that is, putting out a paper and being students as well—they want to be able to choose their own courses to make this dual career feasible.[3]

The reaction of vocal Harvard students to the proposals for a core curriculum originally put forward by Dean Henry Rosovsky can serve to make more concrete what has been said and to make clear that the issue is not a simple one of uniform student resistance to constraint. The original committee that was assigned the task of framing core-curriculum proposals included two student members, who were serious and hard-working (the same was true of the student members of the Task Force on Student Life, on which I contemporaneously served); these students came to support the idea of a core curriculum—in fact, what was in some ways an imaginative one. But from the beginning, the Harvard *Crimson* was adamantly and vehemently antagonistic to all curricular restraints and to the very idea of a core curriculum, while also deriding the present general-education program for its alleged aimlessness.

---

[3] I speak here as an assiduous but unsystematic reader of the student press over a period of decades and want to make clear the limits of my knowledge. I am most familiar with the daily papers of major state and private universities—the *Daily Princetonian*, the *Michigan Daily*, the *Daily Illini*, the *Daily Texan*, the *UCLA Bruin*, the *Stanford Daily*, and so on. Weekly student papers, such as the Chicago *Maroon*, the Williams *Record*, the Ramapo *Horizons*, and the Rhode Island College *Anchor*, are on the whole different and commonly, though not invariably, less adversarial and probably less influential. (The weekly *Carletonian*, with its editorials, letters, news stories, and serious discussion of issues, is a notable exception.) Some dailies, such as the Florida State University *Flambeau*, take minimal interest in educational issues other than those affecting students directly, such as library hours, overenrolled courses, tuition, the cafeteria, or bookstore prices. In fact, such papers' lack of interest in educational reforms proceeding on their own campuses has often been harmful to the reforms; for example, the effort at Florida State University to create in a few educational units a so-called Curriculum of Attainments was to my knowledge referred to only a single time in three years' issues of the *Flambeau*.

(The student weekly, the *Independent*, also opposed the core curriculum.) These students were not acting out of self-interest, for any reforms would not take effect until long after they graduated. The same was true of the student members of the student-faculty Committee on Undergraduate Education, a subcommittee of the Faculty Council, an elected body created in the reforms of governance of the sort already referred to.

I sought in vain to persuade any student editors or members of the Committee on Undergraduate Education with whom I spoke, over a period of several years, that they were potentially doing a disservice to the many "invisible" bewildered students who would not want to admit their dependence on adult guidance but who were often desperately in need of it. A poll the *Crimson* took of student opinion may be interpreted to offer some support for this view. It indicated that well over 80 percent of the entering class was opposed to a core curriculum, compared with 54 percent of the graduating class. In all public discussion at faculty meetings, student representatives used only aggregate figures and did not break down the data in this way. This disaggregation might indicate that, once students had established their independence, a substantial percentage were ready by the time of graduation to be willing to indicate that they might have been better off in a more guided setting.

Harvard, of course, belongs to that small group of university colleges that could ask almost anything of their students and still be overapplied. Eventually the majority of the faculty voted to support a core curriculum but, by that time, one considerably diluted from the original plan—with some faculty opponents citing student opposition as a significant factor in their own arguments.

Student Influence over Professors

The foregoing are examples of student influence, as distinct from student market power. Student influence is of course no novelty, no invention of the 1960s. An ideal-typical German Herr Doktor Professor, Professor Ordinarius, might not care what students thought, but surely Professor Hegel cared to have bright student disciples to carry forward his ideas. And it may well be that Professor Thorstein Veblen's contumacious disregard for undergraduates was partly a realistic judgment on the collegiate life of his day and partly a defense against the threat of being wounded by the lack of student interest in what he cared about—the wound that professors continually receive from students who may not even be aware they are inflicting it. Students exercise this influence continuously: by the level of effort they are prepared to make; by their responsiveness to what interests them and their indifference or even disappearance when they are bored, as they so often claim to be—an outcome that students almost never feel reflects on themselves, but only on the teacher or the subject matter.[4]

Everywhere, and over a period of many years, I have met students who say they are bored. I have sought on occasion to engage such students in dialogue. I have asked them whether there is anything they could do of an active sort that might make them less bored. They might then tell me about a particular professor of English literature who speaks in a monotone, reads from ancient lecture notes, gives examinations that are farcically easy. Perhaps such professors are survivors of pedants, similar to those who taught in the colonial colleges, who continued to teach in American colleges and universities at least down to the early part of the twentieth century. I do not believe that most faculty members, even in the avant-garde institutions, are capable of more than fifteen or so lectures that are truly creative in organizing old material in a new way or presenting new material at the edge of the unknown. Inevitably, therefore, most lectures will contain considerable elements of redundancy. But it does not follow that they are "boring"

---

[4] Parents will of course recognize similar phenomena vis-à-vis their own children. Among adolescents, only the most sensitive and discerning are aware that such powerful, seemingly omnipotent adults as their parents can be wounded, indeed in some cases psychically destroyed, by their children's reactions. Psychiatrists, unlike professors with their students, can protect themselves by appealing to the concept of transference, according to which hostile reactions from patients are not necessarily a statement about themselves as individuals, but an element of the therapeutic process. Some therapists have carried the concept of transference to the point at which they can completely absolve themselves of responsibility by interpreting all a patient's reactions as transference, much as a dogmatic Marxist can interpret all behavior of the hated bourgeoisie as based on a tacit or overt conspiracy against the oppressed. For a vivid account of the psychoanalyst's sensibilities, one implicitly related to the sensibilities of other adults who believe themselves to have a vocation for helping others, see Wheelis (1958, chap. 7).

to an alert student. Often I have said to such students that it is important and interesting to see what kinds of discourse are practiced in various parts of the academic aviary. They may not like a particular lecture on Chaucer, but they could find interest in detailed attention to a particular illustration of the academic species of Chaucerians.

When I say this to students, they frequently become furious: they tell me that they did not pay their tuition or give up their time for such a purpose, but rather to receive the professor's wisdom concerning Chaucer. They are not interested in what Gregory Bateson long ago termed "deutero learning," or learning how to learn. They are not curious about the architecture of the classroom or about the sociometry of the way students distribute themselves —for example, whether diligent women sit nearer the front and chattering and bored men nearer the rear. Like most Americans, they can think of only one thing at a time—and the ability to think of more than one thing at a time seems to me a mark of an educated person.

The papers students write—something they are doing less often and less capably (as, apart from professional complaints, data from the Educational Testing Service and elsewhere show)—are also forms of conversation in which students provide, in that now overused word, "feedback" to teachers. The latter, even in institutions where there is no formal system of evaluation of faculty by students, are eager, while not appearing too eager, to learn what students think of their courses.

Often, of course, the information comes indirectly. In research universities, senior faculty members may learn about student reactions from their teaching assistants or from remarks by colleagues. In fact, students are often diffident about giving a teacher direct praise lest they be thought to be apple-polishing or bucking for a good grade or letter of recommendation. Or, attributing the same omniscience to teachers as formerly to parents, students assume that teachers know when they are giving a good lecture or a good course and that it would be superfluous to tell them so. Understandably, younger teachers make an effort to appear more self-possessed than they are; they assume, along with students, that older teachers who appear reasonably relaxed in the

classroom have this assuredness and self-possession. But in my observation as well as in my personal experience, this is rarely the
case, and it might even be laid down as a not entirely correct but
often useful generalization that the best teachers are those who
remain anxious about their teaching, for whom it has not become
ritualized, but an ever-renewed experiment with an uncertain
outcome—although it is also true that there are many genuinely
self-confident and quite charismatic teachers whose polished performance becomes self-confirming, with students tending to share
the teacher's own satisfaction with his performance. (This complete
self-assuredness appears somewhat less common among women
faculty members, at least in major universities, where they are still
in the minority and are often torn between the perfectionism that is
an older tradition especially among women students and professors and the current standards of supposed "naturalness" and compulsory relaxation.)

The Faculty Branch of the Student Grapevine. Among the influences
that students bring to bear in these many informal ways on their
teachers, the influence of the judgment of other teachers plays
a larger role than is generally recognized. I am not speaking of
situations in which competition for retention or tenure leads to
malicious faculty gossip about potentially rival colleagues.[5] Rather,
I have in mind situations such as one still finds in the most selective
and academically oriented institutions, where a large proportion of
students are paying attention to what faculty members are saying
about one another, looking for navigational clues as well as for
gossip. An example is the fate of some faculty members who, contrary to prevailing legend, have been given permanent positions in
major research universities mainly on the basis of their teaching
and their evident concern for undergraduates. But when students
come to realize that these faculty members lack respect from their

[5] On the role of malicious gossip in contemporary society in reducing the work and
life of people of eminence to ordinary or less than life size, see the subtle analysis in
Sisk (1978). Sisk makes a distinction between "humanizing" gossip, which renders
the great approachable and in fact more interesting, and the near-paranoid "black"
or "pornographic" gossip, now so rampant in our society generally, which demeans
achievers and achievements so as to lessen the requirements on everyone, to make
achievement itself a target because it must hide something discreditable.

peers in their discipline—because they do not publish or because they are seen as crowd pleasers or both—student respect itself tends to dissolve. In one such instance, as already mentioned, a faculty member who was an intelligent interpreter of the field in which he taught but who did not advance the field by publication left Harvard to sing in the Metropolitan Opera.

In an earlier era of overapplied colleges, judgments of this sort did not suffice to threaten retention of a faculty member, since even had there been a loss of student traffic—and this did not always happen in more or less required elementary courses—there was no financial exigency. (For a discussion of recent litigation concerning claims of financial exigency as a reason for releasing faculty members on tenure, see "Current Litigation," 1978.)

Combating Disparagement. Faculty members subjected to derogatory comments from their colleagues have a variety of ways of fighting back to maintain their standing among students and hence, in some situations, their jobs. For one thing, if the disparaging professors are senior and scholarly, they can in turn be disparaged as stuffy pedants by faculty members of all ages who show themselves to be "with it," on the side of the students against the institution—or of "the people" against the society. In all situations in which a professional group seeks to control what it defines as quackery, the "quack"—defined (in conversation) by Everett Hughes as someone who has more appeal to clients than to colleagues—may be more original or may merely exhibit the going totems of originality. Some such people conscientiously seek to reach students already discouraged by lack of stimulation, while others simply dress up traditional wares so as to appeal to particular student clienteles who can be counted on to form defense squads when issues arise within the department and the institution. As already suggested, students in women's studies programs are an important and growing cadre, following the model originally set by primarily black faculty members establishing black studies departments.[6]

[6] Since the foregoing was written, *Time* magazine ("Hard Sell for Higher Learning," 1978) has taken note of the kinds of advertising that both individual faculty members and colleges are pitching to students. Although the article quotes me as saying, "The free market works very badly in higher education," referring to academic

As would be expected from what was said in Chapter One about faculty power in the major national law schools, the postbaccalaureate institutions preparing students for careers in law or medicine or business administration remain sufficiently in control of their own turf so that they do not in general need to mobilize strategies of defense against student consumer sovereignty. This does not mean that there may not be struggles over curricular division of labor or over those portions of student time, varying among professions and institutions, that are more or less elective. In fact, precisely because the medical schools do possess a monopoly of training for what is still the most sought-after profession, and because of the traditions represented in the Hippocratic oath, the clinical professors in a teaching hospital may monitor one another's work, especially in such fields as surgery or obstetrics, and were doing so long before malpractice suits made the practice of "defensive medicine" endemic and often harmful. (In the light of the prevailing cynicism in academic as well as general circles regarding organized medicine, I should make clear that I am referring here mainly to the top-flight teaching hospitals that maintain clinical review committees. These, for example, monitor operations and will withdraw the license to use the hospital from a surgeon who has been shown by the pathologist or by the records to have performed too many unnecessary operations or to be simply incompetent. More rarely, state and local medical associations may remove the license to practice of physicians who are fraudulent or plainly incompetent, and the same is true of permission to use some good non-university-connected hospitals [see Bosk, 1979]. There is no similar monitoring of faculty members who do not meet their classes, turn in grade sheets or reports on dissertations, or keep office hours—a Carnegie Commission survey shows that 12 percent of faculty members have no office hours. Seduction of students of either sex, which of course is sometimes initiated by the student, is tolerated, if not vicariously enjoyed. For astringent and

---

integrity, it notes that professors are paying more attention to their lectures; I have already indicated that "more attention" does not necessarily mean more substantial lectures. Although the free market may work badly in higher education as in other areas, it does not always follow that federal regulation works less badly. See the discussion of the argument over voluntary accrediting associations in Chapter Ten.

penetrating essays on the apparently growing normlessness of the academic professions, see Rieff, 1973; Shils, 1977.)

Furthermore, the medical faculty, especially in the clinical areas, comprises the gatekeepers to the preferred internships and, later, the residencies that will establish physicians-in-training as qualified specialists. The faculty members hold a reasonably high consensus about the responsibility practitioners should possess, both in and out of hospital settings, not to go beyond the bounds of their own expertise; and a great effort at continuing education of physicians is constantly being made, as well as warning doctors about newly discovered dangers of various treatment procedures or drugs. (Peterson and others [1956] investigated the poor quality of private practice by doctors for whom this curriculum of warnings appeared to have minimal effect.)

What has been said is not meant to imply that medical schools are a homogeneous lot, only that they maintain a relatively high degree of faculty autonomy. In some, a new field, such as community medicine, or topic, such as bioethics, may be treated disparagingly by many faculty members or even more by students. Those who teach in such areas or devote particular study to them may be thought to lack serious scientific concerns and may have to fight against the prevailing currents for the legitimacy of what they do. In contrast, in the medical school of the University of Kansas when studied in the 1950s, it was the research scientists on the faculty who had a hard time establishing their importance compared with those practitioners, often adjunct faculty members, who seemed to hold the key to how to treat patients (Becker and others, 1961).

And of course what has been said earlier about the degree to which professors care what students think of them when it cannot affect their positions in their fields would also vary in degree among medical schools. Compared with the emphasis put on teaching in the best graduate schools of business administration and law schools, the medical schools have not in the past been much concerned with the quality of teaching, although this appears to be changing—and of course there are many kinds of teaching, from retooling in the basic sciences (which may repeat what was learned at the undergraduate level) to "hands-on" training in the hospital emergency room, surgical amphitheater, or on the ward.

Unionization as Self-Protection Against the Free Market. I have already made reference to faculty unions in Chapter Three, in connection with noting the beginnings of realization among activist, consumer-oriented students that faculty unions are not necessarily in the students' interest. Indeed, unions are often the first line of defense to which faculties turn, particularly in the public sector, as a way of limiting administrators' ability to respond rapidly to shifts in the student "market" by closing out departments with falling enrollments even if that means letting tenured faculty members go.

Furthermore, since students have achieved many concessions to demands for participation and sit, for example, on committees that influence decisions on retention and promotion, a union becomes not only a substitute for such committees but also a forum where faculty members can talk among themselves in the absence of students and feel that this is legitimate.

Collective bargaining generally sets up grievance procedures to protect faculty members from dismissal—a situation that, during the period of growth, led to virtually instant tenure in many two- and four-year public institutions. For a thoughtful defense of this pattern on the ground that it leads to higher morale because faculty members are not put in competition with one another, see Livingston (1973). Read against Cottle's poignant essay (1973) about the agonies of seeking and yet hating oneself for seeking tenure at Harvard, Livingston's article, though it appears to have great merit, runs into difficulties in at least two ways: With declining enrollments and heavily tenured faculties, not everyone can gain tenure in every field. Moreover, as long as there exist major scholarly and research-oriented colleges and universities that insist on research as one price of tenure and, increasingly, also on demonstrated ability in teaching, some able individuals will prefer to take their chances at such an institution for the opportunities, stimulation from colleagues, and excellent students it offers, surrendering the relative safety that the publicly financed and occasionally still growing state institutions can supply. However, just in the last several years of evident decline and a future of much steeper decline in the number of tenure places in the major elite institutions, a number of people have made Livingston's choice and have preferred to stay at a state institution where they are virtually assured of tenure, turning down invitations to come as assistant professors or nontenured lecturers to such institutions as Princeton, Chicago, or Harvard, where tenure is not guaranteed or even highly probable.

At a number of institutions I have observed faculty members who have jumped into collective bargaining out of antagonism to a particular administration or, notably, a systemwide control that robs institutions of a good deal of autonomy. Faculty members have believed that they could hold onto such privileges as faculty senates or merit increases but have discovered that the collective bargaining contract signed on their behalf by union leadership, often in the state capital and embracing an entire state system, has sacrificed privileges they had had. Ordinarily, the union provides a certain minimal security in the form of grievance procedures and at least a temporary rise in salary, even if the budget of the whole institution is cut by a resentful or simply tax-conscious legislature. (A recent study comparing unionized and nonunionized institutions provides evidence that unionization does not raise salaries over the long term. Perhaps the conclusion has to be qualified by recognizing that fear of unionization may be one factor raising salaries at the nonunionized institutions.)

I am not sufficiently an expert on collective bargaining and all the ways it has operated at various levels of academic quality and organization to contribute to the immense literature already extant in this developing field. (See, for general discussion, Garbarino, 1975; for sympathetic accounts, see Osborne, Ryor, and Shanker, 1977.) But I would like to mention one interesting discovery that has been made by a number of presidents of large, unionized state universities—namely, that unions of professionals such as faculty members (the same might be true of high-level civil servants or of physicians or members of a law firm) seldom reach the relative equanimity that one can sometimes find in industry, even among unions such as the United Auto Workers, which are known to be tough bargainers and quite prepared to use the strike weapon. I recall one president of a leading university in Michigan, who had on his board of trustees both auto-industry executives and top UAW officials, remarking that in ten years they had not reached the established mutuality of relations that operated on a day-to-day basis between the companies and the UAW. One reason may be that faculty members have in almost no case been unanimously prounion. Ladd and Lipset (1975, chap. 10) have data indicating that even the younger faculty members, over half of whom regard unions as beneficial, include a third who think otherwise. Thus, when an institution does vote for a union, and when faculty members find themselves bound by a union-dues checkoff (without which many would take advantage of whatever benefits the union provides and might even be sympathetic with the union but would not pay dues), there is bound to be a dissatisfied minority. And while this is also the situation, of course, in many unionized factories and offices, it remains on the whole true that union members outside academe are more prepared to pay dues for the security of a union. Moreover, despite efforts toward greater worker participation, most workers in the United States do not seem prepared for the responsibilities of managing either the company or the union. In a factory, union members do not generally feel that their own workload has increased because their shop steward spends a lot of time on union business—that is what they have elected him to do. But in academic life, one of the ironies of collective bargaining is the frequent disparagement by faculty members of their own local union activists, who are neither in general productive scholars nor carrying their full load as faculty members—so much so that in one case, when the contract permitted merit increases to be handed out by faculty members, those lowest on the list included some of the very union activists who had procured the limited bonanza. In some instances efforts have been made to decertify a union (as well as to change to another union, supposedly a more aggressive one), although most of these fail. (The reverse situation also has its ironies. In several private universities where the president and/or the board of trustees have fought against a union, or its definition of the appropriate bargaining unit, before the National Labor Relations Board prior to the *Yeshiva* decision, the presidents have said to me that the faculty is so angry that, even if under that decision the union is not certified, the institution will almost be worse off, because the embittered faculty members have no collective channel through which to express their resentments.)

In a meeting in 1974 with the sociology department of Florida State University, I argued against unionization in a forum where all but one or two members of the department were either mildly or passionately prounion. I recall one tenured faculty member striking the table with his fist and saying, "We want clout!" I observed that this is something that the strike weapon does not bring to a campus, for unlike police officers, fire fighters, transport workers, or sanitation workers, we do not provide essential services. There is no truancy law for college students, and as I have noted before, a strike is against their interests, but it is not against society's or, in many cases, even their parents' vital interests. I believe that a faculty union strike can be broken (although doing so may not be worth the cost of lowered morale) especially when there are a large black student population and an overwhelmingly white faculty, black students can be mobilized to protest the strike and to complain that they are surrendering potential earnings and are not being taught. Liberal faculty members will find it hard to resist this plea, nor would the press be particularly sympathetic with faculty members posing as proletarians.

Still, elaborate grievance procedures can so delay the flexibility of administration response to market conditions as to lead to bankruptcy[7] (consider the Bloomfield College case already mentioned). Under AAUP rules, it is possible to close down a whole department if it can no longer be afforded but not possible then to retain a single especially versatile and useful member of that department. Sometimes when I have talked to faculty union activists, I have reminded them of the fate of the railroad labor unions; nor are the steelworkers, with their high wages and pension benefits, notable examples of security in the face of foreign competition. Protection furnished by grievance procedures cannot be absolute in a situation of a labile student body, not bound by requirements and of course not bound to attend any particular institution. The

[7] The faculty of Ithaca College in Ithaca, New York, voted for a union at the time of the arrival of the current president, James Whalen, who had already experienced the death of the college he formerly headed, Newton College of the Sacred Heart. It appears from conversations with faculty members and from correspondence that some faculty members in the liberal arts and sciences were seeking to limit the president's power, for example, to shift resources to the popular field of music education by reducing staff in "unproductive" departments. However, the board of trustees refused to recognize the union, and the issue is now on appeal in the Second Circuit Court of Appeals, while an ever more militant group of faculty members assert their rights.

fact that the State University of New York is unionized did not prevent the regents from closing down the doctorate in history at SUNY-Albany; litigation ensued, as it generally does, but the regents, with their constitutional power over all of education in the state of New York, won the verdict.

Furthermore, unionization is unlikely to protect the non-tenured faculty member from repeatedly negative evaluations by students, supplemented by visits to one's classes by colleagues and by a student course guide that repeatedly pans a particular instructor. It is of course possible that a union activist could protect himself or herself by that very fact, making his or her own release appear an unfair labor practice and hence raising the threat that the case might be taken to the National Labor Relations Board or its state-level counterpart. As was suggested earlier concerning unionization at community colleges, it is an overstatement to declare that unionization destroys a sense of colleagueship, for it may never have been present, or unionization may make it, as it were, official that colleagueship has already been destroyed. But polarization between union activists who may not bear their full departmental load and their departmental colleagues may further impair colleagueship, and there is no guarantee of union solidarity on behalf of someone who weakens the appeal of a particular department, which has to fight for student customers to maintain or increase its intramural market share. Hence, in the absence of a special reason to claim discrimination, unionization may shorten the time needed to acquire the relative—but only relative—permanence of tenure, but it cannot guarantee tenure or guarantee that tenure itself will assure permanent employment. Each faculty member must do that on his or her own, both in competition with other members of the department and in competition with other departments offering enticing bills of fare.

In the larger, comprehensive colleges and multiversities, interdepartmental competition is increased by the kind of incremental change that goes on constantly within the boundaries of what appears to the outsider to be a single field. For example, in a large department of political science, one can find faculty members who are primarily political philosophers, competitors with the philosophy department; political historians and even psychohistorians; political sociologists, hard to distinguish from sociologists of politics; students of public opinion, hard to distinguish from social psychologists or members of the department or school of mass communications; model builders, hard to distinguish from some members of the department of management; and area specialists, often hard to distinguish from anthropologists. Moreover, in many multiversities, one finds more than a single department harboring members of a particular specialty. For example, the engineers in a university, like the faculty of the school of business, may want their "house," or "captive," economists, who will attend to the applied needs of their field rather than to the intramural, semiautonomous growth of the disciplines within economics. Similarly, one will find psychologists in the department of psychology, the medical school, the school of management, the school of education, and—dealing, for example, with training in skills of negotiation or advocacy—in the law school.

On many campuses, a not especially eager scavenger can pick up horror stories of the way student opinion can be manipulated by assiduous and unscrupulous faculty members to assure their retention in the face of peer disapproval and even contempt. Just as the demand for Laetrile has conquered the apparently more scrupulous cancer researchers, so the "Laetriles" of academia are often retained in the face of peer judgment. I shall leave to the reader's imagination the questions of the effect on the person who is thus forcing himself or herself on an unwilling department and the quality of departmental relations when it does not prove possible to come to terms with, and form a genuine colleagueship with, someone who has won entry in this fashion.[8]

[8] I am reminded of a discussion with a group of presidents of public institutions, many of them former teacher's colleges, at which there had long been a number of women faculty members who were bringing suits for alleged sex discrimination and repeatedly winning the suits. As some of the presidents complained, the court could properly have ordered a removal of the discrimination and a reexamination of the case; what the court seemed invariably to order was that the plaintiff be promoted to tenure—a position that, even in the absence of discrimination, could not be justified by the institution's own standards. In other words, as so often in the regulatory and judicial processes, the remedy has been disproportionate to the supposed offense—in effect, a punitive remedy with long-run consequences for all concerned. I have mentioned the University of Minnesota consent decree, in which a woman chemist sued who had been denied a tenure-track position; the decree not only awarded

Some union contracts, as at Oakland University in Michigan, call for compulsory arbitration if, after the grievance procedures have been followed, the administration still does not agree to grant tenure. So far as I have been able to determine, the arbitrator generally sides with the person bringing the grievance, in part because in the open proceedings, faculty members will hardly ever testify against a potential colleague, and thus the record in the hands of the arbitrator is already tilted (even if the union officials do not believe the person should have tenure); faculty members who have critical private assessments of the candidate for tenure are afraid to put these in writing because, with the general decline of confidentiality, both in "sunshine laws" and in practice, the critics fear reprisal. (On the consequences of the decline of confidentiality, see the comments by the former president of San Jose State University, Bunzel, 1975; on the ethics of writing letters of recommendation to try to shift the burden to another institution, see Callahan, 1978.)

Changing Institutions Versus Changing Students

We are living today in an era of political and pedagogic protectionism sometimes termed "conservative" or "neoconservative." These labels are misleading. Since the disappearance of the Federalist party, there has been very little in the United States that could be called truly conservative. Most of our public figures who term themselves "conservative" are active interventionists in foreign affairs, eager to spend more money not only on defensive but also on strategic offensive weapons. They are reckless toward the environment, whether this is viewed as the international context in which this country must operate or as the domestic environment of land and resources that limits growth and the radical change growth brings. They express conservative attitudes on spending for social and welfare programs, on sentimentality toward criminals, and so forth, but they are not conservative in the sense of wanting to

---

$100,000 to the plaintiff and imposed on the chemistry department a quota requiring that two of the next five tenure-track openings must be filled by women, but also called for a special master who "will resolve all past or future sex-discrimination claims, will have power to award cash damages or faculty positions (including tenure), and will oversee the hiring of the University until 1989" in all departments, not only chemistry (Broad, 1980).

preserve a traditional America, and they are quite eager to seek government help not only for the cost-plus beneficiaries of the defense industries but also for other ailing industries for which they demand tariff protection and, where needed, government subsidy. Still, the mood of the country is opposed to adventure and experiment except in foreign affairs, where a xenophobic reckless-ness is often manifest.

For individuals who are still concerned with change, one re-sult has been to internalize the desire for change—to seek to realize one's own potentialities as an individual, rather than as a member of a social or communal group. Even on campuses where the ma-jority of students are oriented toward vocationally useful pro-grams, there remain a flourishing interest in the arts and a turn away from sociology, planning, urban studies, toward psychology and toward noncurricular experiments in self-realization—some-times in new religious cults and sometimes in what might be called the religion of psychologism (see Gutmann, 1978).

At its best, this inward turning has a certain monastic quality that is not isolating or bent purely on personal salvation, but seeks a few like-minded persons with whom to develop, for example, a work-sharing group, as in some of the more idealistic communes. At its worst, the inward turn takes forms variously described as the new narcissism, me-ism, or heightened egocentrism (Lasch, 1979; Riesman, 1979a, 1980a). In either case, the world at large is given up as a lost cause, and the turn is toward the smallest unit—either the self or a small group such as one might find in a civil defense shelter like the one Margaret Mead two decades ago considered trying to set up in Greenland so that a few might escape annihila-tion by fallout from nuclear weapons.

In a period when many students have moved away from pre-vious activism, anyone who seeks to alter student attitudes as an effective means of educational reform has to guard against en-couraging the already powerful consumerist attitudes prevalent in many student bodies. In spite of the discouraging prospects of reforming institutions in a period of scarcity, I believe that efforts at reforming educational institutions need to continue, and I count myself over many years of efforts as an only slightly chastened and still active reformer. Neither at Chicago nor at Harvard have I sought reforms at wholesale, but only at retail, skeptical whether an entire institution could be changed even by so effective and self-confident a dean of faculty as McGeorge Bundy or Henry Rosovsky. (I was equally allergic to attempts at wholesale reform in the society at large, seeking both in education and in other areas for small-scale pilot experiments before anyone would be encouraged to plunge ahead along lines that might not prove workable.)

We are now in an era when even reforms at retail are unlikely to be feasible except in the handful of overapplied institutions that can afford to turn students away by making greater demands on them for curricular coherence and in the evangelical colleges, where students (and faculty) remain subordinate to the overriding mission of the institution. This mission may be an unstable amalgam of a particular version of Christianity with a particular version, not always traditional, of the liberal arts and sciences.

From time to time in recent years, I have been called in by experimenting institutions in search of guidance—and sometimes of promotional puffery. I have come as a sympathetic skeptic. One reason for skepticism arose out of observation of experiments that lacked any sense of the limits and tradeoffs of human energy and resourcefulness. As Gerald Grant and I have described matters in viewing a few such experiments, faculty members tended on quite short order to become exhausted by endless committee meetings, demanded of them by their efforts to preserve their own pedagogic and curricular version of the ideal and by their ideological commitments to racial justice and equality and also to egalitarian participation by everyone involved in the enterprise (Grant and Riesman, 1978). Thus, the experiments we observed seemed quite frequently to have a short half-life, as faculty members withdrew either physically or psychologically, believing their hopes defeated, and in any event drained and exhausted. Many of the experiments proceeded, like some devotees of the counterculture, with Rousseauistic hopes that equality could be achieved among people unequal in persuasiveness, manipulativeness, and pertinacity—an aim of equal participation that often got in the way of effective management of what under optimal circumstances would be almost intractable problems of curricular change. (On some of the problems of participatory democracy, see Mansbridge, 1980.) I also thought that the increasingly prosperous industry built up around evaluation, made up primarily of people recruited from psychology, lacked any ethnographic sense of context and hence came up with trifling results when it sought to assess the actual impact of a change in curriculum on student learning, since one knew so little about either the particular students or the context; in other words, one could not transfer what was found at one institution to others—while one overaggregated data from many institutions and often came out with pessimistic results, much as in the famous Coleman Report, which led many readers to conclude that nothing made much difference. (I experienced the vicissitudes of evaluation firsthand as a member of a group studying instances of competence-based learning and teaching—mostly outside the field of teacher education—in a variety of postsecondary institutions [Grant and others, 1979].)

I have not given up as an educational reformer. I have defended the experimental interdisciplinary curriculum at Evergreen State College against its critics in the legislature and in the governor's office. I have remained close to what I regard as the most interesting cluster of experiments in a major institution: the colleges of the University of California at Santa Cruz, whose fate I have followed from the very earliest days of planning.

The reading of academic history, notably Bell (1966), Rudolph (1962, 1977), and Veysey (1965), and my own observations led me to believe in the "great man" (today we would say "great person") theory of academic change or reform. Although individual faculty members might seek to make changes, they were almost invariably unsuccessful without support from the top, and it was often in fact the academic leaders, especially those in an earlier era who had authority and long tenure, who had a view of the whole and wanted to leave their stamp on an institution as well as to keep up with its rivals and thus were less provincial than their faculties. Today we have seen how limited is the leverage of a college or university president and how short the average tenure (now five years). The president is hemmed in on all sides and, if authority is exercised too strenuously, will be resisted by faculty members, who will resort to unionization if they have not already done so, frequently in an effort to inhibit change that might be to their personal disadvantage. Another constraint on the president is systemwide management, which often levels institutions and denies autonomy to leaders of units in a multicampus system.

Ways of Countering Student Passivity

As already remarked, continual change goes on within departments as the progress of research alters and enlarges material available to particular courses, creates new subspecialties, and slowly eliminates certain subfields as these lose intellectual vitality. Most change is unconscious and not recognized as such; it proceeds incrementally, requiring no presidential sanction, though it may be halted by budgetary or other veto or by the departure of frustrated faculty members who are unable to shake a department loose in order to introduce new topics in line with new research.[9] If one is thinking of what is consciously labeled "reform," the number of institutions that have attempted anything of a systematic sort might be as many as 250 out of 3,000 institutions. And even in this small number, the students affected in any appreciable degree by the changes are likely to be a minority.

Furthermore, students "vote" for or against reforms by their attention or abstention; many have killed reforms without even knowing it, just as some have saved reforms without being aware of their power. A good example of the latter comes from the Harvard freshman seminar program. When it was first proposed, many faculty members thought freshmen were satisfied with the extant program, and they saw no reason to devote money to freshman seminars. As it turned out, freshmen have registered for the seminars every year in double the numbers for whom seminars have been available. This fact muted faculty criticism when the program came up for review three years after its inception, and there has been no formal review since that time in the twenty-year life of the pro-

[9] I have referred to Donald Campbell's essay (1979–80), which contends that it will be particularly difficult in an era of retrenchment to create new subspecialties, where these depend on individuals marginal to the core of their own original departments who have found colleagueship across departmental boundaries. Such individuals are the most likely to be eliminated in a period of retrenchment, since the departmental core will not support them for tenure, and the allies they have made in neighboring fields are unlikely to be able to assist them vis-à-vis departmental autonomy.

gram. Furthermore, in spite of the lack of grades, freshmen outdid themselves in seriousness in most of the individual seminars. Not yet wholly jaded and blasé, choosing a subject and a professor voluntarily, and not wanting to appear foolish in a small-group setting, freshmen proved that they were capable not only of doing highly sophisticated work "at the frontiers of knowledge," as the seminar brochure puts it, but also of doing diligent work even in the face of competition from graded courses in which their records would be relevant for such overapplied fields of concentration (majors) as social studies, history and literature, or history of science, as well as for postbaccalaureate preferment.

Even while pursuing my subsidiary career as an educational reformer, hoping to influence presidents, academic deans, and on occasion faculty members, I was also seeking to persuade students, especially undergraduates, that they could do far more to improve their own education than curricular design could accomplish, particularly as their short stay would not allow them to see the fruits of larger reforms they had helped to support or even sponsor. I followed the lead of Everett Hughes (in conversation) in dividing academic institutions into four categories. In the first category, which is small in number but large in influence, students have to make an effort to avoid acquiring an education; these are the institutions dealt with in this book where students are clearly subordinate to faculty hegemony and have internalized faculty values. Those who cannot perform this internalization are inclined to withdraw, either by leaving the institution and going somewhere else or by what in Eastern Europe is called internal emigration, in which the physical body remains on hand while the psychological self has practiced withdrawal of effort to a point consistent with survival. The second, far larger category embraces most major state universities, most private research universities, and those first-class liberal arts colleges not included in the first category. At these institutions, the student has a fairly even chance of getting an education; the opportunities and facilities are there, and there are no obstacles of a peer or institutional sort against exploiting them, but one can get by without doing so. The third category includes the majority of institutions—namely, the unselective state and regional comprehensive colleges and universities and the almost entirely unselective private institutions (although among these, there are very considerable variations, and some rise above their vulnerability to student pressure through firm leadership and devoted faculty efforts). At these, one has to make an effort to discover an education. At first glance, the peer culture appears wholly philistine, the faculty culture philistine or indifferent or both. It is in such institutions that an honors program may rescue individual students, bringing them together with like-minded fellows whom they might not otherwise meet and with faculty intellectuals who would otherwise give up on students as beyond redemption. Many graduates of such institutions have gone on to do graduate work at first-rate universities, having caught fire from a particular professor who may have been a transient in an earlier era of faculty mobility, perhaps someone in the process of earning money to complete the doctorate. Everett Hughes' fourth category is the residual one of institutions where, no matter what the effort of the student, it is impossible to get an education. There is no one on the faculty who has ever studied with a truly cultivated person, nor anyone who has made up for such a deprivation by heroic efforts as an autodidact.

In what is necessarily a limited personal experience, I have yet to discover an institution in this fourth category. I do know from visitors, however, that there are some institutions, often small and isolated, where "rock around the clock" is so pervasive that peer pressure prevents any student who is not heroic from seeking out faculty members who might help him or her overcome the deficiencies characteristic of the majority of the students at the institution, who are there for the credential and the collegiate good times more typical of an earlier era. Faculty members are subject to similar peer pressure. If they made more demands on themselves than their colleagues, they would be seen, much like self-propelled students, as rate busters and would be ostracized, and in such institutions there are many petty ways of punishing a faculty member, even one who has presidential support, who incites fairly uniform peer disapproval. Illustrations would be the piling on of great masses of committee work, while departmental secretaries refuse to do any work for the boycotted pariah; classes scheduled at times, such as 8:00 A.M., discordant with the prevailing student night life. Students could also defeat such a faculty member by avoiding his or her classes and thus leading, if the person does not have tenure, to dismissal for failure to carry an adequate load.

No doubt it is my good luck that I have not yet seen such an institution. Naturally, I would hardly be invited to one, and when, on the academic-freedom survey (Lazarsfeld and Thielens, 1958), I visited institutions unbidden, many of them at the bottom of what I then called the academic procession. I was able to discover faculty members eager to talk with someone like myself because they had so little opportunity for intellectual commerce at their institution. Students could have learned something from them.

Of course, even the poorest college has a library (although one hears of rare instances in which a library has literally been borrowed for purposes of accreditation and returned when the accrediting team has departed), and in some of these institutions the librarian, even if not a subscriber to the *Library College Bulletin,* may welcome students who are eager readers and who can educate themselves quite apart from what the faculty can make available.

Nevertheless, long before the present era of overt consumerism, students have very rarely seen themselves as academic and intellectual self-starters. In colleges of Hughes' first type, where students have to work hard to avoid getting an education, they also can, of course, be passive about it. MIT offers a dramatic example of students with exalted verbal as well as mathematical test scores who are awed by one another and who have in the past been among the more subordinated students in top-flight postsecondary institutions. Like Cal Tech, MIT sought to take pressure off the first year by abolishing grades, but that did not abolish students' anxiety over their adequacy—in some cases only enhancing it.

Student Research. But MIT did something else: it established UROP, the Undergraduate Research Opportunities Program. The tenth-anniversary issue of the *MIT Student Research Opportunities Directory* (Undergraduate Research Opportunities Program, 1979) gives an excellent picture of the variety of opportunities that have been provided in many fields and by many faculty members. (I am also indebted to Edwin Taylor, professor of physics at MIT, one of the main faculty supporters of the program [personal correspondence; see also Taylor, 1974].)

Any student can come with a project and use UROP as a

switchboard to discover a faculty member who will help the student become involved in research, and I am informed that this is the easiest way in which an MIT student turns from passive consumer and absorber to active agent. As mentioned in Chapter One, such progression is easiest in some of the sciences, where the field is moving so quickly and is so fluid that a bright undergraduate can make a contribution. Biology is outstanding in this respect, as a study by Fulton and Trow (1975) has shown. Trow himself has been a consultant to MIT, responsive to the institution's awareness that, for all the giftedness of both faculty and students, it has been for many a deadening place (see Snyder, 1967). MIT has, of course, many faculty members engaged in research who enjoy working with student apprentices; given a mechanism by which students can overcome diffidence and engage themselves with such professors in active work, they become producers and not simply stuffed and anxious consumers.

The National Science Foundation has established a program of small grants to undergraduate liberal arts colleges, allowing one or more students to organize a research project and seek out a faculty member as their mentor, or a faculty member can himself or herself recruit undergraduates to the NSF program through the use of the NSF grants. These grants operate not only in the natural sciences but also in such fields as anthropology, where a faculty member can encourage students who want to do a bit of empirical field research, not something that will be definitive, but rather exploratory and heuristic. As many research universities recruit fewer and fewer graduate students in fields with no prospect of immediate faculty employment, many faculty members in such institutions may also learn, what many of the scientists already know, that undergraduates are capable of doing research that in the best cases will be publishable in either the regular journals of the discipline or journals particularly set up as a forum for student work.

Verne Stadtman (1978), associate director of the Carnegie Council, notes that "only" 5 percent of students nationally have taken a hand in designing their own curriculum. In fact, this is a very considerable number, higher than I would have myself thought likely—the glass is not half full, but neither is it empty.

Raising the level in the glass might in the long run be helped by cooperative student effort, both to secure more opportunities for individuated programs and to involve a larger proportion of their fellow students. But there can be a considerable tension between looking after one's own educational chances and seeking to institutionalize these on behalf of one's fellow students. Student activists and educational reformers rarely stay in college long enough to profit from seeing their proposals institutionalized, though their successors may benefit. Moreover, especially at present, when many students are working part-time even in selective institutions in order to meet mounting costs, time and energy spent in efforts at educational reform may be at the expense of their own academic development. Furthermore, in an era in which it is cool to be cool, students in the more cosmopolitan institutions are especially unlikely to reveal enthusiasms they have discovered on their own. And, too, such enthusiasms may encounter a skeptical response from many faculty members.

I can illustrate this last point with a meeting I recently attended, arranged by the head tutor in the sociology department for those seniors who were planning to write senior essays. I had been asked to speak and began by saying that one interesting feature of sociology for undergraduates was that it was a "backward" field in which most of the important aspects of contemporary society were hidden from its members and that many students would have access to some aspect of that society which would be news to their professors. Sociology and anthropology, like archeology and geology, are fields in which amateurs can make a contribution even if they lack conceptual sophistication. They can tell us about something on which we ourselves have not had a chance to stumble. However, I was immediately followed by a colleague who took just the opposite line: it is unlikely that students in a senior thesis will discover anything original, and so they should consider the thesis a kind of finger exercise that will give a feeling of completion and accomplishment for its craftsmanship, not its discoveries. Of course, I am all in favor of craftsmanship, but I thought that the comment, though it might have inhibited some student grandiosities, overlooked the fact that much originality is in the eye of the beholder: if one sees something freshly, let us say about friendship, the fact that Aristotle observed similar phenomena should not destroy one's pleasure in the use of one's powers. In fact, Aristotle may have been wrong, or his views may be less applicable to today's society. Consequently, he does not stand in the way of a student who is exploring friendship as, for example, a finding in chemistry of a new organic compound stands in the way of a student who wants to explore a similar molecular arrangement.

Yet I do not mean to suggest that students cannot also be active in the natural sciences, outside of the obvious examples of biology and geology. They can work in the laboratory of a professor in the natural sciences where teamwork is the rule rather than the exception, and many students do just that, sometimes in summer, even while in secondary school.

Another way students can become active is through teaching a subject they have just learned, to fellow students or to underclassmen. Few institutions make adequate use of supervised student teachers (except as laboratory assistants). Yet it seems to me that there is no better way to turn passivity around than to teach a subject that one learns best by having to instruct someone else and hence to clarify one's own previously perhaps inchoate understanding.

A quite different way students can become active is through learning a foreign language and then making use of it—for example, in tutoring in bilingual schools or in taking one of the many opportunities for travel abroad that many American academic institutions offer. A student exploring another culture, who is fluent in its language or becoming fluent, is no tourist. He or she is an active agent seeking to understand the ways of different peoples— an activity without which it seems to me impossible to have an adequate understanding of one's own country.

An Example of Scholarly Extracurricular Activities. It is also important for students who want to become producers to discipline themselves not to expect the instant gratification consumerism promises. I can illustrate my point best with an example. In the late 1950s, Professor H. Stuart Hughes and I organized a group of Harvard students, mainly undergraduates, concerned with nuclear disarmament; the group called itself TOCSIN, meaning the bell or signal that sounds the alarm. Hardly any of these students were natural scientists. But they realized that in order to deal with issues of arms control between the Soviet Union and the United States, they had to learn something about seismic detection, and finding at Fordham University the best seismic laboratory available to them, some of the students went to Fordham to see whether in fact it was possible, as the Russians claimed and some Americans denied, to tell the difference between a nuclear explosion and an earthquake. They concluded that it was possible, and three of them took their conclusions to one of the recurrent arms-control conferences then in slow motion in Geneva. Their work also required that they learn something about the intramural politics of the Soviet Union in order to counter arguments about Soviet heavy nuclear weapons and growing strength of Soviet armed forces generally. They understood what many of the critics of the SALT II treaty prefer not to understand—the extent to which the Soviet Union is armed against its own people, its captive nationalities, its restless "peoples' democracies," its incompetent modes of production (even the heavy weapons, which so impress Americans who think in terms of tonnage rather than effectiveness). Some of these students wrote speeches for congressmen who had been elected in 1958 on peace platforms, in a Democratic off-year victory over the Republicans, and who were coming up again to much more difficult battles in 1960 in the wake of a Democratic presidential candidate, John Kennedy, who was talking utter nonsense about an alleged "missile gap" and complaining about the danger of Cuban Communism "ninety miles from home."

Only much later did comparable student interest find a place in the curriculum, as in two general-education courses in the social sciences: one offered by Karl W. Deutsch, "Problems of Peace, Justice, and the Processes of Change," which dealt only in small degree with disarmament but covered all kinds of intra- and international conflicts and their peaceful resolution, and the other by Roger Fisher of the law school (one of the original supporters of TOCSIN), "Coping with International Conflict," suggesting practical ways of breaking conflict down into manageable bits concerning which students were to make inventive contributions, notably in Arab-Israeli relations and in southern Africa.

For a time, TOCSIN leaders overshadowed in importance the Oberlin-based Student Peace Union, although the two groups periodically collaborated. An early opponent of involvement in Vietnam, TOCSIN was swept aside as the antiwar movement became less interested in Vietnam and satisfied simply with anti-Americanism: knowledge of Southeast Asia was not required, but only the chanting of slogans about America as racist, imperialist, and seeking to destroy the Vietnamese for the sake of tin or some other commodity. As against the close study of American public opinion characteristic of TOCSIN supporters, the later antiwar protesters in major universities saw the war as the work of liberal (or "mandarin") intellectuals, completely ignoring the earlier role played by the Asia-Firsters, who had suffered unhappily through World War II, and by Cardinal Spellman and his many followers. Convinced of the righteousness of their cause—and indeed, in my judgment, it was righteous—the antiwar protesters did not bother with anonymously writing speeches for congressmen, but preferred demonstrations that aroused the ire of patriotic Americans who were themselves becoming uneasy, or indeed opposed to the war, but were even more opposed to the protests. Already one could see in the later stages of the antiwar movements a need by students and many faculty members for instant response—so much so, that the universities themselves often became the enemy because they were accessible and vulnerable, while in contrast the political process was inevitably slow and, to the neophyte, opaque. Naturally, I except from these comments the many who worked devotedly for Eugene McCarthy, some of them former TOCSIN supporters, and later for Robert Kennedy.

I value student idealism as against the prevailing cynicism and careerism. What I find sad is that the idealism has so often been misdirected—and, as in the later anti–Vietnam war protests, in my judgment actually counterproductive. Indeed, in Vietnam the disproportionate means used to an end that was itself doubtful from any point of view, military or geopolitical, led to an international series of attacks by students almost everywhere—again, as in the United States, with little attention paid to Vietnam itself and much to what was deemed rotten in America.

The antiwar protests, greatly influenced by the concerns and spirit of the counterculture, have been the model for the protests against nuclear power plants by groups of young people, including many students, capable of mobilizing several hundred thousand followers if sufficient media stars (Ralph Nader, Jane Fonda, Tom Hayden, Robert Redford) are on hand—a combination of teach-in, civil disobedience, and Woodstock. Just as the anti–Vietnam war movement spread to other countries, notably Japan, so has the attack against nuclear power plants, present and projected. This attack may be interpreted as one aspect of a much larger environmentalist movement that began with the patricians who cared about the preservation of scenic beauty and wildlife areas, notably Gifford Pinchot and Theodore Roosevelt. Like other once-upper-class movements and tastes, environmentalism has been socially mobile downward, affecting many in the educated middle and upper middle classes and often constituting covert class warfare against the working class, many of whose members would also like scenic amenities and pollution-free air and lakes but for whom jobs and automobiles and the income that derives from the generation of power are indispensable. Efforts by a few, including myself, to persuade the present generation of student idealists who are demonstrating against nuclear power plants that the worst consequences these plants could have would be minor in comparison with nuclear war have been unsuccessful. Paradoxically, New England is at once the area that suffers most from lack of its own energy resources and also a locale where environmentalists have been especially powerful, reflecting the many liberal arts colleges in the region and the antitechnological bias shared by many in these colleges. The environmentalists themselves, though not greedy for goods, would certainly not be able, any more than the working class, to endure a severe energy shortage; they travel light, but they do travel, and their stereo equipment and loudspeakers would be silenced if there were a real power shortfall. (None of the foregoing is meant to suggest that work to explore the potentialities of "soft" energy options, such as some kinds of solar heating, windmills, and the harnessing of tides and of still unharnessed rivers, is not useful. However, one now finds some of the New England anti-nuclear-power protesters also protesting the conversion of public utility plants and heating plants from oil or gas to coal, leaving no way out for the interim period of vulnerability from a cutoff of oil, which is essential not only as fuel but as a source of pharmaceuticals and other products which at present can be made only from once-living matter and which no amount of "soft" energy can readily replace.)

In the protest against nuclear power, the sense of political powerlessness among the demonstrators, combined with their impatience with the electoral process, leads to almost exclusive reliance on civil disobedience (see Sharp, 1970, 1973). The coerciveness of civil disobedience is attractive to those who sometimes rationalize and sometimes believe that parliamentary, democratic, and constitutional government is a sham and for whom the patient work of listening to and then seeking to persuade voters, legislators, and the general public appears hopelessly slow if not altogether impossible. Civil disobedience also has been democratized, whether the protesters are farmers driving excessively expensive tractors through the streets of Washington or whether government employees are holding the public hostage by strikes. Its progress makes a vicious circle, since at best parliamentary processes are difficult to manage and, when interrupted by civil disobedience, become even more so, raising the specter of the collapse of the power to govern and the call for a "strong man" who will take charge, curbing "the interests" (that is, other people than oneself and one's companions). The other great shortcut, to which recourse is increasingly made, is the judiciary. Almost any group that claims to represent the public interest can find a sympathetic judge who will issue an injunction to stop some ongoing productive process—a "veto group" of one, as our federal judiciary loses all sense of restraint vis-à-vis what would once have been thought of as political questions outside the orbit of the courts. (See, for example, Glazer, 1978; Miller, 1977; Thernstrom, 1979.)

A few years ago, at the nuclear power plant at Vernon, Vermont, a young man used dynamite to topple a tower that carried a mechanism for testing radiation in the atmosphere—that is, a protective device. His trial in district court was attended by admiring fellow demonstrators, and when he was freed by a liberal judge, he was cheered by spectators as if he had been a Freedom Rider in the days of the civil-rights movement. His action, similar in style if not in target to some of the violent antiuniversity actions of the late 1960s, could not differ more from the work of Denis Hayes, president of Stanford's student government in 1968–69, founder of

"Earth Day," and author of a serious study of the possibilities and problems of the use of solar energy (Hayes, 1977).

Of course, if one thinks in terms of age cohorts, it is quixotic to suppose that the cohort old enough to remember the controversy about nuclear weapons and the arguments over the test ban in 1963 would have the same outlook on life as those who came of age in a later decade, when the very fact that nuclear war had not occurred served to still doubts and dissipate the nightmares of nuclear destruction common among the earlier cohort (see Keller, 1978; Ryder, 1965). Still, as in any society, there are continuities among cohorts. One of these is the organizational talent that the educated upper middle class possesses, whatever cynicism it may have toward large organizations and whatever criticism it may level against those of its members who are thought to be taking "ego trips" by organizing even those demonstrations of which many fellow students approve. In part, this ability to organize comes from self-confidence; in part, from attendance at selective colleges by groups of affluent students who are the children of capable organizers and who have early on learned to organize their own lives and to travel on their own and have used voluntary associations in their high schools as practice grounds for their organizing talents. The discontinuity arises when it comes to the time span involved in any organizing effort. Where students form a substantial political plurality or even majority in a college town, such as Madison, Berkeley, or Ann Arbor, one does find students who are prepared to do the necessary canvassing and make use of their strength at the polls to capture the major elective offices.

Interest in Nonfashionable Topics. Furthermore, no cohort comes at all close to being a "total institution," and there are always many exceptions to any generalization about an age group. To return to the curricular arena, from which I have momentarily digressed, I have been impressed with the rise (to be sure, a very modest one) in the study of classics at the very time when most students are not interested in any epoch outside their own immediate milieu. (A similar rise has occurred also in the United Kingdom, despite the dropping of Latin and Greek from the curriculum of most secondary schools, including some of the more famous ones.) One source of interest in Greek mythology comes from the more scholarly supporters of the women's movements, such as Philip Slater, author of *The Glory of Hera* (1968). And, too, some students have concluded that a vocational curriculum will not necessarily provide them with "meaningful work"; they know from summer and part-time jobs that they can make a living, and they look to college as supportive of interests that only in the rarest case will serve as a vocation (Arendt, 1958, chaps. 3, 4; Green, 1968). This is one source of the continued interest in the performing arts, not only among affluent students who can afford the risks, but among students in unselective colleges who often harbor unrealistic hopes, which they can ill afford, that they can become actresses or actors or can make a living as filmmakers or musicians; to be sure, some of the students in these colleges who major in the arts harbor no such hopes, but they have no immediate vocational aims or none that appear pertinent to the job market. In a way, this development is a flight from the preoccupation with social "relevance" of the 1960s, an aspect of the turning inward already referred to, but lacking the narcissistic implications that the inward turn often has when immediate gratification is sought rather than the artist's craft and durable furniture for the mind.

The interest in Greek is to some extent related to a revived interest in religion—not the new cults that flourish especially in California but reexamination of traditional religion, often by young people from agnostic and highly secular backgrounds.

Just as in academic institutions of Everett Hughes' third and fourth types, students may not discover one another without institutional help in the form of an honors program or some other locus where they can gather with like-minded faculty members, so students with such offbeat interests as traditional religion on large secular campuses tend to live in the condition sociologists term "pluralistic ignorance"; that is, each thinks he or she is quite alone, having no way in the prevailing climate of intolerance for non-Eastern religious outlooks of finding others of similar persuasion. Of course this is not true of those whom adults seek out, such as Roman Catholic students or Latter-day Saints, who are numerous enough to justify providing, if not a campus chaplain, then Mormon wards or even a "stake" in the vicinity. But for students not attached to a particular denomination, there is no such facility.

Only six divinity schools are attached to universities; all the rest are separate institutions, and even where they are attached (as at Harvard or Yale), the connection is peripheral. Sympathetic adults such as myself can be important in such a setting, for students seek me out, sometimes because I have noted my interest in religion in the faculty handbook of the sociology department or my residential House, and the word gets around. Using me as a switchboard and agent of legitimation, such students can find one another—but I know no secular campus where they provide any sizable cadre whose values are at variance with the larger age cohort to which all of them belong. There were enough such students in Harvard College in the last few years to overcome faculty objections to a field of concentration in the study of religion, although cautious faculty members restricted enrollment to a relatively small number and drew primarily on the divinity school to provide sufficient offerings.[10]

I have drawn on my own observations at Harvard College or neighboring MIT for examples of student self-help that has made use of modest faculty assistance, in which active-minded students have become vigorous producers rather than either passive or alienated consumers. In a period of large-scale faculty demoralization and students' desires to be entertained and awarded with little effort the credentials to which they believe themselves entitled, I have no formula for turning a whole generation of students into self-starters. I believe it is nevertheless necessary to make the effort not to surrender to prevailing moods, but to combat them. Moods and attitudes that seem well-nigh universal are often less powerful than they appear: the attitudes are often held with inner ambivalence, and individuals may be ready to respond to leadership that is at the same time realistic and hopeful.

Furthermore, although the United States appears to many

---

[10] I am speaking here of an interest in religion as divorced from ethnicity. Jewish studies are increasingly popular on many university campuses, and here also there is a tendency of young people to go beyond their parents' nominal adherence to Judaism and devoted adherence to Jewish philanthropy and to the fate of Israel. These students wear yarmulkes, spend terms on a kibbutz if they can, and learn Hebrew not because their parents have sent them to Hebrew school but out of their own interest—in part, perhaps, a reflection of what the historian Marcus Hansen called the "third-generation revival" of ethnicity. See, however, Gans' skeptical view (1979) of the "new ethnicity."

Americans, as to most foreign observers, as increasingly a uniform national culture, spread by the mass media and individual mobility, there are still great differences among regions and among subcultures. Already noted is the example of Furman University in Greenville, South Carolina, a sectarian Baptist college I had the opportunity of visiting in 1967. Elite Northern institutions had turned violently against the Vietnam war, but at this college the majority of students and faculty and folk of the surrounding community were solidly in favor of the war. Yet there was an active group of students, quietly tutoring and doing other social service work among blacks in the community, who had begun to question the war pretty much on their own. To illustrate: As an institution with strong denominational controls, and with a powerful line drawn between church and state in the Baptist tradition, the institution had acted on the religious belief in noninvolvement with the state by turning down the offer of a federal science building (much as Brigham Young University and Hillsdale College still refuse federal help). But these students observed that the institution had a strong ROTC chapter, subsidized by the armed services, surely a branch of the state; was there not an inconsistency here? It was hardly a popular question, and it was not aggressively asked. These students had arrived at their views in a climate that was largely hostile; I concluded that they deserved more credit than those who regarded themselves as nonconformist on liberal campuses for holding similar but locally prevalent views. The Southern students had found support in a social-service mentor who was not a faculty member, and they also discovered faculty members who were willing to consider the issue, but not yet in a public way. The college existed in an evangelical environment much more conservative than the college itself. My service to the students was to assure them that they were not "freaks" or unpatriotic and that in fact I had in my own conversations discovered members of the armed services who quietly harbored similar doubts.

This example is intended to suggest that the forms in which students can become self-starters depend very much on the local context and cannot be gathered in surveys of aggregate opinion. In a way, students at a college of the sort just mentioned have a great advantage, lacking in the more cosmopolitan institutions, of discovering books their own professors have not read and ideas their own professors may have encountered but have not openly voiced. I have mentioned earlier my practice of asking students whether they have discovered books their professors do not assign in class. The answer is generally in the negative. (If one asks students why they have bought so few nonrequired books, they will complain about the high and increasing price even of paperback books, although books have not risen faster than either private college tuitions or the general price level.)

There is an additional and paradoxical factor in the spread of the paperback book, which has had many advantages in allowing students in earlier college generations to build up personal libraries at low cost. The possibility of assigning relatively inexpensive paperbacks has had the drawback of making available to avant-garde instructors the very latest in radical (and sometimes pornographic) writing, just as films and television also make such material widely available. The opportunity for gradual student self-development in quiet maturation is truncated by such availability, which, in a paradoxical way, turns potential producers into quick consumers. Paradoxically, also, the very fact that students now have the privilege as educational consumers of demanding that a new course be taught as soon as they have developed an interest in some topic denies them the opportunity to develop that interest on their own in the absence of the "rewards" of credit and academic legitimacy. Thus do independent student interests tend to be driven to the very fringes of academia: to areas such as astrology, although I assume that some institutions now offer courses in astrology, just as some offer courses in parapsychology and other subjects once considered outside the framework not only of what Thomas Kuhn would consider "normal science" but even of those scientific revolutions that result from slow shifts within normal science. Even when students have an interest as idiosyncratic for young people as death and dying, there will be courses and readings in Kübler-Ross, Robert J. Lifton, and other writers to provide for their newfound wants. In the multiversity and its counterparts, any wish can be turned into a pedagogic topic, no matter how outré it would once have seemed to an academic senate confident of its conservative principles.

Triumph of the Adversary Culture

César Graña, who teaches sociology at the University of California at San Diego, wrote a book a few years ago entitled *Bohemian versus Bourgeois* (1963), describing the conflicts between the generally staid French bourgeoisie of the first part of the 19th century and the bohemian artists who needed their patronage and despised their values while resisting the relatively mild constraints those values imposed on their work. In the United States, the minority of Americans, mainly in the East, who concerned themselves with what was defined as high culture also resisted innovation. As late as the Armory Show of 1913, which introduced Americans to current avant-garde European painting, there were echoes of this generation's old struggle and hostility to what was thought of as decadent art. American patrons of art were oriented to "classical" European forms and were insecure about their own judgments and hence unable to accept novelty, even when imported. When I was an undergraduate in that milieu half a century ago, there still were "secret books"—for example, in contemporary English and American literature and in the art of Weimar and Vienna. We students went around quoting T. S. Eliot's *Waste Land* to one another at a time when American literature was hardly taught at Harvard College, and English literature, much of which still had a philological cast, focused—at least as far as undergraduate teaching went—on writers such as Coleridge; Dickens was thought vulgar, George Eliot scarcely mentioned.

But even by that time, change had begun. European refugees brought with them the avant-garde culture of Central Europe, as they did so notably to Black Mountain College, as Duberman (1972) has described it. Psychoanalysis began to be assimilated into medical schools (much against Freud's belief in lay analysis), and what Harold Lasswell, in a memorable phrase, had called "restriction by partial incorporation" began—a less conspiratorial and more accurate phrase than Herbert Marcuse's "repressive tolerance."

But it was not until after the Second World War that the few remaining cultural arbiters lost belief in themselves as well as credibility with others, and we entered an era in the arts that Daniel Bell

(1976) has called "the eclipse of distance." America, now a world capital for the arts, began to be populated by artists who enjoyed playing games with their patrons, seeing what outrageous stunts they could get away with and finding these highly praised and even lucrative. The cultural limits had been removed or pushed to the far corners of an allegedly obscurantist hinterland. The "herd of independent minds," to use the famous phrase of the art critic Harold Rosenberg, was in the ascendant in the major intellectual and academic centers.

It is important to emphasize these wider developments in the culture because they are not often discussed when academicians argue about the core curriculum, the liberal arts, the effort to reimpose requirements after the concessions of the 1960s to what were believed to be student wants. That is, requirements were disappearing also in many fields of scholarship, outside the more consensual fields of. mathematics, the natural sciences, and the more quantitative social sciences, such as economics. Faculty hegemony was not reestablished in subordinating students to traditional definitions of scholarship, because these very definitions had come under devastating attack from within. To some extent, students turned to professors who had won their confidence in the hope of validating judgments about their own adequacy. For these were often students who had been told since childhood that they were "original" and "creative" and found themselves in an institution in which there were a great many other students who had received the same message.[11] As the aim for many students as well as for adults became, in Abraham Maslow's term, "self-actualization," or, in the more common parlance of the human potential movement, "self-realization," an unlimited ceiling became visible: "mere" accomplishment using a skill—for example, a senior essay

[11] In the opening chapters of his biography of Gregory Bateson, David Lipset (1980) describes the very different attitude of his subject's father, the pioneering geneticist William Bateson, who discouraged his second son, Martin, from pursuing a career in the arts on the ground that such work was only for the genius, the extraordinarily creative person, while "we Batesons" were capable only of doing the painstaking work of scientific discovery. (My mother held an almost identical attitude, a legacy of late romanticism, that ordinary people could do the work of the world, including science and scholarship, but only the genius could reach the heights of Bach in an earlier day or Picasso in hers.)

at Reed—would not suffice unless it could also be defined both in terms of one's personal growth and in terms of the norms of one's reference group as an authentic statement about the qualities of the self.

For that small minority of students I have spoken of as self-starters, the new freedoms provided in this way, to explore both themselves and the greatly expanded curricular and extracurricular milieus, created awesome and inspiring opportunities. In the "little magazines" of poetry, photography, or criticism, published today by undergraduates working together with faculty members, one can find work of remarkable quality, often at a level of sophistication far beyond that of earlier student generations. Many of these students are not activist and therefore are regarded as apathetic by people who judge them from the vantage point of the minority of activists of the late '60s, as if the latter represented the entire age cohort. But if one thinks of activity in less time-bound and ideological terms, these students are as active as any who have ever attended American colleges and universities. Indeed, many are in attendance who in an earlier day would have avoided college as unduly constricting and pedantic. For example, many attend liberal arts colleges even though they are headed for careers in dance or painting or musical composition, because they want a broad liberal arts education as a foundation for a professional career. Philip Glass, who graduated from the college of the University of Chicago before attending Juilliard and then earned his living as a plumber until he had established himself as an internationally recognized composer whose first concerts were often at colleges and local art museums, rather than in larger settings, illustrates this pattern.

But today the college of the University of Chicago, like other liberal arts colleges, is filled with students for whom the college is rarely a place for intellectual activity, but rather a way station en route to medical school, law school, or other postbaccalaureate or professional work. (For a critical comment on the anti-intellectual nature of the typical pre-med curriculum, see Thomas, 1979.) These students are active in the sense of hard-working; they are passive in the sense of not taking control of their own educations apart from calculations of what will best serve their postbaccalaureate vocational interests. It would be absurd to blame students for running scared in the face of an uncertain occupational future. But it is also important to realize that such students, even if requirements are reimposed, will simply go through the motions of doing the requisite work; they will be passive in the sense that they will not be intellectually engaged with what they are studying—an intellectual engagement that, as I trust this book has made clear, has never been common among students in the United States, whose aims have always been, like those of most of their teachers, either directly or covertly pragmatic and utilitarian.

Implicit in what I have said is a view of personal development influenced by psychoanalytic theory and perhaps also by American Puritanism—namely, that one must struggle against obstacles in order to develop one's capacities fully. I do not refer here to any directly "oedipal" belief, patriarchal by its very nature, that sons must struggle against fathers. Rather, I refer to the belief that people of whatever age who want to gain a sense of purpose and accomplishment must struggle against the intrinsic difficulties of their subject matter and that there is a danger that adults in general and faculty members in particular lack the convictions that give rise to creative struggle with the actual materials of scholarly work, including that branch of work now fitted under the rubric of "creativity" in cognitive terms and perhaps "independent study" in curricular ones.

In this constellation, there is at work a subtle egalitarianism. In the "softer" social sciences and humanities, students will say about a piece of work they have done that they "feel" this or that, not that they "think" or "speculate" this or that. And there is a widespread belief that all feelings are equal and are entitled to equal weight. Thus students can and do contend that no one is entitled to judge their feelings, as represented in a piece of work, because it represents their true feelings, and that is the end of it. Quite apart from the unawareness in the general culture and, of course, among students as well that the judgment of what are one's "true feelings" is not automatic, it simply is not true that feelings are equal, any more than that other affective qualities are equal. Feelings can be more or less discriminating—indeed, I would contend that feelings can be more or less rational. To illustrate: feelings of contempt for others may represent a mixture of narcissism and sadism; they may also represent the highest moral judgments of a person who has not succumbed to the prevailing moral relativism of his or her peers.

The question naturally asked by faculty members and administrators is how one can inculcate these qualities of active responsiveness among students, alertness to the world around them, curiosity and willingness to learn from all sources, whether approved or otherwise. I have no assured or single answer. Experience as student, teacher, and colleague has led me to emphasize the importance of mentorship. Good mentors offer contagious examples; unfortunately, authoritarian or exploitative mentors may sometimes also spread contagion, unless their behavior is so obviously wretched as to create a negative reaction. The continuing ability of the top-flight liberal arts colleges to recruit students who might be, and often are, admitted to bigger, "brand name" institutions in the Ivy League or to Stanford testifies to the realization by a small proportion of students (no more than 5 percent of the college-going population) that it is worth paying high tuition to find what I have sometimes termed the new *in loco parentis*, substitute "parents" who can provide mentorship outside the domestic milieu, where parent/child relationships (as we did not need to learn from psychoanalysis) are contaminated by relations of authority and by the understandable fears of childhood and the anxieties of parenthood. Support for this view comes from the work of Daniel Levinson. His book *The Seasons of a Man's Life* (1979) emphasizes the importance of mentorship in one's student days and also later, as well as the frequent need to transmute mentorship into colleagueship after a certain time has passed; in due course, those who have profited from generous mentorship may in turn become mentors.

In an aggregate way, there are clues to be found in Alexander Astin's *Four Critical Years* (1977b), which emphasizes the importance of residential education and of student involvement in the institution in extracurricular as well as in curricular ways. Paradoxically, Astin finds that working part-time (provided it is no more than 20 hours per week) has a positive impact on student development as measured by various psychological indices, as if to suggest that working students are likely both to be more highly motivated and to learn better how to organize their time.

I have noticed at my own and similar institutions that the drive to find summer employment among affluent students who do not need it to pay their college costs has grown greatly in the last few years. Some of the positions are of an internship sort, obviously useful in deciding on potential careers and establishing linkages to such careers. For others, the desire to work, for example, as a waitress or stock clerk, represents a belief that one should come closer, if raised in affluence, to "real life," although how "real" such experiences are when known to be temporary is an open question. What is lost in such decisions is the pattern traditional in British universities of reading parties during the summer, subsidized even for nonaffluent students by the grants provided for everyone attending university in the United Kingdom. To be sure, a number of affluent students still travel abroad during summer vacations and some of these seek to perfect their knowledge of another language, but this is less the case in the present era of diminished facility for speaking another language and a greater acceptance of the desire of non-Americans to practice their English.

All I have been suggesting is that desirable outcomes do occur and that they are more likely at some types of institutions than at others. I can also make some negative statements about environments that will be harmful to the cultivation of the qualities of the self-starter: environments in which everyone's motto is "do your own thing" and in which there are requirements neither of curriculum nor of qualitative judgment of any sort on the part of adults. I can also declare that I do not see the teaching of ethics, now so often sought at the undergraduate level, as responsive to the issues raised here, for although it may make students more aware of what the appropriate answers are, let us say on a scale of conventional morality, and may occasionally alert previously unawakened students to ethical questions that then become serious for them, there appears to be little evidence of how students will behave in actual situations or how active they will be in response to such situations.

The Alleged Death of Student Idealism

Levinson's book analyzes a group of men at a particular midlife point, following them backward through careers in what is often a reconstruction of chance sequences. There appear to be timetables that approximately fit this cohort; for example, mentors are generally about ten years older than mentees, and many mentor/mentee relationships last a certain amount of time and then either explode in animosity or dissolve into more peerlike relationships of friendly colleagueship. Levinson would not claim that the stages distinguished in his sample are universal, nor, as Rossi (1980) has pointed out, has he examined the physiological variables that affect middle life and aging, as they affect childhood and adolescence. (In any event, such variables would differ between the sexes, and Levinson's subjects were all men.) No such scruples of cultural history and timing affect the many observers—academics, journalists, students themselves—who have declared that "the students" of the 1960s were idealistic and generous, while those of the 1970s have become conservative, self-seeking, and cynical. Since I have in the preceding paragraphs been critical of what I regard as misplaced student idealism, as in the protests against nuclear power and in the methods of civil disobedience, I want to make clear my differences from this now familiar perspective.

Ordinary language about American history since the end of the First World War has been obsessed with decennary judgments: people speak of "the twenties," "the thirties," or "the sixties" as a way of interpreting the flow of events and too easily accounting for discontinuities (see Riesman, 1978c). There is, however, one area in which poll data are fairly conclusive—namely, the enormous drop in confidence in American institutions, including institutions of higher education, beginning about 1965 and leveling off in the late 1970s at a point where all the major institutions lacked legitimacy with perhaps three quarters of the population (see, for example, Lipset, 1979). So thoroughgoing, in fact, is this cynicism, notably among the educated, that one could say that those students who continue to show concern for others and belief in social, cultural, and economic improvement must indeed have great strength of conviction to carry them against the current of nihilism.

Furthermore, these students have in many of the more academically selective schools and colleges had many teachers who were themselves euphoric activists for civil rights in the 1950s and early 1960s and against the war in Vietnam in the late 1960s and early 1970s. For a number of these faculty members (many of them now mentors), a euphoric hope that everything could be changed—what seemed to me at the time an extravagant optimism—has been replaced by a soured determinism, often some version of Marxism that sees the fate of individuals as wholly the result of social conditions and "capitalist" conditioning. (Unlike earlier Stalinists or more recent idolators of Castro or Mao, the majority of these Marxists, who term themselves socialists, appear not to see a country on earth in which they can place their hopes. They may be on the side of revolutions in the less developed countries, barely formed as yet into nation-states, but they are not particularly charmed by Swedish Social Democracy or by the Mao of the Cultural Revolution; they have no model for the United States.)[12]

There is a somewhat older cohort of faculty members, influential for some students, who were enthusiastic admirers of John Kennedy's presidency, especially after his assassination. Convenient amnesia blinds them to the fact that no other president, nor the chief executive of any nuclear power, has threatened the world with destruction as Kennedy did at the time of the Cuban missile crisis—a manufactured crisis partly created by Kennedy's own rhetoric in the election campaign against a successor to Dwight Eisenhower. And it was Kennedy who first sent military advisers to Vietnam and left to surround his successor, Lyndon Johnson, a

---

[12] There is a small group of idealists whose motto, "Small Is Beautiful," has become well known and who hope to develop in enclaves what might be the seedlings for a larger social order. But their preoccupation is primarily with the viability of the seedlings, and there has not been much thought for how these could be applied to so huge and diverse a population as that of the United States. In some respects, they remind me of the "Fugitives" group at Vanderbilt in the 1920s: those Southern writers and their allies who were in favor of a more decentralized America. They differ very much from these intellectual forebears in that the "Fugitives" were politically and culturally conservative, whereas the present explorers of minuscule, manageable enclaves think of themselves as radical. But it would not be the first time that "extremes" on the standard political spectrum, joined by their libertarian goals, turned out to resemble each other.

core of self-confident strategists who were insistent on continuing the war.[13]

Student interest in peace had been active in the United States and in England before the Second World War; it began to revive in the 1950s in the face of the Cold War and McCarthyism. Efforts toward integration in the South began shortly after the *Brown* decision of 1954, many Southern white liberals risking ostracism or worse at the hands of segregationists, whose most recent illustration of civil disobedience is the minuscule revival of the Ku Klux Klan. Tutoring of black children was a natural extension of the social service activities on many college campuses in the late 1950s and early 1960s; a number of more selective white colleges arranged exchange programs with private black colleges during the same period. (The Free Speech Movement at Berkeley in the fall of 1964 was itself an outgrowth of civil-rights activism by movement leaders who had been in the Deep South and then wanted to recruit on the Berkeley campus for actions closer to home on their return. Chancellor Strong's prohibition of such activities within the Berkeley gates touched off the initial demonstrations.)

The students who were active in this way were always a small minority, but virtually everywhere they had strong support, even incitement, from leading faculty members. Periodically, they could bring large numbers of students to take part in demonstrations, especially if they could maneuver university or other authorities into behaving in what appeared to be brutal ways. Like the guerrilla fighters they often became, they generally swam in a sympathetic sea—and many patriotic students who thought otherwise on the major campuses neither controlled the student paper nor had the attention, and in some cases the sympathy, of the metropolitan and television media.[14]

[13] It is only fair to state that, though General Eisenhower's intentions were usually pacific, seeds of the Vietnam combat were in part a legacy of the refusal of John Foster Dulles, Eisenhower's supermoralistic secretary of state, to sign the Geneva Accords of 1954.

[14] On the attitudes of what he terms the national media elite, see Rothman and others (1977). His work stresses the salient role of cosmopolitan Jewish students in the activism of the 1960s. Correspondingly, the concern of many of these students later and of their Jewish successors with Zionism and the fate of Israel has tended to swing them in an anti-Soviet direction, even turning many into the leading hawks; only a small minority of truly radical Jews, and a few liberal non-Zionist Jews, have

The assassinations of Martin Luther King, Jr., and Robert Kennedy in 1968 eliminated both the leading proponent of nonviolence (already under sharp and bitter attack by black-power activists and their white fellow travelers) and the presidential candidate who could appeal to a much wider spectrum of both black and white students than his older brother ever had. But students became disillusioned not only by these tragedies but by one another as, especially after the Cambodian uprising, many became aware that they had been manipulated by a small minority and as splintering developed within that minority, with a number of SDS fragments resorting to terrorist violence. The image of student idealism was itself tarnished.

Nevertheless, when in post–Vietnam war years new issues arose, students could still be mobilized—for instance, in the environmentalist movement, especially the attack on nuclear power. Issues involving race could also mobilize a campus. Many selective colleges have had protests over university investments in or connections with South Africa. There have been boycotts or attempted boycotts of corporations regarded as antiunion (J. P. Stevens or the Cottrell Company, traditional makers of caps and gowns) or as exploiting the impulse toward the "modern" in encouraging bottle feeding in Africa and elsewhere (Nestlé). Both white and black campus activists have monitored their institutions' commitment to recruitment of nonwhite students, teachers, and administrators—and on many campuses they have done so even at a time when desperate competition for scarce jobs preoccupies the majority of students, as it preoccupies all who suffer the ravages and inequities of inflation.

Above all, as suggested earlier, the women's movements have had a more profound effect on our society than any other movement of protest since the Second World War. They have pro-

---

supported the Palestinian cause or familiarized themselves with the situation of the Palestinians in the occupied territories.

For a report on three successive surveys of students in a sample of on the whole fairly selective colleges and universities, see Kesler (1979). The survey indicates the drift of students toward a position they themselves define as more conservative on the majority even of such liberal campuses as Reed College or Sarah Lawrence, but of course the survey cannot probe the shift of standards by which students define themselves as "radical" or "conservative," as the case may be.

foundly altered the aspirations of educated women and influenced the attitudes of educated men. These movements have proceeded, not by large demonstrations—although these have occasionally occurred—but by smaller consciousness-raising groups of women. Although France and some Latin and Islamic countries have an active minority of feminists, there is in no other country anything comparable to the power and intensity of women's active organizing in the United States. I include national organizations such as NOW, the caucuses that have led many professional groups to avoid holding meetings in states that have not passed the Equal Rights Amendment, and the extensive use of networks of women in the various professions to act as mutual support groups, often generating far more intense and effective pressure than the less self-conscious "old boy" network (which continues to exist in some fields and which remains a repeated target of attack even where its power has been attenuated).

To be sure, the women's movements have activated a backlash of hostility from culturally traditional women, much as the antiwar movement generated antibodies because of its strident anti-American symbolism and cultural as well as political radicalism. Even so, the women's movements have proceeded from the upper, educated strata well into the ranks of working-class women.

Finally, it must be noted that one reason for the apparent quiescence and acquiescence of contemporary students is that they have won many victories, which the more radical see as a form of cooptation: they have gained the right from parents, teachers, and other adults to their own modes of dress, their own "life-styles" in general. Treating marijuana laws as their grandparents treated Prohibition, they have made smoking pot almost mandatory in many schools and colleges and have succeeded in decriminalizing its possession in a number of states. In the professional schools, there are cohorts of critics who want to practice preventive medicine or community medicine, though these are everywhere a minority, as are their counterparts in law schools who insist that any law firm they join practice nondiscriminatory policies in hiring and give them time for public-interest work. Even though the country may have grown more conservative in some respects (although nowhere is big business liked or even trusted), educated elites have remained vulnerable to guilt and hence to causes.

In sum, the notion that there are radical discontinuities in the outlook of students, coincident with decades, is largely fallacious. The great change is the overwhelming sense of powerlessness and the accompanying cynicism that prevail currently and make even more dramatic the continuing evidences that students who can afford the luxury of involvement are as capable of it as heretofore.

10

Protecting Students by Voluntary Action: Regional Accrediting Associations

Until Andrew Carnegie's creation of the Carnegie Foundation for the Advancement of Teaching, there was no clear definition of what a college was. It was his concern over the absence of any provision for the retirement of faculty members and his wish to establish a pension plan that made it necessary to decide what a college was and hence who might be eligible. (Before the creation of the Carnegie Foundation for the Advancement of Teaching, many faculty members could not afford to retire, though long since obsolescent or even senile; even if an individual institution could make provision for retirement, such arrangements were not portable, and any faculty members who had moved to another institution were stranded.) The Carnegie Foundation for the Advancement of Teaching created a national network, but one that excluded institutions established for profit, those for religious training, and academies or prep schools that termed themselves "colleges." Thus, "Carnegie units" came into existence to distinguish a college from a high school by specifying the number of units of credit a student required before entering college, while college itself was defined in terms of a sequence of credits for what was ordinarily a four-year course of study.

A comparable necessity occurred when, under the GI Bill of Rights after the Second World War, the Veterans Administration had to decide what educational institutions were to be defined as entitled to the payment of veterans' tuition. They turned to the regional associations which cover the country and which were used to accredit general-purpose colleges (schools were in their purview also but are outside our concern here). The accrediting associations proved insufficient for VA purposes, since they did not deal quickly enough with the institutions newly established to take advantage of the quick money to be made from veterans, nor did they deal with proprietary or many other kinds of postsecondary institutions that were often handled by state licensing laws, such as schools of cosmetology, barbering, or secretarial science, or language schools, such as Berlitz. However, they had enough experience of visiting institutions to see to what extent they obeyed what were then fairly standard definitions of a college, such as having a library with a certain number of books, covering recognized arts and sciences subjects, and having procedures for the admission of students and their passage by stages to either the associate or the baccalaureate degree.

Accreditation by Professional and Disciplinary Associations

The accrediting associations originally were created by the various professions and academic disciplines. Since they can more readily achieve consensus on professional aims, it is sometimes considered that they are too restrictive.

Consider in this connection Worcester Polytechnic Institute when it went on its "New Plan" at the beginning of the 1970s. That plan had originally been developed in a series of memoranda written by faculty members, most of them "home guard," graduates of WPI. These unusual innovators, men of great patience and pertinacity, had spent most of their professional lives at WPI. The documents they wrote called for a dramatically altered curriculum in what had been a standard, local engineering school, drawing like other such schools on students of lower-middle-class and working-class backgrounds without family histories of college attendance, giving them grounding deemed solid by the accrediting associations in the usual fields of engineering—civil, mechanical, electrical, and so on. The American Association for Engineering Education had long argued in favor of requiring engineering schools to devote 25 percent of their curriculum to the humanities and the social sciences, but the AAEE had only the power of persuasion; the actual power to accredit lay with the various guilds within engineering already mentioned. At any rate, WPI had already met the voluntary standards of the AAEE in their traditional humanities, with a sufficient basis of courses in English literature, history, music, and art. However, dealing as in many other tech schools with "first generation in college" undergraduates whose eye was on the many opportunities for employment (which continue to this day) in engineering, only the most exceptionally gifted instructors (I speak from my observation of classes) were able to draw students into subjects that were remote from engineering and were regarded by many as "cultural bull." Many faculty members felt as isolated in their concerns as if they had been teaching in other kinds of directly vocational programs—for example, teaching philosophy or history of education to prospective elementary school teachers or Dostoevsky to students in the criminal-justice program in a community college or four-year comprehensive state or private college. Some found a certain relief in occasional chances to teach part-time at nearby Clark University.

The niche of WPI seemed modestly secure as long as engineering enrollments held up; its graduates gained employment, and a few of its professors secured grants for research and inaugurated some small doctoral programs, drawing students mainly from overseas—for example, Turkey, India, or Taiwan. Of course, WPI could not hope to compete for students with MIT, and it was generally second choice for students in the area to Rensselaer Polytechnic Institute, larger and better known; it was also beginning to suffer competition from the increasing quality as well as the wide tuition gap that made the college of engineering at the University of Massachusetts at Amherst attractive even in a region where public higher education had long had lower status.

In these circumstances, WPI found itself a new president in George Hazzard, who had had experience both in academic administration and in working in an engineering capacity for General Electric and who had considerable skills as fund raiser and publicist for a transforming institution. A large National Science Foundation grant, combined with money from the Carnegie Corporation, the National Endowment for the Humanities, and other sources, made it possible to carry through some of the ideas that had been percolating under the previous administration; Dean William Grogan, a WPI alumnus who had been on the faculty throughout his academic career and was widely respected for his unusual combination of willingness to experiment, common sense, and empathy for troubled faculty members, provided continuity under a new president.

The New Plan was to develop "humanistic engineers" who were no less skilled in the craft of their engineering specialty than heretofore but who had also worked on projects or in settings of social relevance—perhaps best illustrated by the Washington office that WPI established, which allowed students to work for the Environmental Protection Agency or the Office of Technology Assessment and to gain experience of the wider implications of what engineers traditionally have done. The curriculum, previously tight and required, was loosened—at least, so it seemed to many students—to a frightening degree: there were fewer classes, and more individual work on self-paced instruction was required, as well as on "interactive projects," which sought to bring together a social problem and an engineering solution—a task requiring great effort and inventiveness of both faculty and students. I might add, just to indicate how radical was the transformation at WPI, that admissions tests and screening were abolished, and students were allowed to admit themselves if, after counseling and study of the wholly revised and quite alluring catalogue, they believed that they could make it at WPI. (This last change was finally abandoned, as it was impossible to convince students that an institution that admitted rather than selected them could be of high quality.)

Many students continued to come to WPI because it remained for them the available college, often as commuters or spending weekends at home within a fifty-mile radius. The new students recruited by the New Plan itself tended to be more intellectual, much more demanding of faculty time, but in the early years not of sufficient "critical mass" to provide much personal support for one another. More important for our purposes here were the disparities among faculty members: a number of them strongly resisted the New Plan, some because it seemed too elaborate and unworkable, others because the heavy demands of the revised undergraduate program would take energies away from actual or proposed postbaccalaureate programs, and others because they found support among the still resistant students. Many feared WPI would lose the stamp of respectability that it needed to stay in business—the Food and Drug Administration label of purity.

These fears proved groundless. WPI did not lose its respectability or its accreditation. Its changes were only a more dramatic example of efforts to revise the engineering curriculum also taking place at other institutions—for example, Illinois Institute of Technology. WPI had the backing of its distinguished NSF Panel and of national publicity for its efforts.

However, there are some areas in which professional associations can have decisive impact on undergraduate professional programs. This is true at undergraduate schools of education, which need the imprimatur of the National Association of Colleges for Teacher Education; without accreditation, graduates are not permitted to take the examinations or otherwise become certified to teach in the public schools. Similarly, undergraduate programs in nursing require approval if their graduates are to be employable in hospitals or to become RNs. (See the involvement of the Oregon State Board of Nursing in the experimental effort to establish a competence-based nursing program at Mount Hood Community College; Olesen, 1979, pp. 351–359.)

In contrast with the professional associations illustrated here by engineering, disciplinary associations in the sciences will also give accreditation to programs, notably in chemistry, at the undergraduate level. These associations exercise a much less severe sanction than the power of the engineering societies to withhold accreditation, in effect, from an entire institution. Many liberal arts colleges simply do not bother to ask the American Chemical Society to determine whether their undergraduate program has sufficient academic breadth, laboratory facilities, qualified staff, and so on for accreditation, which might be of particular use only to those few students who want to continue with work in chemistry and would not necessarily be relevant even for them.

State System Reviewing

Then there is another kind of program review undertaken by state systems of higher education and therefore applicable only in the public sector (which in most states, of course, is the primary and overwhelmingly numerous sector), not directly to protect potential students in their roles as consumers, but to protect them at best indirectly by limiting wasteful duplication of programs, particularly at the graduate level. A notable example is the pattern held to in California, whereby only the University of California is in general entitled to grant the Ph.D., although some of the state colleges and universities can do so in conjunction with a branch of the university system. Naturally, this limitation on some of the more eminent state universities (San Diego State, San Francisco State, San Jose State) is bitterly fought by the latter as humiliating, discriminatory, "elitist," and so on. Similarly, the University of Wisconsin-Madison, though merged into a statewide system, has maintained almost a monopoly of the doctorate; thus, the University of Wisconsin in the major city of Milwaukee does not grant a doctorate in sociology, though it does in social sciences, as well as in psychology and some other fields. (There are also differences in selectivity within the system at the undergraduate level, and some of the regional campuses have virtual open admissions.) In New Jersey, Connecticut, and Massachusetts, only the flagship campus of the state university is empowered to grant the doctorate. In Louisiana, fifty-eight master's programs have just recently been eliminated at public universities by decision of the state board of regents—mainly programs in precollegiate education ("Fifty-eight Degree Programs to Be Eliminated," 1980). Although Michigan is not a "system state," Oakland University in Rochester, Michigan, had to pass the scrutiny of a state commission in order to gain permission to grant doctorates in several specialized fields. In this last case, as in others, outside consultants were called in, cooperatively selected by the institution and the state board of higher education or similar agency, to offer recommendations.

I have already referred to the procedure followed by the board of regents of the State University of New York to withdraw accreditation from the Ph.D. program in history at the Albany SUNY campus. But this decision was taken in a field in which there are virtually no jobs for Ph.D.s, even for most graduates of highly selective world-class universities. It was one episode that helped lead Dorothy Harrison, of the New York State Department of Education, in collaboration with Professor Ernest May of Harvard's history department, to establish the beginnings of a program for preparing Ph.D.s in history and eventually in the other humanities for work in government service (for example, the Foreign Service), public life, and banking. Naturally, after losing its case in the courts, the decision was humiliating and a blow to morale at SUNY-Albany. And conceivably, an undergraduate at SUNY-Albany could argue that his or her degree means just slightly less because of this verdict. But on the whole, it has been the hope of SUNY administrators that the shrinkage in doctoral programs will lead to more concentration on the quality of undergraduate teaching—an outcome likely only if the faculty members in question are not too demoralized, have not become too dependent on graduate teaching assistants, and are prepared to make more than perfunctory efforts to teach the students they have, rather than to long for the students no longer available to them at the postbaccalaureate level.

Voluntary Regional Associations

Failure of the Regional Idea in Government Policy. In many fields of policy, at the very beginnings of the "First New Nation," arguments have occurred between those who might be called federalizers and those who term themselves states'-righters. It was possible to pass the Morrill Act of 1862 only because the Southern states, with their traditional emphasis on states' rights, were not represented in the Congress. During the New Deal era, legislation dealing with social security, agriculture, and other fields of policy was often fought out between centralist and decentralist factions. When similar conflicts arose in Lyndon Johnson's Task Force on Education, the compromise of setting up regions to oversee administration of new educational programs—regions comparable to those of the Federal Reserve Board or the Federal Circuit Courts of Appeal was deemed unavailing, and on the whole the federalizers, in some cases motivated by the euphoria of the Great Society, won out. However, there is one area in which most federal agencies have been willing (though with increasing misgivings) to delegate power to regional groupings —namely, the voluntary regional accrediting associations, such as the North Central Association of Colleges and Schools, the New England Association of Schools and Colleges, and many other associations that cover the country. These agencies, created by the institutions themselves, have the delegated power to determine the eligibility of institutions to receive federal money, either directly or channeled through students carrying federal grants with them. Along with the professional accrediting associations, the regional ones are represented in Washington by the Council on Postsecondary Accreditation, an organization now in the process of reorganization.

Operation of Regional Associations. Regional associations, such as those just noted, the Southern Association of Colleges and Schools, and the Western Association of Schools and Colleges, are not-for-profit groups. Each has a commission on institutions of higher education that deals exclusively with postsecondary education and has the power to accredit and to reaccredit two-year and four-year not-for-profit academic institutions. A new institution or one newly seeking accreditation must apply for candidate status and follow rules set up by these voluntary bodies. The general practice is to assign a member of the commission or a staff member of the association, and sometimes both, to help the applicant institution prepare for the visit of an accrediting team—a process that ordinarily lasts some four or five years.

Some institutions receive only provisional accreditation, after a short period of review. However, accreditation is never permanent. There are variations in the timetables set for revisits, but ordinarily each institution must be visited at least once a decade. In accreditation visits at Harvard College, MIT, Amherst College, and other places like them, the accrediting teams and the supervising regional association must waste a good deal of valuable time to find out whether they have remained reputable institutions. (Even so, not all the time is wasted; visiting teams have pointed out, for example, situations in which undergraduate teaching appears to be neglected or there are inadequate procedures for review of grievances, so that such visits can serve in a mild admonitory way.)

The regional associations have a loose central body: the Council on Postsecondary Accreditation (COPA), formerly directed by Kenneth Young (see Jacobson, 1980). Within the American Council on Education there is also an Office of Self-Regulating Initiatives, which, in Kenneth Young's words, "is collecting codes of good practice, identifying areas where such codifications of generally accepted behavior should be developed (or updated), working with other appropriate groups to prepare new or revised codes, and planning dissemination and education activities. (For example, the National Association of College and University Business Officers is working on proposed guidelines for tuition refund policies.)" (personal correspondence, January 25, 1979; also Young, 1978).

It is widely believed that there are great differences in the quality of the work of accrediting teams in the different regional associations. The North Central Association publishes a quarterly journal of more or less scholarly articles, but it does not follow that any of its particular accrediting teams will do a thorough job of investigating the financial and curricular quality of a particular institution, especially as such measurable indices as the number of books in the library or the number of Ph.D.s on the faculty may say little about the quality of education conveyed or the forms of marketing in use to recruit and retain students. Thurston E. Manning, Director, Commission on Institutions of Higher Education of the North Central Association, has described in an essay how the first efforts to establish standards of excellence focused on an increasingly long list of measurable indices of the sort just mentioned: books in the library; Ph.D.s on the faculty; number of departments; limits to the size of laboratory sections; and so on. But in 1928, Floyd Reeves and John Dale Russell surveyed 29 colleges in terms of the quantitative measures that the North Central Association had adopted, such as average expenditure per student and student/faculty ratios; however, on the basis of visits to colleges and qualitative assessments of a holistic sort, it was clear that there was no substantial correlation between these quantitative measures and what sagacious and knowledgeable observers would agree was educational excellence. The result was the abandonment of the formal standards and the alteration of the criteria to take account of an institution's purposes and the degree to which those purposes, assuming their legitimacy, were in practice being met. Abandoning the abstract measures, as Manning puts it, "allows the rich flowering of educational institutions that has occurred" (Manning, 1978, p. 8); however, the qualitative assessments now required, although Manning believes them superior to the Veterans Administration's formalistic standards, also raise questions about who is doing the assessments and how they can be supported, in all their inevitable subjectivity, against attack.

Moreover, in the few instances when going concerns have had their accreditation removed, which for all practical purposes amounts to a death sentence, there has been controversy and generally litigation. The former bombastic president of Parsons College in Iowa, who cheerfully accepted *Life* magazine's label of "Flunk-Out U.," almost invited a visit from the North Central Association, not only because he widely advertised the college as prepared to accept any student who had graduated from any high school, but also because he offended many private college officials by his repeated contention that it was possible with good business management to run a private institution without any support from private philanthropy, and to pay high faculty salaries as well, on a cash-customer basis—statements not supported by Parsons College's books. (President Millard Roberts maintained that many Midwestern private college officials who attacked him for his blatant open-door policy only claimed to be selective; having turned down someone in the spring and then finding themselves underenrolled as the fall term was about to open, they might get in touch with the same person and say that a reexamination of his or her record indicated that the person was, after all, qualified and would be admitted. For discussion of a valuable effort among some faculty members at Parsons College to redeem the apathetic and inept, and the burial of its virtues under its misleading salesmanship, see Gusfield and Riesman, 1968.)

As attacks mounted in the 1960s on traditional postsecondary education and a number of new, self-proclaimed "nontraditional" institutions began, the accrediting associations did not want to appear to stifle potentially valuable experiments. They made clear, as the North Central Association had already done, that their mission was to be defined in terms of the goals of the institution itself: they were to examine whether, for example, a contract system of learning lived up to its own imperative to possess quality control, so that contracts were monitored in some fashion and were not simply bargains between a faculty member and a student that demanded nothing in the way of serious work of either a traditional or a nontraditional sort. It has always been evident that the United States, with its immense diversity of institutions, could never possess the nearly uniform standard of a degree from a German university or the platinum standard of degrees at university level in the British Commonwealth (including the degrees of the "nontraditional" Open University, which proceeds by correspondence, television, and occasional conferences with mentors). Nor could one expect impoverished private colleges—especially, perhaps, in the South—to come close to the standards, for example, of Bowdoin College (which is highly selective but does not require SATs), Wellesley, Carleton, or Whitman.

But some of those who looked at the makeup of the accrediting teams that visited some of the newer institutions, either begun or transformed in the surge toward the nontraditional in the last fifteen years, might be pardoned for a touch of cynicism. They would be quick to note that the individual chairing the team was herself or himself the president or dean of another relatively new nontraditional institution. Of course, such a selection could be defended on the ground that only such an innovator would understand and be reasonably sympathetic with the efforts of another nontraditional institution—at least this could be true when such institutions were springing up in large numbers in the 1960s and were, given the flood tide of students, in only marginal competition with one another. In addition, the cynics might miss several things, including the makeup of the entire team, which, in every case that I can recall, included some more traditionally academic faculty members. Furthermore, the college awaiting accreditation had to prepare an elaborate self-study with a great deal of documentation on student test scores and rates of attrition, for example—often an extremely bulky volume that informed the faculty itself of what was happening in its own institution, of which some had been able to remain innocently or evasively unaware. And one could never tell whether the accrediting team would in fact be sympathetic; one could only hope so—usually correctly. For the college being accredited, the process was never as pro forma as it seemed to some outsiders, including some officials in the Federal Trade Commission and a minority in the Office of Education who regard it as anomalous that private, voluntary associations have the power to determine what institutions will or will not receive federal funds. To such officials, the accrediting associations appear to be "special interests" like any other, concerned with the survival of their members, good, bad, indifferent—failing to appreciate that the survival of the great majority depends on elimination, through withdrawal of accreditation or refusal to grant it, of the scandalous abuses of a few.[1]

The Holdouts. There are a handful of institutions which have refused to accept any federal or state subsidy and which, although accredited, are on principle refusing to comply with HEW questionnaires and directives. As mentioned in Chapter Five, this group includes large and distinguished Brigham Young University, which has ample support from the Latter-day Saints and maintains high standards. Since HEW regulators could not find any violation of federal rules in the actual conduct of the campus, they attacked the institution because students living in the campus town of Provo, Utah, find off-campus accommodations that are rented exclusively either to men or to women. They see this as sex discrimination practiced by the landlords, while Brigham Young University maintains that it has no control over the traditional rental policies of private enterprises. This conflict is, in my judgment, an example of the degree to which HEW officials will pursue an institution that appears to disobey its mandate. (Another example has occurred at Berkeley, where, in an effort to prove discrimination in hiring against women and minorities, HEW officials have insisted on seeing letters written in confidence about particular candidates, while the faculty members to whom such letters were addressed believe it would be immoral to violate the confidentiality originally promised.)

More interesting are the secular institutions that have been

[1] As I learned from discussion with officers and members of the Committee on Institutions of Higher Education of the New England Association, there have been a number of situations in which the association is aware of abuses but is slow to remove accreditation for fear of litigation and even libel suits; this fear inhibited the association from proceeding promptly in the Windham College case discussed in Chapter Seven, despite awareness among the relevant members of the committee concerning actual and potential abuses. Even state licensing authorities have sometimes hesitated to move quickly unless they feel they have evidence against an institution that will stand up in court.

fighting regulation as such. Two examples will suffice. One is Hillsdale College, with fewer than a thousand students in a small Michigan town. Though no longer church-related, it does not grant the A.B. to students who do not fulfill the language requirements (it gives them a Bachelor of Liberal Studies degree for study in English of French, German, or Spanish and Latin American civilizations), and it maintains a strict rule against alcohol, coed dormitories, or intervisitation. It has been attacked through its students, some of whom arrive carrying federal grants or loans, and HEW has claimed in administrative semijudicial hearings, now being appealed, that accepting such students requires a college to obey all HEW mandates. Hillsdale College's president aggressively advertises a conservative "free enterprise" philosophy and hopes to survive as a distinctive college by reason of this very battle, although if his students cannot receive any form of federal grant or loan, this may not be feasible. Similarly, Grove City College in Pennsylvania, United Presbyterian in origin, has fought an analogous battle both with HEW and with the activist Pennsylvania Department of Public Instruction. An HEW hearing found that in fact Grove City does not discriminate on the basis of gender or race, but it does not agree to abide by the regulations on the "handicapped," a category reported to include alcoholics, addicts, and others that the college does not want (Kirk, 1979). Concerning Grove City's outlook, a student leader reports in Cass and Birnbaum (1979, p. 184) the "seeming paradox—students apparently have more influence on curriculum than on rules governing their social life. . . . in direct contrast to the great majority of campuses across the country. Pressures for academic achievement appear moderately strong." Whatever their diverse motives, these institutions are paradoxical in another sense: they are seeking to maintain a hegemony characteristic of the academic revolution, although it is in general a hegemony of a forceful president and a supportive board of trustees rather than of the faculty as such.

Improving the Performance of the Regional Associations. In discussing over the years the work of the accrediting teams and the varying performance of the regional associations, I have become convinced that their performance could be greatly improved. I know from personal experience how intensely alert a team must be to make a review of a departmental program in a first-rate university, judging its effectiveness for that institution's already high purposes, even where nothing is consciously concealed from the visiting team. In contrast, those who enjoy serving on accrediting teams have in the past sometimes been junketeers, tired professors glad for an expense-paid trip to another institution and with nothing much better to do. Such freeloaders have allowed the person chairing the team to do most of the work of writing the report, which is in turn to a considerable extent based on the self-study submitted by the institution itself. The review of the report by the association's officials may then be more or less perfunctory, extending credence to the visiting team whatever inner misgivings about its quality of detailed scrutiny there may be.

The Commission on Institutions of Higher Education of the New England Association has shown how it is possible to improve the process of orienting prospective visiting teams and to improve staff work at the association's headquarters. With support from John R. Proffitt, director of the Division of Eligibility and Agency Evaluation in the Bureau of Postsecondary Education of the Office of Education, the New England Association secured a small grant, which it used in a training program for evaluators both for institutions of higher education and for a separate Commission on Vocational, Technical, and Career Institutions. The Commission on Institutions of Higher Education used the grant to develop self-study guide materials and Institutional Data Profiles enabling "an institution to 'take its own pulse' and evaluate trends over a five-year period" (letter from Richard J. Bradley, executive director of the New England Association, to John R. Proffitt, November 2, 1979.) The grant provided funds to run a workshop for evaluators. But it did not allow for any expansion of the staff. I would hope that further such experiments could be tried that could assist the often overworked staffs of the regional associations, providing them with greater opportunity to recruit, during a period of faculty oversupply, some older but still sagacious faculty members who would be prepared to spend substantial time in evaluation visits and to help educate neophyte members of visiting teams concerning the kinds of inquiry necessary to avoid being taken in by the "Potemkin villages" that institutions being evaluated can erect, seeing to it, for example, that the students with whom the visiting team will be allowed contact are both well scrubbed and well briefed to give their blessing to the institution as it currently operates.

There is no doubt that there is considerable variation, not only within each region in terms of particular teams visiting particular institutions, but among the regions; some are more experienced and scrupulous, others more relaxed. (California, for example, poses special difficulties because its state licensing laws apparently allow what are little more than degree mills to spring up, call themselves law schools or graduate schools of management, and recruit by mail or emissary all over the country—these are established with such rapidity that the Western Association of Schools and Colleges can hardly catch up with them!) But it goes much too far to share the wholly negative outlook of the critics of voluntary accreditation, including some within the Federal Trade Commission and others in the Office of Education. Just as in the attack on the Educational Testing Service, dealt with in Chapter Four, many have taken an adversary point of view toward all private institutions. They regard accrediting associations as mutual back-scratching operations that too rarely impose sanctions, warnings that they will withdraw accreditation, or in fact do so; as it is sometimes colloquially put, "the fox is set to watch the chickens"— the chickens being the students. In fact, however, the accrediting associations have two motives to improve the strictness of the accreditation process. One, already indicated, is to prevent debasement of the academic coinage, for the sake of the reputation of the majority of reasonably above-board academic institutions. The other is to avoid what is felt in a cumulative way as the increasingly heavy hand of federal regulation, with its tendency toward uniform standards, legalistic elaboration of regulations, and reporting requirements that could easily be met by major publicly funded universities but hardly by smaller, especially private institutions, which already have difficulty complying with the demands of state and federal regulation. Furthermore, if there are differences among the different regional accrediting associations, the experience with federal regulation, for example of affirmative action or the protection of the handicapped, provides no evidence at all that the different regional offices or even different officials apply a uniform set of standards; some seek to apply the standards reasonably to deal with varying local conditions, while others are either blindly literalistic or determined to "Get the bastards!"

By no means all college presidents with whom I have discussed these issues share my belief that the accrediting process can be improved with sufficient celerity to provide assurance of quality and to stave off federal regulation. One of the difficulties, already conceded, is the unevenness of quality, either present or in prospect, among the different regions. Perhaps a greater difficulty exists in dealing with those institutions that, accredited in a particular region, establish branch campuses in other regions. They sometimes set up shop rapidly without notice to local authorities. This is not a new development; for example, the University of Maryland has long had campuses on army bases in many parts of the world. Many of the new boundary-hopping institutions are the result of the demographic falloff in local enrollments; some of these are also located on army bases and compete with the military itself for part-time student customers. Members of regional accrediting commissions have told me they rely primarily on the accreditation provided at the institution's home base, which they may supplement with information about a particular branch, but they are certainly capable of enforcing standards on branches located within their own jurisdiction.

Where Voluntarism May Not Work

State Licensing and Branch Campuses. The voluntary accrediting associations deal only with those postsecondary institutions that are what we ordinarily think of as colleges or universities: institutions governed by a board of trustees or its equivalent and run not for profit but for a presumed public purpose. In the next chapter I discuss diploma mills, which are a conspiracy between the profit-making institution and the customer, who buys, in effect, a forged degree. States license schools of cosmetology, mortuary science, hairdressing, tavern keeping, and a host of other activities. Some state laws are lax when it comes to proprietary institutions. California, as just mentioned, and Florida, until recently, have been notorious examples—in effect, chartering piracy in the way in which Delaware became the haven of so many corporations at the time of the building of many national corporate enterprises. Or, to use another analogy, such institutions are like vessels flying the Panamanian flag, not inspected for seaworthiness within recent memory.

Other states, such as Pennsylvania, New York, and quite recently Massachusetts, have been eager to enforce licensing laws and to put shoddy enterprises out of business. Massachusetts was flexible enough to give prima facie licensing and hence accreditation to Simon's Rock Early College, which took students in after the tenth grade and, provided they performed sufficiently capably, granted them a baccalaureate after four years of study (Whitlock, 1978). However, the state also had, in Assistant Attorney General Paula Gold, a consumer advocate who reluctantly felt compelled to withdraw state approval from private Grahm Junior College for want of financial stability, while recognizing that in the very act of doing so she created a self-confirming prophecy.[2]

When universities cross a national boundary and set up campuses overseas, either for their own students or in a consortium of students from several institutions, accreditation problems are not seriously raised, because the home-base institution is still subject to the accrediting association of its own region, and its overseas activities will be examined as part of the examination of the whole curriculum. Indeed, ever so many American institutions, public and private, have campuses overseas, such as Berkeley has had for years successfully in Göttingen, or Amherst in Japan, or Stanford in Tokyo, Paris, Berlin, Salamanca, Vienna, and elsewhere. Consortia, such as the Associated Colleges of the Midwest, have also established centers in France, Italy, Japan, England, and elsewhere. Until the fuel shortage put it out of business, World

---

[2] Albert Ullman reports that the committee of the New England Association agreed that Grahm Junior College should close, and they recently and reluctantly reached the same conclusion concerning Annhurst College in Woodstock, Connecticut, a small Catholic college for women conducted by the Daughters of the Holy Spirit, one of the many private colleges that have been engaged mainly in teacher education and are now in trouble, when there is a surplus of schoolteachers; with the departure of a handful of sisters who could keep Annhurst College afloat, the institution was headed for bankruptcy.

Campus Afloat, run out of Chapman College in Orange County, California, provided a valuable year of travel for students taking a year out with some very distinguished faculty members, studying the limited number of places that would be visited in the course of a year—by no means a tourist junket. Indeed, given the provincialism of Americans, our growing monolingualism, our ignorance of much of the world, any ventures of this sort that are not wholly composed of fun and games seem to me advantageous and worthy of support.

So, also, Antioch started to set up branch campuses, as did Goddard College, well before the present collapse of the student market; these varied greatly in quality, but some of them, such as the former branch of Antioch in Columbia, Maryland, or its teacher-training branch, which started in Putney, Vermont, and moved to Keene, New Hampshire, provided valuable services for people seeking advanced degrees on a part-time basis. Nevertheless, both for Goddard and for Antioch, quality control at a distance has always been difficult. And for some of the new institutions recently launched or, for example, New York institutions that have set up master's degree programs in other states—as the College for Human Services has done (Grant and Riesman, 1978, chap. 5)—when New York State education authorities denied the institution similar privileges within New York or at least held its petitions in abeyance, great difficulties are created—ones with which COPA has not been able to cope. In effect, what we are seeing develop are educational conglomerates, often competing at a distance with local institutions by offering more reward for less work.

I can certainly offer no ready solution for the lacunae in the accreditation process. Up to this time, the dangers have seemed to me to lie more in the general demoralization of already threatened academic standards, such as they are, than in the harm done to particular students by border-hopping institutions; federal regulation of these institutions would not at this point seem worthwhile in cost/benefit terms, but rather would resemble the use of an elephant gun to kill mosquitoes. As the mosquitoes get noisier and more numerous, however, I believe that the regional accrediting associations must take responsibility for off-campus operations not only by detailed examination of the home campus but also by trips to its outlying branches as part of the normal accrediting routine. If the operations are clearly fraudulent, they may be caught by vigilant state licensing authorities in the jurisdictions where they have set up shop, but the local accrediting associations have little hold on such enterprises, which in any case often operate by offering degrees at a distance. In the worst cases, the mail-fraud statutes may be helpful to catch up with such institutions as Walden University in Florida, which in effect sells doctorates to buyers all over the country. The main responsibility should fall on the Southern Association and perhaps on Florida licensing authorities as well.

Foreign Students. In Chapter Seven I have already dealt with some of the problems of recruiting foreign students as an aspect of the mismatching of students in general with academic institutions in general. It is time now to return to the question of foreign students with the possibility of some kind of federal regulation in mind, for there is no doubt that foreign students are being recruited to American institutions with increasing avidity (see Scully, 1980). As Chapter Eight made clear, I believe that a great deal can be done by and on behalf of students to improve their information about institutions without resorting to federal regulation (see Carnegie Council on Policy Studies in Higher Education, 1979a). For example, disinterested educational brokerage services can be extended far beyond the metropolitan areas where they now exist by means of computer terminals to allow students and those seeking to help them cope with the flood of marketing to do a better job of consumer research in matching themselves to institutions. However, these protections do not operate overseas, and as institutions become eager not only to fill underenrolled dormitories and classrooms but also to recruit students from such oil-rich countries as the Arab states of the Persian Gulf[3] or potentially even Libya,

---

[3] Since the foregoing was written, Iranian students in the United States have been, almost like hostages, pawns in the conflict between the two countries. For a time, it looked as if all who did not ask for political asylum would be deported, forcing a choice on many students who were eager to return to Iran when political conditions might become less turbulent and who had no intention of remaining here permanently. After representations at the State Department and the White House

Nigeria, or physically near but psychologically distant Mexico, it may be that the need for controls beyond the capacities of those that now exist will require further federal intervention. The magnitude of the problem is shown by the fact that the number of foreign students studying in the United States has doubled in ten years (Fiske, 1980a, 1980b).[4]

The problems of students from overseas are often only heightened versions of the problems of "foreign" students native to the United States. Many overseas students speak better standard English, with whatever colorful and socially attractive accents, than American-born students of limited educational preparation. Or consider the adjustments required of Chicanos recruited to Eastern Ivy League institutions from Spanish-speaking, often devoutly Catholic migrant-laborer families in the small towns of the Imperial Valley of California or of south Texas.

In some of our Midwestern states (Michigan, in particular) good support for foreign students can be found. To mention a few examples, Western Michigan University in Kalamazoo has made efforts over a number of years both to encourage its own students

---

by university officials and others (I was myself involved in this effort), a decision was reached that most Iranian students could stay in the United States, at least if currently enrolled in a regular baccalaureate or graduate program. A few students, however, have been caught as virtual stateless persons—in one case, because of having gone to Iran to help interpret for an American television crew, but not now permitted to return; in others, because negotiations for a postbaccalaureate fellowship had not been completed. (See, in general, Middleton and Scully, 1980.) Xenophobia has erupted on some campuses—and of course the national pressure for expulsion, earlier supported by the White House and carried out in registration by the Immigration and Naturalization Service, reflects the growing American truculence.

[4] Edward Fiske has shared with me his notes on more or less fraudulent practices in recruiting that were not included in his published articles. For example, some proprietary agencies have branches all over the country to teach English, and quality control is difficult to maintain. Reading Fiske's notes, I am struck by the number of small and isolated private colleges that have sought to stave off dissolution by recruiting foreign students, even on no-need scholarships—although one makes use of a professional recruiter with long experience who seems able to make reasonable matches. One man told Fiske: "I have a double standard that I apply to and for domestic students . . . to recruit in hard times, you have to take shortcuts. You want the kid here fast, because you want the money—bring the money, and we'll find a situation for you—not the right one. . . . It is a blind date—it is an arranged marriage."

to study abroad and to look after students from abroad, notably from the Middle East. This regional state university of some 20,000 students offers a handful of doctoral programs and can provide undergraduate training in engineering and other technical subjects often desired by non-Americans. A number of persons at the university have served in the Peace Corps and thus are not provincial. Kalamazoo College, a private college of high quality (originally American Baptist) with 1,500 students, has 80 percent of them participating in its Foreign Study Program and has centers not only in France, Germany, and Spain but also in Colombia, Sierra Leone, and Japan and has also some exchange programs with Western Michigan. Kalamazoo College is sophisticated, but the town itself is conservative. Students of the Islamic faith are less likely to meet culturally offensive displays or ideological attack than would be true in some East Coast and West Coast metropolitan areas. (Information based on conversations and personal correspondence with Western Michigan University and Kalamazoo College officials.)

Michigan State University has 1,200 foreign students, including a number of Palestinians, who have found assistance from some faculty members and fellow students when, as sometimes occurs, they have claimed to be harassed as real or alleged PLO activists through visa troubles with United States immigration authorities. Michigan State is perhaps the most outstanding of America's land-grant universities, and its agricultural outreach programs are symbolized by the fact that its dynamic president of an earlier era, John Hannah, became the director of the AID program on leaving the university; there have also been other technical missions overseas. These far-flung connections at Michigan State have helped make it possible for such faculty members as John and Ruth Useem, mentioned earlier, to help prepare foreign students for the "reverse culture shock" likely to be experienced by returnees as often more traumatic than the experience of study in the United States, as the returnees realize or rediscover that what they have taken for granted in academic protocol and research procedures in the United States finds little echo in often highly politicized, and yet still rudimentary, research establishments back home. Torn between one's disciplinary aspirations and one's national loyalty and recognition that one was helped to go · verseas in order to return and assist one's native country, some individuals seek to cope with this dilemma by shuttling between research centers in their home country, where they lack any feeling of colleagueship, and research centers in the United States, where they feel the guilt of self-imposed expatriation.[5]

The National Association for Foreign Student Affairs, headquartered in Washington, D.C., along with the Institute for International Education in New York, seeks to act as a switchboard for foreign students, and so do the cultural attachés of American embassies. In an earlier day, when there were more vocations and less opposition to American overseas evangelism, missionaries often provided avenues of access for foreign students who had attended mission schools. Such a connection landed the aristocratic Japanese wife of former Ambassador Edwin Reischauer at Principia College, the Christian Science institution in the far south of Illinois. Amherst House, on the campus of Doshisha University in Kyoto, was originally a missionary school, and it fosters exchange with Amherst and some comparable liberal arts colleges, such as Carleton and other members of ACM, the Associated Colleges of the Midwest. However, none of these informal connections and arrangements is adequate for handling the problem. I would be quite prepared to see some kind of federal supervision and regulation set up in this area.

Postscript. Since the foregoing was written, Harold Orlans has reminded me that it is unlikely for the federal government to assist the regional accrediting associations do a better job without at the same time being brought more closely into supervision of the accrediting process. Nor would it be likely to establish ongoing support for the regional associations while excluding the professional accrediting agencies or the regional commissions that accredit vocational schools. Orlans also shares the skepticism of a number of college and university presidents whom I have consulted as to whether most of their institutions would put up the money for a really thorough work on accrediting, especially in the light of the fear and expense of litigation to which the text refers (personal correspondence).

[5] Here also, there are domestic analogues. Minority students from within the United States are very commonly under tremendous pressure to return "home" and to serve "their people" if they obtain postbaccalaureate degrees, especially in medicine and law. In an earlier era, no such pressure was placed on the first generation of immigrants who secured higher education; their individual achievements were taken as wholly sufficient service to the ethnic group.

11

Government Intervention for Consumer Protection

This chapter will deal with efforts of federal (and, to a lesser extent, state) government to protect students, viewed in their role as consumers, from educational fraud and deception. But before turning to this currently hotly contested arena, I want to make clear some of the ways the federal government influences student choice by means of its financial aid policies.

Access Versus Diversity

Liberalization of federal and state aid to students has helped make access to college available to the vast majority of Americans. The arguments first advanced after the passage of the Higher Education Act amendments of 1972 that many students are bribed to attend college are much more potent today with the great increases in student aid to middle-income families (Finn, 1978, chaps. 3, 4; Grant, 1972b). Veterans' benefits have been perhaps the most striking case: there is no need component for eligibility, and some students can actually make money by attending college. Well-to-do students who declare themselves "independent" can obtain loans at low interest and reinvest the money in certificates of deposit or other investments that pay the prevailing high rates of interest. Such students may then even default on their loans, and protections for privacy of student records may make it difficult to track them down.

The federal government does not, of course, dictate which postsecondary institution a student shall attend. But the federal and state governments have a decisive impact on the choices students make by means of direct financial aid and, through institutions, by means of the distribution of work-study funds. Similarly, states affect student choice by the amount of subsidy they provide for public institutions and, in a rare handful of states, for private institutions—a list of states to which Florida must recently be added in spite of its relatively small and not especially distinguished roster of private colleges and in spite of the belief of the public institutions dominating the state that they are underfinanced. It makes a great deal of difference, moreover, whether the states follow the plan of so-called Bundy aid of New York, which gives awards for every degree granted and thus rewards an institution for holding onto students who might be better off transferring. It penalizes an institution that does the handicraft labor of remedial work with students if it loses those students—in part as a result of its own contribution—to institutions from which they graduate, since the latter institutions will receive the Bundy aid. Pennsylvania maintained fully portable grants until recently, fighting off legislative provincialism, and now permits students to take half of the aid that would be allowed them for in-state enrollment to colleges outside the state. And Pennsylvania has also been prepared to assist institutions that are fundamentally private, such as the University of Pennsylvania and Lincoln University, which are called "state-related," giving money in the same way to Temple University while taking over the University of Pittsburgh as primarily a state institution when it began to falter as a private one. (Incidentally, the continuing hegemony of private higher education in the Northeast is illustrated by the fact that, once Pittsburgh became known as a public institution, heavily dependent on commuter students, it lost a great deal of its appeal for out-of-state students; 91 percent of its students now come from Pennsylvania.) Pittsburgh did not change as much as its image did—it still has relatively high test scores in the college of arts and sciences and, of course, in the schools of engineering and of nursing; it also retained some independent members of the board of trustees.

The interviews my assistants and I have done on how students choose colleges, though not systematic, reinforce the widespread conclusion of more systematic studies that students who are the first in their families to attend college often overestimate the actual cost to them of attending a private institution and underestimate the cost of a low-tuition public one. On the one side, they do not realize that the stated tuition figure of many private institutions is a nominal figure and that financial aid packages in many cases reduce it for the majority to a manageable level, especially if students are willing to take out loans whose repayment need not start until after graduation and whose interest rate is usually subsidized. To some extent, private institutions, as they market their wares more aggressively, are making students aware of such possibilities and are sometimes awarding financial aid on a merit basis (as has been common for years in athletics) as well as on a basis of need.

Even so, a student from a lower-middle-class or working-class background may feel that a college or university with a nominal price tag of $7,000 for tuition will attract students who will be socially alien, although in fact just such institutions make an effort to attract students from a wide diversity in economic as well as in racial and ethnic terms. Conversely, students who live at home and commute to local schools are only in modest measure aware of the costs of attending college in the earnings forgone because they can usually work only part-time at low-paying jobs, rather than full-time at better-paying ones. That more young men than women have got this message is illustrated by the fact that today for the first time there are more women entering college than men. Furthermore, if students board at home, the costs of living at home seem to come out of the family budget with no particular accounting for those costs; and only recently, with the rise in the price (and sometimes the decline in availability) of gasoline, has commuting by car seemed a particularly expensive mode of access to a commuter college. (Apart from the cost of feeding often voracious students at home, families must sometimes bear the hidden cost of having a gregarious son or daughter who brings friends home whose diurnal rhythms differ from those of the family!)

But the significant cost is the one that Alexander Astin emphasizes in *Four Critical Years* (1977b)—namely, that commuting students are much more likely to drop out of college before completion either of an associate or of a baccalaureate degree; their usually minimal involvement in extracurricular activities is tied to tangential involvement in the curriculum itself. Administrators and faculty members constantly complain that commuter colleges cannot bring students back for cultural events in the evenings or on weekends—if the campus is in a high-crime area, it is apt to be deserted then, just as the central city core, once flourishing, may be deserted. All the studies with which I am familiar, including Astin's massive ones, make clear that attending the local college on a commuter basis is a short-run saving and a long-run loss of opportunity. Of course, in some cases, there is no choice, where the student has a job near home, falls between stools in terms of financial aid that would permit attending a residential college, having a part-time work-study job on campus, and having to worry only about the costs of transport during vacations.

Nevertheless, there is some awareness among students that selectivity means something. Hence, even when the Permanent Charity Fund of Boston made a systematic effort to persuade students from community colleges to transfer to four-year private institutions, promising financial aid that would make up the difference between the costs of public and private upper-division work, few students thought themselves sufficiently capable academically or comfortable socially to make the shift. However, a study of the sample of students who successfully transferred to more or less selective private institutions is interesting in indicating that these students were willing to start their college work in a community college because they believed themselves academically inferior; if they received good grades and got encouragement, they overcame their self-mistrust, and after having thought of themselves as not "college material," now began to think of themselves as "transfer material." A study of those we termed "the community college elite" indicated the ups and downs of this process and how some students could temporarily be demoralized by radical faculty members who ran down the community college and said that grades in this small frog pond meant nothing—these were usually faculty members with "good" degrees who regarded themselves as alienated and conveyed the message to students that they were not in a "real college." But the more resilient students were not troubled by this and, with encouragement from other faculty members, successfully completed a baccalaureate program in a private institution and often went on to postbaccalaureate study, grateful for the opportunity to start in a place where they would not be too humiliated by their anticipated academic awkwardness (Neumann and Riesman, 1980).

To be sure, most institutions successful in making use of the program of the Permanent Charity Fund were not notably selective: Northeastern University, already referred to for its entrepreneurial inventiveness; Suffolk University, an upgraded law school turned into a liberal arts college primarily through the use of adjunct faculty; and Bentley College, whose enterprising president, Gregory Adamian, offers business programs to appeal to community college students in a nonthreatening environment.

As fewer and fewer private institutions can afford to be selective, though they may maintain a pretense of selectivity, there have in recent years been some dramatic instances in which an increase of selectivity in the public sector has resulted in an increase of student applicants. That this occurred at the University of Florida flagship campus in Gainesville is not surprising; when students are prepared to pay the costs of residential education and want a brand-name degree, they will select the flagship campus if they can be admitted. What is striking is that Florida had more applicants when it raised its entrance standards, while its traditional competitor, Florida State University, lowering its standards of entry, lost enrollment. It is not clear whether this correlation can be interpreted as causal. But it is also true that the University of Wisconsin-Parkside (in Kenosha), a commuter college that opened in the late 1960s as an unselective, open admissions institution, has recently raised entrance requirements and discovered that this made it more attractive to students, although not as attractive as Wisconsin-Oshkosh, with the salience of its technical programs, including the health professions. Reference has already been made to Northern Illinois University, whose president has said in correspondence that its venture of increasing requirements and selectivity is a gamble, with the result as yet uncertain.

Narrowing of Veterans' Options. Chapter Two described the extraordinary impact on the colleges of the GI Bill of Rights after World War II, which paid students' tuitions wherever they went and thus allowed choice, not only of private institutions of high selectivity, but of out-of-state institutions as well. As noted earlier, the Vietnam veterans receive a flat stipend with no requirement of showing need, and thus well-to-do veterans (not that there are many) receive the same stipend as impoverished ones (Finn, 1978, chap. 1). The result is that veterans are likely to choose low-cost commuter colleges where their costs will be fully covered, and they may even have some additional money to spend. Veterans are also eligible for Basic Educational Opportunity Grants, which provide half the cost of education up to $1,800. The half-cost provision is meant to provide some protection for private colleges through the incentive for students to attend institutions with tuitions over $1,800. The public sector has lobbied to remove the half-cost provision. This may occur in graded steps (Hook, 1980).

We have already seen that in some public institutions, such as Michigan State and, notably, Santa Cruz, there are options of small-scale programs, but generally these are residential universities where the costs for out-of-state students often approach those of the less costly private institutions.[1] This is a severe limitation on freedom of choice, especially in light of the fact that, even for in-state students, most state universities offer relatively low tuition but cannot meet the costs of travel and subsistence, let alone those of income forgone. Moreover, since so many of the flagships and land-grant state universities are located (reflecting an old American pattern) in relatively small communities, the opportunity to find jobs in the immediate environs, other than the limited roster of work-study positions offered on campus, is curtailed. (The University of Minnesota is perhaps the most notable exception, and UCLA has attained almost flagship status in Southern California.) Thus, the low tuition of the major state universities is a subsidy, often hidden under populist rhetoric, for the relatively affluent as

[1] With the voting age now set at 18, it has been relatively easy for students, most of whom are that age or older, to claim resident status and financial independence of parents in a short time, a year at most. The number of students who are declaring themselves independent for the sake of securing state and federal financing has risen dramatically. For a discussion of possible devices enabling students to jump state "tariff" barriers and equalizing costs of attendance among the different regions of the country, see Blaydon (1978).

well as the academically adept in-state students,[2] with special provisions made for the recruitment and full support of minority students through a combination of federal, state, and private subsidy (and the more or less sub rosa recruitment of athletes, often with help from alumni).

Symbolism of the Tuition Tax Credit. In mid-October 1978, in the last moments before congressional adjournment, it appeared that Congress would pass the tuition tax credit proposed by Senators Moynihan and Packwood (which would give modest aid to middle-income families though not be limited to them) as a means of aiding private colleges. The amount was so small ($250) that the only higher education lobby to come out in favor of this regressive tax credit was the American Association of Community and Junior Colleges. The congressional Conference Committee managed to substitute for the tax credit a greatly raised upper limit on the family income that would permit dependent students to receive direct federal student aid through the BEOGs and other grant programs. Since the tuition tax credit could not really help middle-income families, the large amount of support it received, requiring the administration greatly to enlarge the number of middle-income families whose children would be entitled to a federal subsidy, would seem to have depended on a desire among relatively well-to-do taxpayers to withhold from the federal government money that would otherwise go to needy recipients of student aid (much as some "peaceniks" have withheld their telephone tax or other taxes calculated to support the war effort), without private colleges being substantially aided.

However, when in the second session of the 96th Congress, Senator Moynihan proposed what was called the "baby BEOGs" grant for needy children attending nonpublic schools, the amendment was overwhelmingly defeated (71 to 24) both on the basis of constitutional misgivings concerning the church/state First Amendment issue (which Senator Moynihan argued should be left for the

[2] For an overview of these matters, see Danière (1964); also, among many reports and sponsored studies of the Carnegie Commission and its successor Council, see Anderson, Bowman, and Tinto (1972) and the Carnegie Commission's own report *Higher Education* (1974).

Supreme Court to decide, for it was not a clear-cut issue) and out of the power of the National Education Association and other lobbies, which share the belief that any support for nonpublic schools will further weaken the already troubled public schools—an alternative already available to the well-to-do (*Congressional Record*, 1980, pp. 68–85). The tuition tax-credit idea may not be dead—Senator Tower spoke in its favor but against the Moynihan amendment—but it seems unlikely to be revived soon.

Broadening Student Choice in Education: The Voucher Idea. The vast majority of private colleges have no endowment, and many that have had endowments have dipped deeply into them in order to keep tuition costs down in the face of inexorably rising per-student costs—a rise that obviously is due to inflation, the quadrupled costs of energy (for heating in the North and air conditioning in the South), and the increasing costs of compliance with government regulations.[3]

During the lush 1960s, many of the leading private colleges, although anxious about their long-run future, were reluctant to make an issue of the growing tuition gap between themselves and the public sector for fear of being accused of elitism and opposition to open access. Private and public institutions sought to present a united front to the federal government, even though there were occasional battles at the state level.

Shortly after the end of the Second World War, a number of economists began to make proposals for something like a voucher system or what came to be termed the national Educational Opportunity Bank, with the aim of providing a freer market for student customers. Both economists dubbed "conservative," such as free-market advocate Milton Friedman, and Keynesian liberals, such as the late Seymour Harris, favored such a plan.

---

[3] One tiny, private liberal arts college in New England that teeters every year on the edge of bankruptcy was recently asked by an HEW official to appoint an affirmative action compliance officer—this although the college exists in an area with virtually no black or Spanish-speaking population, and although the administration is so minuscule that most of the president's letters are written by him in longhand. Having to care full-time for a single paraplegic or blind student in this mountainous terrain under the regulations for the handicapped might be just enough to put this college out of business.

In the late 1950s I worked with Seymour Harris and others in a seminar at Harvard to develop the details of such a proposal. Our aim was to make it possible in principle for students to take out income-contingent loans in which their bet on their later earnings, collected through the Internal Revenue Service by an add-on to the income tax, would be shared by the pool of borrowers, with some administrative costs and possibly lowered interest rates[4] provided by the federal government as its contribution. Such a plan would permit sufficiently ambitious students to jump over the state tariff barriers, which are now of two sorts: inducements through state scholarship plans to attend in-state institutions, and the cost barrier increasingly separating residential from commuter colleges and private from public colleges—although it should always be emphasized that there exist some low-cost, unselective private colleges that are hardly more expensive than many public institutions (and in the East are sometimes sought out on grounds of status even though the public sector provides more options and better market buys).

The Educational Opportunity Bank idea never got a serious hearing from the Administration or Congress. Indeed, it presents a number of technical difficulties in addition to the obvious political liabilities of a plan so strongly opposed by the Washington lobbyists for public-sector institutions, increasingly hard pressed by rising costs and taxpayer resistance, which fear that under such a plan state legislatures would raise public college tuitions—and we have seen in the case of CUNY how passionately the alumni and adherents of public institutions cling to the belief that zero or negligible tuition is, despite federal and state grants to students, the sole road to open access or, at any rate, the shining symbol of such access. (This fear is by no means entirely self-serving. The requirement of filling out forms may inhibit low-income students from families of limited education from obtaining even the widely avail-

---

[4] In the light of steeply rising interest rates, and hence opportunities for affluent students to borrow from the federal government or to obtain insured government loans at low interest and put the money, for example, into Treasury notes paying high interest, I no longer believe that interest rates should be subsidized. This lack of interest subsidy and the income-contingent feature differentiate the plan from the TAP (Tuition Assistance Plan), for which President John Silber of Boston University has become a leading spokesman (Silber, 1978; also Jencks and Riesman, 1968, chap. 6).

able BEOG assistance, and in any event this program—with its limitation, almost certainly to be altered, that the grant can cover no more than half the cost of tuition—does not cover the entire cost of even a low-tuition college, including the cost of books, subsistence, forgone earnings, and so on. Much depends also on whether a particular student has available a public community college within easy commuting distance, on the quality and even the probity of financial aid officers, and on their ability—given not only the vagaries of financing but the often dramatic oscillations in the number and the need of students seeking aid in any particular year—to give prospective students absolute assurance of presumptively available aid.)

Representatives of unselective, relatively low-cost private colleges drawing students from their local areas were also opposed to the Educational Opportunity Bank concept, fearing that students would be drawn from their catchbasins to superior institutions, either public or private, in-state as well as out-of-state. Today many of these colleges, which have no reputation beyond their locale or their particular denomination, are still caught by the ever-increasing tuition gap between the private and public sectors even though they have kept costs down, and hence they might be less opposed to such a concept.

In fact, the great majority of the members of the Carnegie Commission were wholly opposed to a national Educational Opportunity Bank of the sort described. However, a unanimous commission, a number of whose members were subjected to intense personal pressure and even abuse from their fellow members of the major higher education lobbies, proposed that federal aid be channeled directly to students, the course later followed by the Higher Education Act amendments of 1972, with additional grants to institutions accepting such students—federal assistance that proved not to be forthcoming.

To become eventually self-sustaining, a national Educational Opportunity Bank would have to appeal to students who think themselves likely to strike it rich as physicians or educational consultants in order to increase the size of the pool; it would have to permit those earning very high postbaccalaureate incomes to buy out of the scheme at some fair price so that they did not continue to pay indefinitely or leave a legacy of payments to their heirs. (Those of us who favored the idea wanted the largest possible pool of users of such a bank for an additional reason: to help create a barrier between the bank and the federal government, so that the anger of a particular congressman about some institution or its students would not lead to the imposition of loyalty oaths or other restrictions or to a cut in the bank's necessary initial subsidy.)[5] It should also be added that the IRS was inimical to the idea from the beginning; it thought it had enough to do without taking on the task of collecting what was in effect postponed tuition and other educational expenses.

One of the aims of the Educational Opportunity Bank idea was to avoid two deleterious effects that educational loans can have. On the one hand, for conscientious students, the need to repay can dictate vocational plans by requiring sufficiently lucrative employment so that the loan and interest can be paid off without excessive strain. The Educational Opportunity Bank, geared to earnings reported to the IRS, would lengthen the repayment period, if not forgive the loan, for the minority for whom higher education does not pay off financially—for example, some artists and ministers (and their spouses) and members of many other useful callings with low earning power.[6] On the other hand, for less conscientious students, the Educational Opportunity Bank would have prevented the scandalous defaults on student loans that have put the

[5] Just as Senator Proxmire enjoys attacking individual grants by scrupulous federal agencies such as the National Science Foundation, so also there have been illustrations in the states of the dangers of legislative monitoring of scholarships. For example, an earlier version of the Pennsylvania state scholarship plan, which required that students be deprived of scholarships who refused to register for the draft or were otherwise civilly disobedient—a provision fought by some of the private colleges, such as Haverford, Bryn Mawr, Sarah Lawrence, and Harvard—was eventually knocked out as unconstitutional. Similarly, arguments regularly occur over the annual legislative appropriation the Commonwealth of Pennsylvania makes to the support of the "state-related" but still private University of Pennsylvania. Thus, during the academic year 1977–78, a group of students cooperated with the Teamsters to portray the university as antilabor because of an on-campus strike and thus jeopardized a $17 million state appropriation on which the university utterly counts for its continued solvency.

[6] No implication is intended that higher education per se is the "cause" of increased earnings for any particular student, although for special groups, such as medical and dental students from nonaffluent backgrounds whose educational costs are largely subsidized, the case would seem fairly clear in the aggregate. See the arguments over genetics, family background, and "luck" in explaining occupational placement and income inequality in Jencks and others (1972).

whole loan program into jeopardy—a complicated issue dealt with in *Next Steps for the 1980s in Student Financial Aid*, a report of the Carnegie Council on Policy Studies in Higher Education (1979c).

My own aims in supporting an Educational Opportunity Bank did not include increasing what already seems the irresponsibility of many affluent parents who make no sacrifices, let alone set aside any savings, for their children's education. The Educational Opportunity Bank, as originally designed, did not require a parent's report to the College Scholarship Service. This would free students from pressure from parents who might pay for attendance at their own college but not at some other institution. Or, as in some of the instances our interviewing has turned up, students would have an alternative in responding to parents willing to make a deal with their college-age children to encourage them to attend a low-cost but socially respectable community college for two years, often a deal abetted by the offer of a new car and perhaps a trip to Europe. At the same time, it was the hope of the proponents of an Educational Opportunity Bank that conscientious parents might be shamed into assisting children determined to optimize their opportunities for a useful, enjoyable, and productive life through further education by contributing to their college costs and thus reducing the amount of stipend needed from the bank.[7] Furthermore, as student and faculty protests spread in the late '60s, I expected an adult backlash more rapid and more severe than occurred over the sight of what seemed to be relatively prosperous young people at public institutions such as Berkeley, incited by or joined by faculty members, attacking the sacred cultural symbols of nation, church, and family; I believed that adult "taxpayer" resentments would be moderated if it were clear that these young people would eventually pay part of the cost of their educations. Furthermore, I quite agree with those opponents of the Educational Opportunity Bank who emphasize the social, as against the individual, benefits of education (for example, Bowen, 1977;

---

[7] Students rarely pay the full cost of educating themselves, except perhaps in proprietary schools and, at least until quite recently, in continuing education. Furthermore, the stated tuition of a private institution is in fact a ceiling, or maximum; price discounting occurs at all levels of quality and selectivity (Ihlanfeldt, 1980). At many private colleges the maximum amount of financial aid provided by the college at least equals the tuition, although it may not pay all the cost of board and room, let alone what no institution pays—the cost of income forgone.

Hyman, Wright, and Reed, 1975); on an aggregate basis, their case seems amply made.

To put the same point another way, my support for the Educational Opportunity Bank idea was not intended to limit the responsibility of relatively affluent parents to offer their children choice as well as access well beyond their attaining voting age. Even before the federal government became involved, the residential state universities were in effect subsidizing the reasonably affluent at the expense of the very poor, whose children often do not even finish high school, or the well-to-do, who may encourage their children to attend elite private universities. (See Jencks and Riesman, 1968, chap. 3, especially pp. 107–120; also, in chap. 6, pp. 257–279 and sources there cited.)

Government Action and Lobbying for Students as Consumers

There has been a mobilization of students locally and nationally to be heard on certain issues that plainly affect them in their role as purchasers of educational services—tuition, for example, or, in one case, charges against a whole group of students for vandalism, to which the students responded by filing a motion for an injunction. For example, a volume by Shark, Brouder, and Associates (1976) discusses the fight by students at the University of Bridgeport to have their evaluations of instructors taken seriously in decisions on retention and promotion. (It should come as no surprise that the AAUP union was "negative about any further student involvement, feeling that students had made no real contribution to the process in the past and in fact created a problem for them by violating the confidentiality of the collective bargaining relationship in their statements to the press" [p. 93].) In another case, that of the University of Cincinnati, faculty members in the AAUP union hoped students would support their demands against the administration, and there was also anxiety about the noncontinuity of student representation. Here again the issue of student evaluations was raised (chap. 7).

The volume under discussion makes clear that a cohort of experienced students is developing who recognize both alignments and differences of interests between students and faculty and are prepared, like any group of consumers involved in a collective bargaining negotiation but not generally present at the table, to try to have their voices (failing their votes) attended to. The student demand to sit in on collective bargaining negotiations is especially ambiguous at institutions, both public and private, where students have won the right to sit on boards of trustees, as in all public institutions in Massachusetts: are they then "management" who are doubly represented at the bargaining table?

At any rate, it is clear that not only are students quite commonly organized on individual campuses (though in student government elections, as in local, state, or national elections, very few students actually vote[8]) to represent what they regard as the student interest—for example, in low tuition or bookstore and food prices or in evaluations of faculty members—but a movement is beginning for statewide organization of students, as in Sacramento, to press for further support for the universities in cooperation with administrators, or in Washington to work with the national education lobbies, to pressure Congress for more generous student assistance policies.

These lobbies in Washington and in such state capitals as Sacramento, Albany, and (by no means always on the same side) Harrisburg, serve to remind legislators that students have the vote and that parents also do; the enormous pressure built up in Washington in 1978 for tuition tax credits and/or liberalization of grant and loan policies to enable students from middle-income families to participate showed the power in straight political terms of organized "consumer" groups in the area of postsecondary education. We may also recall that some activist students have been involved in the campaign against testing, especially as allies of Ralph Nader—a crusade in which some members of the Federal Trade Commission and what is now the Department of Education may have been sympathetic, although not visible.

However, it is very doubtful that student lobbies can move

[8] In 1972 the National Committee for a Student Vote was set up to help clear away obstacles to the registration of students to vote at their campuses in the 1972 elections and to encourage students to make use of the new facilities made available to them. The results were disappointing: many students on the Left attacked voting as playing the traditional game rather than the activist extraparliamentary game, and young people followed the long-standing American tradition of voting less than their parents or other elders do. Still, what students lack in voting power, their activist minorities can compensate for in organizational strength, as had been demonstrated in the presidential campaigns of Eugene McCarthy and Robert Kennedy as well as in a number of local contests.

fast enough and effectively enough to cope with the increasing danger of fraudulent marketing practices by colleges desperate for students. Where individual faculty members, desperate for students, compete for them by an automatic grade of A and by demanding minimal amounts of work, this unprofessional (though understandable) strategy can scarcely be called fraudulent, since the students are eager rather than deceived consumers. Alston Chace, former chairman of the Department of Philosophy at Macalester College, describes such practices in a barbed essay (1978). And although the federal and some state courts have been active in this area, as in so many other areas where pliable judges serve, so to speak, at the pleasure of the activist bar, court actions are also too uneven, even when combined with organized student pressures, to serve as adequate protection against the sorts of abuses that the FTC has policed in the sale of other consumer products.

External Degree Programs. Cases of clear fraud can be put aside in which the purchaser of educational credentials is not deceived, but is buying a credential without performing the kinds of study or exhibiting the kinds of competence generally thought to warrant such a credential. The fraud here is practiced on other properly credentialed persons (or in competition with people also possessing slightly less spurious degrees) and on the general public, which may also be deceived by such degrees. Clearly, state legislation and enforcement should put out of business such enterprises, often consisting of no more than a post office box and a cooperative printer or lithographer; and as for enterprises that do business across state lines, perhaps the mail-fraud enforcement agencies can assist in policing the traffic.

However, there is a gray area containing external degree programs that demand a certain amout of work by correspondence and perhaps a brief visit to the nearest branch of far-flung campuses, allowing the doctorate (ordinarily in education but sometimes the Ph.D.) to be "earned" on the basis of truly minimal performance—far less, for example, than would be required of a Princeton senior writing the regulation senior essay. Here also there is no fraud on the student consumer who knows what he or she is buying, often at quite large fees, in order to continue to work and reside full-time somewhere else while picking up a credential that will bring added income and status, for example, within the hierarchy of a school system. Some of these enterprises are so clearly shoddy that they barely stay one step ahead of the sheriff. A further, quite considerable step takes us to the diverse array of external degree programs offered by such institutions, already re-ferred to, as Goddard College or the Antioch Network; some of these are serious educational ventures, while others have been more loose and careless. (For the Antioch Network as it existed in an earlier day, see Grant, 1972a; on Goddard, see the critique by Miles, 1973; and for a general discussion of the need for standards in external degree programs and a description of issues involved in attaining these, see Bowen, 1973, and Houle, 1973.)

The frenzied hunt for tuition-paying students that leads to setting up both baccalaureate and master's degree programs in great numbers, either at a makeshift locale or at the underenrolled campus of an extant institution, can be seen by examining the educational advertisements in the Sunday *New York Times,* just as in the *Chronicle of Higher Education* one finds many advertisements by educational consultants who will set up such programs for a desperate institution. The desperation springs not only from the demographic drop in the immediate post–high school age group but also in the decision of many white males who graduate from high school with respectable grades that they are better off enter-ing the labor market immediately than enrolling in college—a case made for a popular audience by Carolyn Bird in *The Case Against College* (1975) and by Richard Freeman in *The Overeducated Ameri-can* (1976b). Indeed, the Carnegie Council itself has recognized that youth should have other options after high school than going im-mediately to college, as set forth in its report *Giving Youth a Better Chance: Options for Education, Work, and Service* (1979b). What might be thought of as the higher education industry has fought back directly, not only by extensive efforts to recruit older students or students recently out of high school who are working part-time, but also by lobbying for increased grants for student aid at both state and federal levels, even in some states by building new com-munity colleges or expanding physical facilities of extant ones (as is currently being planned in Massachusetts despite an overabundance of places in already existing institutions). But there is also an indirect mode of defending higher education: requiring a college degree for more and more positions even though the work itself does not demand the kinds of learning most colleges impart (although one might argue that college is, at least to a modest degree, a screen for motivation[9] and in that sense useful to employers)—in other words, credentialism. It is thanks to this protection that college graduates are able to "bump" high school graduates in the labor market except in those relatively rare cases in which they are considered overqualified and hence likely to be transitory. (In the same way, credentialism operated to help teacher's colleges in California when that state required a master's degree earned in one postbaccalaureate year for certification to teach in public schools, though it would be very difficult to show on the basis of tests of competence that those with master's degrees are more qualified teachers than the graduates of the more selective liberal arts colleges and universities.)[10]

As pointed out earlier, however, not all learning-at-a-distance programs are shoddy and diluted. Empire State College perhaps comes closest to the model of the British Open University, some of

[9] An illustration of the point can be drawn from the experience of the army with high school dropouts in comparison with high school graduates. The army will make exceptional efforts, superior to the remedial work in many regular academic institutions, to provide dropouts with the education that will give them a high school diploma; nevertheless, the dropouts are 50 percent more likely not to serve out their full term of military service than those who have completed high school.

[10] To be sure, in *Griggs* v. *Duke Power Company*, the United States Supreme Court decided that tests must bear some relation to the task to be performed. (In that case blacks had charged that they were discriminated against in employment by tests bearing no connection to their competence to do the work.) However, the lower federal courts have been reluctant to apply the test of *Griggs* to degrees from academic institutions; this was a case of a test administered by an employer and thus seems to have been given less sanctity in judicial scrutiny. There are also pending suits against bar examinations, based on similar allegations of discriminatory impact, for example, against the graduates of black law schools or against black law graduates in general, although I myself would argue that there is a fairly clear relation between ability to master the relatively minimal demands of a bar examination and ability to be a reliable lawyer for a client of whatever race. It seems conceivable that courts could strike at academic credentialism—and if not they, then perhaps the taxpayers who pay doubly: for the training and for the added salary for public servants who are required to have the training.

whose modules it has adapted at its Saratoga Springs headquarters for the less proficient American population on which it draws. It provides not only learning at a distance but local centers to which students can come for counseling on programs and careers, periodic bouts of formal teaching, and work with mentors by correspondence, completing carefully prepared modules that have the great advantage of allowing students of all ages, as in the British Open University model, to remain at home, working at least parttime, while completing a bachelor's degree started but interrupted for marriage, the army, a job, or many other reasons. Thomas A. Edison College in New Jersey; Metropolitan State University, an upper-division institution in the Twin Cities; the University of the Air, whose headquarters are at the University of Nebraska at Lincoln—all these programs are serious and scholarly and originate from state universities or state systems or consortia of undoubted academic legitimacy.

As is evident, I am opposed to government regulation either by agencies or by courts in consumer protection if the failings in the present system—though *system* is hardly the right term for any part of the American postsecondary scene—can be dealt with on a more or less voluntary and self-policing basis by institutions themselves and the accrediting associations designed to monitor their performance.

Once we leave the arena of collusion between the purchaser and vendor of educational credentials and start thinking of students as consumers buying educational services, we realize that the picture of them as simply or merely consumers is a distortion. Students are at once the producers and the consumers of their own educational development; one of the major aims of that development is to help them become more active producers, less passive and simply receptive consumers. Even though we know that education can be dangerous to moral equilibrium and even to mental health,[11] we do not "buy" an education in the way that we buy an automobile that has a defect requiring recall or a household appliance or a pharmaceutical product that turns out to have hidden dangers.

---

[11] For a reflective discussion of the misgivings concerning the potential moral havoc of a widely disseminated avant-garde "adversary" culture, echoing misgivings that go back to Rousseau and to Plato, see Chace (1978–79).

Action by Federal Agencies. At times, on a "Naderite" model, students themselves have brought suit for what might be termed educational malpractice, contending, for example, that they have been given a baccalaureate but have not been given an education (as in a suit brought against the University of Bridgeport several years ago); a similar class-action suit was brought against the business school of Vanderbilt University by a group of students who contended that the school was mismanaged, its service overpriced. But such efforts at consumer protection have generally arisen when third parties, notably a federal agency, are paying for education.

As already mentioned, the Veterans Administration has tried to control what it regarded as malpractice by institutions that enrolled GIs making use of educational benefits provided by law. Not only did the VA discover, after the Second World War, that some institutions were raising their tuitions to take advantage of the then-generous provisions of the GI Bill of Rights, but it also discovered a number of institutions that were springing up overnight to take advantage of these veterans and the tuitions they could bring with them. Indeed, what had been the valuable bonus not only to veterans but to the diversity of American higher education in allowing veterans to have choice as well as access—and the costly choice of high-quality residential, usually private institutions away from their original homes—was abused to such an extent that at the time of the Korean War the VA decided that it would limit tuitions, thus preventing abuse but at the same time restricting veterans' orbits (see Finn, 1978, chap. 1).

Similarly, the VA felt it had to step in to monitor the disingenuousness of a number of proprietary institutions set up or expanded to take advantage of the tuitions of veterans seeking vocational training and credentials under the less open-handed benefits, as far as tuitions are concerned, of the revised GI bill, soon due to expire. Some proprietary institutions are covered by their own accrediting agencies, but these lie outside the orbit of the better-known regional accrediting agencies of nonprofit two-year and baccalaureate institutions. And local monitoring in the fifty states is either nonexistent or dilatory (Fiske, 1979a, 1979b), so that the VA moved in on its own, with minimal consultation with the established educational agencies in HEW or elsewhere in the federal government. For one thing, it required institutions serving veterans to provide a clearly stated refund policy so that the profiteers could not "take the money and run." But it also instituted measures which seemed obviously useful on their face but which turned out to have antieducational consequences. An example is the rule that no course could count for GI-bill credit if more than 85 percent of those enrolled were veterans. The purpose was to prevent the creation of instant courses simply to garner veterans' dollars. But the same regulation struck down the very careful development of an orientation program by the community college system of Vermont precisely to assist the readjustment of veterans and veterans only. It required considerable effort for the proper exemption to be made for such a creditable attempt to help the veterans readjust to the college milieu. (The GI bill has no means test; wealthy veterans can get educational benefits, although the assumption naturally was, especially for Vietnam veterans, that most would be needy and also in need of consumer protection.)[12]

If the Veterans Administration led the way, there were those in the Office of Education and the Federal Trade Commission who were not far behind in their wish to protect students in their role as consumers. Those students who fell within the orbit of their concern were those to whom the federal government was providing aid either through outright grant or work-study programs or through federally insured student loans; as with the enforcement of the Occupational Safety and Health Act or affirmative action requirements, the leverage of federal dollars could be used to enforce, or so some officials have thought, better protection for the loan- and grant-assisted students.

The Federal Interagency Commission on Higher Education

---

[12] There was one hazard against which the VA could not provide protection. It is, in my judgment, a shameful episode in the history of some of the more selective or avant-garde academic institutions: namely, their treatment of veterans as "war criminals"—an attitude that made many conceal their veteran status or hesitate about enrolling in institutions that might have been optimal for them. Veterans were persecuted by students who had escaped the draft because they were sufficiently adept and well off to be for many years exempt as students or to know other devices, less extreme than expatriation or prison, that would keep them out of the service. (One such device was to hide out from one's draft board in an inconspicuous junior college in a state far from one's home—a practice I have learned of from Verne Stadtman.) Such attitudes are by now considerably attenuated, although they can still be found, as a number of veterans have reported to me who are at universities that were centers of antiwar protest in the '60s and early '70s.

has prepared a report on the need for greater consumer protection and federal monitoring of educational programs, which, I gather from correspondence with her, has the approval of former Assistant Secretary Mary Berry, the forceful sub-Cabinet official in HEW responsible for educational programs. (As this manuscript goes to press, President Carter has just succeeded in fulfilling his promise to the National Education Association of creating a separate Department of Education, a proposal opposed by me and many others whose concern has been with the independence of higher education—and secondary education also—from further federal intervention and with the protection of private, nonunionized institutions from pressures brought about by the legislation's powerful sponsor. The belief held by many proponents of the legislation that to give Cabinet status to education would also give it greater importance and visibility is in my judgment an illusion; what will be visible is the weakness of education, rather than its strength, when removed from the greater powers of HEW and the close tie to the AFL-CIO and organized labor in the congressional committees that supervise both education and labor.)

There are undoubted abuses and lacunae of information even in accredited institutions, as were turned up in the study by the American Institutes of Research (1977)—for example, failure to state refund policy when students drop out, failure to note courses that are unlikely to be taught because professors are on leave,[13] lack of any data whatsoever concerning placement rates of

[13] At Harvard University during the academic year 1979–80, undergraduates complained because a large number of history courses were not being taught that year, owing to, on the one hand, long-planned sabbaticals and, on the other hand, unpaid leaves of absence that professors had taken in accordance with the cycle of their own work and their ability to win grants and fellowships. Dean Henry Rosovsky was forced to warn department heads to monitor such leaves through a five-year program, to make sure that such unexpected lacunae in staff would not recur. Yet, one of the privileges of teaching in a major research university, almost regarded as part of academic freedom, has been the opportunity to take leaves of absence, subject only to the mildest of departmental constraints, if, for example, one can win a coveted Guggenheim Fellowship or a Fulbright or a year at one of the centers or institutes for advanced study. In contrast, in a small liberal arts college, faculty members are much more likely to subordinate their personal ambitions to departmental and collegewide requirements, especially since the departments are often so small that, if an extra person in a department unexpectedly goes on leave, there are not enough people to teach courses required for the major.

graduates. (Data on placement rates is a difficult area because much higher education does not aim at placement, but the issue arises in those vocational programs that point to the high salaries and superior jobs held by people in the field for which they are presumably preparing their students.) Similarly, Arthur Levine of the Carnegie Council staff has been studying both malpractice on the consumer by educational institutions and the generally far less examined issue of malpractice by the consumer—for example, the student who falsifies his or her previous academic records or who signs up for a program in order to get government benefits without any intention of continuing in the program (sometimes in collusion with tuition-hungry institutions) or who takes out a loan without the slightest intention of repaying it. The very existence of these forms of what Arthur Levine terms student "me-ism" indicates the one-sidedness of regarding students simply in their role as consumers, rather than simultaneously seeing them as producers who are beneficiaries of capital investment and educational expenses largely borne by others.

I have mentioned the students who have well-to-do parents or spouses but declare themselves "independent" in order to become eligible for subsidies—whose costs are often borne in part by the non-well-to-do who could not afford to attend college. There are a number of cases—only a few of which become public—of wealthy parents who refuse to meet their obligations for the education of their children, much in the way that they may refuse to pay required alimony. A good example is the lawsuit reported in the *Washington Post* ("Daughter Sues Father to Pay College Fees," 1979) of Adrienne Zimmerman against her attorney father, reputed to earn more than $100,000 a year, for failing to keep his promise to pay for her education. If the father were an institution, he could be charged with sex discrimination, since he had paid the fees of her brothers—of course, a very common discrimination in the country at large, though less common in well-to-do, professional Jewish families.

College Catalogues as Registration Statements? There has been discussion in the federal government that catalogues should be audited in the form described in Chapter Eight with the illustrations of Barat and Irvine—similar audited catalogues were prepared by some eight other institutions as a result of grants from the Fund for the Improvement of Postsecondary Education—and, further, an insistence that institutions file documents comparable to those filed for the Securities and Exchange Commission by corporations wishing to offer securities to the public.

The SEC analogy is more than a little frightening to someone like me, who, trained as a lawyer, is aware that the SEC regulations are enormously beneficial to large legal and accounting firms, which can secure the complicated kinds of information and prepare the necessary papers for registration statements—an expense so great that smaller corporations have difficulty in securing access to the equity market because the expense of filing and defending a registration statement is greater than the amount of money they would be able to raise.[14]

The information it would be nice to have, which the federal officials now considering greater intervention on behalf of educational consumers would like to have, is often difficult if not impossible to obtain. How can one tell whether, when a graduate gets a position in a field not directly related to the program pursued as an undergraduate, this was a result of the college experience? Many institutions, especially among community colleges and in the public sector, have no way of keeping track of commuter students who disappear, leaving no return address: they do not see an exit counselor; they may simply pick up their latest check and, in the old American style, take off for parts unknown. (One Midwestern institution has added to the battery of letters at the registrar's dis-

[14] Similarly, the Humphrey-Hawkins "Full Employment bill" seems likely only to create full employment for lawyers, whose habitual dichotomous thinking is not necessarily the optimal way to handle complex tradeoffs either in dealing with public services in our cities and states or in the intricacies of helping postsecondary institutions in a time of retrenchment do a fairer and more commendable job vis-à-vis those who work for them or attend them. Of course, the American belief in legalism is one that goes back to the fact of our written Constitution and Chief Justice Marshall's successful ingenuity in giving the Supreme Court and the lower federal courts the final say on what the Constitution means. What has changed is the degree of federalization—our new imperial bar and judiciary, as the Warren Court abandoned the earlier effort at judicial restraint and subsumed under the Fourteenth Amendment the entire Bill of Rights and applied it to the states; this is one only partly understood form of the nationalization or federalization that has occurred in the last decades.

posal, such as *I* for *Incomplete*, the mark of *V* for a student who has simply "Vanished.") Any intensive efforts to discover the location of former students are likely to meet with cries of "Big Brother" and interference with privacy. (However—in my judgment, fortunately—the Internal Revenue Service is now cooperating with the efforts of the Office of Education to track down student defaulters on loans who are on the federal payroll or otherwise earning enough that they could easily at least begin payments on their indebtedness.)

Furthermore, many colleges simply do not know how many students will show up and hence how many faculty members they will need; if more show up than anticipated, they can recruit adjunct faculty or even, in the present market, full-time faculty often of higher quality than their already established faculty. The uncertainty of enrollments in an institution, and certainly within particular programs or courses, may reflect the irresponsibility of students who are "no-shows,"[15] leading institutions to overadmit in order not to be left stranded—sometimes with the result of overcrowded living conditions, about which students in their role as consumers loudly complain.

As an example, when in the last several years, the yield, as admissions officers term it, of students applying to Tufts University greatly increased over the experience of previous years, some of the excess students were housed in the by no means uncomfortable civility of the Sheraton Commander Hotel in Cambridge, with bus service to take them back and forth to the Tufts campus not far away. Their situation was perhaps not optimal, compared with living on campus, but compared with the situation of students in most

[15] Deidre Kedesdy, dean of admissions of the University of Massachusetts at Amherst, has called my attention to a growing practice of students who apply to high-tuition and selective Ivy League institutions and also to the state university. They would once have regarded the latter application as a "safety" school to attend if denied admission to unpredictably selective private university colleges. Today, Dean Kedesdy notes, students who have every intention of attending the state university will apply to Ivy League institutions simply in order to define themselves as adequate; once admitted, they turn down the Ivy League offers to attend the low-tuition University of Massachusetts, whose quality, along with that of other flagship campuses in New England, has been increasingly recognized by the public—thus leading to unexpectedly high yields at the university campus and again to overcrowding there.

parts of the world and indeed much of the United States, it was idyllic. Yet some students are planning to bring suit on the ground that they have been the victims of educational malpractice. Furthermore, the requirement that the VA has instituted concerning tuition refunds, which is also likely to be mandated by federal regulations generally, may not adequately compensate residential colleges for students who vacate dormitory rooms, which cannot at any particular moment be refilled, and stop paying board bills.

I can illustrate from personal experience the difficulties caused by students' irresponsibility in their behavior as comparison shoppers in an academic supermarket. For nearly twenty years I directed a large (about 200–500 students) general-education course in the social sciences with the assistance of a staff recruited in accordance with expected enrollments. Harvard has no pre-registration. Students would come in great numbers to the introductory meetings, fill out questionnaires, and often write special pleas to me explaining why they should be admitted to a course that they could see from the crowded room was likely to be overenrolled. Again and again, in the first several weeks, I would plead with students that, if they intended to drop the course, they should notify my secretary on the university switchboard, which most could do without charge or difficulty, so that someone else, excluded in the first lottery of acceptances and eager to take the course, could be admitted. (All this was set up so that students would not have to speak personally to me to say they were dropping the course, which they might have found awkward if they sufficiently misjudged my own attitude.) However, students almost never did this for the sake of other students, with the result that we would overadmit to a certain degree, but, wanting small discussion groups, could not overadmit to any large extent. We occasionally found ourselves with more students than the available staff could handle or more than could fit into the lecture and section-meeting rooms, long since arranged, but often we would find ourselves underenrolled when it was too late for students who had been eager to take the course to change their programs in order to do so. No amount of pleading and explanation of this situation influenced the "no-shows"—a problem that also existed in assigning students to sections, some of which were too large for fruitful discussion and some below critical mass.

Indeed, the behavior of students as self-indulgent consumers is a problem all schooling faces today. Activist groups concerned with "student rights," though they may correct one or another injustice, also add to the feeling of students that they have rights but no responsibilities, as if they were all of them by definition a handicapped and powerless group, rather than, as in the present situation of declining enrollments, a mostly unorganized bloc of "voters" by their presences and absences within the polity of postsecondary education.

State Action. An increasing number of activist state attorney generals' offices, like some contemporary state utility and insurance commissioners, are seeking to make their reputations and to fulfill what they see as their obligations in the protection of consumers' rights. For example, in Massachusetts, Paula Gold, director of the consumer-protection division of the state attorney general's office, has been much concerned with policing college marketing. I have already noted her initiation of action against Grahm Junior College on the ground that its financial condition was shaky, even while many students still hoped that they could somehow manage to keep the place afloat. Of course, after such action (which was probably wise), any such chance was lost. Paula Gold herself recognized the dilemma; as Nina McCain of the *Boston Globe* reported, "Requiring colleges to tell students if they are in financial trouble almost ensures that students will stay away and make the troubles worse. But [Gold] says 'I don't know what you can do but disclose the information. It's not fair to students not to disclose' " (McCain, 1977, pp. 49, 54).

State action has the obvious advantage over federal action of greater closeness to the particular academic setting. The difficulty is that the states are unevenly equipped to deal with postsecondary education; even the concept of 1202 Commissions, which every state is required under federal legislation to create or designate, assumes that there are fifty cadres of civic-minded boards and well-trained commissioners and their staffs, whereas only some (by no means all) major and populous states and a few enlightened smaller states are likely to have such volunteer and paid officials on whom to call.

Students as a Minority Group. We live in a cultural climate in which many groups once discriminated against have gained considerable political and more obliquely persuasive power, but their leaders recognize that there is still political gain and moral righteousness to be earned through the belief that one remains in a minority deserving of special protection from foundations, government agencies, and state and federal courts. (The newly won power is uneven in its spread: some institutions are extremely vulnerable, for example, to any charge of racism or sexism and bend over backward to avoid any such allegation, while other areas are still relatively untouched by such pressures, especially outside major cosmopolitan centers.) Today, students are in a somewhat similar position. It is convenient for their activist leaders and for those who speak on behalf of students to behave as if students were an oppressed cadre, as they often were during the triumph of the academic revolution in a few institutions, although they always had the privilege of departure and although these institutions were never, in Erving Goffman's phrase, "total institutions."

The argument of this volume has been that, as valued customers in that vast majority of institutions which are underenrolled in whole or in particular schools, students currently have the upper hand even if they do not have formal power—though they often have that too in the mechanisms of governance set up in the late 1960s and early 1970s. For them, also, it is convenient to believe that they are in a minority. And when, as in the case of aggressive academic marketing, there are undoubted abuses, there is understandable pressure both from student groups and from concerned government agencies to enter the arena with regulations or at least with investigations. Moreover, student lobbyists, underestimating the power of students as customers, have voiced their distrust even of such agencies as the College Entrance Examination Board, which they see as in the hands of enemies or, at best, benign paternalists who may not be acting in the students' interests. The same, as we have seen, is true of the Educational Testing Service. Moreover, I have already noted that some lawyers in the Federal Trade Commission and some officials in the Office of Education regard the use of voluntary accrediting associations to establish eligibility for student aid as anomalous: these accrediting agencies are run by, and therefore presumably on behalf of, the institutions, whereas the only firm source of supervision could be a government agency acting on behalf of isolated and still largely unorganized student customers and potential customers. To put it in the terms in which I have heard federal officials speak: the regional accrediting associations are dismissed out of hand as private and voluntary, seen as representing the interests of the academic, not-for-profit institutions—interests regarded as of necessity adversarial to those of students. The opponents of reliance on accreditation as the main device to monitor abuses of students' rights in the practices of colleges and universities note that accreditation was not intended to homogenize or standardize the practices of academic institutions, but rather to see whether an institution lives up to the goals it has set for itself—and since in theory, at least, these goals can be lax and cursory, accreditation comes to be virtually automatic.

The belief that interests necessarily are in conflict between student "consumers" and educational institutions draws part of its strength from the general atmosphere of American litigiousness, with its yes/no dichotomizing tendency, plaintiffs and defendants, and zero-sum legal games, which stands in such a marked contrast to the Japanese attitude of seeking to make compromises among interests that are seen as only partly in conflict and partly in potential harmony. For discussion, see Vogel (1979). This general American pattern of legalism has been greatly expanded in recent years by what seems to me an almost paranoid belief, especially prevalent among young people but widespread in the country as a whole, that large organizations, even nonprofit ones, are almost inevitably at odds with those they serve. (For an illustration of the Ralph Nader view of testing as a racially biased conspiracy, see *The Testing Digest*, 1979.)

Federal Aid to Students and Expansion of Federal Regulation

When, as mentioned earlier, I visited Furman University in South Carolina in the middle 1960s and discovered that it had refused to accept federal money for a needed science building because of Baptist strictness in keeping church and state separate, I found that, for most of the responsible Furman administrators and faculty members, the issue was one of doctrinal purity, but others feared that inevitably federal money meant eventual federal control. At the time, their fears struck me as excessive. I recalled that the post–World War II GI Bill of Rights had given veterans the widest possible freedom of choice: they could attend a private college with high tuition or a state university in another state than their original residence; in either case, the tuition would be paid directly to the institution, and each veteran would receive supplementary grants for additional costs of education. The National Defense Education Act of 1958, a post-Sputnik measure, provided fellowships and traineeships for students entering certain fields deemed relevant to the national security, such as engineering or nursing, and "defense" was interpreted with wide latitude, so that it did not lead to any militarization of the campuses to which students went. (Even the term *defense* in the legislation, as some members of Congress privately declared, had been inserted not because of any militaristic bias on their part but to protect them from conservative "taxpayer" constituents who might object to their "wasting money" on educating youth at national expense, something previously considered a local or state responsibility.)

As the foregoing pages have suggested, matters look very different today. The threat of withdrawal of federal money, coming to colleges via aid to students, is being used to diminish diversity, as well as to require, from institutions already suffering from many uncontrollably rising costs, the heavy burden of reporting and of seeking to show compliance with regulations. Even colleges that follow the older Southern Baptist attitude and accept no federal grants, such as those previously available for building dormitories or supporting libraries, may find themselves pursued by federal regulators because their students are receiving money from the various federal student aid programs. As noted earlier, Presbyterian Grove City College has followed the Southern Baptist formula and refused all federal aid, but it was nevertheless threatened by HEW with a cutoff of government funding of students for failure to fill out Form 639A (Assurance of Compliance with Title IX)—Title IX applies to women the provisions against discrimination already incorporated for blacks and other ethnic minorities in earlier legislation. Grove City College is fully coed, does not discriminate, and provides equal facilities, athletic and otherwise, for women. In an unusual move, it took the initiative and brought suit to block the HEW action, winning the case in Pittsburgh Federal District Court, Judge Paul Simmons declaring that the government has no legal right to penalize individual students as "a remedy for coercing the college." The judge added that Form 639A went beyond the mandate of Title IX, which applies only to students, since the form also contains inquiries concerning sexual discrimination in faculty hiring ("Sundae Punch," 1980).

But it is rare for colleges to take the initiative by bringing suit themselves. More commonly, public-interest law firms will bring suit in a federal jurisdiction of their own choosing in order to force compliance with regulations, and individual plaintiffs, sometimes supported by such firms, will bring suit, as in the suits now being brought under the one-sentence law concerning discrimination against the handicapped by, for example, blind students who insist that a college provide them with a reader or paraplegic students who insist that they be furnished with someone to help them navigate through the campus. The lengthy regulations developed by HEW to implement the law covering discrimination against the handicapped forbid the formation of consortia, which might specialize in facilities so that paraplegics could be directed to the many barrier-free campuses, or blind students or deaf students could be grouped together in an institution that has facilities providing for them. (Drug addicts and alcoholics have been included by the regulations as among those to be considered "handicapped," almost certainly not groups within the original congressional intent. One former HEW official told me that there was no doubt that the regulations were "vindictive.")[16]

[16] The vindictiveness of regulations and of enforcement proceedings is often the result of a vicious circle, not simply of zealotry or antiuniversity attitudes among the many lawyers and other officials involved in the regulatory process. In the case of legislation on behalf of the handicapped, although a number of colleges and universities had taken the trouble in the last several decades to build barrier-free campuses for the sake of paraplegics, the lobbies representing higher education in Washington made no effort to get in touch with representatives of the organized lobbies for different handicapped groups and to try to work out a *modus vivendi* prior to legislation. Moreover, colleges and universities, including some of the most liberal, have been increasingly bewailing the web of regulation and interference as such, in an indiscriminate way, making it appear as if they were obstinately opposed,

One of the most important efforts by litigation and federal regulatory action to limit diversity, and hence the options available to students, began as a lawsuit, *Adams* v. *Morgan*, in the Fifth Federal Circuit Court of Appeals in New Orleans—a case brought by the NAACP Legal Defense and Education Fund to require what was then HEW to enforce Title VI of the Civil Rights Act of 1964 by cutting off federal funds from every public institution of higher education in the South that did not have a sufficient number of white students (in predominantly black institutions) or black students (in predominantly white ones). The case was first brought to my attention by a white student at Newcomb College who, at school in New Orleans in an earlier day of white resistance to desegregation, had fought on behalf of desegregation. But now she realized that the result of a successful lawsuit would be, in effect, the partial submergence of predominantly black Southern University, both students and professors, by the often more academically adept students and more demanding professors in neighboring Louisiana State University, both in Baton Rouge and in New Orleans. Applied throughout the South, such a ruling would destroy the symbols of black pride and identification with blacks' public institutions. At the time I first learned of the suit, LSU had average SAT scores of around 450, Southern University of about 300 (and ACT

---

for example, to equal treatment of women and of minorities, rather than making specific complaints against specific excesses. Furthermore, a number of the advocates for higher education have taken the position that they should not be treated as commercial firms are treated in often the identical legislation, including the Occupational Safety and Health Act, but that they are entitled to special autonomy and special consideration; while nonprofit institutions do have the argument that they cannot pass on additional costs to the consumer, there is a latent snobbery in this judgment that there is a firm line separating educational institutions from all others which would justify exemption of the former. (Indeed, such arguments often succeed in convincing me that many businesses are the victims of indiscriminate regulation, variable enforcement policy, and elements of vindictiveness; furthermore, there are many borderline cases, for example, of corporate laboratories, such as Bell Labs or RCA Labs, that face problems in dealing with affirmative action litigation comparable to those of the more selective research universities.) The attitude of the universities has led some government lawyers, and of course public-interest law firms, in devising regulations and in enforcement proceedings, to be motivated by a drive to "get the elitists," setting up in turn a defensive reaction on the part of the affected institutions, which may willfully delay compliance (though delay is more usually the result of the complexity of demands by the regulators, who are often ignorant of internal university procedures).

about 11). The situation of the public black institutions had already been weakened by the "brain drain" of able black faculty members and students to predominantly white institutions both North and South.

The leading NAACP counsel who brought the suit are Yankees, several of them white. If they had consulted any Southern black educators, they would only have been told what many have told me—namely, that their institutions cannot recruit a "proportionate" number of whites. The Southern public black institutions have evoked intense alumni loyalty; their fraternities and sororities have a lifelong quality, unlike the usual situation in the North, where only a few alumni continue to care about the fraternity after graduation. Whether scholars approve or not, the athletic teams and marching bands of such Southern institutions as Florida Agricultural and Mechanical University provide rallying points for blacks, much as football and basketball teams in the North, often including many black athletes, serve as symbols of identity for whole cities as well as for academic institutions. We are not dealing here with race as such, for blacks from Africa or the Caribbean have a quite different cultural outlook, as do upper-middle-class blacks in metropolitan centers whose children attend predominantly white private schools and leading predominantly white universities.

As the litigation moved slowly, the Office of Civil Rights put pressure on what was then HEW to use the threat of cutting off federal funds to force compliance by Southern state systems of higher education.[17] The leading black educator Andrew

---

[17] An interim strategy was to establish, in effect, magnet professional schools on the black campuses; for example, schools of architecture and of pharmacy were established at Florida A&M. Business management was transferred from predominantly white Armstrong State to predominantly black Savannah State, with education moving the other way. Enrollments suffered at both schools. Since both architecture and pharmacy require more knowledge of mathematics and science than the Southern black students attending college are apt to have, these schools have become, on both the faculty and student levels, resented white enclaves on the predominantly black campuses. Where whites and blacks compete on a more equal footing, as in applications to law school on black campuses, as I have observed at Texas Southern Law School (which fought off an effort to merge it with the University of Houston Law School some years before the litigation discussed in the text began), or at North Carolina Central University, a predominantly black university in

Billingsley, president of Morgan State University in Baltimore, has expressed views common to administrators, faculty members, and students in the predominantly black colleges and universities throughout the South, in commenting on an effort to merge: "Part of it is the assumption that black schools are inferior, but the truth is that the academic standards at Morgan are higher than in many of the white schools. . . . The other fallacy is that every individual school ought to reflect the makeup of the entire population. The salt-and-pepper test has nothing to do with education. The Constitution does not require salt-and-pepper but open access. The black schools already have open access" (Raspberry, 1980; Glazer, 1980).

Federal actions and proposed actions to protect student consumers are geared to making sure that they are given proper information by colleges, that they can get proper refunds of tuitions if they leave, and so on, but in no case are such efforts aimed at seeing that student options are maintained at least at their present level by supporting the diversity inherited from an earlier era—diversity that, for many students, is obviously still attractive (see Cunnigen, 1978), however those of us who, like me, prefer universalistic values to ethnically self-protective ones may judge these complex issues. Diversity exists in any event, owing to the still very great heterogeneity of the United States, so that even federal district judges, although all nominally appointed by the president, tend in some measure to reflect the climates of their locales and often render diverse opinions, which, after a period of confusion, the Supreme Court, itself divided, is asked to reconcile. Yet this very uncertainty of enforcement and the diversity of actions and attitudes taken by the local governmental enforcers do not change the feeling expressed to me by the affirmative action officer of a major research university—namely, that the threat of a lawsuit is felt like a "knife at the throat." Federal agencies charged with enforcement of regulations they have themselves drafted are of

---

Durham, the black students bitterly resent the white ones and make life difficult for them. Charles Levy's book *Voluntary Servitude: Whites in the Negro Movement* (1968) describes for a somewhat earlier day the situation of a white faculty member teaching in a predominantly black college and the onion rings of suspicion and distrust with which such a person is surrounded.

course aware of the uneven vulnerabilities of academic institutions, and they are apt to go after those most likely, for reasons of local or national public relations or fear of a polarized faculty and student body, to accept a consent decree, which can then be used in other, very different types of situations. Thus a regulation intended to be uniform, lacking respect for local hardships and local options, often turns out in fact to have an uneven impact and, for any one institution, an unpredictable *in terrorem* one.

Government and Private Assistance in Student Choice

Both the College Entrance Examination Board and the American College Testing Service make extensive efforts to increase the sophistication of students and their families concerning the lifelong importance of decisions whether and where to go to college. A number of cities already contain centers, accessible to the bulk of the urban population, where students can get disinterested computer-assisted advice on institutions that might be available to them, given their interests, their test scores and high school grades, their financial needs, and their willingness or ability to live away from home. *The College Board News* is widely circulated, addressed to students and parents, but like other such printed material, it rarely reaches isolated or urban impoverished groups. I have already referred to the efforts of the Bush Foundation in St. Paul and of the Permanent Charity Fund in Boston to acquaint community college students with the possibility of foundation-assisted transfer to private colleges at the upper-division level.

But regions of the country vary greatly in the availability of information of this sort. On the one hand, as just indicated, federal regulation and judicial intervention are unwise if they fail to take account of the fact that, in many ways, the South is still different from the rest of the country. On the other hand, private agencies need to recognize that the Preliminary Scholastic Aptitude Test, a practice run taken in the junior year in many nonaffluent Northern high schools, permits serious consideration of options concerning where to apply to college rather than the nearest available college and seems almost never to be offered in Southern secondary schools, even when many students will be taking the SAT as seniors. It seems possible that the federal government can extend the kinds of knowledge available at the metropolitan centers to remote regions by computer hookups.

More generally, if we want to help students become more active producers of their own education, then we need not only to overcome the passivity that is so depressing in many of our elementary and secondary schools but also to experiment much more than we have with the Early College idea, in which students are removed from slack secondary schools to what is, ideally, the greater seriousness and strenuousness of a college program. Students need to be persuaded that they have a choice and shaken out of the assumption that some colleges are out of the question for them because they could not get financial aid—an assumption that they do not check, perhaps because they are protecting their dignity by not applying where they may be turned down. Furthermore, students need diagnostic testing, not only at the end of their high school careers and not only for the sake of interschool comparison, as in the growing vogue for competence-based testing, but in order to individuate counseling and to give counselors more clues toward further inquiry concerning particular students. Here again, one needs to experiment with tests of noncognitive qualities in order to identify the "overachievers," the ones who can be counted on to perform up to and beyond the level of their measured achievement and who should take a chance on being stretched to that limit, although not taxed beyond it to the point of humiliation.[18]

In the present situation of serious concern with marketing on the part of colleges to recruit students, the hope for countering salesmanship by disinterested advice may appear quixotic. But I am convinced, as these pages have emphasized and as many people have pointed out without too many students listening, that college is the most important "purchase" a young person is likely to make—a purchase that is always costly in terms of income forgone

[18] Warren Willingham of the Educational Testing Service has been engaged in extensive investigation of tests of noncognitive qualities, although his essays and those of his associates on this subject are as yet unpublished because of the difficulty of establishing reliable measures of such qualities. However, ETS has helped launch a program of National Arts Awards to provide recognition for students' artistic talents, as well as the already available tests of academic achievement and capability (Hechinger, 1980).

and in time and effort, even if it is subsidized by third parties. Students rarely see the cost of college attendance as an investment that can be amortized over a lengthy period and paid off, thanks to inflation, with dollars of lower purchasing power. In lower-income and even many middle-income families, price differences between colleges may loom large, and yet they would seem trivial if viewed as lifetime investments. In addition, even students at the postbaccalaureate level are often swayed by offers of financial aid as an indication of how much the institution values them, realizing neither their own value to the institution nor the tie-in requirement of the cost of accepting the offer as against any less lucrative offers from elsewhere. Thus, graduate students can sometimes be tempted to stay on at universities where they have been undergraduates by an offer of a seemingly generous teaching fellowship, when they have in large measure "run out of school" at that institution and should move to another that offers them less in immediate terms but more opportunity to learn, a chance to see another part of the academic forest, and a potential source of later placement. Sometimes acceptance of the higher offer from a place of lesser quality, eager to develop its doctoral program, is used to rationalize the student's fear of the unknown.

One might even argue that subsidization of most of the costs of college is damaging because it minimizes the seriousness of the choice—one reason for my favoring the Educational Opportunity Bank idea, for if more students regarded college as something that they had to purchase (even on the retroactive installment plan) as against other potential purchases, they might be apt to make a more serious choice to attend or not. And if they decided to attend, they might not feel that they were having a subsidized lunch whose nutritional quality need not be examined as carefully as if one were paying out of one's own eventual pocket.

In any government or philanthropic effort along the lines just described, it is important to take account of the widespread cynicism in the general population, including students, that everything is a "sell," including college. Such cynicism protects people from gullibility at the price of depriving them of potential opportunity. Students need to learn some simple precautions, especially about those programs that promise immediate vocational benefits, but for a large part of the American population, an increase of cynicism is hardly requisite: the dosage is sufficient now. Rather, one needs to tap the residual sources of idealism that cynicism tends to cover over, sources of a desire to extend oneself in an era of seeming hedonism, and the belief that one has some power over one's fate.

Such a position is in flat contradiction to the view that the "value added" by college is, if not negligible, at least not measurable. Many believe that what matters is the "input" into colleges and that colleges differ little in what they accomplish—they only differ in those they recruit or admit. In the aggregate, this may well be so, but every teacher knows that, for individual students, individual institutions and one's trajectory within them make a tremendous difference. Institutions that recruit cadres identical on such measurable factors as test scores and socioeconomic background have very different impacts on students. Paired comparisons of such institutions can make this clear, even if such differences wash out when one uses gross measures of college "productivity," such as the number of people going on to graduate and professional education, the number who graduate at all, or the income earned by graduates. But this says nothing about variations in the degree of push one will get toward securing an education at one institution or another. Some colleges, and some programs within colleges, leave a stamp on people—for worse as well as for better. These differences do not wash out, and in some degree they can be anticipated—that, at least, is my premise and hope.

Bibliography

Adelson, J. "The Teacher as a Model." In N. Sanford (Ed.), *The American College: Psychological and Social Interpretations of the Higher Learning.* New York: Wiley, 1962.

American Association of University Professors, Committee A. "Academic Freedom and Tenure: Philander Smith College (Arkansas)." *Academe,* May 1980, pp. 198–206.

American Institutes for Research. *Safeguarding Your Education: A Student's Consumer Guide to College and Occupational Education.* Santa Ana, Calif.: Media One, 1977.

Anderson, A., Bowman, M. J., and Tinto, V. *Where Colleges Are and Who Attends: Effects of Accessibility on College Attendance.* New York: McGraw-Hill, 1972.

Anderson, Q. "John Dewey's American Democrat." *Daedalus,* 1979, *108,* 145–159.

Arendt, H. *The Human Condition.* Chicago: University of Chicago Press, 1958.

Astin, A. W. "Equal Access to Postsecondary Education: Myth or Reality?" *UCLA Educator,* Spring 1977a, pp. 8–17.

Astin, A. W. *Four Critical Years: Effects of College on Beliefs, Attitudes, and Knowledge.* San Francisco: Jossey-Bass, 1977b.

Astin, H. S., Harway, M., and McNamara, P. *Sex Discrimination in Education: Access to Postsecondary Education.* Report prepared with the Education Division, National Center for Education Statistics, U.S. Department of Health, Education, and Welfare, 1976.

Bailey, S. K. "Marketing Perspectives: Student and National Interests." In *Marketing in College Admissions: A Broadening of Perspectives.* Papers from the Wingspread Colloquium, Racine, Wisc., November 8, 1979. New York: College Board, 1980.

Balderston, F. E. *Managing Today's University.* San Francisco: Jossey-Bass, 1974.

Baltzell, E. D. "The Protestant Establishment Revisited." *American Scholar,* 1976, *45,* 499–521.

Baltzell, E. D. *Puritan Boston and Quaker Philadelphia.* New York: Free Press, 1979.

Banfield, E. C. *The Unheavenly City: The Nature and Future of Our Urban Crisis.* Boston: Little, Brown, 1970.

Barbato, J. "For Adults Only: The Possible Dream." *Change*, September 1979, pp. 20–21.

Bassis, M. S. "The Campus as a Frog Pond: A Theoretical and Empirical Reassessment." *American Journal of Sociology*, 1977, *82*, 1318–1326.

Bateson, M. C. " 'The Figure of Tinsel': A Study of Themes of Hypocrisy and Pessimism in Iranian Culture." *Daedalus*, 1979, *108*, 125–134.

Bayer, A. E., and Astin, A. W. "Campus Unrest, 1970–71: Was It Really All That Quiet?" *Educational Record*, 1971, *52*, 301–313.

Becker, H. S., Geer, B., and Hughes, E. C. *Making the Grade: The Academic Side of College Life.* New York: Wiley, 1968.

Becker, H. S., and others. *Boys in White: Student Culture in Medical School.* Chicago: University of Chicago Press, 1961.

Bell, D. *The Reforming of General Education: The Columbia College Experience in Its National Setting.* New York: Columbia University Press, 1966.

Bell, D. *Cultural Contradictions of Capitalism.* New York: Basic Books, 1976.

Ben-David, J. "The Fate of Liberal Education in the Seventies." *Contemporary Sociology*, 1980, *9*(4), 505–508.

Bennett, W. J., and Delattre, E. J. "Moral Education in the Schools." *Public Interest*, no. 50 (Winter 1978), 81–98.

Berger, B. Letter. *Character*, April 1980, pp. 2–3.

Berger, P. L., and Berger, B. "The Blueing of America." *New Republic*, April 3, 1971, pp. 20–23.

Bernard, J. S. *Academic Women.* University Park: Pennsylvania State University Press, 1964.

Bird, C. *The Case Against College.* New York: McKay, 1975.

Birenbaum, W. *Something for Everybody Is Not Enough: An Educator's Search for His Education.* New York: Random House, 1971.

Blackburn, R., and others. *Changing Practices in Undergraduate Education.* Berkeley, Calif.: Carnegie Council on Policy Studies in Higher Education, 1976.

Blaydon, C. C. "State Policy Options." In D. W. Breneman and C. E. Finn, Jr. (Eds.), *Public Policy and Private Higher Education.* Washington, D.C.: Brookings Institution, 1978.

Bonham, G. W. "The Open University: Lessons for the Future." *Change*, November 1978, pp. 14–15.

Boorstin, D. J. *The Americans: The National Experience.* New York: Random House, 1965.

Bosk, C. L. *Forgive and Remember: Managing Medical Failure.* Chicago: University of Chicago Press, 1979.

Botstein, L. "A Proper Education: The Trade-off Between Method and Motive." *Harper's*, September 1979, pp. 33–37.

Bowen, H. R. "Financing the External Degree." In Commission on Non-Traditional Study, *Diversity by Design.* San Francisco: Jossey-Bass, 1973.

Bowen, H. R. *Investment in Learning: The Individual and Social Value of American Higher Education.* San Francisco: Jossey-Bass, 1977.

Boyd, W. M. "SATs and Minorities: The Dangers of Underprediction." *Change*, November 1977, pp. 48–49, 64.

Boyer, E. L., and Kaplan, M. "Educating for Survival: A Call for a Core Curriculum." *Change*, March 1977, pp. 22–29.

Brann, E. T. H. *Paradoxes of Education in a Republic.* Chicago: University of Chicago Press, 1979.

Breneman, D. W., and Finn, C. E., Jr. (Eds.). *Public Policy and Private Higher Education.* Washington, D.C.: Brookings Institution, 1978.

Brill, H. *Why Organizers Fail: The Story of a Rent Strike.* Berkeley: University of California Press, 1971.

Broad, W. J. "Ending Sex Discrimination in Academia." *Science,* 1980, *208,* 1120–1122.

Brouder, K. *Report on Student Involvement in the College Board.* Mimeograph, 1978.

Bryson, L. "Notes on a Theory of Advice." In L. Bryson (Ed.), *Communication of Ideas.* Institute for Religious and Social Studies. New York: Cooper Square, 1964. (Originally published 1948.)

Bunzel, J. H. "The Faculty Strike at San Francisco State College." *AAUP Bulletin,* 1971, *57*(3), 341–351.

Bunzel, J. H. "The Eclipse of Confidentiality." *Change,* October 1975, pp. 30–33.

Cahn, S. M. "Appendix: The Uses and Abuses of Grades and Examinations." In S. M. Cahn (Ed.), *Scholars Who Teach: The Art of College Teaching.* Chicago: Nelson-Hall, 1978.

Callahan, D. "When Friendship Calls, Should Truth Answer?" *Chronicle of Higher Education,* August 7, 1978, p. 32.

Campbell, D. T. "Novel Narrowness." *Syracuse Scholar,* 1979–80, *6*(1), 78, 208.

Carnegie Commission on Higher Education. *Less Time, More Options: Education Beyond the High School.* New York: McGraw-Hill, 1971.

Carnegie Commission on Higher Education. *Higher Education: Who Pays? Who Benefits? Who Should Pay?* New York: McGraw-Hill, 1974.

Carnegie Council on Policy Studies in Higher Education. *The States and Private Higher Education: Problems and Policies in a New Era.* San Francisco: Jossey-Bass, 1977.

Carnegie Council on Policy Studies in Higher Education. *Fair Practices in Higher Education: Rights and Responsibilities of Students and Their Colleges in a Period of Intensified Competition for Enrollments.* San Francisco: Jossey-Bass, 1979a.

Carnegie Council on Policy Studies in Higher Education. *Giving Youth a Better Chance: Options for Education, Work, and Service.* San Francisco: Jossey-Bass, 1979b.

Carnegie Council on Policy Studies in Higher Education. *Next Steps for the 1980s in Student Financial Aid: A Fourth Alternative.* San Francisco: Jossey-Bass, 1979c.

Carnegie Council on Policy Studies in Higher Education. *Three Thousand Futures: The Next Twenty Years for Higher Education.* San Francisco: Jossey-Bass, 1980.

Cass, J., and Birnbaum, M. *Comparative Guide to American Colleges.* (8th ed.) New York: Harper & Row, 1977.

Cass, J., and Birnbaum, M. *Comparative Guide to American Colleges.* (9th ed.) New York: Harper & Row, 1979.

Chace, A. "Skipping Through College: Reflections on the Decline of Liberal Arts Education." *Newsletter of the International Council on the Future of the University*, December 1978, pp. 1–8.

Chace, W. M. "Lionel Trilling: The Contrariness of Culture." *American Scholar*, 1978–79, *48*, 49–70.

Chait, R. "Tenure and the Academic Future." In *Three Views, Tenure*. New Rochelle, N.Y.: Change Magazine Press, 1979.

Chickering, A. W. *Commuting Versus Resident Students: Overcoming Educational Inequities of Living Off Campus*. San Francisco: Jossey-Bass, 1974.

Clark, B. R. "The 'Cooling-Out' Function in Higher Education." *American Journal of Sociology*, 1960a, *65*, 569–576.

Clark, B. R. *The Open Door College: A Case Study*. New York: McGraw-Hill, 1960b.

Clark, B. R. *The Distinctive College: Antioch, Reed, and Swarthmore*. Chicago: Aldine, 1970.

Clark, B. R. "The Cooling-Out Function Revisited." In G. B. Vaughan (Ed.), *New Directions for Community Colleges: Questioning the Community College Role*, no. 32. San Francisco: Jossey-Bass, 1980.

Clark, B. R., and Trow, M. "The Organizational Context." In T. M. Newcomb and E. K. Wilson (Eds.), *College Peer Groups: Problems and Prospects for Research*. Chicago: Aldine, 1966.

Cohen, A. M., and Brawer, F. B. *The Two-Year College Instructor Today*. New York: Praeger, 1977.

Cohen, M. D., and March, J. G. *Leadership and Ambiguity: The American College President*. New York: McGraw-Hill, 1974.

College Entrance Examination Board. *On Further Examination: Report of the Advisory Panel on the Scholastic Aptitude Test Score Decline*. New York: College Entrance Examination Board, 1977.

College Entrance Examination Board. *College Times: Facts for Your Future from the College Board*, no. 2. New York: College Entrance Examination Board, 1977–78.

Commission on Non-Traditional Study. *Diversity by Design*. San Francisco: Jossey-Bass, 1973.

Committee on Race Relations. *A Study of Race Relations at Harvard College*. Prepared for the Office of the Dean of Students. Cambridge, Mass.: Harvard College, 1980.

Committee on the Objectives of a General Education in a Free Society. *General Education in a Free Society: Report of the Harvard Committee*. Cambridge, Mass.: Harvard University Press, 1945.

Congressional Record, 96th Congress, 2nd session. Vol. 126, no. 105. June 24, 1980.

Cottle, T. J. "Pains of Permanence." In B. L. Smith and Associates, *The Tenure Debate*. San Francisco: Jossey-Bass, 1973.

Cottle, T. J. *Time's Children: Impressions of Youth*. Boston: Little, Brown, 1974.

Cottle, T. J. *College: Reward and Betrayal*. Chicago: University of Chicago Press, 1978.

Cross, K. P. *Beyond the Open Door: New Students to Higher Education*. San Francisco: Jossey-Bass, 1971.

Cross, K. P. *Accent on Learning: Improving Instruction and Reshaping the Curriculum*. San Francisco: Jossey-Bass, 1976.

Cunnigen, D. "The College Preferences of Black College Students in the South." Unpublished paper, Department of Sociology, Harvard University, May 1978.

"Current Litigation." *Academe*, December 1978, pp. 2, 4, 9.

Danière, A. *Higher Education and the American Economy.* New York: Random House, 1964.

"Daughter Sues Father to Pay College Fees." *Washington Post*, July 25, 1979, p. 8.

Davis, J. A. "The Campus as a Frog Pond: An Application of the Theory of Relative Deprivation to Career Decisions of College Men." *American Journal of Sociology*, 1966, 72, 17–31.

Decter, M. *Liberal Parents, Radical Children.* New York: Coward, McCann & Geoghegan, 1975.

Deitch, K. M. "Financial Aid in American Private Elementary-Secondary Education: Some Introductory Observations." Unpublished paper prepared for the National Association of Independent Schools, 1980.

DeLamater, J. "Intimacy in a Coeducational Community." In A. A. Harrison (Ed.), *Explorations in Psychology.* Monterey, Calif.: Brooks/Cole, 1974.

Diggins, J. P. *The Bard of Savagery: Thorstein Veblen and Modern Social Theory.* New York: Seabury Press, 1978.

Dreyfuss, J. "Ethnic Studies: A Springboard, Not a Trap." *Change*, February 1979, pp. 13–16.

Duberman, M. *Black Mountain: An Exploration in Community.* New York: Dutton, 1972.

Dugger, R. *Our Invaded Universities: Form, Reform, and New Starts.* New York: Norton, 1974.

Eckland, B. K. "College Dropouts Who Came Back." *Harvard Educational Review*, 1964, 34, 402–420.

Educational Testing Service. *Public Interest Principles for the Design and Use of Admissions Testing Programs.* Princeton, N.J.: Educational Testing Service, 1980.

Fallows, J. "The Tests and the 'Brightest': How Fair Are the College Boards?" *Atlantic*, February 1980a, pp. 37–48.

Fallows, J. "Sheepskins Are for Sheep: Credentials Look Great on the Wall, but They Don't Get the Job Done." *Washington Monthly*, March 1980b, pp. 9–17.

Feldman, K. A., and Newcomb, T. M., *The Impact of College on Students* (2 vols.). San Francisco: Jossey-Bass, 1969.

"Fifty-Eight Degree Programs to be Eliminated at Louisiana's Public Universities." *Chronicle of Higher Education*, January 14, 1980, p. 6.

Finn, C. E., Jr. *Scholars, Dollars, and Bureaucrats.* Washington, D.C.: Brookings Institution, 1978.

Fischer, R. "Pace University: How to Ignore the Steady State." *Change*, November 1977, pp. 32–39.

Fiske, E. B. "Baruch and City Start 'No-Need' Scholarships." *New York Times*, January 25, 1978, p. 39.

Fiske, E. B. "Job-Training Schools Grow Along with Cries of Abuses." *New York Times*, July 25, 1979a, pp. A-1, B-2.

Fiske, E. B. "State Seeks Tighter Control of Vocational Education." *New York Times*, July 27, 1979b, pp. B-1, 4.

Fiske, E. B. "The Marketing of the Colleges." *Atlantic*, October 1979c, pp. 93–98.

Fiske, E. B. "Problems Arise as Colleges Recruit Students Overseas." *New York Times*, February 24, 1980a, pp. 1, 40.

Fiske, E. B. "Colleges Face Problems on Overseas Recruiting." *New York Times*, February 25, 1980b, p. D-8.

FitzGerald, F. *America Revised: History Schoolbooks in the Twentieth Century.* Boston: Atlantic/Little, Brown, 1980.

Foster, W. T. *Administration of the College Curriculum.* Boston: Houghton Mifflin, 1911.

Freedman, M. "CCNY Days." *American Scholar*, 1980, *49*, 193–207.

Freeman, R. B. *Black Elite: The New Market for Highly Educated Black Americans.* New York: McGraw-Hill, 1976a.

Freeman, R. B. *The Overeducated American.* New York: Academic Press, 1976b.

Fulton, O., and Trow, M. "Research Activity in American Higher Education." In M. Trow (Ed.), *Teachers and Students: Aspects of American Higher Education.* New York: McGraw-Hill, 1975.

Gamson, Z. F. "Performance and Personalism in Student-Faculty Relations." *Sociology of Education*, 1967, *40*, 279–301.

Gamson, Z. F., Boyk, B., and Gipson, G. "Experimental College Grads: Getting Theirs." *Change*, September 1977, pp. 48–49.

Gamson, Z. F., Peterson, M. W., and Blackburn, R. T. "Stages in the Response of White Colleges and Universities to Black Students." *Journal of Higher Education*, 1980, *51*(3), 255–267.

Gans, H. J. "Symbolic Ethnicity: The Future of Ethnic Groups and Cultures in America." In H. Gans and others (Eds.), *On the Making of Americans: Essays in Honor of David Riesman.* Philadelphia: University of Pennsylvania Press, 1979.

Garbarino, J. W. *Faculty Bargaining: Change and Conflict.* New York: McGraw-Hill, 1975.

Geertz, C. "Blurred Genres: The Refiguration of Social Thought." *American Scholar*, 1980, *49*(2), 165–182.

Gerzon, M. *The Whole World Is Watching: A Young Man Looks at Youth's Dissent.* New York: Viking Press, 1969.

"Getting Testy: The Rebellion Gathers Steam." *Time*, November 26, 1979, pp. 11–17.

Glazer, N. "City College." In D. Riesman and V. A. Stadtman (Eds.), *Academic Transformation: Seventeen Institutions Under Pressure.* New York: McGraw-Hill, 1973.

Glazer, N. "Conflicts in Schools for the Minor Professions." Harvard Graduate School of Education *Bulletin*, Spring 1974a, pp. 18–24.

Glazer, N. "The Schools of the Minor Professions." *Minerva*, 1974b, *12*, 346–364.

Glazer, N. "Should Judges Administer Social Services?" *Public Interest*, no. 50 (Winter 1978), 64–80.

Glazer, N. "University and College Admissions in the United States: The Government Impact." *Newsletter of the International Council on the Future of the University*, May 1980, pp. 1–6.

Glenny, L. A. "Demographic and Related Issues for Higher Education in the 1980's." *Journal of Higher Education*, 1980, *51*(4), 363–380.
Goldsen, R. K., and others. *What College Students Think*. New York: Van Nostrand, 1960.
Goldsmith, J. "Collective Behavior in an Academic Community—A Case Study." Unpublished essay, Reed College, 1971.
Goldsmith, J. "Youth in the Public Sector: Institutional Paths to Social Membership." Unpublished doctoral dissertation, Department of Sociology, University of Chicago, 1973.
Goleman, D. "Leaving Home: Is There a Right Time to Go?" *Psychology Today*, August 1980, pp. 52–61.
Gordon, M. S. *Youth, Education, and Unemployment Problems: An International Perspective*. Report of the Carnegie Council on Policy Studies in Higher Education. New York: Carnegie Foundation for the Advancement of Teaching, 1979.
Graña, C. *Bohemian Versus Bourgeois: French Society and the French Man of Letters in the Nineteenth Century*. New York: Basic Books, 1963.
Grant, G. "Let a Hundred Antiochs Bloom." *Change*, September 1972a, pp. 47–58.
Grant, G. "Universal B.A.?" *New Republic*, June 1972b, pp. 13–16.
Grant, G., and Riesman, D. "An Ecology of Academic Reform." *Daedalus*, 1975, *104*, 166–191.
Grant, G., and Riesman, D. *The Perpetual Dream: Reform and Experiment in the American College*. Chicago: University of Chicago Press, 1978.
Grant, G., and others. *On Competence: A Critical Analysis of Competence-Based Reforms in Higher Education*. San Francisco: Jossey-Bass, 1979.
Green, T. F. *Work, Leisure, and the American Schools*. New York: Random House, 1968.
Gross, T. *Academic Turmoil: The Reality and Promise of Open Education*. New York: Doubleday, 1980.
Gusfield, J. R., and Riesman, D. "Innovation in Higher Education: Notes on Students and Faculty Encounters in Three New Colleges." In H. Becker and others (Eds.), *Institutions and the Person: Essays in Honor of Everett C. Hughes*. Chicago: Aldine, 1968.
Gutmann, D. "Psychology as Theology." *Social Research*, 1978, *45*(3), 452–466.
"Hard Sell for Higher Learning: With Enrollments and Budgets Down, Colleges Cater to the Kids." *Time*, October 2, 1978, p. 80.
Hartnett, R. T., and Feldmesser, R. A. "College Admissions Testing and the Myth of Selectivity: Unresolved Questions and Needed Research." *AAHE Bulletin*, March 1980, pp. 3–6.
Hassenger, R. "Adoption/Adaptation of Open University Courses in American Universities: Focus on Empire State College (State University of New York)." British Open University Foundation, *Occasional Newsletter*, no. 4 (March 1979), pp. 1–3.
Hassitt, J., and others. "Report of the *Ad Hoc* Committee on the Collegiate Seminar Program." Berkeley, Calif., June 14, 1979.
Hawkins, H. *Pioneer: A History of the Johns Hopkins University, 1874–1889*. Ithaca, N.Y.: Cornell University Press, 1960.

Hayes, D. *Rays of Hope: The Transition to a Post-Petroleum World.* New York: Norton, 1977.

Heath, R. *The Reasonable Adventurer.* Pittsburgh: University of Pittsburgh Press, 1964.

Hechinger, F. M. "About Education: Program Aims to Encourage in U.S." *New York Times,* July 1, 1980, p. C-4.

Herrnstein, R. J. "In Defense of Intelligence Tests." *Commentary,* February 1980, pp. 40–51.

Hochschild, A. "Inside the Clockwork of Male Careers." In F. Howe (Ed.), *Women and the Power to Change.* New York: McGraw-Hill, 1975.

Hodgkinson, H. L. *Campus Senate: Experiment in Democracy.* Berkeley: University of California Press, 1974.

Hofstadter, R. *Anti-Intellectualism in American Life.* New York: Knopf, 1963.

Hook, J. "House-Senate Panel Approves Higher Student Grant Limits." *Chronicle of Higher Education,* July 28, 1980, pp. 1, 4.

Houle, C. O. *The External Degree.* San Francisco: Jossey-Bass, 1973.

Huntington, S. P. "The Changing Cultures of Harvard." *Harvard Alumni Bulletin,* September 1969, pp. 51–54.

Hyman, H. H., Wright, C. R., and Reed, J. S. *The Enduring Effects of Education.* Chicago: University of Chicago Press, 1975.

Ihlanfeldt, W. *Achieving Optimal Enrollments and Tuition Revenues: A Guide to Modern Methods of Market Research, Student Recruitment, and Institutional Pricing.* San Francisco: Jossey-Bass, 1980.

Institute for Social Research, University of Michigan. "Deepening Distrust of Political Leaders Is Jarring Public's Faith in Institutions." *ISR Newsletter,* Autumn 1979, pp. 4–5.

Itzkoff, S. W. "Review of Eva T. H. Brann, *Paradoxes of Education in a Republic.*" *American Journal of Education,* 1980, *88,* 260–263.

Jacobson, R. L. "The Great Accreditation Debate: What Role for the Government?" *Chronicle of Higher Education,* June 16, 1980, pp. 8–10.

Jencks, C., and Riesman, D. "The Viability of the American College." In N. Sanford (Ed.), *The American College: A Psychological and Social Interpretation of the Higher Learning.* New York: Wiley, 1962.

Jencks, C., and Riesman, D. "Shimer College." *Phi Delta Kappan,* 1966, *47,* 415–420.

Jencks, C., and Riesman, D. *The Academic Revolution.* New York: Doubleday, 1968.

Jencks, C., and others, *Inequality: A Reassessment of the Effect of Family and Schooling in America.* New York: Basic Books, 1972.

Jencks, C., and others. *Who Gets Ahead? The Determinants of Economic Success in America.* New York: Basic Books, 1979.

Jerome, J. *Culture out of Anarchy: The Reconstruction of American Higher Learning.* New York: Herder & Herder, 1970.

Johnson, R. R. "The Myth of Leadership Among Colleges." *North Central Association Quarterly,* Summer 1979, *54,* 25–32. (Shorter version, "Leadership Among American Colleges," *Change,* November 1978, pp. 50–51.)

Julian, A. C., and Slattery, R. E. *Open Doors 1975/6–1976/7.* New York: Institute of National Education, 1978.

Jung, S. M., and others. *Improving the Consumer Protection Function in Post-Secondary Education.* Palo Alto, Calif.: American Institutes for Research, 1976.

Kahl, J. "Educational and Occupational Aspirations of 'Common Man' Boys." *Harvard Educational Review*, 1953, *23*, 186–203.

Karabel, J. "Community Colleges and Social Stratification: Submerged Class Conflict in American Higher Education." *Harvard Educational Review*, 1972, *42*, 521–562.

Kato, H. *Education and Youth Employment in Japan.* Report of the Carnegie Council on Policy Studies in Higher Education. New York: Carnegie Foundation for the Advancement of Teaching, 1978.

Katz, J. "Epilogue: The Admissions Process—Society's Stake in the Individual's Interest." In H. S. Sacks and Associates, *Hurdles: The Admissions Dilemma in American Higher Education.* New York: Atheneum, 1978.

Katz, J., and Cronin, D. "Sexuality in College Life." *Change*, February-March 1980, pp. 44–49.

Kauffman, J. F. *At the Pleasure of the Board: The Service of the College and University President.* Washington, D.C.: American Council on Education, 1980.

Kellams, S. E. *Emerging Sources of Student Influence.* ERIC Higher Education Research Report no. 5. Washington, D.C.: American Association for Higher Education, 1975.

Keller, M. "Reflections on Politics and Generations in America." *Daedalus*, 1978, *107*, 123–135.

Kemerer, F. R., and Young, D. A. "United They Stand: Growth of the Student Unions." *Change*, December 1977, pp. 16–21.

Kennedy, D. "How the Law School Fails: A Polemic." *Yale Review of Law and Social Action*, 1970, no. 71.

Kerr, C. *The Uses of the University.* Cambridge, Mass.: Harvard University Press, 1963.

Kesler, C. R. "The Movement of Student Opinion." *National Review*, 1979, *31*(47), 1483–1491.

Kett, J. *Rites of Passage: Adolescence in America, 1790 to the Present.* New York: Basic Books, 1977.

Kevles, D. J. *The Physicists: The History of a Scientific Community in Modern America.* New York: Knopf, 1978.

Kirk, R. "From the Academy: Grove City Goes to Court." *National Review*, 1979, *31*, 13, 70.

Klein, R. "Universities in the Market Place." *New Universities Quarterly, 33* (3), 306–320.

Klitgaard, R. E. "The Decline of the Best? An Analysis of the Relationships Between Declining Enrollments, Ph.D. Production, and Research." Discussion Paper Series, no. 65D. John Fitzgerald Kennedy School of Government, Harvard University, 1979.

Klitgaard, R. E., and others. "Merit and Admissions Policy: Case Studies from Pakistan." *Comparative Education Review*, June 1979, pp. 271–282.

Knapp, R. H., and Goodrich, H. B. *Origins of American Scientists.* Chicago: University of Chicago Press, 1952.

Knapp, R. H., and Greenbaum, J. J. *The Younger American Scholar: His Collegiate Origins.* Chicago: University of Chicago Press, 1953.

Kuhn, T. *The Structure of Scientific Revolutions.* Chicago: University of Chicago Press, 1962.

Ladd, E. C., Jr., and Lipset, S. M. *The Divided Academy: Professors and Politics.* New York: McGraw-Hill, 1975.

Lamont, L. *Campus Shock: A Firsthand Report on College Life Today.* New York: Dutton, 1979.

Lasch, C. *Haven in a Heartless World: The Family Besieged.* New York: Norton, 1977.

Lasch, C. *The Culture of Narcissism: American Life in an Age of Diminishing Expectations.* New York: Norton, 1979.

Lavin, D., Alba, R. D., and Silberstein, R. A. "Open Admissions and Equal Access: A Study of Ethnic Groups in the City University of New York." *Harvard Educational Review,* 1979, *49*(1), 53–92.

Lazarsfeld, P. F., and Thielens, W., Jr. *The Academic Mind: Social Scientists in a Time of Crisis.* New York: Free Press, 1958.

Lerner, B. "The War on Testing: David, Goliath & Gallup." *Public Interest,* no. 60 (Summer 1980), 119–147.

Levine, A. *Handbook on Undergraduate Curriculum.* San Francisco: Jossey-Bass, 1978.

Levine, A., and Weingart, J. *Reform of Undergraduate Education.* San Francisco: Jossey-Bass, 1973.

Levinson, D. *The Seasons of a Man's Life.* New York: Ballantine, 1979.

Levy, C. *Voluntary Servitude: Whites in the Negro Movement.* New York: Appleton-Century-Crofts, 1968.

Lifton, R. J. *Death in Life: Survivors of Hiroshima.* New York: Random House, 1967.

Lipset, D. *Gregory Bateson: The Legacy of a Scientist.* Englewod Cliffs, N.J.: Prentice-Hall, 1980.

Lipset, S. M. "Whither the First New Nation." *Tocqueville Review,* Fall 1979, pp. 64–99.

Litten, L. H. "Marketing Higher Education: A Reappraisal." In *Marketing in College Admissions: A Broadening of Perspectives.* Papers from the Wingspread Colloquium, Racine, Wisc., November 8, 1979. New York: College Board, 1980.

Litten, L. H., Jahoda, E., and Morris, D. "His Mother's Son, Her Father's Daughter: Parents, Children, and the Marketing of Colleges." Paper presented at the Middle States Regional Assembly of the College Board, Philadelphia, 1980.

Litten, L. H., and others. "Twixt Cup and Lip: Some Evidence on the Effect of Financial Concerns on College Choice." Paper presented at the Midwestern Regional Assembly of the College Board, February 18, 1980.

Livingston, J. C. "Tenure Everyone?" In B. L. Smith and Associates, *The Tenure Debate.* San Francisco: Jossey-Bass, 1973.

London, H. *The Culture of a Community College.* New York: Praeger, 1978.

London, H. "In Between: The Community College Teacher." *Annals of the American Academy of Political and Social Science,* March 1980, pp. 62–73.

Luke, L. P. E. "Equal Access Admissions at Harvard/Radcliffe: The View from Financial Aid and Alumni/ae Giving." Senior honors thesis, Departments of Sociology and Economics, Harvard College, 1979.

Lynch, G. E. "*The Brethren*: As Seen from Below." *Columbia College Today*, March 1980, pp. 8–9.

McCain, N. "The College Catalogues Get Low 'C' in Candor." *Boston Sunday Globe*, August 28, 1977, pp. 49, 54.

McCarthy, C. *The Wisconsin Idea*. New York: Macmillan, 1912.

Maccoby, E., and Jacklin, C. N. *The Psychology of Sex Differences*. Stanford, Calif.: Stanford University Press, 1974.

Maccoby, M. "Egocentrism, Narcissism, and Egoism: A Response to David Riesman." *Character*, April 1980, pp. 1–2.

Mankoff, M. "Waiting for Lefty on Campus: The Prospects for Political Activity." *Commonweal*, April 11, 1980, pp. 207–211.

Manning, T. E. "Pursuing Excellence." Address at the annual meeting of the New England Association of Schools and Colleges, Boston, December 7, 1978.

Mansbridge, J. *Toward Adversary Democracy*. New York: Basic Books, 1980.

Medsker, L. L. *The Junior College: Progress and Prospects*. New York: McGraw-Hill, 1960.

Merton, R. K. "Insiders and Outsiders: A Chapter in the Sociology of Knowledge." *American Journal of Sociology*, 1972, *24*, 9–47.

Merton, R. K., Reader, G., and Kendall, P. (Eds.). *The Student Physician: Introductory Studies in the Sociology of Medical Education*. Cambridge, Mass.: Harvard University Press, 1957.

Meyersohn, R., and Katz, E. "Notes on the Natural History of Fads." *American Journal of Sociology*, 1957, *62*, 494–601.

Middleton, L., and Scully, M. G. "Most Iranian Students Can Stay in U.S., Despite Severing of Diplomatic Relations." *Chronicle of Higher Education*, April 14, 1980, pp. 1, 10.

Miles, M. "Second Thoughts on the External Degree." *Change*, September 1973, pp. 6–7, 64.

Miller, H. L. "The 'Right to Treatment': Can the Courts Rehabilitate and Cure?" *Public Interest*, no. 46 (Winter 1977), 96–118.

Mitzman, B. "Reed College: The Intellectual Maverick." *Change*, September 1979, pp. 38–43.

Morgenthau, H., and Person, E. "The Roots of Narcissism." *Partisan Review*, 1978, *45*(3), 337–348.

Morris, J. (Ed.). *The Oxford Book of Oxford*. New York: Oxford University Press, 1978.

Morrison, J. L., and Freedman, C. P. "Community College Faculty Attitudes, Socialization Experiences, and Perceived Teaching Effectiveness." *Community Junior College Research Quarterly*, 1978, *2*, 119–138.

Moynihan, D. P. *Coping: On the Practice of Government*. New York: Random House, 1973.

Muscatine, C., Director, Collegiate Seminar Program. Memorandum to Donald A. Riley, Associate Vice-Chancellor, Academic Development. Re: Our staff comment on the Trow Committee report. University of California, Berkeley, 1979.

Myers, K. "Antioch Law School Loses Court Battle, Deans Fired." *Chronicle of Higher Education*, January 21, 1980, p. 11.

Nader, R., and Nairn, A. "Tests That Perpetuate Inequality." *Washington Post*, April 8, 1980, p. A-19.

National Academy of Education. *Improving Educational Achievement*. Report to the Assistant Secretary for Education. Washington, D.C.: National Academy of Education, 1978.

National Student Educational Fund. *Report for the Years 1977–1979*. Washington, D.C.: National Student Educational Fund, 1979.

Neumann, W., and Riesman, D. "The Community College Elite." In G. B. Vaughan (Ed.), *New Directions for Community Colleges: Questioning the Community College Role*, no. 32. San Francisco: Jossey-Bass, 1980.

"New Exams to Assess English Skills." *College Board News*, February 1980, p. 8.

Nisbet, R. "Hutchins of Chicago." *Commentary*, July 1964, pp. 52–55.

Oates, M. J. "Organized Voluntarism: The Catholic Sisters in Massachusetts, 1870–1940." *American Quarterly*, 1978, *30*, 652–680.

O'Connell, B. "Where Does Harvard Lead Us?" *Change*, September 1978, pp. 35–40.

Olesen, V. "Overcoming Crises in a New Nursing Program: Mount Hood Community College." In G. Grant and others (Eds.), *On Competence: A Critical Analysis of Competence-Based Reforms in Higher Education*. San Francisco: Jossey-Bass, 1979.

Orlans, H. "The End of a Monopoly? On Accrediting and Eligibility." *Change*, February-March 1980, *12*(2), 32–37.

Osborne, W. B., Ryor, J., and Shanker, A. "Three Union Leaders Talk About the Academic Future." *Change*, March 1977, pp. 30–35.

Pace, C. R. *The Demise of Diversity? A Comparative Profile of Eight Types of Institutions*. New York: McGraw-Hill, 1974.

Parker, G. T. *The Writing on the Wall: Inside Higher Education in America*. New York: Simon & Schuster, 1979.

Patterson, O. "Toward a Future That Has No Past—Reflections on the Fate of Blacks in the Americas." *Public Interest*, no. 27 (Spring 1972), 25–62.

Patterson, O. *Ethnic Chauvinism: The Reactionary Impulse*. New York: Stein and Day, 1978.

Perry, W., Jr. *Forms of Intellectual and Ethical Development in the College Years*. New York: Holt, Rinehart & Winston, 1970.

Peterson, M. W., and others. *Black Students on White Campuses: The Impacts of Increased Black Enrollments*. Ann Arbor: Institute for Social Research, University of Michigan, 1978.

Peterson, O., and others. "An Analytic Study of North Carolina General Practice, 1953–1954." *Journal of Medical Education*, December 1956, *31*, Part II.

Peterson, R. E., and Associates. *Lifelong Learning in America: An Overview of Current Practices, Available Resources, and Future Prospects*. San Francisco: Jossey-Bass, 1979.

Pitts, J. R. "The Hippies as Contrameritocracy." *Dissent*, July-August 1969; reprinted in *Dissent*, Spring 1974, pp. 305–316.

Plumb, J. H. "Eccentrics Flowered." *New York Times Book Review*, August 6, 1978, p. 12.

Radner, R., and Kuh, C. V. *Preserving the Lost Generation: Policies to Assure a Steady Flow of Young Scholars Until the Year 2000.* Berkeley, Calif.: Carnegie Council on Policy Studies in Higher Education, 1978.

Raspberry, W. "Student Checkup." *Washington Post,* October 1, 1979, p. A-21.

Raspberry, W. "The State and Morgan State." *Washington Post,* February 14, 1980, p. A-19.

Rathbone, C. "The Problems of Reaching the Top of the Ivy League . . . and Staying There." *London Times Higher Education Supplement,* February 8, 1980, pp. 10–11.

Record, W. "Some Implications of the Black Studies Movement for Higher Education in the 1970's." *Journal of Higher Education,* 1973, *44,* 191–216.

Record, W. "White Sociologists and Black Students in Predominantly White Universities." *Sociological Quarterly,* 1974, *15,* 164–182.

Record, W. "Review of William Julius Wilson, *The Declining Significance of Race: Blacks and Changing American Institutions* (Chicago: University of Chicago Press, 1978)." *American Journal of Sociology,* 1980, *85,* 965–968.

Reich, C. A. *The Greening of America: How the Youth Revolution Is Trying to Make America Liveable.* New York: Random House, 1970.

Rever, P. R. "The Dynamics of Admission to the Less-Selective Public and Private-Sector Colleges." In H. S. Sacks and Associates, *Hurdles: The Admissions Dilemma in American Higher Education.* New York: Atheneum, 1978.

Ricks, D. "Tests and Scholarships: A Cautioning Tale." *Financial Aid News,* no. 3 (March 1961), pp. 3–5.

Rieff, P. *Fellow Teachers.* New York: Harper & Row, 1973.

Riesman, D. *Thorstein Veblen: A Critical Interpretation.* New York: Scribner's, 1953; New York: Seabury Press, 1975.

Riesman, D. *Constraint and Variety in American Education.* Lincoln: University of Nebraska Press, 1956.

Riesman, D. "Field Report: Some Observations on the Interviewing in the Teacher Apprehension Study." In P. F. Lazarsfeld and W. Thielens, Jr., *The Academic Mind: Social Scientists in a Time of Crisis.* New York: Free Press, 1958.

Riesman, D. "Notes on New Universities, British and American." *Universities Quarterly,* 1966, *20,* 128–146.

Riesman, D. "Notes on Meritocracy." *Daedalus,* 1967a, *96,* 897–908.

Riesman, D. "The Urban University." *Massachusetts Review,* 1967b, *8,* 476–486.

Riesman, D. "The Collision Course of Higher Education." *Journal of College Student Personnel,* 1969a, *10,* 363–369. (Revised version, "Universities on a Collision Course," *Trans/Action,* September 1969, pp. 3–4.)

Riesman, D. "The Search for Alternative Models in Education." *American Scholar,* 1969b, *38,* 377–388.

Riesman, D. "An Academic Great Depression?" *Universities Quarterly,* 1971, *26,* 15–27.

Riesman, D. "The Mission of the Urban Grant Universities." *Journal of General Education,* 1974, *27,* 149–156.

Riesman, D. "Educational Reform at Harvard College: Meritocracy and Its

Adversaries." In S. M. Lipset and D. Riesman, *Education and Politics at Harvard*. New York: McGraw-Hill, 1975a.

Riesman, D. "The Future of Diversity in a Time of Retrenchment." *Higher Education*, 1975b, no. 4, 461–482.

Riesman, D. "Preface." In A. Miller (Ed.), *A College in Dispersion: Women of Bryn Mawr, 1896–1975*. Boulder, Colo.: Westview Press, 1976.

Riesman, D. "The Anti-Organisational Syndrome: Of Generational Gaps." *Encounter*, 1978a, *51*(3), 52–68.

Riesman, D. "Community Colleges and Social Stratification: Some Tentative Hypotheses." *Catalyst*, 1978b, *8*(2), 1–5.

Riesman, D. "1968, Ten Years On: Spoilt American Heirs Still Turn to Great Cathedrals of Learning." *London Times Higher Education Supplement*, May 5, 1978c, pp. 8–10.

Riesman, D. "Thoughts on the Decline of Student Writing." Talk to the Writing Center, Harvard University, March 22, 1978d.

Riesman, D. "A Conversation with Simmons College." *Journal of General Education*, 1979a, *31*, 79–108.

Riesman, D. "Encountering Difficulties in Trying to Raise Academic Standards: Florida State University." In G. Grant and others, *On Competence: A Critical Analysis of Competence-Based Reforms in Higher Education*. San Francisco: Jossey-Bass, 1979b.

Riesman, D. "The Self-Centered Society." In *Collier's Year Book, 1980*. New York: Macmillan Educational Corp., 1979c.

Riesman, D. "The Undergraduate Sociology Curriculum: The Liberal Arts Function." Paper presented for panel on "Issues in Teaching: Alternative Curriculum Models" at meeting of the American Sociological Association, Boston, August 1979d. (Also in *Journal of General Education*, in press.)

Riesman, D. "Egocentrism." *Character*, March 1980a, pp. 3–9.

Riesman, D. "The Overriding Issue." *Commonweal*, 1980b, *107*(10), 299–301.

Riesman, D., and Denney, R. "Football in America: A Study in Cultural Diffusion." *American Quarterly*, 1951, *4*, 309–325.

Riesman, D., Denney, R., and Glazer, N. *The Lonely Crowd: A Study of the Changing American Character*. New Haven, Conn.: Yale University Press, 1950.

Riesman, D., and Glazer, N. *Faces in the Crowd: Individual Studies in Character and Politics*. New Haven, Conn.: Yale University Press, 1952.

Riesman, D., and Riesman, E. T. *Conversations in Japan: Modernization, Politics, and Culture*. New York: Basic Books, 1967.

Riesman, D., and Roseborough, H. "Careers and Consumer Behavior." In L. Clark (Ed.), *Consumer Behavior*. New York: New York University Press, 1955.

Robins, L. "On Being a Sociological Sleuth." *Radcliffe Quarterly*, September 1979, pp. 7–10.

Robinson, A. L., Foster, C. C., and Ogilvie, D. H. *Black Studies in the University: The Symposium*. New Haven, Conn.: Yale University Press, 1969.

Rodriguez, R. "Beyond the Minority Myth." *Change*, 1978, *10*(8), 28–34.

Rose, P. I. *"Nobody Knows the Trouble I've Seen": Some Reflections on the Insider-*

Outsider Debate. Northampton, Mass.: Smith College at the Davis Press, 1978.

Rosenberg, M. J., Verba, S., and Converse, P. E. *Vietnam and the Silent Majority: The Dove's Guide*. New York: Harper & Row, 1970.

Rossi, A. S. "Aging and Parenthood in the Middle Years." In P. B. Baltes and O. G. Brim (Eds.), *Life-Span Development and Behavior*. Vol. 3. New York: Academic Press, 1980.

Rothman, S. *The Radical Impulse*. New York: Oxford University Press, in press.

Rothman, S., and others. "Ethnic Variations and Student Radicalism." In S. Bialer (Ed.), *Sources of Contemporary Radicalism*. Boulder, Colo.: Westview Press, 1977.

Rudolph, F. *The American College and University*. New York: Knopf, 1962.

Rudolph, F. *Curriculum: A History of the American Undergraduate Course of Study Since 1636*. San Francisco: Jossey-Bass, 1977.

Ryder, N. B. "The Cohort as a Concept in the Study of Social Change." *American Sociological Review*, 1965, *30*, 843–861.

Ryor, J. "Who Killed Collegiality?" *Change*, 1978, *10*(6), 11–12.

Sacks, H. S. " 'Bloody Monday': The Crisis of the High School Senior." In H. S. Sacks and Associates, *Hurdles: The Admissions Dilemma in American Higher Education*. New York: Atheneum, 1978.

Sammartino, P. *I Dreamed a College*. South Brunswick, N.Y.: A. S. Barnes, 1977.

Sammartino, P. *A History of Higher Education in New Jersey*. South Brunswick, N.Y.: A. S. Barnes, 1978.

Scarf, M. *Unfinished Business: Pressure Points in the Lives of Women*. New York: Doubleday, 1980.

Schelling, T. C. "Comments on the Uses of Course Examinations." In L. Bramson (Ed.), *Examining in Harvard College: A Collection of Essays by the Harvard College Faculty*. Cambridge, Mass.: Committee on Educational Policy, Faculty of Arts and Sciences, Harvard University, 1963.

Schelling, T. C. "On the Ecology of Micro-Motives." *Public Interest*, no. 25 (Fall 1971), 59–98.

Schudson, M. "Organizing the 'Meritocracy': A History of the College Entrance Examination Board." *Harvard Educational Review*, 1972, *42*, 44–69.

Scully, M. G. "Abuses in Foreign-Student Recruiting Tarnish U.S. Colleges' Image Abroad." *Chronicle of Higher Education*, April 7, 1980, pp. 1, 17.

Seidler, M. B., and Ravitz, J. "A Jewish Peer Group." *American Journal of Sociology*, 1955, *61*, 11–15.

Select Committee on the Curriculum. *Education at Amherst Reconsidered: The Liberal Studies Program*. Amherst, Mass.: Amherst College Press, 1978.

Seligman, J. *The High Citadel: On the Influence of Harvard Law School*. Boston: Houghton Mifflin, 1978.

Sennett, R., and Cobb, J. *The Hidden Injuries of Class*. New York: Knopf, 1972.

Sewell, E. "Bensalem College: Dreams Start with People." In G. B. MacDonald (Ed.), *Five Experimental Colleges*. New York: Harper & Row, 1973.

Shark, A. R., Brouder, K., and Associates. *Students and Collective Bargaining*. Washington, D.C.: National Student Educational Fund, 1976.

Sharp, G. *Exploring Nonviolent Alternatives*. Boston: Porter Sargent, 1970.

Sharp, G. *The Politics of Nonviolent Action: A Study Prepared Under the Auspices of Harvard University's Center for International Affairs*. Boston: Porter Sargent, 1973.

Shattan, J. "The No-Nuke Wind Ensemble." *American Spectator*, March 1980, pp. 7–12.

Shils, E. *Center and Periphery: Essays in Macrosociology*. Chicago: University of Chicago Press, 1975.

Shils, E. "The Academic Ethos." *American Scholar*, 1977, *47*, 165–190.

Shklar, J. "Let Us Not Be Hypocritical." *Daedalus*, 1979, *108*, 1–26.

Silber, J. "The Tuition Dilemma: A New Way to Pay the Bills." *Atlantic*, July 1978, pp. 31–36.

Simmons, A. "Harvard Flunks a Test: Vintage Curriculum in New Bottles." *Harper's*, March 1979, pp. 20–27.

Sisk, J. P. "The Bitter Truth of Gossip." *American Spectator*, October 1978, pp. 10–14.

Slack, W. V., and Porter, D. "The Scholastic Aptitude Test: A Critical Appraisal." *Harvard Educational Review*, 1980, *50*, 154–175.

Slater, P. E. *The Glory of Hera: Greek Mythology and the Greek Family*. Boston: Beacon Press, 1968.

Sloan Commission on Government and Higher Education. *Program for Renewed Partnership*. Cambridge, Mass.: Ballinger, 1980.

Snyder, B. R. "How Creative Students Fare Inside Science." In P. Heist (Ed.), *Education for Creativity: A Modern Myth*. Berkeley: University of California Press, 1967.

Somers, R. H. "The Mainsprings of Rebellion: A Survey of Berkeley Students in November 1964." In S. M. Lipset and S. S. Wolin (Eds.), *The Berkeley Student Revolt: Facts and Interpretations*. New York: Doubleday, 1965.

Sowell, T. *Black Education: Myths and Tragedies*. New York: McKay, 1972.

Sowell, T. "The Plight of Black Students in the United States." *Daedalus*, 1974, *103*, 179–196.

Sowell, T. " 'Affirmative Action' Reconsidered." *Public Interest*, no. 42 (Winter 1976a), 47–65.

Sowell, T. "Patterns of Black Excellence." *Public Interest*, no. 43 (Spring 1976b), 26–58.

Sowell, T. (Ed.). *Essays and Data on American Ethnic Groups*. Washington, D.C.: Urban Institute, 1978.

Sowell, T. "Myths About Minorities." *Commentary*, August 1979, pp. 33–37.

Spady, W. G. "Peer Integration and Academic Success: The Dropout Process Among Chicago Freshmen." Unpublished doctoral dissertation, University of Chicago, 1967.

Stadtman, V. A. "The College Curriculum in American Higher Education." Lecture at Hiroshima University, March 15, 1978.

Stanford University. *The Study of Education at Stanford*. Stanford, Calif.: Stanford University, 1968.

Stanley, J. C. Letter. *Harvard Educational Review*, 1967, *37*, 275–276.

Stanley, J. C., and Porter, A. C. "Predicting College Grades of Negroes Versus Whites." Mimeograph, University of Wisconsin at Madison, 1966.
Stark, J. S. *The Many Faces of Educational Consumerism.* Lexington, Mass.: Heath, 1977.
Stebbins, R. A. "Toward Amateur Sociology: A Proposal for the Profession." *American Sociologist,* 1978, *13,* 239–247; comments by R. Altahauser, E. C. Hughes, C. Perin, D. Riesman, and P. H. Rossi, pp. 247–251.
Steinem, G. "Getting Organized: The Time Factor." *Ms.,* March 1980, pp. 9, 45.
Stone, A. "Legal Education on the Couch." *Harvard Law Review,* 1971, *85,* 392–418.
Strout, C., and Grossvogel, D. I. (Eds.). *Divided We Stand: Reflections on the Crisis at Cornell.* New York: Doubleday, 1970.
"Sundae Punch: Grove City vs. Form 639A." *Time,* March 24, 1980, p. 70.
Suslow, S. "A Report on an Interinstitutional Survey of Undergraduate Scholastic Grading, 1960's to 1970's." Unpublished paper, Office of Institutional Research, University of California at Berkeley, 1976.
Taylor, E. "What to Ask of a College." Unpublished manuscript, 1974.
The Testing Digest. Middletown, Conn.: Project to De-Mystify the Established Standardized Tests, 1979.
Thelin, J. R. *The Cultivation of Ivy: A Saga of the College in America.* Cambridge, Mass.: Schenkman, 1976.
Thernstrom, A. M. "The Odd Evolution of the Voting Rights Act." *Public Interest,* no. 55 (Spring 1979), 49–76.
Thernstrom, A. M. "E Pluribus Plura—Congress and Bilingual Education." *Public Interest,* no. 60 (Summer 1980), 3–22.
Thomas, L. "Natural Science." *New England Journal of Medicine,* 1973, *288,* 307.
Thomas, L. *Lives of a Cell: Notes of a Biology Watcher.* New York: Viking Press, 1974.
Thomas, L. *The Medusa and the Snail: More Notes of a Biology Watcher.* New York: Viking Press, 1979.
Thorne, B. "Girls Who Say 'Yes' to Guys Who Say 'No': Women and the Draft Resistance Movement." Paper presented at the meeting of the American Sociological Association, New Orleans, 1972.
Tinto, V. "Does Schooling Matter? A Retrospective Assessment." *Review of Research in Education,* 1977, *5,* 201–235.
Tobias, S. *Overcoming Math Anxiety.* New York: Norton, 1978.
Tobin, J. "On Improving the Economic Status of the Negro." In T. Parsons and K. B. Clark (Eds.), *The Negro American.* Boston: Houghton Mifflin, 1966.
Trilling, D. "We Must March My Darlings." In D. Trilling, *We Must March My Darlings: The Critical Decade.* New York: Harcourt Brace Jovanovich, 1977.
Trow, M. "The Second Transformation of American Secondary Education." *International Journal of Comparative Sociology,* 1961, *2,* 145–166.
Trow, M. "The Campus as a Context for Learning: Notes on Education

and Architecture." Address at colloquium on education and architecture, Sarah Lawrence College, 1968.

Trow, M. "The Public and Private Lives of Higher Education." *Daedalus,* 1975a, *104*(1), 113–127.

Trow, M. (Ed.). *Teachers and Students: Aspects of American Higher Education.* New York: McGraw-Hill, 1975b.

Trow, M. *Aspects of American Higher Education, 1969–1975.* Berkeley, Calif.: Carnegie Council on Policy Studies in Higher Education, 1976a.

Trow, M. "Higher Education and Moral Development." *AAUP Bulletin,* Spring 1976b, p. 24.

Trow, M. "Departments as Contexts for Teaching and Learning." In D. E. McHenry and Associates, *Academic Departments: Problems, Variations, and Alternatives.* San Francisco: Jossey-Bass, 1977.

Turnbull, W. "Foreword." In *Annual Report of the Educational Testing Service for 1977.* Princeton, N.J.: Educational Testing Service, 1978.

Undergraduate Research Opportunities Program. *MIT Student Research Opportunities Directory, 1979–80.* Cambridge: Massachusetts Institute of Technology, 1979.

Vaughan, G. B., Elosser, B., and Flynn, T. "Consumerism Comes to the Community College." University of California Topical Paper No. 55. Los Angeles: ERIC Clearinghouse for Junior Colleges, 1976.

Veblen, T. *The Higher Learning in America: A Memorandum on the Conduct of Universities by Business Men.* New York: D. W. Huebsch, 1918.

Veysey, L. *The Emergence of the American University.* Chicago: University of Chicago Press, 1965.

Veysey, L. *The Communal Experience: Anarchist and Mystical Communities in Twentieth-Century America.* Chicago: University of Chicago Press, 1973a.

Veysey, L. "Stability and Experiment in the American Undergraduate Curriculum." In C. Kaysen (Ed.), *Content and Context: Essays on College Education.* New York: McGraw-Hill, 1973b.

Veysey, L. "The Humanities in American Universities Since the 1930s: The Decline of Grandiosity." Paper presented at conference on humanistic disciplines, Society for the Humanities, Cornell University, November 29, 1979.

Veysey, L. "Undergraduate Admissions: Past and Future." In *Marketing in College Admissions: A Broadening of Perspectives.* Papers from the Wingspread Colloquium, Racine, Wisc., November 8, 1979. New York: College Board, 1980.

Vogel, E. F. *Japan as Number One: What the United States Can Learn from Japan.* Cambridge, Mass.: Harvard University Press, 1979.

von Rothkirch, C. *Field Disaggregated Analysis and Projections of Graduate Enrollment and Higher Degree Production.* Technical Report No. 5. Berkeley, Calif.: Carnegie Council on Policy Studies in Higher Education, 1978.

Waller, W. *The Sociology of Teaching.* New York: Wiley, 1932.

Watters, P. "Faith, Hope, and Parity." *Change,* 1969, pp. 10–13.

Weiss, R. S. *Loneliness: The Experience of Emotional and Social Isolation.* Cambridge, Mass.: M.I.T. Press, 1973.

Weiss, R. S. *Going It Alone: The Family Life and Social Situation of the Single Parent.* New York: Basic Books, 1979.

Wells, P. "Applying to College: Bulldog Bibs and Potency Myths." In H. S. Sacks and Associates, *Hurdles: The Admissions Dilemma in American Higher Education.* New York: Atheneum, 1978.

Wheelis, A. *The Quest for Identity.* New York: Norton, 1958.

Whitlock, B. W. *Don't Hold Them Back: A Critique and Guide to New School-College Articulation Models.* New York: College Entrance Examination Board, 1978.

Whyte, W. F., Jr. *Street Corner Society.* Chicago: University of Chicago Press, 1943.

Woodward, R., and Armstrong, S. *The Brethren: Inside the Supreme Court.* New York: Simon & Schuster, 1980.

Yale Daily News (Ed.). *Insiders' Guide to Colleges.* New York: Berkley, 1978.

The Yellow Pages of Undergraduate Innovations: A Guide to Innovations in Higher Education. New Rochelle, N.Y.: Change Magazine Press, 1974.

Young, K. "Evaluating Institutional Effectiveness." *Educational Record,* 1978, *57*, 45–52.

Young, M. *The Rise of the Meritocracy, 1870 to 2033: An Essay on Education and Equality.* New York: Random House, 1959.

Zorza, R. *The Right to Say "We."* New York: Praeger, 1970.

Name Index

Subject Index

and Hispanic students, 237–239; information role of, 226–240; and inner-city black students, 233–237; institutional visits by, 228–229; trust in, 236
Counterculture: backlash against, 98–104; and defeat of the meritocracy, 81–86; impact of, on higher education, 6–7, 31
Credit: for independent study, 72–76; for off-campus involvement, 71–76; for remedial work, 78–80
Creighton University, 57
Curriculum: in arts, 149–153; in black, ethnic, and third world studies, 140–148; and brain drain, 153–156; cycles in, 248n, 272; diversity in, 197–224; expansion of, 136–156; and land-grant colleges, 137–138; student influence on, 273–277; in women's studies, 138–140

Dallas, University of, 177
Dartmouth College: mathematics at, 20–21; as selective, 264; students at, 169. *See also* Ivy League
Davidson College, 171–172
Deborah P. v. *Turlington*, 161
Decorah College: decompression role of, 158; and recruitment, 52
Deep Springs College, 28
DeFunis case, 129n
Degrees: external, 116–117, 358–361; Master of Arts in Teaching, 60, 87; three-year, 184
Demographic trends, impact of, 7–8
Dental schools, and student choice, 212
Department: as faculty base, xx; power of, 100–101; stability of, 272–273
Disciplines. *See* Fields of study
District of Columbia, University of the, and foreign students, 222
Diversity: and foreign students, 218–224; within institutions, 205–210; and recruitment of minorities, 202–204; restrictions on, 197–224
Doctoral programs: faculty dominance of, 11–27; misinformation on, 245–247; oversupply of, 212–213
Dormitories, coresidential, 166n
Doshisha University, 221, 343
Douglass College, 155
Duke University, 168; changes at, 229n; and recruitment, 53, 56; as selective, 27, 124; student choice of, 230
Dutch Reformed colleges, 172

Education: bilingual, 91–92, 202, 238; change in, and great persons, 293–294; change in, and student consumerism, 271–321; mark of, 279; residential, 110, 314, 346–347; vouchers for, 232, 351–356. *See also* Higher education
Education Commission of the States, 240
Educational brokerage services: and foreign students, 340; information from, 225–226, 377; and marketing, 214
Educational Opportunity Bank, 213–214, 351–356, 379
Educational Testing Service (ETS), xvii, 60, 62, 72, 82, 123, 124, 125n–126n, 130–131, 132, 133, 134, 135, 136, 156, 214, 222, 279, 336, 370, 378n, 385
Elementary and Secondary Education Act, Title VII of, 201–202
Elmira College, 205
Elon College, 168–169
Empire State College, and external degrees, 116–117, 180, 360–361
Environmental Protection Agency, 73, 325
Erskine College, 166–167
Ethical responsibility, academic code of, 29n
Ethnic colleges, decompression role of, 156–159
Ethnic groups, and demographic trends, 7n
Ethnic studies: and ethnic revival, 148; expansion of, 140–148
Evangelical colleges: analysis of, 162–178; attrition at, 173; choice of, 163–164; flexibility of, 162–163; as halfway houses, 156–159, 172–175; individuality at, 164; profiles of, 165–172; secularization of, 175–178
Evergreen State College: architecture of, 209n, closing threatened at, 106; contract system at, 93; as reform, 293
Examinations, use of, to teacher, 247n
Experiment in International Living, 219
External degree programs: and consumer protection, 358–361; spread of, 116–117

Faculty: advising by, 257–259; attitudes of, 271–273; black, 141; burnout by, 122, 195; as coach rather than